THE
FIRST FAMILY

RANDOM HOUSE
NEW YORK

THE
FIRST
FAMILY

—

MIKE DASH

TERROR,
EXTORTION,
REVENGE,
MURDER,

AND THE

BIRTH OF THE
AMERICAN
MAFIA

Published in the United States by Random House,
an imprint of The Random House Publishing Group,
a division of Random House, Inc., New York.

Originally published in the United Kingdom
by Simon & Schuster.

RANDOM HOUSE and colophon are registered
trademarks of Random House, Inc.

Photograph credits can be found on page 377.

LIBRARY OF CONGRESS CATALOGING-IN-PUBLICATION DATA
Dash, Mike.
The first family : terror, extortion, revenge, murder, and
the birth of the American mafia / Mike Dash.
p.   cm.
ISBN 978-1-4000-6722-0
1. Mafia—United States—History.   2. Mafia—United
States—Biography.   3. Criminals—United States—
Biography.   4. Organized crime—United States—
Case studies.   I. Title.
HV6446.D35   2009
364.1'060973—dc22   2009005681

Printed in the United States of America on acid-free paper

www.atrandom.com

2 4 6 8 9 7 5 3 1

FIRST EDITION

Book design by Barbara M. Bachman

Between the law and the Mafia,
the law is not the most to be feared.

PREFACE

HUNDREDS OF BOOKS HAVE BEEN WRITTEN ABOUT THE MAFIA, but this one is different from the rest. Its focus is the birth of the American branch of the fraternity during the years between 1892 and 1930—a period that has, to my astonishment, been almost entirely neglected until now. Few writers have ever asked how, exactly, the Mafia came into existence in the United States. *The First Family* does.

The vast majority of "Mafia books" are also notoriously unreliable: compiled from rumor, hearsay, wild assumptions, and the endlessly recycled errors of earlier authors. *The First Family* sets out to correct these faults. The book is painstakingly rooted in primary sources—not least the detailed records of the U.S. Secret Service, the New York bureau of which was the only federal, state, or city agency to keep the earliest Mafiosi under systematic surveillance. This bureau's daily reports covering the key years from 1899 to 1916 fill fifty-nine huge volumes, each well over a thousand pages long, and among them they make up by far the greatest trove of reliable information on the Mafia's formative years; they form the bedrock on which my narrative has been erected. To my bafflement, I found no sign that any other writer on the subject has ever bothered to examine them.

The balance of the story has been drawn from other important but neglected records: more than ten thousand pages of century-old trial transcripts, the detailed confession of a key member of an important Mafia counterfeiting ring—which turned up in the Hoover Presidential Library, of all places—and the letters and personal memoirs of several participants, not least William Flynn, who was the chief of New York's Secret Service bureau, with a single brief hiatus, from 1901 until 1917.

Flynn's recollections, which were serialized in various contemporary newspapers, have likewise escaped attention until now, and they have been supplemented with the copious daily coverage of crime provided by well over a dozen early-twentieth-century papers. Taken together, this material makes it possible to reconstruct the events of a century ago in often-minute detail.

The story that emerges differs in many vital respects from the accounts that have been offered hitherto, most of which are heavily polluted with misinformation. When I first began my research four years ago, I read that Giuseppe Morello, the first great boss of the New York Mafia, was born in 1863 or 1870—or, some said, perhaps in 1880. Contacting the registry office in his Sicilian hometown, Corleone, I discovered that the correct date was May 2, 1867—a fact his own family seems to have been unaware of, since his gravestone bears the 1870 date. Another account held that Giuseppe had a brother, Antonio, who preceded him as boss in New York, and who once shot dead the dreaded leader of a rival criminal society, the Camorra. The battered transcripts of Antonio Morello's 1892 murder trial, rescued in the early 1980s from a dumpster and now archived in an obscure law library, reveal that he was neither a member of the Mafia nor any relation to his more celebrated "brother," and also that the man he killed was a one-armed organ grinder with no criminal record who had crudely insulted Morello's wife.

Since the story that emerged from my own years of research is frankly astonishing, I also want to make it clear that nothing of what follows is fiction or "imagined" history. None of the conversations reported in these pages is invented; each was recalled, word for word, by one of the participants, or noted down by a newspaper reporter. As any historian should, I have listed my sources of information paragraph by paragraph, and line by line where necessary, and these can be verified in the endnotes.

The First Family, in short, is not a rehash of the cursory, inaccurate, invented tales you may have read before.

This is how it really happened.

MIKE DASH
London, April 22, 2009

CONTENTS

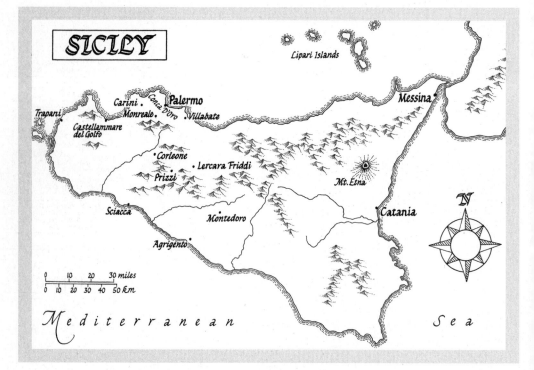

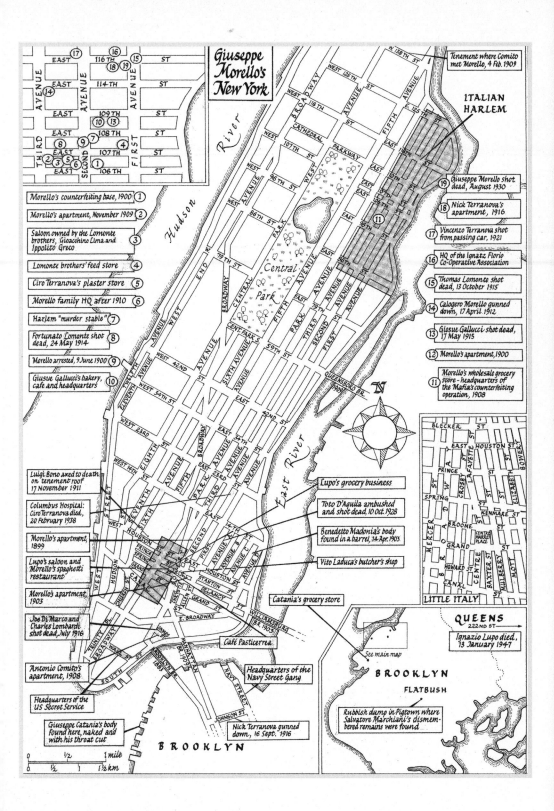

Giuseppe Morello's New York

ITALIAN HARLEM

Map legend (numbered locations):

1. Morello's counterfeiting base, 1900
2. Morello's apartment, November 1909
3. Saloon owned by the Lomonte brothers, Gioacchino Lima and Ippolito Greco
4. Lomonte brothers' feed store
5. Ciro Terranova's plaster store
6. Morello family HQ after 1910
7. Harlem "murder stable"
8. Fortunato Lomonte shot dead, 24 May 1914
9. Morello arrested, 9 June 1900
10. Giusue Gallucci's bakery, café and headquarters
11. Morello's wholesale grocery store – headquarters of the Mafia's counterfeiting operation, 1908
12. Morello's apartment, 1900
13. Giosue Gallucci shot dead, 17 May 1915
14. Calogero Morello gunned down, 17 April 1912
15. Thomas Lomonte shot dead, 13 October 1915
16. HQ of the Ignatz Florio Co-Operative Association
17. Vincenzo Terranova shot from passing car, 1921
18. Nick Terranova's apartment, 1916
19. Giuseppe Morello shot dead, August 1930

Other labelled locations:

Tenement where Comito met Morello, 4 Feb. 1909

Luigi Bono axed to death on tenement roof 17 November 1911

Columbus Hospital: Ciro Terranova died, 20 February 1938

Morello's apartment, 1899

Lupo's saloon and Morello's spaghetti restaurant

Morello's apartment, 1903

Joe Di Marco and Charles Lombardi shot dead, July 1916

Antonio Comito's apartment, 1908

Headquarters of the US Secret Service

Giuseppe Catania's body found here, naked and with his throat cut

Lupo's grocery business

Toto D'Aquila ambushed and shot dead, 10 Oct. 1928

Benedetto Madonia's body found in a barrel, 14 Apr. 1903

Vito Laduca's butcher's shop

Catania's grocery store

Café Pasticceria

Headquarters of the Navy Street Gang

Nick Terranova gunned down, 16 Sept. 1916

LITTLE ITALY

QUEENS
222ND ST
Ignazio Lupo died, 13 January 1947

BROOKLYN
FLATBUSH

Rubbish dump in Pigtown where Salvatore Marchiani's dismembered remains were found

See main map

BROOKLYN

Hudson

East River

Central Park

N

0   ½   1 mile
0   ½   1   1½ km

The MORELLO FAMILY TREE

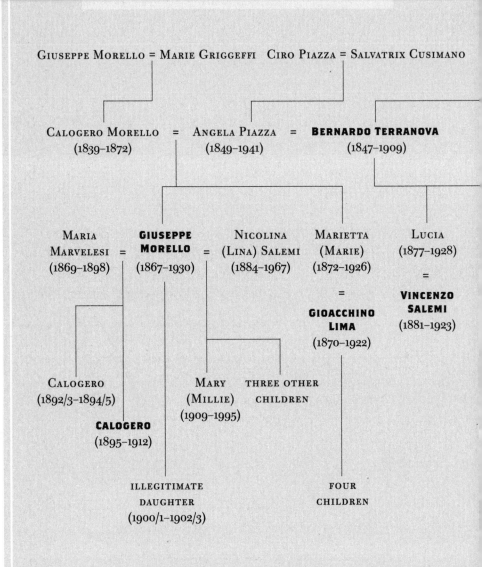

GIUSEPPE MORELLO = MARIE GRIGGEFFI   CIRO PIAZZA = SALVATRIX CUSIMANO

CALOGERO MORELLO = ANGELA PIAZZA = **BERNARDO TERRANOVA**
(1839–1872)   (1849–1941)   (1847–1909)

MARIA   **GIUSEPPE**   NICOLINA   MARIETTA   LUCIA
MARVELESI =   **MORELLO** =   (LINA) SALEMI   (MARIE)   (1877–1928)
(1869–1898)   (1867–1930)   (1884–1967)   (1872–1926)
                                                                    =

                                                    =   **VINCENZO**
                                                                    SALEMI
                                                    GIOACCHINO   (1881–1923)
                                                    LIMA
                                                    (1870–1922)

CALOGERO   MARY   THREE OTHER
(1892/3–1894/5)   (MILLIE)   CHILDREN
                                 (1909–1995)
         CALOGERO
         (1895–1912)

         ILLEGITIMATE   FOUR
         DAUGHTER   CHILDREN
         (1900/1–1902/3)

Figures with a known involvement in
organized crime appear in **BOLD.**

md 2008

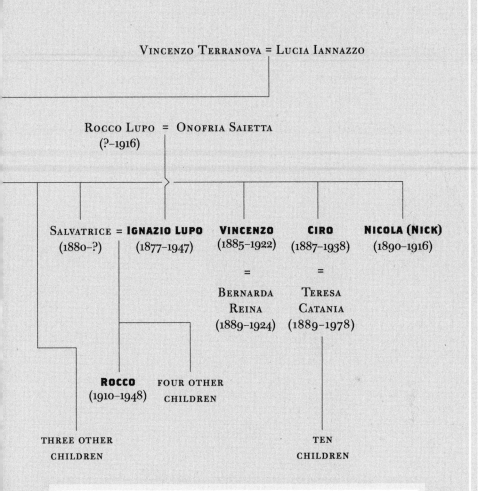

Vincenzo Terranova = Lucia Iannazzo

Rocco Lupo = Onofria Saietta
(?–1916)

Salvatrice = **Ignazio Lupo**   **Vincenzo**   **Ciro**   **Nicola (Nick)**
(1880–?)   (1877–1947)   (1885–1922)   (1887–1938)   (1890–1916)

=   =

Bernarda   Teresa
Reina   Catania
(1889–1924) (1889–1978)

Rocco   Four other
(1910–1948) children

Three other   Ten
children   children

SOURCES

Certificates of births, marriages, and deaths, Ufficio Anagrafe, Corleone • Passenger and crew lists of vessels arriving at New York, U.S. National Archives • U.S. federal censuses of 1910, 1920, 1930 Certificates of births, marriages, and deaths, New York Municipal Archives • Index to New York deaths 1950–1982, New York Public Library • Federal transcripts, Morello Flynn, *The Barrel Mystery* • *Washington Post,* July 12, 1914 Private information from the Morello family

ROGUES' GALLERY

===

THE MORELLO FAMILY

GIUSEPPE MORELLO aka "The Clutch Hand," "Little Finger," and "One Finger Jack." Founder and leader of the first Mafia family in New York and "boss of bosses" of the American Mafia until 1910. Born in Corleone, Sicily, in 1867; suspected of murder and cattle rustling there and found guilty of counterfeiting. Arrived in the United States in 1892; arrested on charges of counterfeiting in 1900 and in connection with the Barrel Murder in 1903; lead suspect in the unsolved disappearance and probable murder of a teenage servant girl; New York Police Department (NYPD) rap sheet shows further arrests on suspicion of kidnapping and bomb throwing; organized extensive extortion ring and numerous rackets; suspected of involvement in up to sixty murders. Imprisoned 1910–20; on his release was sentenced to death by the Mafia's general assembly. Overturned death sentence and became an influential adviser to the second generation of Mafia bosses. Murdered August 1930 by rival Mafiosi.

MARIA MARVELESI Morello's first wife; born Corleone, Sicily; immigrated to the United States 1893; mother of two sons, both named Calogero. Died 1898.

LINA MORELLO Née Nicolina Salemi. Morello's second wife; born Corleone, immigrated to the United States 1903 and married Morello the same year; four children. Complicit in various criminal schemes; hid Mafia correspondence and extortion letters in her child's diapers. Outlived her husband by thirty-seven years.

IGNAZIO LUPO Palermo Mafioso better known as Lupo the Wolf. Immigrated to the United States around 1898; married Morello's sister. Found guilty of murder in Sicily; suspect in the murder of Giuseppe Catania in Brooklyn, 1902; suspect in the Barrel Murder case, 1903; NYPD rap sheet shows further arrests for arson, sending threatening letters, kidnapping, and issuing death threats. Set up Mafia money-laundering schemes. Ran chain of grocery stores; bankrupted 1908; convicted of counterfeiting 1910 and sentenced to thirty years. Paroled 1920. Sentenced to death with Morello by the Mafia's general assembly and fled to Sicily; returned 1922 and ran fruit and bakery rackets; suspect in a 1930 murder; charged with another killing, 1931; rearrested 1936 and returned to jail to serve out the remainder of his 1910 counterfeiting sentence. Released 1947 and died three weeks later.

—

GIUSEPPE BOSCARINI Corleone man who sold Morello counterfeits in Pennsylvania.

GIUSEPPE CALICCHIO aka "the Professor." Neapolitan printer hired for Morello family counterfeiting operation. Long experience of forgery in Italy; printed fake banknotes for impoverished noble families. Arrested January 1910, sentenced to seventeen years.

GIUSEPPE CATANIA Brooklyn grocer and Mafia counterfeiter; associate of Lupo's; talked while drunk and found on the Brooklyn waterfront with his throat cut and his naked body stuffed into a potato sack.

ANTONIO CECALA Sicilian who headed Morello family's insurance rackets; proud professional arsonist; became head of the family counterfeiting operation 1908; arrested and tried 1910, sentenced to fifteen years; shot dead 1928 while running a crooked insurance business.

SALVATORE CINA A violent bandit in Sicily and a farmer in upstate New York; provided base for Morello counterfeiting operation and sold counterfeit bills throughout the United States. Arrested and tried 1910, sentenced to fifteen years.

SALVATORE CLEMENTE aka "Dude." Sicilian counterfeiter, member of the Stella Fraute gang and confidant of the Terranova brothers. Long prison sentences in 1895 and 1902. Arrested again 1910 and turned informant, becoming Flynn's key man inside the Morello family.

ANTONIO COMITO aka "the Sheep." Calabrian printer coerced into working for the Morello gang. Printed thousands of dollars' worth of counterfeit bills, 1908–1909. Arrested January 1910, turned informant, and gave evidence leading to conviction of Morello and eight other members of his family. Placed in protective custody by Flynn; left New York for South America 1911 and became a successful businessman.

JOE DIMARCO Sicilian gambling lord whose alliance with the Terranova brothers turned sour. Murdered on Nick Terranova's orders, July 1916.

GIUSEPPE DI PRIEMO Morello counterfeiter arrested in Yonkers, December 1902, and sentenced to four years in jail. Attempts by his brother-in-law Benedetto Madonia to free him led to the Barrel Murder, 1903. Returned to Italy on his release; conflicting stories have him dying en route or in a shooting in Carini just after landing; either way a likely victim of Morello's.

JOSEPH FANARO Striking gangster—red-haired, stood six feet four. Arrested in connection with the Barrel Murder and suspected of luring the victim, Benedetto Madonia, to his death. Suspect in the murder and dismemberment of Salvatore Marchiani, 1907; admitted to playing cards with him hours before his death. Fell out with Terranova brothers circa 1911. Murdered by members of the Morello and Mineo families, November 1913.

GIUSEPPE FONTANA Influential Sicilian involved in the 1893 Notarbartolo murder; arrived in New York circa 1901 and joined Morello family. Murdered by gunmen from two Mafia families after falling out with the Terranova brothers, November 1913.

MESSINA GENOVA Butcher and partner of Lupo in a Prince Street saloon. Arrested in connection with the Barrel Murder, 1903, and thought by the police to have administered Madonia's deathblow. Brother in

New Orleans was also a Mafioso. Moved to Ohio and murdered there 1908.

VINCENZO GIGLIO Cina's brother-in-law, a Mafioso from Tampa who was related by marriage to the important Trafficante family. Convicted of counterfeiting 1909; died in prison 1914.

IPPOLITO GRECO Saloon owner and partner in the "Murder Stable" who supplied the gunmen who murdered Barnet Baff. Had rivalry with Tom Lomonte. Shot ten times by unknown assailants in his stable, 1915.

PIETRO INZERILLO Café owner in Little Italy; supplied barrel in which Benedetto Madonia was interred, 1903. Shot three times by unknown assailants in New York, late 1908; survived. Fled to Milan late 1909 to avoid arrest and later involved in counterfeiting in Italy.

VITO LADUCA aka Vito Longo. Born Carini, Sicily; served in Italian navy. Butcher and extortionist in New York. "Dread bulwark of the Black Hand." Arrested on charges of passing counterfeit notes, Pittsburgh, 1903. Suspect in the disappearance and probable murder of Jasper Barcia, 1903. Arrested in connection with the Barrel Murder. Chief suspect in the kidnapping of Antonio Mannino, 1904; working in Pittsburgh, circa 1906; returned rich to Carini circa 1907; shot dead there February 1908.

SAM LOCINO "Queer-pusher" who sold Morello notes in Pittston, Pennsylvania, and provided the tip that led to Flynn convicting the Morello leadership six months later. Shot twice in the head soon after Morello's conviction.

FORTUNATO LOMONTE Sicilian gang leader; owned feed store on East 108th Street near the infamous Murder Stable; installed as joint boss of the Morello family circa 1911 on the Clutch Hand's imprisonment. Largely ineffective; known as a conciliator. Shot dead by unknown gunman, 1914.

TOM LOMONTE Brother of Fortunato, took over Morello family with him in 1911. Shot dead by hired gunman Antonio Impoluzzo, 1915.

BENEDETTO MADONIA High-ranking salesman of counterfeit Morello notes, 1902; sent to Pittsburgh to help free arrested members of the Morello family early 1903. Brother-in-law of Giuseppe Di Priemo; sent a thousand dollars to Morello to pay for his legal aid; on complaining of lack of backing from the Clutch Hand was lured to New York and became the victim in the infamous Barrel Murder, April 1903.

CALOGERO MORELLO Giuseppe Morello's eldest son; a Mafioso at seventeen, murdered in April 1912 as part of the Morellos' vendetta with the Madonias.

TOMMASO PETTO aka "Petto the Ox"; real name Luciano Perrini. Born Carini, Sicily; strongman and enforcer for Morello family. Arrested in connection with Barrel Murder, 1903, and was the only suspect charged with murder; released without trial 1904 and moved to Pittston, Pennsylvania. Murdered there October 1905 by unknown killers.

NICK SYLVESTER Morello bomb thrower, wagon driver, and errand boy, arrested 1909 in connection with the Morello counterfeiting ring, sentenced to fifteen years. Became Secret Service informant in jail.

CIRO TERRANOVA aka "the Artichoke King." Middle Terranova brother. Worked as a plasterer while organizing family vegetable racket. Married, ten children. Plotted murder of inconvenient witnesses; arranged murder of Joe DiMarco, 1916, and took over his gambling interests; tried on associated murder charge 1918 and acquitted on a technicality; Mafia leader in Harlem late 1920s, working for Joe "the Boss" Masseria; heavily involved in lotteries and the artichoke rackets. Forced into retirement by a younger generation of Mafiosi, mid-1930s; harassed by the police thereafter. Died of a stroke, 1938, the only one of the four Morello-Terranova brothers to die in bed.

NICK TERRANOVA aka "Coco." Youngest of the "Terranova boys." Succeeded Lomonte brothers as head of the Morello family. Ran family horse theft ring; extortionist and murderer. Shot dead two of the gang responsible for his nephew's death and vowed to butcher all the rest. Never married. Murdered by Camorra gunmen in a Brooklyn ambush, September 1916.

VINCENZO TERRANOVA aka "the Tiger." Eldest Terranova brother; married into Reina family. Ran family ice racket. Suspect in the murder of "Diamond Sam" Sica, 1908; charged with murder of Charles Lombardi, 1918, but did not stand trial; murdered May 1922 by rival Mafiosi.

PASQUALE AND LEOLUCA VASI Minor family members caught with $3,600 worth of counterfeits under a bed, November 1909.

LULU VICARI Chief assassin used by the Morello family before 1914.

GIOVANNI ZACCONI Arrested in connection with the Barrel Murder, 1903; thought to have driven the wagon that deposited Madonia's body on East 11th Street; became a farmer in Connecticut; shotgunned to death there by unknown assassins 1909.

THE SICILIAN MAFIA

VITO CASCIO FERRO Fearsome Mafia boss from Bisaquino. An ally of Morello's during three years spent in the United States; later became the most influential Sicilian Mafioso of the first third of the century. Suspected of playing a leading part in the Petrosino murder.

PAOLINO STREVA Corleone capo who was Morello's superior in the local Mafia.

BERNARDO TERRANOVA Morello's stepfather, an initiated member of the Corleone Mafia who led the family to New York in 1893. His own three sons also became Mafiosi.

IN CORLEONE

ANNA DIPUMA Neighbor of Giovanni Vella who witnessed his murder and told friends she would testify as to the identity of his killer. Shot in the back outside her home a few days later.

FRANCESCO ORTOLEVA Minor politician framed by Morello for the Vella murder; tried and convicted after extensive Mafia intrigues; served twenty years for a crime Morello had committed. Son sought Flynn's aid in having him freed.

GIOVANNI VELLA Honest head of the Corleone Field Guard, murdered by Morello after getting too close to shutting down a Mafia cattle-rustling ring, 1889.

BERNARDINO VERRO Socialist firebrand and mayor of Corleone, initiated into the Mafia by Morello's stepfather, Bernardo Terranova, early 1893. Later denounced the fraternity and was murdered by it, November 1915.

MICHELE ZANGARA Morello neighbor who overheard a compromising conversation. His body was found, broken and dead, at the foot of a bridge just outside Corleone.

THE NEW ORLEANS MAFIA, NEW ORLEANS POLICE, AND NEW ORLEANS VIGILANTES

DAVID HENNESSY New Orleans police chief mortally wounded in a shotgun ambush, December 1890. Told a friend: "The dagoes did it."

JOSEPH MACHECA Powerful New Orleans shipping boss; Sicilian born and alleged to have been a prominent local Mafia figure.

CHARLES AND TONY MATRANGA Born in Monreale, Sicily, and influential on the New Orleans waterfront. Italian police documents name Tony Matranga as one of the bosses of the New Orleans offshoot of the Monreale Mafia; witnesses in Louisiana describe initiation ceremonies organized by his brother. Tony Matranga lost a leg in battle with the rival Provenzano clan; Charles survived the Parish Prison lynching, March 1891.

WILLIAM PARKERSON New Orleans lawyer and vigilante leader who led the eight-thousand-strong mob that burst into New Orleans's Parish

Prison and murdered eleven Sicilians accused of involvement in the Hennessy murder—America's worst mass lynching.

THE NEW YORK MAFIA

JOE BONANNO aka "Joe Bananas." Influential second-generation Mafia boss and head of one of New York's five families; remained active into the 1960s. Played leading role on the Castellammarese side in 1930s Mafia war; met and described Morello, his enemy.

SALVATORE D'AQUILA aka "Totò." Ruthless Palermo Mafioso and cheese importer who kept a low profile and headed his own family in Harlem from at least 1912 in rivalry to Morello's. After the Clutch Hand's imprisonment, had himself declared America's boss of bosses in succession to him; later arranged for Morello and Lupo to be sentenced to death. Shot dead in 1928 ambush and succeeded by Masseria.

SEBASTIANO DOMINGO aka "Buster from Chicago." Mafia gunman imported from Illinois to fight in the Castellammare War. Deadly sharpshooter. Victims included Giuseppe Morello, Manfredi Mineo, and Joe "the Baker" Catania, nephew of Ciro Terranova. Shot dead in Manhattan, 1932.

SALVATORE LUCANIA aka Charlie "Lucky" Luciano. Born Lercara Friddi, Sicily. Highly influential Mafia boss of the 1930s and 1940s; decades earlier, a key aide of Masseria; his decision to betray his boss brought the Castellammare War to a sudden end.

SALVATORE MARANZANO Highly educated, ambitious, a killer: the boss of the Castellammarese side in the 1930 Mafia war led the faction that killed Morello and Masseria. Murdered at the behest of Luciano and other Mafia leaders when he in turn became too grasping, September 1931.

GIUSEPPE MASSERIA aka "Joe the Boss." Mafia boss of bosses after D'Aquila's death. Rose to power during Morello's imprisonment; a key ally and protector of the Morello-Terranova clan during the 1920s. Morello and Ciro Terranova were both his lieutenants.

MANFREDI MINEO aka Al. Palermo Mafioso who formed his own family in Brooklyn around 1910. Allied with the Morellos against D'Aquila in 1911–12. Later a Masseria ally; killed during the Castellammare War.

NICOLA SCHIRO aka "Cola." Founder of the second of New York's Mafia families; allied with Morellos against D'Aquila in 1911–12. Led Castellammarese Mafia faction in Brooklyn. Ousted by Maranzano and returned to Italy.

JOE VALACHI aka "Joe Cago." Neapolitan burglar recruited by the Castellammarese during the 1930 Mafia war. Sworn enemy of Ciro Terranova; friend of Alessandro Vollero; memoirs gave first inside look at the Morello-era Mafia.

UMBERTO VALENTI aka "the Ghost." Cruel and effective Morello ally, then rival; member of the D'Aquila family. Had Vincenzo Terranova murdered, 1922; killed in revenge three months later.

THE PITTSBURGH MAFIA

NICOLA GENTILE Born Agrigento, Sicily; American Mafia killer and diplomat whose smooth journey through half a dozen U.S. families gives vital insight into the fraternity in Morello's time. Helped save the Clutch Hand's life in 1920. Died in Sicily sometime after 1974.

THE CAMORRA

RALPH DANIELLO aka "the Barber." Real name Alfonso Pepe. Low-level Camorra cocaine dealer and gunman who turned informant when his bosses refused to help his wife and family. Betrayed entire Camorra leadership and cleared up twenty-three unsolved murders; his evidence led to half a dozen capital trials and the jailing of Alessandro Vollero and Pellegrino Marano. Given a suspended sentence as a reward for his information. Later served five years for felonious assault. Murdered in Newark soon after his release from prison, 1925.

PELLEGRINO MARANO Camorra boss in New York. Ran the Coney Island gang. Jailed on Daniello's evidence after trial for second-degree murder.

TONY NOTARO Camorra gunman who turned informant to save his life and helped convict the Neapolitans' New York leadership.

ANTONIO PARETTI aka "Tony the Shoemaker." Camorra gunman who took part in numerous murders. Fled to Italy. Returned to New York, 1925, and was convicted and executed for his part in the Nick Terranova slaying.

ALPHONSE SGROIA aka "the Butcher." Camorra gunman who killed four. With Daniello and Notaro, turned informant to save his life; gave evidence against fellow Camorrists including Paretti.

ALESSANDRO VOLLERO Camorra boss in Brooklyn; led Navy Street gang. Allied with Terranova brothers against Giosue Gallucci, then turned on the Harlem Mafia and tried to seize control of its rackets. Was winning "Camorra war" when Daniello turned traitor; subsequently convicted of murder, had capital sentence overturned on appeal, and served fifteen years in Sing Sing. Met Joe Valachi in jail; fearing Mafia vengeance, retired to Italy on his release.

NEW YORK ORGANIZED CRIME

GIOSUE GALLUCCI aka "the King of Little Italy." Influential Neapolitan politician and racketeer who rose to power in Harlem after Morello's 1910 conviction. Ran highly profitable "Royal Italian Lottery." Had numerous enemies—ten bodyguards were killed defending him. Survived half a dozen assassination attempts and two serious bullet wounds in all, but was killed by a group of Mafia and Camorra gunmen sent by Nick Terranova and Alessandro Vollero, 1915.

JACK GLEASON Irish member of the 1900 Morello counterfeiting gang. Mollie Callahan's sweetheart; gave Secret Service information relating to her disappearance.

EDWARD KELLY, CHAS BROWN, AND JOHN DUFFY Irish queer-pushers arrested in North Beach, May 1900, for passing Morello bills.

PAUL KELLY Real name Paolo Vaccarelli. Intelligent and able early Italian gang boss who fell from power after the rise of the Mafia. Moved to Harlem under Morello's protection and reinvented himself as an early exponent of labor racketeering.

LUIGI LAZZAZZARA Partner of Pasquarella Spinelli in the Murder Stable. Chief suspect in her murder; took control of the property and ran it until stabbed to death outside the premises, February 1914. A likely Morello family victim, police theorized.

ANIELLO PRISCO aka "Zopo the Gimp." Freelance extortionist who fell foul of Gallucci; murdered December 1912.

TOM SMITH Irish blacksmith and boodle carrier associated with the 1900 Morello counterfeiting gang.

GIULIANO SPERLOZZA Leading Black Hand extortionist and Morello enemy, victim of extremely inventive assassination, 1908.

PASQUARELLA SPINELLI Sicilian owner of the East 108th Street Murder Stable. A Morello ally; murdered on the premises March 1912.

HENRY THOMPSON aka "Dude." Irishman who headed a gang of queer-pushers responsible for passing Morello's crude 1900 counterfeits.

THE NEW YORK POLICE DEPARTMENT

THEODORE BINGHAM Army general and New York police commissioner; dispatched Petrosino on his fatal mission to Sicily.

ARTHUR CAREY Detective sergeant; homicide specialist who investigated the Barrel Murder, 1903.

MICHAEL FIASCHETTI Born in Rome; a leading member of the Italian Squad after Petrosino's death; investigated Camorra in Naples and Mafia "Good Killers" gang in New York and New Jersey, 1921.

JOE PETROSINO Best-known detective in New York. An Italian, born Padula, Naples; immigrated to the United States in 1870s and worked as a shoeshine boy and foreman on the garbage scows; recommended to the NYPD by Captain Alexander "Clubber" Williams despite his diminutive height and joined the police in 1883. Promoted to detective by Police Commissioner Theodore Roosevelt a dozen years later; investigated Barrel Murder, 1903; lieutenant in charge of the Italian Squad, 1906. Sent to Sicily in 1909 to gather information expected to lead to the deportation of Italian criminals; murdered in Palermo with the knowledge and active collusion of the Morello family.

ANTONIO VACHRIS Genoese head of the Italian Squad in Brooklyn. Investigated the Catania "sack murder" in 1902 and the Salvatore Marchiani murder and dismemberment five years later. Warned Petrosino against traveling to Sicily.

THE U.S. SECRET SERVICE

THOMAS CALLAGHAN Teenage agent sent into the Morellos' tenement home to gather evidence of the internal layout. Survived an encounter with the Clutch Hand to become head of the agency's Chicago bureau.

WILLIAM FLYNN Native New Yorker born to Irish immigrant parents; former plumber and jailer; a highly talented natural detective who headed the Service's New York bureau for fifteen years. Pursued Morellos for more than a decade; provided vital evidence in the Barrel Murder case and convicted forty-five members of the gang in 1909–10.

Ran the only intelligence operation that penetrated the Mafia's inner councils before the 1970s. Later highly effective counterintelligence chief during World War I; investigated anarchist bombings 1919–20; preceded Hoover as head of the FBI, then ran a private detective agency in New York until his death.

JOHN HENRY Long-serving New York operative involved in both the 1903 and 1909 Morello counterfeiting investigations.

CHARLES MAZZEI Italian counterfeiter and informant who gave Flynn valuable inside information about the Morello family's activities.

LARRY RICHEY Born Ricci. Philadelphia Italian who joined the Secret Service at sixteen after stumbling into a counterfeiters' lair; investigated 1903 Morello counterfeiting ring; later became a journalist and eventually the highly influential private secretary of President Herbert Hoover.

PETER RUBANO Flynn's top Italian agent, infiltrated outer reaches of the Morello gang in the years 1906–10.

JOHN WILKIE Washington-based head of the Secret Service; a former Chicago newsman who penned the original "Indian Rope Trick" hoax.

INNOCENT BYSTANDERS

BARNET BAFF Feisty poultry dealer who refused to accept the prices imposed by the chicken cartel of Washington Market. Murdered by four hired gunmen, 1914.

LUIGI BONO Italian grocer from Highland, New York; axed to death on a tenement rooftop, 1911, and found horribly mutilated, apparently a Mafia victim suspected of talking to the police.

MOLLIE CALLAGHAN Maid hired to clean Morello's rooms in 1899; discovered evidence of counterfeiting and disappeared that Christmas. Neither she nor her body was ever found.

KATRINA PASCUZZO Antonio Comito's mistress; endured months with him in the Morello gang's upstate headquarters.

SALVATORE ROMANO Doctor, born in Corleone, duped into treating sixty members of the Morello family for free and later into testifying in Morello's favor at his 1910 counterfeiting trial. Lied on the stand; tried later for perjury.

THE
FIRST FAMILY

CHAPTER 1

THE BARREL MYSTERY

===

THE ROOM FELT LIKE THE BOTTOM OF A GRAVE. IT WAS DAMP, LOW ceilinged, windowless, and—on this raw-boned New York night—as chilly and unwelcoming as a policeman's stare.

Outside, on Prince Street in the heart of Little Italy, a fine drizzle slanted down to puddle amid the piles of rotting garbage strewn along the edges of the street, leaving the cobbles treacherous and greasy. Inside, beneath a billboard advertising lager beer, a featureless, cheap workingmen's saloon stretched deep into the bowels of a dingy tenement. At this late hour—it was past three on the morning of April 14, 1903—the tavern was shuttered up and silent. But in the shadows at the far end of the bar there stood a rough-hewn, tightly closed door. And in the room behind that door, Benedetto Madonia sat eating his last supper.

The place was advertised as a spaghetti restaurant, but it was in truth an eating house of the most basic sort. An old stove squatted against one wall, belching fumes. Musty strings of garlic dangled from the walls, mingling their odor with the smell of boiling vegetables. The remaining fittings consisted of several rough, low tables, a handful of ancient chairs, and a rusting iron sink that jutted from a corner of the room. Gas lamps spewed out mustard light, and the naked floorboards had been scattered with cedar sawdust, which, at the end of a busy day, coagulated in a thick mix of spit, onion skins, and the butts of dark Italian cigars.

Madonia dug hungrily into a stew of beans, beets, and potatoes, hearty peasant food from his home province of Palermo. He was a powerfully built man of average height, handsome after the fashion of the time, with a high forehead, chestnut eyes, and a wave of thick brown hair. A large mustache, carefully waxed until it tapered to points, offset the sharp slash of his Roman nose. He dressed better than most workingmen, wearing a suit, high collar, tie, and well-soled shoes—all signs of some prosperity. Exactly how he earned his money, though, was scarcely obvious. If asked, Madonia claimed to be a stonemason. But even a casual observer could see that this was a man unused to manual labor. His forty-three-year-old body had begun to sag, and his soft hands—neatly manicured—bore no trace of an artisan's calluses.

After a while the solitary diner, sated, thrust his bowl aside and glanced across the room to where a handful of companions lounged against one wall. Like him, they spoke Sicilian—a dialect so rich in words drawn from Spanish, Greek, and Arabic that it was scarcely intelligible, even to other Italians—and, like his, the jewelry and the clothes they wore were quite at odds with their supposed professions: laborer, farmer, clothes presser. Yet there was no mistaking the fact that Madonia was an outsider here. Immigrants though all those in the restaurant were, the others had become New Yorkers and now felt quite at home amid the teeming streets of the Italian colony. Madonia, on the other hand, had first come to Manhattan just a week ago and did not know the city. He found it disconcerting that he required an escort to find his way round Little Italy. Worse, he was growing increasingly alarmed at the way these men he barely knew muttered together in low voices, and spoke so elliptically that he could not grasp the meaning of their words.

Madonia had little chance to grapple with this mystery. The Sicilian had barely finished his meal when, with a click that echoed loudly through the room, the solitary door into the restaurant swung open and a second group of men appeared. In the sickly flicker of the gaslight Madonia made out the face of one he knew: Tommaso Petto, an oval-faced hulk of muscle and menace whose broad chest, strong arms, and limited intelligence had won him the nickname of "the Ox." Behind him, another figure lurked, silhouetted momentarily against one wall of the saloon. It was that of a man of slender build and middling height, his eyes twin drops of jet, like black holes bored into his skull. The newcomer's face was expressionless and gaunt, his skin rough, his chin and cheeks unshaven. He wore his mustache ragged, like a brigand's.

The Ox stepped instinctively aside, allowing the slight figure to step into the room. As he did so, a spasm of anxiety ran through the other figures in the restaurant. This was their leader, and they showed him fearful deference. Not one of the half-dozen others present dared to return his gaze directly.

Madonia himself was not immune to the terror that the black-eyed man inspired. The newcomer's voice, when he spoke, was parched, his gestures undemonstrative and minimal. Above all, there was the disconcerting way he swathed the right side of his body in a voluminous brown shawl. The arm that he kept hidden was, Madonia knew, appallingly deformed. The forearm itself was stunted, no more than half the length of any normal man's. Worse still, its hand was nothing but a claw. It lacked, from birth, the thumb and first four of its fingers. Only the little finger, useless on its own, remained, like the cruel joke of some uncaring deity. Black eyes' name was Giuseppe Morello, but his maimed appendage had earned him the nickname "Clutch" or "the Clutch Hand."

Morello wasted little time on ceremony. A single gesture from his good left hand sufficed; two of the men who had been lounging along the wall jerked up and pinioned Madonia, each seizing an arm as they dragged the diner to his feet. Their prisoner struggled briefly but without effect; grasped none too gently by his wrists and shoulders, he had no chance of escape. To shout out was hopeless; the room was too far from the sidewalk for even a full-blown scream of terror to be audible. Half standing, half supported by his captors, he writhed helplessly as the black-eyed man approached.

Exactly what passed between Madonia and the Clutch Hand is uncertain. There may have been a brief but angry conversation. Most likely the word *nemico,* enemy, was used. Perhaps Madonia, aware, far too late, of the lethal danger he was in, begged uselessly for mercy. If so, his words had no effect. Another gesture from the black-eyed man and the two associates restraining the prisoner dragged him swiftly across the floor toward the rusty sink. A rough hand seized Madonia by the hair, yanking his head back and exposing his throat. At this, a third man lunged forward wielding a stiletto—a thin-bladed dagger, honed to razor sharpness and some fourteen inches long. A second's pause, to gauge angle and distance, and the blade was thrust home, sideways on, above the Adam's apple.

The blow was struck with such brutal strength that it pierced Madonia's windpipe from front to back and continued on till it struck bone. The men holding the captive felt his frame collapse, limbs rubbery and unresponsive, as the weapon was withdrawn. Using all their strength, they hauled the dying man back to his feet as Petto the Ox stepped up, his own knife in his hand. A single sweeping slash from left to right, so fierce it cut right through Madonia's thick three-ply linen collar, severed both throat and jugular vein, all but beheading the prisoner.

Shocking though this violence was, it was premeditated. As life left Madonia in gouts, the men gripping his arms forced his head over the sink so that each succeeding pulse of blood drummed against the iron and gurgled down into the drains. The little that escaped fell onto the victim's clothes or was soaked up by the sawdust underfoot. None reached the floorboards to stain them and leave lasting evidence of the crime.

It took a minute, maybe more, for the awful flow of blood to ebb. As it did, thick fingers reached around Madonia's gashed neck and tied a square of gunnysack around his throat. The coarse fabric absorbed the dying trickle from the wounds as the corpse was doubled, lifted bodily, and carried to the center of the room. There other hands had dragged a barrel, three feet high, of the sort supplied by wholesalers to New York's stores. A layer of muck and sawdust, scooped up from the floor, had been spread inside to absorb any remaining blood, and the dead man's body was forced inside with uncaring savagery.

One arm and a leg projected from the barrel, but that was immaterial; Morello and his men had no interest in concealing the body. Madonia's corpse was meant to be discovered, and the savage wounds it bore were a deterrent. Still, there was no point in chancing premature detection. An old overcoat, its labels carefully removed, was spread over the protruding limbs and the barrel wrestled and maneuvered back into the saloon and thence through a door that opened onto an alley. A decrepit one-horse covered wagon stood there, waiting in the darkness. Several of the Sicilians combined their strength and heaved their burden onto it; two men, hunched now in heavy cloaks, climbed on. And, with a creak of springs and clop of hooves, Benedetto Madonia embarked upon his final journey.

AN HOUR OR SO LATER, shortly after dawn, a cleaning woman by the name of Frances Connors left her apartment on the East Side and set off to the nearest bakery to buy rolls.

Her neighborhood was desperately impoverished. Connors's tenement stood between a failing livery stable, its business proclaimed in peeling paint, and a collapsing row of billboards buttressed with iron scrap. To her right, as she turned out of her apartment, the East River slopped a tide of stinking effluent against crumbling wharfs. To her left, a warehouse full of cackling poultry leaned hard against a factory. And directly ahead, where East 11th Street met Avenue D, her route to the nearest bakery took her past the scarred exterior of Mallet & Handle's lumberyard.

Mallet & Handle's was just as filthy and decrepit as East 11th Street itself. The yard smelled sourly of refuse, and its walls were pocked with unwashed windows swathed protectively in chicken wire. Most days deliveries piled up haphazardly outside, forcing passersby to pick their way through ragged piles of timber. This morning, though, another obstacle blocked Connors's path. A barrel, covered with an overcoat, sat squarely in the middle of the pavement.

The lights were coming on in nearby tenements and the rain had all but ceased, but it was still too early for the stevedores and sweatshop workers of the neighborhood to be about. No one saw Mrs. Connors chance upon the barrel. No one watched her size up the obstruction, or lift a corner of the cloth to peer inside. They heard the Irishwoman, though. What Connors saw brought a scream to her lips so full of terror that heads came thrusting out of windows up and down the street. The cleaner had exposed the right arm and the left leg of a corpse. And below them, peering out from sawdust dark with blood, a face with a high forehead, chestnut eyes, and thick brown hair.

Connors's cries brought the local watchman running. He, in turn, ran for the police. Patrolman John Winters, who hastened up from his post nearby, pulled away the coat and saw at once that the man in the barrel was dead; his gashed throat and the chalky pallor of his skin were proof of that. Long blasts on the policeman's whistle brought reinforcements rushing to the scene. One man was sent to phone the men of the Detective Bureau while the others set about examining their find.

It was a horrific job. Everything that Winters touched was sticky with gore; the face and body of the dead man were spattered, the clothes saturated; blood oozed between the barrel's staves. But there was little to show how the corpse had found its way to East 11th Street. Rain had wiped out traces of the covered wagon's journey; footprints had dissolved to mud, cart tracks had been obliterated. And though Sergeant Bauer, of the Union Street station house, had passed the lumberyard at 5:15 A.M. and was quite certain that the barrel had not been present then, door-to-door inquiries along both sides of the street failed to reveal a single person who had seen the wagon as it rumbled down the road or had any idea how it could have been unloaded by Mallet & Handle's without anybody noticing.

Forensic science was still in its infancy in turn-of-the-century Manhattan; fingerprinting, just introduced by Scotland Yard, had yet to be adopted by the New York Police Department (NYPD), and the notion of preserving a crime scene was unheard of. Not bothering to wait for the detectives of the 14th Precinct to appear, Winters prized Madonia's body from the barrel—a difficult job, as it was wedged firmly inside—and stretched it out amid the puddles to examine it for clues. No effort was made to protect the body from the elements, but the patrolman did observe two details of importance: the coat that had covered the barrel was only slightly wet, despite the drizzle of that night, and the body beneath it remained warm to the touch. Plainly the butchered corpse had been abandoned only recently, and the man himself had not been dead for long.

It was left to Detective Sergeant Arthur Carey to start a systematic search. Carey, the first policeman with experience of murder to reach the spot, tagged the contents of Madonia's pockets; they consisted of a crucifix, a date stamp, a solitary penny, and several handkerchiefs, one of them, small and drenched with perfume, evidently a woman's. A watch chain dangled from the corpse's waistcoat, but the watch was gone; there was no wallet, and no name sewn anywhere into the clothing. Even the labels in the victim's underwear had been removed. "There was," the detective conceded, having checked, "not a scrap of information on the body to establish identification."

Carey felt more confident in guessing the dead man's nationality. The corpse's looks were clearly Mediterranean. More tellingly, a brief note, written in Italian in a woman's hand, had been found crumpled in a trouser pocket. Both earlobes had been pierced for earrings, a practice commonplace in Sicily, and the stiletto wounds on Madonia's neck also looked bloodily familiar. In the course of his career, the detective had examined the victims of several Italian vendettas. Most likely, he concluded, the man had died in one of the murderous feuds common in Little Italy.

Not all of Carey's colleagues were so certain; in the first hours after the murder, some officers were working on the theory that the dead man might have had his throat cut by a vicious robber or was even the victim of a deranged crime of passion. The possibility that the corpse was Greek or Syrian was also mooted. Most policemen, though, concurred with the sergeant's swift deductions. There were, after all, dozens of murders every year in the Italian sections of the city, and most were the products of exactly the sort of deadly feuds with which Carey was so familiar. Few cases of this type were ever solved; New York's police (nearly three-quarters of whom were Irish) did not pretend to understand what went on in Little Italy, and faced with witnesses and suspects who rarely spoke much English and seldom sought to involve the authorities in their disputes, detectives found it almost impossible to solve even incidents in which the murderers' identities, and the reasons for the killing, were common knowledge in the immigrant community.

It was clear from the outset, though, that this murder would not go uninvestigated. The brutality of the assault, and the unprecedented circumstances of the barrel's discovery, had all the makings of a great sensation; by the time Carey had concluded his initial examination, at about 6:15 A.M., the sidewalks outside Mallet & Handle's were already clogged with gawkers who milled about in the hope of glimpsing the now shrouded body. A squad of police reserves, summoned from nearby station houses, had to link arms to keep back a crowd that quickly swelled to several hundred people. The first newspapermen appeared as well, scrawling down their shorthand summaries of what was known about the case. Bloody murder was always front-page news.

By breakfast time, indeed, the fresh whiff of sensation had brought a gaggle of inspectors all the way up from police headquarters. Among the senior officers keen to reap the attendant publicity was George McClusky, the head of the Detective Bureau, who took full charge of the investigation. A tall, good-looking man with handsome hair and a thick mustache, McClusky had served more than a decade with the bureau and possessed so much swagger and self-confidence that he was universally known behind his back as "Chesty George." But the inspector's high opinion of his own abilities was not matched by reality. McClusky was a clumsy investigator, too certain of the rightness of his own opinions and lacking the subtlety and intuition of the best detectives. He tended to be hasty, too, and all too often rushed into premature arrests. A genuinely baffling case—which Arthur Carey already feared the barrel mystery would turn out to be—might easily confound him.

Fortunately for the police, Carey had already taken steps to remedy the situation. His tentative identification of the barrel victim as a Sicilian had prompted him to call for help, and within the hour it arrived in the unlikely shape of a squat man in a shapeless overcoat, his face half hidden beneath a derby hat. The newcomer was Sergeant Joseph Petrosino, born in Padula, south of Naples, but now New York's great expert on Italian crime. Quite possibly the most recognizable officer in the entire department, Petrosino was smallpox-scarred, strong-featured to the point of ugliness, and short even by the standards of the day—he stood a mere five feet three and customarily wore lifts in his shoes to augment his height. The detective's diminutive stature, though, was as deceptive as the look of blank-eyed stupidity that he often wore upon his face; the sergeant tipped the scales at close to three hundred pounds, and much of that bulk was muscle. "He had," a member of the district attorney's office who knew him well once wrote, "enormous shoulders and a bull neck, on which was placed a great round head like a summer squash. His face was pock-marked and he rarely smiled, but went methodically about his business, which was to drive Italian criminals out of the city and the country."

It took Petrosino only a few minutes to examine the yard, the body, and the handful of effects that had filled Madonia's pockets. Then he and Carey turned their attentions to the barrel in which the dead man had been found. It had been cheaply made, without hoops, and now that the corpse had been removed, the detectives could see that a three-inch thickness of sawdust coated its base. Taking turns, the two men reached inside and sifted through the blood-saturated cedarwood, discovering a hairpin, onion skins, and several black cigar butts that Petrosino said were of Italian make—detritus, the detective noted, from a restaurant floor. Carey, running a finger along the inside of the staves, felt tiny granules grind against his skin. Several lodged under his fingernails; lifting his hand to his mouth, the sergeant touched the tip against his tongue and tasted sugar. That suggested the barrel had at one time been the property of a candy store, a pastry shop, or a café.

It was only as the morning brightened into daylight that the most important clue emerged. Peering for the first time at the barrel's base, Carey made out the faint marks of a stencil. There, in muted ink, he read the legend "W&T." And, stamped along the side of a stave, was a faint serial number: "G.223." The two detectives glanced at each other. Here at last was a lead worth following.

NEW YORK'S PRINCIPAL SUGAR refineries sat bunched together on the far side of the East River, belching smoke along the waterfront. Carey spent the remainder of the morning and part of the afternoon trudging from one to another, until at last he found a factory where clerks recognized the stencil marks. "W&T," the detective was told, were the initials of one of the refinery's customers: Wallace & Thompson, a grocer on Washington Street. "G.223" denoted a recent consignment consisting of six hoopless barrels of sugar.

The man at Wallace & Thompson was just as helpful. He recalled the order and told Carey that all six barrels had already been sold. Half of the consignment had been broken up and disposed of in ten-pound lots, but the other three barrels had been sold entire.

"Have you got any Italian customers?" Carey asked.

"Only one," replied the clerk. "Pietro Inzerillo, who has a pastry shop in Elizabeth Street." Inzerillo had purchased two barrels of sugar for his Café Pasticceria, a popular meeting spot for working-class immigrants that stood just around the corner from the Prince Street saloon.

Sending word for Petrosino to join him, Carey hastened off to Little Italy.

AN AMBULANCE BROUGHT Madonia's body to the city morgue midway through the morning. The coroner's surgeon, Dr. Albert Weston, was waiting; he performed a quick, efficient autopsy, noting a physical description, listing wounds, and informing the police that their anonymous victim had died sometime between 3:30 and 4 A.M. The examination uncovered several other clues as well. Seventeen separate wounds had been carved into the man's face after he died—suggesting, the coroner thought, the motive of revenge. And the scarcely digested Sicilian meal that Weston found in the man's stomach was the first firm evidence McClusky had as to Madonia's nationality and to what he had been doing at the time that he was murdered.

The autopsy complete, Weston laid the corpse on a bed of ice. In this way the remains could be preserved, at least for several weeks, while attempts were made to discover its identity. Soon after lunch, the first in a long line of policemen and potential witnesses began calling at the morgue, sent there by McClusky in the hope that someone would recognize that striking face; in time, more than a thousand people would file hopefully past the body. Weston even allowed a photographer from William Randolph Hearst's muckraking *New York Journal* to snap a picture of the cadaver as it lay on the slab. That sort of thing was usually frowned on, but the *Journal*, with its screaming headlines, simple text, and ample use of illustrations, boasted a larger circulation among the immigrant community than any other New York paper. By evening half a million of its readers would have seen the dead man's face. Surely one of them would recognize it.

McClusky fed Weston's information to his men. Nobody could say that the police were not making every effort to solve the case; hundreds of detectives from precincts all over the city had been pulled off their normal duties to question informants and to hunt for clues, and virtually the whole of the uniformed force was sucked into the investigation, too; even long-serving Manhattan crime reporters could scarcely remember a time when so great a proportion of police resources had been devoted to a single case. Yet by mid-afternoon, Carey and Petrosino aside, not one of the NYPD's thousands of officers had come up with a worthwhile lead. The mystery man in the rickety barrel seemed to have sprung from nowhere; no one had seen him loitering around the city, noticed anything suspicious, or had the least idea how a well-dressed Sicilian with chestnut eyes might have come to such an awful end.

No one, that is, but a man sitting in an anonymous Wall Street office who had glimpsed Madonia just once, the day before the murder.

THE MOST ATTENTIVE READER of the evening papers sprawled behind a desk in Manhattan's Treasury Building, leafing with growing interest through pages dense with coverage of the barrel mystery.

William Flynn was chief of the New York bureau of the U.S. Secret Service, which made him the most important agent in the country outside Washington. A native of Manhattan, the son of an Irish immigrant, and educated in the city's public schools, Flynn did not look much like anyone's idea of a government man. He was thirty-six years old and tall, close-cropped, and bullet-headed, with the powerful build of the semi-professional baseball player that he had been in his twenties and a face that too much desk work was beginning to turn jowly. Flynn had an unlikely background for a Secret Service agent, too; he had left school at fifteen to be a plumber and later worked for several years as a guard in a New York jail. But he was a great deal cleverer than his bland looks and sausage body might suggest. In the six years since he had joined the service, Chief Flynn had blazed such a trail through New Orleans, Washington, and Pittsburgh that John Wilkie, the agency's director, had personally selected him to tackle the toughest posting that the service had to offer. Now here he was on Wall Street, the U.S. government's most senior detective.

Flynn's job was to keep the biggest city in the country free from counterfeiters and forged bills. Although best known today for guarding the president, the Secret Service was, and remains, a department of the Treasury. It had been founded after the Civil War, at a time when nearly half of all the cash in circulation was counterfeit, and its first duty has always been to maintain robust public confidence in the value of the dollar. The agency came by its close protection role by accident—one of Flynn's predecessors in the New York office had actually been demoted for informally assigning men to guard President Cleveland—and even in 1903, after the assassination of William McKinley had forced Washington to take that problem much more seriously, nine-tenths of Secret Service manpower, and practically all its budget, was devoted to the war on counterfeiting. The work demanded men of unusual ability; forgers rarely committed messy, headline-grabbing crimes, they could work from almost anywhere and were noted for their brains. Tracking them down and procuring evidence against them called for patience, thoroughness, and cunning. In all these qualities, Flynn excelled.

The counterfeiting problem in New York was particularly bad. Large quantities of fake notes and bad coins were in circulation. A few of these were first-rate forgeries; most counterfeit currency, though, consisted of badly printed notes on poor-quality paper and crudely struck half-dollar coins and quarters. These unskillful fakes were never intended to fool bankers or Treasury men; they were put into circulation by small-time crooks known as "queer-pushers," who bought them at a discount from the men who forged them and took their chances palming them off on harassed bartenders and shopkeepers. Queer-pushing was far easier when practiced in poor immigrant districts, where crowds were dense and the locals unsophisticated. It was for this reason that counterfeiting was especially common in the Jewish and Italian enclaves of New York—and for this reason, too, that Flynn had spent the evening, a day earlier, loitering outside a butcher's shop on Stanton Street in Little Italy.

The Secret Service had been aware ever since the spring of 1899 that Sicilian forgers were passing bad money in New York, and over the years its agents had arrested a number of queer-pushers who were agents of the gang. Half a dozen of these small fish had been convicted and given sentences of as much as six years; most recently, on New Year's Eve 1902, a group of Italians had been caught in Yonkers passing counterfeit five-dollar bills drawn on the Iron Bank of Morristown, New Jersey. Three of the members of this gang had been convicted a month before the Barrel Murder. They had gone to jail tight-lipped—much to Flynn's frustration—refusing to reveal either the names of their suppliers or the location of their printing works.

It had taken the Secret Service twelve weeks, and a large expenditure of effort, to solve the mystery of the Morristown fives. In the end, however, long hours of covert observation and the careful cultivation of informants drew agents to a dingy butcher's shop at 16 Stanton Street, a two-minute walk from the spaghetti restaurant where Madonia would meet his death. The store, Flynn learned, had changed hands in early April. Its new owner was a large and powerful Sicilian named Vito Laduca.

The trail that had led Flynn to Stanton Street worried the Secret Service chief considerably. For one thing, the previous owner of the butcher's shop, the man who had agreed to sell the store, had vanished on the day the sale was due to be completed, and the police could find no trace of him; they were increasingly convinced he had been murdered. For another, Laduca himself had been arrested for counterfeiting some weeks earlier. He had been picked up in Pittsburgh early in January on suspicion of passing the same forged five-dollar bills that were now circulating in Manhattan, and though the Pennsylvania authorities had been unable to make the charges stick, investigation had established that Laduca's New York associates were not the sort a law-abiding man would choose as friends. Some, such as the confectioner Pietro Inzerillo, whose café stood just around the corner, had no police records but were of growing interest to the Secret Service. Others were known criminals. Of these, by far the most daunting was the counterfeiters' leader, a slight man of nearly forty who came from Corleone, south of Palermo. He had a criminal record on both sides of the Atlantic, having been arrested for a double murder in Sicily and in New York for forging bills. He also had a maimed right hand and jet-black eyes.

William Flynn had built his reputation on a formidable ability to catch the most elusive forgers; in the course of his six-year career he had set out on the trail of dozens of counterfeiters and failed to convict only one. But Giuseppe Morello and his men had proved to be formidable adversaries. Two months earlier, in February, Flynn had asked one of his Italian informants to infiltrate the gang, but the Sicilians were clannish and shunned approaches from strangers. In March, trying a different tack, Flynn ordered a second stool pigeon to strike up a business acquaintance with Messina Genova, who kept a store of his own a little way down Stanton Street. Giovanni La Cava, the most reliable man the Chief had in Little Italy, made the approach with an offer to sell real estate at bargain prices, but Genova haughtily rebuffed him, remarking that Sicilians had had enough of being cheated by crooks from mainland Italy. "La Cava is a good man," Flynn wrote despairingly to Washington, "but he won't connect with [them]. It seems next to impossible for an outsider to break into this gang."

La Cava's failure was a blow to Flynn, who found himself forced to resort to far more time-consuming measures to gather evidence against the counterfeiters. With no man on the inside of the group, long hours of covert observation would be needed to deduce the size and hierarchy of the gang. It was a decision that the Chief would rather not have taken; keeping watch in Little Italy was no easy task, and it placed a huge strain on his limited resources. At least three operatives were required to monitor a single location, and he had only nine agents to deploy across the whole of New York. But, beginning early that April, Flynn's men took up positions on Stanton Street and began to take careful note of every man who went into or out of the butcher's shop.

It was tedious and unrewarding work that required a keen eye and a memory for faces. The surveillance began each day at 8 A.M. and ran until after dark. Flynn's agents, disguised as laborers, hung about in doorways and had to be careful not to say too much, for fear of giving themselves away in a district in which everybody spoke Italian. They rotated duties where they could, relieving one another every few hours to reduce the chances of attracting notice and working usually in pairs, so there was a man available to tail a suspect and another to maintain the watch.

The results of the first two weeks of work were mixed. Several of the most frequent callers to the shop proved to be well known to the Secret Service; in time, with tips and help provided by informants, the operatives put names to almost a dozen members of the counterfeiting gang. But seven or eight others could not be identified, and on April 13, after work, Flynn decided to travel up to Stanton Street himself to make a personal assessment of the situation.

It was a cold and blowy evening, threatening rain, when the Chief alighted from his streetcar on the Bowery, downtown Manhattan's great thoroughfare. Laduca's store stood several hundred yards away, down a busy street clogged with pushcarts thrust hard up against the pavements and peddlers sending up a cacophony of Sicilian slang as they hawked everything from hardware to vegetables from their stalls. Despite the weather, the sidewalk and the street were thronged with men hastening home from work and women dressed in black hunting for bargains, and everywhere there were gangs of rough-clad children, playing in between the carts or scavenging food or change that had fallen in the dirt. Flynn, cocooned in an overcoat and with his head bowed against the wind, forced his way through the crowd until he picked out the first of his agents, Operative John Henry, who was skulking against a doorway across the road from the butcher's store. Henry had been hanging around in the vicinity since 1:15 P.M. Now, he rapidly explained to Flynn, Morello and two of his associates were holding a discussion of some sort in Laduca's shop. A fourth Italian, a stranger Henry had not seen before, had left the shop a little earlier. He was now lounging, smoking a cigarette, against a streetlamp down the street.

Flynn and Henry kept watch as the sky darkened and the conversation in the butcher's store grew more heated. They felt sure that the counterfeiters had not seen them. But, after a while, one of the men inside 16 Stanton Street broke off from the conversation and came to the door carrying a hammer and a curtain. He tacked the cloth across the entrance, barring the interior from view as the muffled voices drifting from the shop rose higher still.

Unable to see or hear anything of importance, Flynn switched his attention to the stranger smoking down the street. In the gathering twilight it was difficult to make out his face. Light from the flickering streetlamp slanted down, throwing most of the Italian's features into shadow as he pulled hard on his cigarette. Still, the Chief was able to get a long look at his suit—brown, it seemed in the fading light—and profile. He felt certain he would recognize the man again.

THE EVENING PAPERS, when they arrived at the Treasury Building next afternoon, led with lengthy coverage of the barrel mystery. The *Brooklyn Eagle,* the *Sun,* and the *Evening World* all reported in the same shocked tones the discovery of the body on East 11th Street and described in vivid detail the wounds that it had borne. Enterprising newsmen had sought out and interviewed Frances Connors and buttonholed Inspector McClusky, who had told them that the murder was most likely an act of vengeance. In the absence of an established motive, the rival papers speculated wildly as to who had killed the victim and why. "Death by torture seems to have been the fate of the man," the *World* suggested, with an almost audible rubbing of hands. "There were no bruises to the body, [and] it appeared as though the man had been held by the arms and legs. . . . This is one of the most interesting murders that has mystified New York in many years."

Sitting alone in his office at the end of the day, Flynn leafed through these reports with interest. The detective in him enjoyed absorbing the details of the case and puzzling over what the newspapers agreed was the most baffling of its mysteries—the problem of the dead man's identity. Beyond the likelihood that the victim was Italian, none of the dozens of journalists and the hundreds of patrolmen who had been scouring Manhattan had any real idea who he was. The *Eagle* focused most of its attention on the torn slip of paper that had been found in the dead man's pocket, which McClusky thought might have been a note sent to lure the man to his death, but the fragment was not much of a clue: "It was exceedingly hard, because of the fact that it was blurred, bloody and burned, to decipher the writing," the newspaper confessed. Only the *Mail and Express* had come up with anything more promising. "An employee of the Street Cleaning Department, named Zido, called at the station and saw the body," it informed its readers. "He said it looked like a man whom he had seen peddling fish on the East Side." But among several hundred East Siders sent by the police to shuffle past the cadaver,

Zido was the only one who thought he recognized that face. "Twenty hours of zealous searching by three sets of detectives and by many reporters have failed to reveal any clue to the identity of the murdered man," confirmed the *Evening World*.

Thus far, Flynn had no reason to suppose that the barrel victim, found on an Irish East Side street, had any connection to his own investigation. It was only when the Chief opened that day's *New York Journal* that he sat up with a start. Hearst's daily had secured the only photograph of the dead man lying on the slab. Its picture had been hurriedly composed and poorly shot—it had been snatched from a low angle and showed the corpse's face only in profile. But there was something deeply familiar about those features.

Flynn felt certain he had seen the man before. Where, though? The Secret Service man closed his door, lit a cigar, and searched his mental files of suspects. After a while it came to him. The face of the man in the morgue was that of the stranger he had watched the previous night slouching against a streetlamp in Stanton Street. He had the same hair, the same straight nose. Folding up his copy of the *Journal,* the Chief summoned Operative Henry. Get down to the morgue as soon as possible, he said. Call back when you have seen the body.

Henry left Wall Street flanked by two other agents who had kept the watch on Stanton Street, and it was past 6:30 P.M. when they phoned in. All three, Henry explained, believed they recognized the dead man from Laduca's store. But there was still at least a little room for doubt. The face of the barrel victim greatly resembled that of the man who had loitered under a streetlamp the previous evening, but his clothes seemed different. The man in Little Italy had been clad in a brown three-piece suit. The barrel victim was wearing blue.

Henry's call bothered Flynn. He thought it highly unlikely that the dead man had changed his clothes in the few hours that separated his appearance on Stanton Street from his violent death. After mulling the problem over for a moment, though, it struck him that he and his operatives might have been the victims of some optical illusion. The man they had watched on Stanton Street had been standing almost directly beneath a slanting electric light that had made it almost impossible to make out the details of his clothing.

The possibility needed to be checked, so Flynn called the East Side precinct house where the body had been taken and arranged to have the dead man's clothes sent over to his office. While he waited for his package to arrive, the Chief rigged up a light over his desk to simulate the streetlight by Laduca's store. He carefully adjusted the fitting so that it shone down at the same angle as the lamp in Stanton Street, then turned off the other bulbs in the office. Soon enough there was a knock at the door and another agent entered with a package that contained the blood-stained suit. Flynn tore off the wrapper and thrust the bundle under the slanting light. He stood well back and squinted.

The cloth looked brown. He reached for the phone on his desk and placed an urgent call to Inspector McClusky.

MEANWHILE, UP IN LITTLE ITALY, Sergeants Carey and Petrosino had found the Café Pasticceria. Its owner, Pietro Inzerillo, was scrawny, almost illiterate, and much older than the other members of Morello's gang—he was a graying forty-four years old and sported an unfashionable mustache. Grudgingly, the confectioner escorted the policemen to his cellar and allowed them to inspect his stores. It did not take Petrosino long to spot a barrel full of sugar that was practically identical to the one that had appeared on East 11th Street. Squatting to examine it more closely, the detective noticed that it bore precisely the same markings: "W&T" stenciled on the base and "G.223" stamped along the staves.

Inzerillo freely admitted that he had purchased two such barrels from Wallace & Thompson and seemed unperturbed when Petrosino wanted to know what had happened to the missing one. When it was empty, the shopkeeper replied, he had taken it upstairs and dumped it in an alley with half a dozen others. He had then sold the lot. Three or four men had come to pick up the empty barrels, but he could not describe them. It was the common practice in the district; barrels were useful things, and he was happy to let his fellow Sicilians purchase the ones that he had finished with.

Petrosino scribbled Inzerillo's statement down. But he did not believe it.

THANKS TO CAREY, FLYNN, AND PETROSINO, the police now knew a good deal more about the barrel victim than they had that morning. They had learned that he seemed to be a stranger to New York and that he had links to an important counterfeiting gang. They knew he had been seen, hours before his death, in the company of several dangerous criminals. They also believed that they had traced the barrel he was found in. But one vital piece of information was still missing. They had absolutely no idea of the dead man's name.

At midnight, responding to Chief Flynn's call, Inspector McClusky arrived at the Treasury Building with two other senior policemen for a briefing on the Morello gang. For the better part of an hour, Flynn ran methodically through everything the Secret Service had discovered about the forgers: their names, their records, and the scale and nature of their operation. Morello, he warned McClusky, was a dangerous individual: cunning, intelligent, and—unlike the great majority of counterfeiters—perfectly willing to use violence. His friends Laduca and Genova were ruthless, too, and the remaining members of the gang were almost as formidable. Among the other members of the group, Flynn pointed out, were Joseph Fanaro, a red-bearded giant of a man—six feet four in his socks—whom Secret Service operatives had seen escorting the barrel victim around Little Italy. Fanaro, the Chief thought, had been assigned to watch over the stranger and ensure that he did not slip away.

It was almost 1 A.M. by the time Flynn finished and the conversation turned to strategy. McClusky, headstrong as ever, was only too aware that his superiors wanted evidence that he was making progress. The press, too, would be expecting action. Now was no time to wait and see how things developed; he and his men, he said, would round up all the members of Morello's gang next afternoon, confident that at least one of them would talk under interrogation. The fact that the arrests would take place in time to feature in the next day's papers was not mentioned, but it was scarcely incidental to the inspector's thinking.

Flynn was utterly appalled. His own investigation would be fatally compromised, he urged, and, anyway, it was too early to be talking of arrests. Likely as it was that Morello and his men knew all about the barrel murder, there was as yet no shred of proof that they were actually involved—and hence there was a real chance that the killers would go free for lack of evidence. The best way forward, the Chief urged, was further observation, which would almost certainly produce new leads. At present Morello did not know that he was being watched. Arrests would simply put the whole gang firmly on its guard.

Flynn pleaded, but McClusky would not be budged and the truth was that the Secret Service had no jurisdiction in a murder case; indeed, the Chief's only role in the operation that was being planned would be to point out the members of the gang to the police. The discussion went on for nearly half an hour, but, in the end, the only concession that Flynn could wring out of Chesty George was a promise that his men would be allowed to search Morello's home after his arrest.

By the time McClusky and his colleagues left the building, it was past 1:15 on the morning of April 16. The Chief stayed just long enough to draft a note to Secret Service director Wilkie explaining what had happened. Ten minutes later, he, too, headed home.

FLYNN'S OPERATIVES WERE back on duty seven hours later, maintaining their usual watch on Stanton Street. Other agents were posted outside Morello's apartment on nearby Chrystie Street and opposite Inzerillo's café; two more loitered on the Bowery. Each group was accompanied by twice the number of plainclothes detectives, which reassured the Secret Service men but made it hard for them to remain inconspicuous.

The police plan was certainly ambitious. It called for almost a dozen members of the counterfeiting gang to be spotted, individually, by Flynn's agents, then followed as they moved about New York until the whole gang was in the authorities' grasp. Adding to the danger that something would go wrong, McClusky was adamant that Morello himself should be the first man arrested. His capture would be the signal for the other teams to move in on their targets—a decision almost as difficult to implement, given the communications available at the time, as the task of following a large number of wary Sicilians around New York for half a day or more without being noticed. To make matters worse, as Flynn had warned, the counterfeiters would certainly be armed.

April 15 proved to be a challenge such as the New York bureau of the Secret Service had not faced before. Almost every agent in the city had been pulled from other investigations and stationed south of 14th Street, while Flynn himself took up position at police headquarters to help coordinate the operation. The members of the counterfeiting gang were nightbirds, not early risers, but the first of Morello's men was spotted as early as 10:45 A.M. and others were acquired one by one until, by midafternoon, Flynn's operatives had five under observation. Snatched phone calls to police headquarters kept the Chief informed of progress, but there was still no sign of Morello. Flynn and McClusky waited, growing gradually more apprehensive, as the afternoon dragged on and the members of the gang flitted to and fro between their homes, Laduca's store, the bar on Prince Street, and the Café Pasticceria. Abetted by frequent showers of rain, several of the Clutch Hand's men lost themselves in the teeming streets, only to be picked up again anxious minutes later.

Flynn's luck held through the long afternoon, but by sunset Morello was still nowhere to be seen. Since there was little prospect of continuing surveillance after dark, McClusky began reluctantly preparing to abandon operations for the night. Then, at 7:10 P.M., the inspector's office door flew open. Standing on the threshold was Secret Service operative Henry, who had run over from Elizabeth Street. Morello had appeared in Little Italy, he said.

The news that Henry brought was critical. The counterfeiter, spotted on Elizabeth Street, had been followed until he entered the Café Pasticceria, where he fell into a long conversation with Inzerillo. McClusky and Flynn had debated what to do in this event and concluded that it would be dangerous to arrest two armed men within the crowded confines of the little café. Better to let Morello conclude his business and leave for home. Better to seize the two men independently.

The lights were coming on across the city as Henry and Flynn hurried out onto a damp Mulberry Street. While Henry hastened back to resume his watch at Inzerillo's, Flynn made instead for the entrance to Delancey Street—a spot he knew, from weeks of observation, that Morello would pass on his way back to his apartment. The Chief splashed through the puddles on East Houston and jogged down the Bowery until he found two more of his operatives and four burly detective sergeants standing against a hoarding on the corner.

The seven men waited impatiently for Morello to appear, but he had not yet left the Café Pasticceria. Flynn's resources were stretched so thin by McClusky's operation that there was no chance of freeing any agents to carry messages, and so no way of getting warning that their man was on the move. The resultant uncertainty made the watch a nervous one, more so as the wait stretched to three-quarters of an hour. It was not until 8 P.M. that the Clutch Hand turned in to Delancey Street, his slight figure silhouetted for a moment against the bright lights of the Bowery. Flynn signaled frantically to the detectives. As he did so, a second man rounded the corner and the Chief saw that Morello had a companion. Petto the Ox was accompanying him home.

The two Sicilians had no chance; McClusky's men were on them in an instant. The four muscular policemen hurled themselves bodily at the counterfeiters, knocking the Clutch Hand to the pavement. Petto, taller and stronger, received a punch between the eyes, swayed for an instant, and then went down as well with two detectives on top of him. The winded counterfeiters tried to reach for their inner pockets, but the policemen knocked their arms away.

Breathing a little heavily, the detectives hauled Petto and Morello to their feet and handcuffed them. Then they began to search their prisoners. Both men proved to be heavily armed. The Ox carried a pistol in a holster and a stiletto in a leather sheath; his boss was concealing a fully loaded .45-caliber revolver in his waistband and had a murderous-looking unsheathed knife strapped to his leg. "A cork," Flynn observed—sounding impressed despite himself—"fixed on the point of the blade prevented it scratching his leg and allowed him to bring it into play with a single motion much more readily than had he carried it in a sheath."

Forcing their way through the crowd of excited onlookers that had rapidly surrounded them, the four detectives frog-marched their prisoners off toward police headquarters, where the two counterfeiters were thrown into separate cells. Inspector McClusky then issued orders for all the other members of the gang to be rounded up, and the results were gratifyingly swift. Secret Service operative Frank Burns and his police escort cornered the Sicilian they had been watching in a basement room in Elizabeth Street and managed to get him out of the building without attracting a crowd. Pietro Inzerillo was arrested without incident in his store, and Joseph Fanaro was seized outside Morello's restaurant on Prince Street. None were given time to draw the weapons they were carrying. The closest McClusky's detectives came to trouble was on the Bowery, where two other members of the gang glanced up in time to see a quartet of policemen bearing down on them. The Sicilians half drew their revolvers, but the policemen disarmed both with their nightsticks, relieving their prisoners of two more guns and a set of lethal stilettos.

Eight members of Morello's gang were arrested that evening, and a ninth at midnight. Almost all proved to be as well equipped as their boss—the next day, newspapermen were invited to photograph a table-top laden with all the daggers and revolvers found on them—and most, to Flynn's considerable annoyance, had permits that entitled them to go about the city armed.

McClusky was jubilant at his success—"radiant," one newspaperman described him, and "all smiles." His men, relieved to have made so many arrests without serious incident, celebrated, too. But, the man from the *New York Sun* observed, "Flynn and his Secret Service agents didn't smile or express any particular joy. The agents who did all the clever work in this case looked bored." The reporter was right to note the difference in the response of the detectives and Flynn's operatives, but he was quite wrong in guessing the reason. The Chief was not bored; he was worried. He felt sure that McClusky had just made a serious mistake.

IT WAS OBVIOUS, as early as the next morning, that Flynn's concerns were justified. Searches of all the prisoners' apartments turned up large quantities of correspondence, written in impenetrable Sicilian, but no sign of any contraband—no forged notes, no bad coins, and no printing plates—nor anything to link the barrel victim directly to Morello's men. Nor were the "strenuous efforts" that the police made to squeeze statements from the suspects any more fruitful, despite application of the brutal methods of the third degree. Not one of the arrested men would talk, and when Flynn took the Sicilians, one by one, down to the morgue to ask them if they recognized the body, none said a word to indicate they did. Morello, whom the Chief's men had seen talking at length to the barrel victim two days earlier, "showed not the slightest sign of recognition or agitation," a disappointed Flynn confessed. "He shrugged his shoulders and volunteered the statement: 'Don't know.'"

In the absence of a confession, McClusky's case remained slender indeed. Several cigars found in Petto's pocket were of a variety identical to the ones Petrosino had discovered on East 11th Street. A sample of the sawdust from Morello's restaurant, which Carey took after the arrest, looked much the same as the bloodstained shavings in the barrel. And a search of the Clutch Hand's dingy attic room on Chrystie Street turned up a collar of the same size and make as the one worn by the dead man. It was enough to impress the newspapermen covering the story, who reported that charges were expected any day, but scarcely sufficient to convince either the district attorney's office or the Secret Service. "The police redoubled their efforts," Flynn recalled, "but to no avail. Every clew, and there were few enough of them, led to nothing. Each new line, which was run down to no purpose, left the case more baffling."

THE BREAKTHROUGH THAT MCCLUSKY had been praying for came three days later, unexpectedly, when a clerk opening the mail at police head-quarters discovered an anonymous letter addressed to the inspector.

"I know the man who was found in the barrel," the note began.

He comes from Buffalo for the purpose of getting money . . . he was condemned for false papers. The police have made the proper arrests, bring the condemned Giuseppe Di Priemo from Sing Sing, promise him his liberty and he will tell you many and many things, do as I write and you will discover all. We salute.

Yours friends S.T.

McClusky read the letter through more than once without feeling much the wiser for it. It had evidently been composed by an Italian with a limited command of English but a rather better knowledge of Morello's gang. The reference to "false papers" suggested that the dead man in the barrel had been a forger, too, and the suggestion that he came from Buffalo made sense—it certainly explained why no one in Little Italy had recognized the corpse. But the name Giuseppe Di Priemo meant nothing to the men of the Detective Bureau; nor did McClusky have any idea why such a person should be locked up in Sing Sing, an infamous prison on the banks of the Hudson River thirty miles north of New York, where a large proportion of Manhattan's criminals spent at least a part of their careers.

Still, if the murder was the product of some counterfeiters' feud, the Secret Service would most likely know more, and a brief phone call to William Flynn was all it took to enlighten the inspector. Flynn was per-fectly familiar with the name: Di Priemo, he informed McClusky, was a middle-ranking member of Morello's gang, one of four Sicilians who had been arrested on New Year's Eve for passing forged five-dollar bills in Yonkers. He was a native of Lercara Friddi, in the Sicilian interior, had lived in New York for three years, and—thanks to his recent conviction in a federal court—had just begun a four-year sentence for counterfeiting. The Chief recalled Di Priemo as uncommunicative to a fault, but, with several years to serve, the desire to cut something from that sentence might just make him willing to talk.

It would take a man a day to travel from New York to Sing Sing and back, but the barrel investigation was going nowhere. McClusky decided to send Petrosino to see prisoner Di Priemo. An Italian speaker would have a much better chance of getting information from the Sicilian than an ordinary detective would.

THE GREAT GRIM BULK of Sing Sing Correctional Facility had been carved out of a hillside on the steep banks of the Hudson at a point where the river swept off in a wide bend to the west, away from New York. The whole prison had been hewn from the gray marble that abounded in the district: the claustrophobia-inducing walls that enclosed the entire complex, the main block with its minute cells (each eight feet long and three feet wide), the death house, and the multitude of workshops in which the jail's thousands of prisoners were set to work each day. It was a terrible place in which to be incarcerated: cramped, rigidly disciplined, and so close to the fast-running river that a chilly dampness permeated everywhere. Each cell held nothing but a cot, a lamp, a Bible, and a slop bucket; the bathing facilities were nonexistent; and the whole prison, in the words of one Sing Sing warden, lay in the grip of "a coldness that hovers like a pall, and a heaviness that presses down upon the spirit like a huge millstone."

For a newly arrived prisoner such as Giuseppe Di Priemo, Sing Sing was very close to hell. The penitentiary squatted on a low bluff half a mile above the village of Ossining and had been carefully positioned so that the men imprisoned there could be made to break rocks in quarries within its perimeter; its very name, a corruption of the Indian phrase *sint sincks,* meant "stone upon stone." The prison, indeed, had been constructed in the 1820s by its own first inmates, and a large proportion of the convicts still worked the local marble, enduring brutal conditions as they cut and shaped each stone. Over the years, though, as the prison grew, it had diversified into several other industries. By 1903, Sing Sing was one of the largest industrial complexes in the United States, and the factories inside its walls made iron stoves, forged chains, and manufactured shoes. The newest prisoners, though, were set to work in the jail's steam laundry, where they labored in what were reputedly the worst conditions in the entire U.S. prison system, washing, drying, starching, and ironing thousands of shirts a day in temperatures that sometimes reached 150 degrees.

It may thus have been sheer desperation that drove Di Priemo to see Petrosino when the detective reached Ossining on the afternoon of April 19. Certainly the prisoner possessed, in full measure, the Sicilian's ingrained antipathy to the police. Di Priemo began the interview cool and uncommunicative, and despite Petrosino's ingratiating Italian, seemed uninterested in answering anything but the most basic questions.

The two men made for an interesting study. They were close in age—Petrosino was thirty-six years old, Di Priemo twenty-eight—and looked not unlike each other. Both men were short and stocky; both were physically strong. But the detective had one great advantage over the monosyllabic prisoner: a surprise to shock him into talking.

"Do you recognize this man?"

Petrosino slid a photograph of the barrel victim across the table. It had been taken in the New York morgue after the undertaker had done his best to patch up the dead man's wounds. The eyes were glassy and the rip in the throat had been concealed by dressing the corpse in a high collar, but the face was recognizable.

Di Priemo glanced down and stiffened. "Yes," he agreed, taken aback despite himself. "I know that man, of course I do. He's my brother-in-law. What's the matter with him? Sick?"

"He's dead," said Petrosino.

Even the detective, with his years of experience, was surprised by what happened next. There was a moment's shocked silence. Then Di Priemo, the tough Sicilian counterfeiter, swayed and collapsed—some sort of faint, Petrosino thought. It took a minute or two to revive him, and longer before he could continue. When he did, his demeanor had changed from suspicious to downright uncommunicative. "My brother-in-law lived in Buffalo," was all he would say. "He had a wife and family there. His name is Benedetto Madonia. His wife is my sister."

Di Priemo gave the Italian detective an address in Buffalo, but he refused absolutely to say more. Petrosino could get not a syllable out of him concerning Madonia's murder or the dead man's relationship with Giuseppe Morello.

He telephoned the news back to New York in any case, and

McClusky called it through to Flynn. The Chief was sitting in his office with a Sicilian translator when the phone rang, working his way slowly through the piles of letter books and correspondence seized from Morello's room. He felt sure that he had seen Madonia's name somewhere earlier that day, and leafing back through the Clutch Hand's untidy ledgers, he eventually found it. Scrawled along the edge of an interior page were the words "Madonia Benedetto, 47 Trenton Avenue, Buffalo, New York." The note, Flynn observed with interest, was in Morello's handwriting. Unlike the other entries on the page, it had been scribbled in red ink.

BY THE TIME PETROSINO got to Buffalo, Madonia's wife had heard what had happened to her husband.

The salacious *New York Journal,* which had better contacts and deeper pockets than any other paper in New York, got word of Petrosino's trip to Sing Sing from an informant at police headquarters as soon as the Italian detective phoned in his report. A hurried telegram to the paper's stringer in Buffalo brought the reporter and a local beat policeman to Madonia's apartment in a two-story frame house that evening. The two men found the oldest of the barrel victim's children, twenty-one-year-old Salvatore, sitting outside enjoying the spring air.

Harry Evans, the Buffalo policeman, was a man of limited tact. Introducing himself, he bluntly explained: "The New York police believe that the Italian who was found with his throat cut is your father."

"I don't know about that," Salvatore answered warily.

"Is your father home?"

"My father is in New York, but we expect him home in a few days."

Evans pressed his point: "Do you know whether or not your father is alive?"

"I guess he is."

It was only when the reporter handed Madonia the *Journal's* photo of his father's body lying in the New York morgue that the news sank in. Badly shaken, the dead man's son burst into tears, then ran blindly back into the house in search of a family portrait. He held the snapshot and the folded copy of the *Journal* side by side. There was no room for doubt; the two photographs depicted the same man.

"You had better come in," the young man told his visitors.

———

PETROSINO ARRIVED at the Madonia house the next morning to find the whole family in mourning and the dead man's wife in bed. Lucy Madonia had been unwell even before word of her husband's brutal murder reached her. Now she looked drawn and ill, older by far than her forty-two years.

It took Lucy a long time to admit that she knew anything of her husband's activities. He was just a mason, she insisted in response to Petrosino's questioning, and had never been in trouble in his life. Yes, Benedetto had done what he could to help her brother when they heard of his imprisonment; he had hurried down to New York to see a lawyer, then journeyed on to Sing Sing to visit Di Priemo. But his purpose was simply to request that his brother-in-law be moved to the penitentiary at Erie, Pennsylvania, where it would be much easier for his family to visit him.

Petrosino persisted. He had experience with interrogation and knew when to hold back information and just when to reveal it. By the time that he had laid out all the police and the Secret Service knew about Benedetto, Lucy Madonia had been compelled to agree that her husband was indeed acquainted with a group of Sicilians in New York. He had "gone out on the road" for them, she admitted, shuttling by rail from Pittsburgh to Chicago and Buffalo. What exactly Madonia had done on his visits to those cities Lucy did not know, she said, but the Secret Service men to whom Petrosino showed her statement on his return to Manhattan recognized the route as one often employed by counterfeiters. This tied in well with the anonymous letter writer's claim that Madonia had a conviction, at home in Sicily, for passing forged bills.

Mrs. Madonia had one more thing to tell Petrosino. Her brother, Di Priemo, she confided, had written to her more than a month ago to say he was in trouble. Soon after that, he had cabled urgently for funds. From somewhere, her husband had raised a thousand dollars—a large sum, and one he dared not send directly. With Di Priemo in custody pending his trial, Benedetto had instead addressed his envelope to an acquaintance in New York. Enclosed with the money was a note instructing the man to take the cash and hand it to a man in a Prince Street saloon.

It was what happened next, Lucy thought, that had sent her husband to his death. Her husband's friends had received the money safely, but they had done precisely nothing to help Di Priemo, neither hiring him a lawyer nor using the cash to bring influence to bear to save him. Nor would they return the unspent dollars to Madonia. Inquiries, and, eventually, letters of entreaty, had no effect on them. In the end the Buffalo stonemason decided that his only chance of recovering the cash was to visit New York himself.

Then Mrs. Madonia added something else, something that made Petrosino start. There was one man, the widow said, who might know why Benedetto had been killed. Her husband had mentioned his name to her, just once, when they were debating how to help Di Priemo. A man called Giuseppe Morello, Madonia had whispered, was the head of a "great society, a secret society, of which he himself was a member, but Morello was against him and would do nothing to aid her brother."

Petrosino knew what that meant. It meant the maimed, implacable Morello was no mere counterfeiter with a ruthless streak.

He was something much more frightening. He was boss of the New York Mafia.

CHAPTER 2

MEN OF RESPECT

=

THE MAFIA, LIKE GIUSEPPE MORELLO HIMSELF, WAS BORN IN WESTern Sicily in the 1860s. It rooted and took shape in a land of stark beauty, grinding poverty, and frequent violence, insinuating its way into the fabric of the island until it exercised a malign, corrupting influence over most aspects of Sicilian life. It became—for the best part of a century— the richest and most successful criminal organization in the world. Yet it remained at base a study in enormous contradictions.

The Mafia was a secret society whose existence was known to every man and woman on the island. Its name was familiar to tens of thousands but was never spoken by its members. It stood for justice—or so it promised its initiates—in places where justice was hard to find, but in reality it worked hand in hand with the landed nobility to keep down Sicily's miserable peasantry. It worshipped honor but lusted after profit—and though, in New York, the society claimed to offer protection to the lowly immigrant, the truth was that, as late as 1920, it preyed exclusively upon the Italian community.

The Mafia thrived on violence. Its fearsome reputation, in both Sicily and the United States, was based on an eternal readiness to kill: men, women, infants, anyone who stood in its way. Its innocent victims—the businesses from which it extorted money, the parents of children held for ransom, inconvenient witnesses who saw or heard more than was good for them—all knew that Mafiosi carried out their threats and that failure to heed their warnings had dire consequences. To all that, though, was added a further diabolical refinement. From its earliest days, the Mafia nurtured an intricate web of working relationships with the people responsible for fighting it. Policemen were bribed. Landowners had favors done for them. Politicians were shown how helpful a ruthless group of criminals could be at election time. In this way, a fraternity that existed to sell protection was protected itself. The real reason why the Mafia was feared—and had its demands met, its orders obeyed—was not simply that it killed. It was that it seemed to be invulnerable. It killed *and got away with it.*

Understanding how and why this murderous society came into existence means understanding a little of the history of Sicily, for the Mafia could have arisen nowhere else. The island, which lies at the tip of the Italian boot, was a place unlike any other. It had been a vitally important crossroads for thousands of years, standing astride trade routes that ran north and south and east and west across the Mediterranean, and its strategic importance meant that it had been fought over ever since Roman times. Greeks, Arabs, Normans, Holy Roman Emperors, the French, and the Aragonese had ruled over Sicily, and all of them had ruthlessly exploited its people. Most recently, in the middle of the eighteenth century, the island had become subject to the Bourbon kings of Naples, a junior branch of the royal family of Spain, which ruled over a fragile patrimony known as the Kingdom of the Two Sicilies. The Bourbon state consisted of the southern half of mainland Italy and the island itself, but there was never any doubt as to which of its pair of provinces was most important. Its kings lived and reigned in Naples, the largest city in all Italy, and visited the island portion of their kingdom as infrequently as once a decade. Even in the Two Sicilies, in short, Sicily itself was seen as a distant, troublesome, and barbarous place—of value for its revenues but too rugged and too rural to befit a king.

For the people of the island, this indifference was to be expected. Centuries of occupation and harsh taxation, of being ruled from afar by men who had no roots on the island and no reason to care for it, bred in the local people a hatred of authority and a deep-rooted unwillingness to settle disputes through the same courts that protected foreign interests and enforced alien laws. Rebellion was commonplace in Sicilian history, and resistance—however mulish and unheroic—was seen as praiseworthy; private vengeance and vendetta were preferable to abiding by the rule of law. Even in the nineteenth century, outlaws were popular heroes there; banditry was more deeply rooted in Sicily than it was anywhere else in Europe, and it endured there longer, too. Little changed even after 1860, when Giuseppe Garibaldi landed on the island on his way to uniting all of Italy. Garibaldi himself was all but worshipped in Sicily because he freed it from its Bourbon overlords. But the Italy that he created, with its capital in Rome, treated Sicily much as the state that it replaced had done, extracting what it could in taxes and giving little or nothing in return. Peace was kept by a garrison of northerners and by police, recruited on the mainland, whose most important duty was not solving crimes but keeping order. The carabinieri did this by setting up and running a huge network of spies and informants to keep an eye on potential malcontents and revolutionaries.

It would be misleading, nonetheless, to think of the Sicily of 1860 as a province united in more than its suspicion of outsiders. There were considerable differences between the eastern districts, where the earth was rich and the local barons still lived on their estates, investing in roads, bridges, and irrigation schemes, and the western portions of the island, where it was far more difficult to wrest a living from the land. Western Sicily was a place of mountains, dust, poor soil, and poorer agricultural towns. A thin strip along the west coast was relatively wealthy; it consisted of the capital, Palermo—an elegant port with little fishing and less industry, many of whose people earned a living as functionaries of the state—and the Conca d'Oro, the Golden Shell, where the island's most important exports, oranges and lemons, were grown in innumerable small citrus groves. The aristocrats of the western hinterlands were mostly absentees, who preferred to live comfortably in Palermo and lease out their estates to grasping tenant farmers known as *gabelloti*. It was in the interest of the barons of Palermo to keep the city's working classes pacified with cheap bread and endless festivals, but the peasants of the distant interior were accorded less respectful treatment. In the eyes of many of the barons, they existed merely to grow food and pay taxes, at rates that, by 1860, required them to hand over half their crops and half their earnings to their landlords and the government.

These demands left peasants practically destitute, a state of affairs rendered more unbearable by the fact that most barons, and even the *gabelloti* who ran their estates, paid practically nothing. One army officer, sent over from the mainland to help keep order, remembered that

> it hurts to see some of the scenes you come across when you live here like I do. One hot day in July . . . I was on a long march with my men. We stopped for a rest by a farmyard where they were dividing the grain harvest. I went in to ask for some water. The

measuring had just finished, and the peasant had been left with no more than a small mound. Everything else had gone to his boss. The peasant stood with his hands and chin planted on the long handle of a shovel. At first, as if stunned, he stared at his share. Then he looked at his wife and four or five small children, thinking that after a year of sweat and hardship all he had left to feed his family with was that heap of grain. He seemed like a man set in stone. Except that a tear was gliding silently down from each eye.

All this was difficult enough when times were good. But times were rarely good for long in Sicily, and the lot of the peasantry worsened considerably in the course of the nineteenth century. The abolition of feudalism, which occurred only in 1812, upset the economy of the interior; it resulted in the dissolution of many large estates, with a consequent diminution in efficiency, and ushered in the rawest sort of capitalism. The *gabelloti*—who paid fixed rents to the barons for the right to farm their lands—had every motivation to extract the maximum revenues from their properties, and wages, where they were paid at all, were driven down by an abundance of labor, a population explosion in the early nineteenth century taking the number of Sicilians to as many as two million. That total far outstripped the numbers that the island could support, and the misery endured by Sicily's peasants was increased by a long succession of natural disasters—floods, drought, and landslides among them—that culminated in the terrible earthquake that destroyed the city of Messina in 1908 and killed as many as eighty thousand people. So great was the poverty in the western districts of the island, and so terrible the destitution, that as much as a third of the population of the island emigrated between 1870 and 1910, at first mostly to the cities of northern Italy but increasingly to the United States. One side effect of this unparalleled movement of men, women, and children was that, after about 1890, practically every family in Sicily had friends or relatives in the great American seaports, particularly New York and New Orleans.

For those who stayed behind on the island, poverty and the lack of opportunity combined to make crime increasingly commonplace in the latter half of the nineteenth century. Given the choice between a lifetime of toil in arid fields, struggling for survival, and the lures of the "bad life," the *mala vita,* thousands of Sicilian youths were tempted into careers of thievery and petty deception; and when, eventually, they were caught and sent to prison, they mixed there with far worse criminals and emerged as likely recruits for far more dangerous gangs. Crime on the island was, moreover, all too often violent. Government authority was never absolute in the depth of the Sicilian interior, and the failure of the Italian state to restrict power and weaponry to the hands of the police and army—to impose what historians would call a "monopoly on violence"—meant that many men habitually bore arms. The annual murder rate in western Sicily, which by 1890 ran at as much as sixty-seven deaths for every thousand people, was fifty times the rate in mainland Italy and paid eloquent testimony to Sicilians' propensity to deploy knives and guns to solve their problems.

One other factor, unique to Sicily, played a part in the emergence of the Mafia, and that was the readiness of large swaths of the island's population to conspire and rebel against hated authority. As early as the late eighteenth century, in the wake of the French Revolution, the Sicilian police began picking up reports of secret societies that met in remote parts of the countryside to swear oaths of loyalty and plot the downfall of the Bourbon monarchy. Although few in number at first, they grew; there were many such groups by the mid-1830s, and more a decade later, when, at the height of the unpopularity of the Naples government, one Palermo nobleman observed that "all the good citizens had begun to organize themselves in Secret Societies." Conditions for the formation of such groups remained propitious even after the unification of Italy in 1860; one of the new regime's earliest proclamations, a demand for universal military service, drove hundreds of Sicilian youths to flee into the interior and turn to banditry, not least because it was widely rumored that young men sent for service on the mainland were castrated.

Sicily's "brotherhoods" and "sects" were generally organized around a capo, or captain, who was often a *gabelloto*. Many borrowed the ideas and symbolism of the Masons, a secretive brotherhood, centuries old, whose notoriety and love of ritual had provided inspiration for any number of similar societies. There were others, though, with different inspirations, which owed loyalty to a radical village priest or which drew for their membership on the armed town militias that participated in uprisings against the hated Bourbons in 1820, 1848, and 1860 and rose again to support a Sicilian nationalist rebellion in 1866. Each of these groups had weaponry and men; each hated the government and the police. The "sects," like criminals and politicians, were in the business of controlling people, and it seemed natural for them to offer to protect their fellow citizens—against the Bourbons at first, then against their personal enemies—and to expect to be paid for their services. Within a year or two, predictably enough, "protection" morphed into protection rackets. Landlords, farmers, and ordinary villagers discovered that they were no longer paying to be shielded against the Bourbons. The protection that they paid for was protection from the "sects" themselves.

WHETHER THE BROTHERHOODS that slowly coalesced in Sicily between 1800 and 1860 possessed any form of central leadership is still debated. Little evidence survives—some early Mafiosi seem to have joined in the revolt of 1866 expressly in order to ransack police stations and burn the confidential reports they contained—and while there are certainly suggestions that the first criminal "families" emerged in and around Palermo and spread outward from there, there is also plenty of evidence that the Mafia meant different things to different people. In some tellings of the story there was a "high Mafia" on one hand—made up of barons, *gabelloti*, priests, and lawyers—and a "low Mafia" on the other, consisting of criminals from the peasant class who committed crimes at the behest of their superiors and were protected by them in turn. The Mafia, in this interpretation, deployed violence to make itself integral to the government in Sicily, which certainly explains why it has proved so hard to keep down. Other writers, though, including several of the policemen charged with keeping order on the island, insisted that "Mafia" was nothing but a state of mind. The word, in these men's view, was nothing but a bit of slang, denoting a sort of insolent self-confidence and pride innate to all Sicilians; there was no secret society at all, they argued, merely groups of men who would not tolerate oppression. It took decades, and the evidence of numerous informants, to prove to everybody's satisfaction that the Mafia was very organized and very real.

The earliest written references to the society's existence date only to 1865, when the prefect of Palermo warned his superiors that "the so-called Maffia" was causing problems in his district. The prefect did not know much about the group, though he thought it had existed for a while—but it was now growing more daring, he suggested, thanks largely to the new government's failure to stamp its authority on Sicily. Over the course of the next four decades, several successive prefects and their chiefs of police shed further shafts of light on the subject without ever really tackling it head-on. The "Maffia" that emerged from these investigations was not a monolithic secret society, with a headquarters and a central leadership; it was an agglomeration of loosely allied gangs known as *cosche,* the Italian name for the tightly bundled leaves of artichokes. These groups, which later writers gave the name of "families," might number anywhere from fifteen to several hundred men. Most towns had only one *cosca*—though there were several in the largest city, Palermo— but it was dangerously misleading to presume that they therefore coexisted peacefully. The Sicilian Mafia is better understood as a rural than as an urban phenomenon, and its families defined themselves by the territory they controlled, territory that generally included large swaths of the countryside outside their city walls. The borders of almost every *cosca's* sphere of influence thus butted against those of other gangs, and this meant that most existed in an uneasy state of mutual suspicion and occasional violent conflict. The resultant murky swirl of shifting allegiances made it difficult for even a family's own members to know exactly where they stood in relation to the Mafias of other towns.

It was vital, in such uncertain times, for each capo to depend upon the loyalty of his men. Many Mafia families had their roots in flesh-and-blood relationships: fathers, sons, uncles, and cousins could trust one another more than they did strangers. Recruits were also required to submit to an intimidating initiation ritual. This practice, the scattering of evidence suggests, was conducted in much the same way in every family, and its basic form was borrowed from Masonic rites. An initiate would be summoned, often at short notice and frequently at dawn, to some remote spot where his capo and several companions were waiting. There, according to a police report dating to 1880, an

> oath was sworn in the presence of three members, one of whom having bound the finger [of the candidate] with a thread, pricked it and sprinkled a few drops of blood upon a sacred image [usually a picture of the Virgin]. This was then burned and the ashes thrown into the wind. The thread denoted the indissoluble bond that united each member to the others; the ashes signified that,

just as it was impossible to give back the paper its original form, so it was impossible for a member to leave the society or to fail in the performance of his contracted observations.

Other bits of ritual paraphernalia served to remind the recruit that he was now a member of a secret society. Because the Mafia had numerous members in many towns, passwords and coded conversations enabled men who belonged to different *cosche* to identify each other. These might take the form of a catechism or make use of Sicilian slang. One of the most common, this one noted in a police report dating to 1875, was a dialogue that began with a complaint about a toothache:

A: God's blood! My tooth hurts! [*points to one of the upper canines*]

B: Mine too.

A: When did yours hurt?

B: On the day of Our Lady of the Annunciation.

A: Where were you?

B: Passo di Rigano.

A: And who was there?

B: Nice people.

A: Who were they?

B: Antonino Giammona, number 1. Alfonso Spatola, number 2 [*etc.*].

A: And how did they do the bad deed?

B: They drew lots and Alfonso Spatola won. He took a saint, colored it with my blood, put it in the palm of my hand, and burned it. He threw the ashes in the air.

A: Who did they tell you to adore?

B: The sun and the moon.

A: And who is your god?

B: An "Air."

A: What kingdom do you belong to?

B: The index finger.

(Pasano di Rigano, it may be noted, is a small town outside Palermo, and Antonino Giammona the name of the most prominent of early Mafiosi. The peculiar references in the conversation to the sun and moon, an "Air," and the index finger are most likely the means of identifying the family to which initiate B belonged.)

There can be no doubt that these ceremonies made newly initiated Mafiosi feel privileged and special, nor that their leaders made a conscious effort to portray themselves as men of dignity and even as defenders of the established order. "The true, authentic Mafioso almost invariably behaves modestly," one nineteenth-century writer on the subject noted, "speaks with restraint and similarly listens with restraint, and displays great patience; if he is offended in public, he does not react at all, but he kills afterwards." For the same reason, initiates spoke of themselves not as Mafiosi—a label imposed on them by outsiders—but as "men of respect" or "men of honor," and talked of belonging to the Onorata Società, the "Honored Society." This concern for law and order (at least in the *cosche*'s warped interpretation of the phrase) manifested itself chiefly in alliances with landowners and the Church against the threat posed by an increasingly revolutionary peasantry—with all the disruptions to the established order that implied. Mafiosi were never merely criminals and enemies of society; they were judges, landowners, and aristocrats as well, and this lent them considerable strength. With friends in all the necessary places, the *cosche* of the nineteenth century had little difficulty in arranging for complaints to be ignored, files and depositions lost, and enemies shotgunned into silence.

Certainly new men of respect soon learned that the Mafia was large enough to have an established hierarchy. Each capo passed orders down to a subordinate, the underboss, and thence to one or more lieutenants, each of whom commanded a small group of initiates and a larger body of associates known as *cagnolazzi*—wild dogs—who were not full members of the society. This hierarchy proved effective and resilient. It protected the capo, whose identity was invariably known to the local police; since he never personally committed a crime, it was practically impossible to obtain the evidence needed to arrest him. It likewise offered incentives to the *cagnolazzi*, whose prospects of gaining admission to the society depended heavily on the loyalty and the ruthlessness that they displayed.

It is scarcely surprising, in these circumstances, that the Mafia flourished in western Sicily. According to a summary compiled in 1900 by Armando Sangiorgi, Palermo's chief of police—a report so comprehensive that it ran to 485 handwritten pages—the eight *cosche* that divided up northern Palermo between them numbered 670 initiates and "wild dogs." Families had been established in more than thirty towns, from Castellammare del Golfo on the northern coast to Agrigento in the south, and though Palermo remained the center of all criminal activities, home to the richest, best-connected, and most powerful of Mafiosi, *cosche* also continued to flourish in the austere hill towns of the scorched interior.

There were significant differences between the Mafia of northern Sicily and the society inland, however. The northern families grew fat on the proceeds of extortion rackets based largely on the citrus groves along the coast—wealthy districts that exported several million cases of fruit every year yet were highly vulnerable, since orange and lemon trees required both careful nurturing and constant irrigation. By the 1890s, campaigns of murder and intimidation had delivered a large number of these estates into the hands of the Mafia, and the society felt strong enough to take direct action against even the most powerful of its enemies. The brutal murder of Marquis Emanuele Notarbartolo—a former governor of the Bank of Sicily whose investigations had threatened to unravel the Honored Society's financial dealings—aroused such anger that it became the subject of two long-running trials. These proceedings were held on the mainland in an effort to minimize the risk of jury tampering, yet even so, the killers went free. Their leader, Giuseppe Fontana of the Villabate *cosca* of the Mafia, was given shelter by a prince and member of the Italian parliament whose estate he protected; when his surrender was eventually negotiated, Fontana was driven not to jail but to Sangiorgi's private residence, and he arrived there in the prince's finest carriage.

The families of the interior lived rather differently. For one thing, they were poorer and much less well connected; for another, they seem to have had yet more ambivalent relationships with the Sicilian police. In Monreale, south of Palermo and one of the earliest Mafia centers, there were two rival associations, which fought for control of the extortion rackets on several large agricultural estates. The older of the two groups, the Giardinieri, were known derisively to their rivals as *scurmi fituzzi,* "rotten mackerels." They were former members of the Monreale militia who had taken part in the revolt of 1866, while their rivals, the Stoppaglieri (a name that can be roughly translated as "stoppered mouths" and thus conveys something of their fabled powers of discretion), were a newer group, founded in the early 1870s by a member of the Monreale carabinieri. The Stoppaglieri's supposed mission was to act as agents provocateurs and help the police wipe out the existing Mafia; in practice, however, they actually took control of many of the Giardinieri's rackets and established themselves as a family to be feared in their own right. There were other, similar examples; in Favera, in the sulfur-mining districts of the south, the local *cosca* expended considerable effort in attempting to control the miners' union. But there were also families whose operations were far more typically rural, involving control of the water supply and cattle rustling. One of these was the Mafia into which Giuseppe Morello was initiated: a family whose income was indeed derived largely from the theft of livestock. It was the *cosca* of a small town in the mountains of central Sicily—a town whose name meant little then but which would become, in time, the most infamous of the society's great strongholds. It was the Mafia of Corleone.

CORLEONE—"LIONHEART"—SQUATTED, flyblown and dispirited, amid the jagged hills of western Sicily. Founded in the tenth century by Saracens, it clung to a strategic spot on bleached stone slopes above the main road to Palermo. Corleone was a fortress town with narrow streets and tiny squares, built to guard the route to the coast; by the second half of the nineteenth century, it had lost its reason for existence. The town's chief industry, by then, was growing food for the Sicilian capital. Beneath its crumbling defensive walls, a patchwork of parched and dusty fields stretched out as far as the eye could see, dotted here and there with darker smears of color marking the location of olive groves. The fields were divided into several vast landed estates, all owned by old baronial families and leased to *gabelloti*.

The countryside around Corleone could scarcely have been less like the rolling, neatly maintained farmland found in the United States and northern Europe. It was sunburned and dusty, and the landowners' willingness to lease their estates to rapacious tenants meant that little was invested in long-term improvements such as irrigation. The land itself was also practically deserted. Perhaps the most striking feature of the Sicilian interior was that it was devoid of villages and farmhouses. Centuries of warfare, and decades more of banditry, had compelled the peasantry to seek the shelter of walled towns; because of this, the land around Corleone was all but lifeless, a limestone fastness whose secret paths were known only to a scattering of locals. It was possible to walk for hours in any direction from the town and see no one but the occasional shepherd on a distant mountainside. One consequence was that the Sicilian hinterland became an ideal hiding place for criminals, more so in the case of Corleone because of the forest of Ficuzza, which ran almost to the walls of the town and was the largest, least-tamed wood in all of Sicily.

For most of Corleone's twenty thousand citizens, conditions were wretchedly primitive. Only the richest of the town's inhabitants enjoyed the luxury of pit toilets, private wells, and glazed windows. The less well off took space in small apartment buildings, most of them lacking in the most basic amenities, including running water. For the very poorest, home was still a low one- or two-room dwelling with dirt floors and no windows. Hovels of this sort were typically no more than ten feet square, a space that the occupants shared with their animals.

Corleone had its share of artisans and functionaries, but most of the town's men labored on the great estates located outside the walls. This meant walks of up to ten miles each way in every weather, and, once there, the work was backbreaking and badly paid. Nor was life conspicuously easier for Corleone's women. While the men toiled on the land, their mothers, wives, and daughters labored at home, cooking, cleaning, spinning, sewing, and fetching water from a nearby well or public fountain. Food was rarely more than eggs, bread, broth, and vegetables; there were elderly peasants in the town who had never tasted meat. A British visitor who passed through Corleone during the 1890s found it horribly impoverished, peopled by "pale, anaemic women, hollow-eyed men, ragged weird children who begged for bread, croaking in hoarse accents like weary old people tired of the world."

It is hardly surprising, in such circumstances, that the Mafia had deep roots in the town. The *mala vita* was especially attractive to men whose one alternative was working in the fields, and petty theft and violence were so endemic in Corleone that one churchman wrote complainingly to his archbishop, pointing out that even the priests there carried guns "by day and by night." Murder was all too common, too, made easier by the narrow, winding streets, lofty windows that served as snipers' perches, and a maze of dusty alleyways that made escape simple and pursuit practically impossible.

Exactly when the Mafia appeared in the town remains uncertain, but it was well established by the 1880s. Giuseppe Valenza, a notoriously brutal landowner from nearby Prizzi, was jailed in 1866 for participating in raids on his neighbors' properties but was freed three years later "through Mafia intrigues." He remained the dominant figure in the district for another decade, murdering rivals and protecting bandits who hid on his land, providing him with firepower and making convenient scapegoats. Forced to flee Sicily in 1877 after being denounced for the role he had played in several infamous kidnappings, Valenza went to Rome, where he lived for a while under what the Italian police described as "the protection of a highly placed and greatly respected personage." Three years later he was back in the neighborhood of Corleone, where he was suspected of arranging at least two murders—together with the shooting of a thief who had unwisely stolen eight head of his cattle, the attempted assassination of two local lawyers, and the wounding of a rival Mafioso who was surprised by Valenza's men while making love to his mistress in a barn.

Valenza remained active well into the 1880s, but by 1884 another ambitious criminal by the name of Luca Patti had formed a gang of his own in Corleone itself. The fledgling Mafia had no central leadership at this point, and no hierarchy that could have decided to establish a branch of the society in the town or appointed a man to lead it. Patti, who had been brought up in the district, organized his own criminal activities, attracting followers until he had the basis of what would, in time, be known as a "family": a leader, advisers, and lieutenants, and a larger group of ambitious minor thugs to carry out his orders. He and his men called themselves the Fratuzzi, which means "brotherhood," and gradually formed working relationships with similar groups in neighboring towns, so that by about 1890 there was a network of loosely connected Mafia families stretching across most of western Sicily.

For all this, Luca Patti had a good deal in common with other early Mafia leaders. He was the son of a watchman paid to guard the fields and a leading figure in an extensive cattle-rustling ring that, a police report filed in 1884 explained, included Mafiosi from nearby Mezzujuso and the port of Termini. Despite his obvious initiative, however, Patti also had several rivals. Over the next five years, as the Fratuzzi of Corleone grew to a strength of forty men, several Corleonesi challenged his right to lead the fledgling family. The result was a period of internal strife that saw the rise and fall of several would-be bosses. It was during these disrupted years that Giuseppe Morello, then in his early twenties, was first heard of as a power in the Mafia.

THERE HAD BEEN MORELLOS in Corleone for generations. Both Giuseppe's grandfather, for whom he was named, and his father, Calogero, were born in the town and lived out their lives there. Morello's mother, Angela Piazza, came from a family with the same deep roots in the community, and poor though he undoubtedly was, and miserable though life in Corleone could be, he always felt a fierce attachment to his home. Morello grew to manhood in Corleone, and when he left, at age twenty-five, he continued to seek the company of fellow Corleonesi. They would be his closest and most trusted allies in New York.

Almost nothing is known of the Morellos' family history but the bare dates of birth, marriage, and death. Yet even these dry, official details are eloquent in their way. Morello's father, for example, was born in 1839 and married, twenty-six years later, to a girl just sixteen years old. Weddings of grooms in their middle twenties and brides who were little more than children were commonplace in Corleone; this union, like many others, was likely entered into by a man who had worked long and saved hard to support a wife, and a girl whose own prospects and expectations revolved entirely around marriage. Giuseppe, the couple's eldest child, was born fifteen months later, on May 2, 1867; a sister, Marietta, followed in 1872. But there would be no more children; Calogero's early death, at the age of only thirty-two, speaks volumes of the harshness of life in the Sicilian interior.

Deprived of his father when he was not yet five years old, Morello acquired a stepfather before he reached the age of six. Widowhood meant penury in Corleone, and Angela Piazza could not afford the luxury of grieving. With two young children to support, she observed the bare minimum of mourning before remarrying in the summer of 1873. Calogero Morello had been dead for fourteen months when his wife wed Bernardo Terranova—another Corleone native, but one much closer to her in age. With Terranova at her side, Angela's prospects improved dramatically. Years later, in papers prepared to gain admission to America, Morello's stepfather would describe himself as a "laborer," which in Sicily meant he worked the land. Other papers, however, show that Terranova was no ordinary farmhand. He was, in fact, an early member of the Fratuzzi, his name known from documents in the Palermo archives compiled by Corleone's sometime mayor. The writer, Bernardino Verro, was a socialist and a firebrand who to his lasting shame allowed himself to be lured into joining the Mafia in 1893, at a time when he was desperate for protection from the local land barons. According to Verro's detailed account, written as a form of exculpation and discovered among his papers twenty-two years later, Terranova was one of the dozen or so Mafiosi who oversaw his initiation early in 1893.

When Terranova himself joined the Fratuzzi is uncertain, but it was probably at some point during the 1880s, when he was still young and strong and had a growing family to feed. Certainly Bernardo's association with the local Mafia helps to explain his stepson's acceptance into the same group, which began at some point later in the same decade. By 1889, when a man named Salvatore Cutrera had secured a brief ascendancy as boss in Corleone, the twenty-two-year-old Morello had risen to the position of lieutenant to one of Cutrera's chief subordinates. He had become a key associate of Paolino Streva—and Streva was the nephew of one of the richest men in town.

The reasons for Morello's rapid rise within the ranks of the Fratuzzi remain unknown, but they can be inferred. The Clutch Hand had his stepfather to teach him. He was a fine organizer, cunning, and ruthless to a degree always valued by the Mafia, as his years in the United States would show. He was also literate—by no means a common accomplishment in the Sicilian interior—and unusually intelligent. All these qualities would certainly have been of value to Streva when, backed by his uncle's money, the Mafiosi became involved in cattle rustling, the most lucrative of rural rackets. They would also serve Morello well when he ran up against that rarest of obstacles in Sicily: an incorruptible policeman.

THERE WERE TWO POLICE forces in Corleone, and Giovanni Vella, the man responsible for catching Streva, was the chief of one of them. Vella was captain of the local Guardie Campestri, the Field Guards, a group of about a dozen men who patrolled the landed estates outside the town walls, mostly on foot. The Field Guards' task was to protect the peasantry from bandits and the cows from rustlers, while the carabinieri—the state police—kept order in Corleone itself.

So far as Streva and Morello were concerned, Vella should have been no more than a minor irritant. The Field Guards enjoyed a mixed reputation in Sicily; unlike the carabinieri, who were generally recruited on the mainland and knew little or nothing of the island when they arrived there, the men of the Guardie Campestri had been brought up in the communities that they protected. That made them, potentially at least, formidable detectives—they certainly possessed a detailed knowledge of the local criminals—but it also meant that they were easily corrupted. Only captains in the Field Guards received regular pay; their men subsisted solely on the rewards handed out by landowners or their *gabelloti*. Since several of these aristocrats and a large proportion of their overseers were active members of the Mafia, the guards were naturally reluctant to pry into their affairs. ("The Campestri," the mayor of Borgetto complained as early as 1884, "far from obeying their leaders, receive their cue from whoever happens to be their protector.") A good number were Mafiosi themselves. As Antonino Cutrera, a Palermo policeman of the period, cynically observed, "Frequently a Field Guard enjoys the reputation of having already committed one or two murders. Once he is surrounded by this aura, his career is made, and he had become a person who demands subjection—a necessary and therefore a better paid person."

Giovanni Vella was not like other leaders of the Field Guards, though. He was "a brave fearless man," one Corleonese declared, and "a great enemy of the Mafia, having sent many of its members to jail." When Streva's cattle-rustling ring began to make its presence felt, stealing dozens of valuable animals and shipping them off to markets on the coast, Vella launched a vigorous investigation. Rustling was an ambitious crime, one that required good organization and considerable resources; with all his contacts in the town, it did not take the captain long to discover who was behind the sudden spate of thefts. "[He] was nearing a solution of some crimes," the same Corleone chronicler learned. "In fact he was ready to make some important arrests."

Vella's problem was that in a place as small as Corleone, the Fratuzzi were just as well informed of his activities as he was of theirs. Streva soon heard of the Field Guards' plans. Knowing Vella's reputation, the Mafioso realized that there was no point in attempting to intimidate or bribe him. The solution to his difficulty would need to be more permanent than that.

There were only two ways to deal with Vella, Streva thought. One was to kill him, but that would invite unwelcome attention from the cara- binieri. The other was to deprive him of his job. The post of captain of Corleone's Field Guards was an elected one, and Vella was due to stand for reelection in the autumn of 1889, a matter of a few weeks away. With the help of the right man, Streva could do more than simply remove a thorn from his side. He could replace Vella with someone much easier to manipulate.

Searching around for a viable candidate—someone electable, a trans- parently honest man, but one more naïve and much less worldly than the incumbent captain of the Field Guards—Streva's choice fell upon Francesco Ortoleva. Ortoleva was forty-one years old at the time, the son of a former mayor of Corleone, and the nephew of one of the most fa- mous priests in western Sicily. He had no Mafia connections and no idea that the acquaintances who came to talk him into running against Vella were actually emissaries from the Fratuzzi. He was perfect for Streva's purposes.

Flattered by the attentions of his visitors, Ortoleva announced his candidacy for the post of captain of the Corleone Field Guards soon af- terward. Streva exulted, but not for long. Vella heard the news almost im- mediately and, bitterly resentful, went straight to a bar, where he drank himself into a stupor. Later that evening, still in an alcoholic haze, he staggered up to his rival's home on the fourth floor of an apartment block and hammered on the door. When Ortoleva opened up, Vella launched into a sozzled tirade. The mayor's son, he slurred, was out to deprive him of an honest living. He was a tool of Paolino Streva and probably a member of the Mafia himself.

Thoroughly alarmed by this performance, Ortoleva told his visitor to leave and, when he would not, pulled a gun from a drawer and bran- dished it in Vella's face. The Field Guard was not so intoxicated that he could not hear the anger in his rival's voice. He reeled off into the dark- ness, unaware that his drunken visit had had the effect that he desired. Upset and just a little frightened, Ortoleva withdrew from the election next day.

It was the worst news imaginable for the Fratuzzi, and Streva pan- icked. The vote was only a few days away, and there was no time to field another candidate. Vella, reelected, would soon complete his investiga- tion of the cattle-rustling ring. He had to go, and quickly.

The job of killing the Field Guard was passed by Streva to his deputy, Morello. Morello knew enough of Vella's routine to feel confident that shooting him ought not to be a problem. Vella patronized the Stella d'Italia café in Corleone and could be found drinking wine there most evenings. Apparently secure in the belief that no one in town dared to touch him, Vella came and went alone. He was also in the habit of taking shortcuts through the backstreets when returning to his wife. Surveying the route, Morello concluded that his target would best be ambushed in an alleyway a few yards from his home.

The Clutch Hand brought in another member of the Fratuzzi to help him—his associate's name was never discovered—and chose a dark night an evening or two later. The two assassins waited at a spot that they knew, presumably from observation, Vella would have to pass on his way home. There was enough light by which to see their intended victim but plenty of shadows in which to hide.

Vella spent that evening drinking at the Stella d'Italia with an old friend—the captain of the Corleone police—and several other public officials. By closing time, as usual, his head was swimming. Passersby watched as the captain rested against a lamppost for a moment and waved away a neighbor who offered to help him to his home. He stumbled through several deserted passageways unmolested and had almost reached his door when he all but walked into the two men waiting for him in the darkness. Stepping aside to let Vella to pass, Morello and his companion drew their guns. Both men were armed with large-caliber revolvers.

It is uncertain whether this was Morello's first murder, but the killing was so poorly handled that it seems likely it was. Taking aim at a range of only a few yards, the Clutch Hand opened fire; several shots rang out, but only one bullet hit Vella, piercing a lung. The Field Guard pitched forward and fell facedown on the cobblestones, his breath coming in wet gasps. Morello did not wait to administer the coup de grâce. The sound of two men running echoed down the alleyway and faded into the night.

The next thing that the neighbors heard was a woman screaming. Vella's wife peered out of a window to see her husband sprawled in the alleyway. Hurrying out, she threw her arms around him, cradling his head in her lap as she called for help. Shutters banged up and down the passage as other householders leaned out to find the cause of the disturbance. Someone ran for the police. By the time help arrived, the wounded man had been carried into his apartment, where his neighbors laid him gently on the bed.

Vella was conscious but dying, blood seeping through his shirt to stain the sheets. It was clear to everyone in the room that he did not have long. His friend the carabinieri captain was the next man to appear; realizing that there was no time to waste, the policeman began asking what had happened. He could get little sense out of Vella. The captain appeared to be delirious and was plainly sinking fast.

"Did you see who shot you?"

"Cows, cows . . . the Mafia," Vella groaned. He meant Streva's gang of cattle rustlers. Then he began to babble a list of names—the members of the Corleone Fratuzzi. The carabinieri man scribbled rapidly, but as Vella rambled on, he interrupted. There were too many names; they could not all have been involved in the shooting. The policeman tried a different tack. Had there been any recent quarrels, he asked—disputes that had taken place in the last few days?

"Yes," the dying man replied. "I quarrelled with Ortoleva yesterday. He wanted to take my job away—take the bread from my mouth." The words came in a bubbling gasp. Vella's lung was collapsing; he was coughing blood, and, worse, air had seeped into his bloodstream. Moments later, the first bubble of oxygen reached his heart, causing a massive cardiac arrest.

Giovanni Vella's dying words posed a dilemma for the Corleone police. There was plenty of evidence that the Fratuzzi had played a part in the Field Guard's murder; aside from Vella's accusation, questioning of members of the crowd still milling in the alleyway produced a witness who claimed to have seen Morello in the passage and to have watched as Morello concealed his gun beneath a pile of rubbish. A search quickly revealed the weapon, which proved to have been recently discharged. On the other hand, the dying Field Guard had also named Ortoleva as a suspect, and Vella's rival was arrested that same night. When the police learned that two men had been seen lurking in the shadows, they also detained another of the candidates for Vella's job.

There are clear hints in what happened next that Streva and the bosses of Corleone's Fratuzzi brought their influence to bear on the police investigation. Morello was arrested and held, pending questioning, but his pistol, the main evidence against him, disappeared soon afterward from the police lockup, apparently removed by a member of the carabinieri who had been paid to dispose of it. Ortoleva, meanwhile, supplied the police with an apparently solid alibi: He had been confined to his apartment, he explained, by a grocery wagon that had parked in the narrow street outside the building, so close that he could not open the front door. Before long, however, several of Giovanni Vella's friends, pursuing inquiries of their own, were approached by a prostitute who claimed to have watched the middle-aged Ortoleva shin down a rope from his fourth-floor apartment just before the shooting. How the mayor's son could have known, in those circumstances, where to find Vella was not explained; nor did anyone ever discover whether the prostitute was sincere, mistaken, or paid by someone to give evidence. What was certain was that the carabinieri investigating Vella's death seemed a lot more interested in Ortoleva than they were in Morello. When, some days after the murder, the Clutch Hand was bailed out, Ortoleva remained in prison, rotting on remand.

But Morello was not quite free of suspicion. Other Corleonesi had seen or heard things that they should not have on the night of the murder. One was a woman named Anna Di Puma, a neighbor of Vella's, who had been returning to her home along the alleyway shortly before the shooting when she saw two men lurking in the shadows. Di Puma recognized one of them as Morello, whom she "knew very well," and when she heard gunfire a few moments later and ran back up the alley to find out what was happening, she found Vella lying at the spot where the men had been. A second possible witness was Bernardo Terranova's next-door neighbor, Michele Zangara. Zangara had been in his apartment when, late one night soon after the Vella murder, he had heard voices drifting through the thin wall between his apartment and his neighbors'. "Peppe, what have you done?" he heard Angela Terranova ask her son. "Now they will come to arrest you." There was a moment's pause before Morello's whispery voice replied: "Shut up, Mother. They have gone on the wrong scent."

Zangara knew enough about Morello and Terranova to say nothing to the police, but Anna Di Puma was much less cautious. She told several of her friends what she had seen, adding that she would gladly give a statement. She was prepared to testify in court as well.

It did not take much time for word of Di Puma's intentions to reach Morello, and it took less for the Fratuzzi to dispose of her. Even in the nineteenth century, even in a place like Sicily, where personal honor supposedly counted for so much, the Mafia never balked at killing women, and Di Puma's intransigence convinced Streva and Morello that she had to be silenced, and quickly. Two days later, as Vella's neighbor sat chatting on a friend's front step, someone shot her in the back.

With the irritatingly honest Di Puma out of the way, Morello had little to fear from the authorities. He was so obviously the chief beneficiary of the woman's death that the police arrested him again and questioned him for several days, but the investigation went nowhere. There were no witnesses to the murder—if any of her neighbors had seen or heard anything to suggest who Di Puma's killers were, they had the sense not to say so in public—and Morello himself produced a solid alibi: He had been in Palermo, he said, at the time of the murder. This was probably the truth; with Streva arranging matters on his subordinate's behalf, the Clutch Hand had no need to do anything so risky as shoot the woman himself. To make quite certain that no charges would be pressed, however, the Fratuzzi brought influence to bear once again. Two eminent lawyers, members of the fraternity, came forward to support the Clutch Hand's alibi, signing affidavits stating that they had seen him in the capital. There was also another killing. Pietro Milone, one of the few policemen in Corleone who believed in Ortoleva's innocence, met his death in another darkened alleyway before he had the chance to pursue his investigations. His assassin, too, was never caught.

The murders of Milone and Di Puma ended any prospect that Morello might be brought to justice for Vella's killing. Francesco Ortoleva was not so fortunate. After four long years on remand, Ortoleva finally came to trial in 1893. Even then, the Fratuzzi took no chances. The defendant's attorneys were bought off, and, having recommended to their client that neither Streva nor Morello should be dragged into the case, the defense team unexpectedly resigned en masse just before the trial was scheduled to begin. A replacement lawyer, brought in at short notice, had little time to grasp the case's numerous complexities. Ortoleva was found guilty and sentenced to life in prison.

GIUSEPPE MORELLO RETURNED to his old haunts in the autumn of 1889 with his reputation burnished. Vella's murder had improved his standing within the Fratuzzi, and so had the way he had handled himself under questioning; there had been no betrayal of Streva or any of the other bosses in the town. The Clutch Hand also had proposals to make—schemes for making more money than the local Mafia had imagined possible.

Morello's new idea was counterfeiting. It made considerable sense. For one thing, it was an urban crime rather than a rural one, and the Vella affair had shown how much easier it was in Corleone to deal with the carabinieri than the Field Guards. For another, it seemed relatively safe; counterfeiting was not then a federal offense in Italy, which meant that responsibility for suppressing it fell squarely on the shoulders of small-town police who were poorly equipped to tackle such sophisticated crime. Most important, they had access to a steady supply of notes produced by a Mafia counterfeiting ring that had begun to operate in Palermo at about this time. The Palermo counterfeiters worked under the protection of Francesco Siino, one of the most powerful Mafiosi in all Sicily, and were probably the source of the bad money that Morello brought into Corleone. The Fratuzzi also possessed, in the reluctant Mafioso Bernardino Verro, the means of passing its forged bills into circulation. By the spring of 1893, at the time of Verro's initiation into the Mafia, the socialist café that he ran in the town was overrun with members of the Fratuzzi gambling with counterfeit notes. The Mafiosi earned the café such a dubious reputation that Verro felt it wise to stay well clear.

Little is known of how Morello's counterfeiting ring was run, who was involved, or how much money the Corleone Mafioso made. Even the circumstances of the ring's collapse remain mysterious. What is known is that the Siino family came under increasing pressure from other Mafia *cosche* along the coast during the early 1890s. These disputes eventually coalesced into a bloody feud between Siino and several branches of the Giammona family, who headed a rival faction in the Sicilian capital, and quite possibly the betrayal by the Giammonas of Siino's allies in Corleone. Whatever happened, it is certain that Morello's operations in the Sicilian interior were compromised sometime in 1892. The Corleone police launched an investigation and several suspects were detained. Eventually, in September of that year, a warrant was at last issued for the Clutch Hand's arrest.

Morello did not wait for the case to come to court—he fled, a fact that did not prevent the Italian government from trying him in his absence during the summer of 1894. So seriously did the Sicilian authorities take the case, indeed, that the trial was moved to the Assize Court in Messina, on the eastern tip of the island, in a part of Sicily where the Mafia's writ did not run and there was little chance that influence or tampered evidence could be brought to bear. The strategy worked; the defendant was found guilty and handed a heavy sentence: six years and forty-five days in solitary confinement.

It barely mattered. By the time the verdict was pronounced, Morello and his family had been in the United States for well over a year.

CHAPTER 3

LITTLE ITALY

=

I T WAS A SPRING DAY, BUT ONLY IN NAME. DARK CLOUDS, PREG-
nant with rain, blew in from the north and sagged low over New York
harbor. Squalls of wind, damp with the clammy moisture of the North
Atlantic, came spinning down around Long Island and darted off across
the germy water, whipping up spume and whitecaps as they hurried for
the Jersey shore. The skies were gray. The city was gray, a jumble of drab
factories and rickety tenements. The sea, green-brown at the mouth of
the Hudson River, swirled with the factory filth that oozed across the
bottom of the harbor until it turned gray as well. And it was cold: the
sort of gooseflesh East Coast chill that the passengers cramming the rails
of the emigrant ship *Alsatia* had never felt in Italy.

The *Alsatia* lay, hove to, in choppy seas just south of Ellis Island.
She was thirty days out of Naples and fresh from a rough Atlantic crossing that had left a large part of her human cargo praying for a land-
fall. That had come on March 8, 1893, a Wednesday. Earlier that day, the
ship's first-class passengers, 150 of them, had disembarked at a Manhattan pier. They were presumed to be above the tests and examinations
that awaited the eleven hundred more or less impoverished Italians still
crammed nervously in steerage. Fourteen months earlier, the U.S. government had opened an enormous immigration center on the island,
staffed by hundreds of inspectors and health officials and capable of
processing as many as twelve thousand men, women, and children in
an hour. There emigrants were questioned as to their employment
prospects—men were required to have a job waiting for them—and
checked to ensure that they possessed sufficient money to support themselves. They were also tested for a number of diseases. Inspectors carried sticks of chalk and marked people's coats with codes: L for lame,

G for goiter, H for a heart condition. The examination for trachoma, an infectious eye disease, was particularly dreaded; it involved having a buttonhook thrust behind an eyelid. Anyone seen bearing a chalk mark was taken off for more interrogation, and most of those who were declared unfit to enter the United States were packed off back to their old countries. A few managed to dodge this fate by smartly brushing off the chalk upon their clothing.

The ledgers that were maintained on Ellis Island record the Terranova family's arrival on the *Alsatia* and give bare details of their circumstances. There was no sign of Giuseppe Morello, for example—the Clutch Hand had slipped into the United States some six months earlier, in the early autumn of 1892. Bernardo Terranova was aboard, however, with his wife, Angela, and all six of their children: Lucia, the oldest, who was just sixteen; her sister Salvatrice, twelve; and Morello's three half brothers: Vincenzo, seven, Ciro, five, and Nicola—Coco to the family— who was only three years old. There, too, was Morello's wife, Maria Marvelesi, whom he had married soon after the Vella murder. Marvelesi came from Corleone and was the same age as the Clutch Hand. She had with her the couple's child, a two-month-old infant christened Calogero in memory of Morello's father.

It was still unusual for families to emigrate together; more than eight Italian immigrants in every ten were men, and more than half of them eventually returned to Italy. Other than that, though, there was little in the Ellis Island records to suggest the Terranovas were anything extraordinary. Bernardo gave his age as forty-three and said his job was "laborer," which was normal enough; most Italians were unskilled, and several hundred of his fellow passengers claimed the same menial occupation. He was the only member of the party who could read or write, and that was common, too. The only clue to Terranova's eminence in Corleone, and to his membership in the Fratuzzi, lies in the notes that the officials made of the *Alsatia*'s baggage. At a time when the average Italian immigrant entered the country with six dollars, carrying a single case, the Terranovas mustered eighteen pieces of luggage among them. No other family on the ship arrived in the United States with so many personal possessions.

From Ellis Island, New York was only a short ferry ride away, but for the *Alsatia*'s wondering Italians it was like entering another world. Gotham was an unimaginable metropolis, a hundred times the size of

Corleone, and filled with the sort of modern innovations and conveniences that were barely even dreamed of in the Sicilian interior. Buildings were lit by gas or electricity, and heated—downtown, at least—by steam; running water was commonplace and not an unimaginable luxury. Travel, hitherto by horse-drawn omnibus, was increasingly by electric streetcar or elevated railway; the first subways were being planned. Telegraphs and telephones were everywhere, and even saloons had ticker-tape machines, to carry the baseball play-by-plays. There were a thousand theaters and music halls and more than ten thousand bars. The tallest building in the city was a church whose spire ascended to a dizzying 290 feet above street level. And everywhere there were people: more than two million of them in 1893, a third of whom were foreign-born, making New York not merely the most vibrant, fastest-growing city in the country, but by a distance the most cosmopolitan.

The largest immigrant communities were still the Germans and the Irish, who between them accounted for more than half a million of the city's population—this at a time when there were fewer than three thousand Chinese in Manhattan, a thousand Spaniards, and three hundred Greeks. They still lived largely in their own communities, the Irish in Five Points and Hell's Kitchen, and Germans in Williamsburg or "Kleindeutschland," east of the Bowery. Immigration from northern Europe had slowed by 1890, though. For the next two decades, by far the greatest number of new citizens would come from Eastern Europe—mostly Jews, fleeing pogroms in the Russian Empire—and Italy. The number of Italians in New York, which was well under 1,000 in 1850 and only 13,000 in 1880, had grown to nearly 150,000 by the turn of the century. By 1910 it had more than doubled again, standing in excess of 340,000. In Italy as a whole, between 1860 and 1914, five million people, one-third of the entire population, left to find work overseas.

The earliest Italian settlers in New York came from the industrial cities of the north. They were skilled workers and middle-class professionals, and they received a cordial welcome. It was not until the 1880s that this pattern changed and much poorer, less educated peasants from the southern provinces began to flood into the city. These Neapolitans and Sicilians were escaping harsh conditions in their homeland: high taxation, an endlessly depressed economy, compulsory military service, and an unprecedented slew of natural disasters—droughts, floods, earthquakes, landslides, and volcanic eruptions—that followed one upon the other so relentlessly that they were seen as signs from God.

Unskilled, illiterate, and speaking mostly in impenetrable dialect, the men of the south were despised even in Italy, where a bit of doggerel popular at the time perfectly described their position in society:

At the head of everything is God, Lord of Heaven.
After him comes Prince Torlonia, lord of the earth.
Then come Prince Torlonia's armed guards.
Then come Prince Torlonia's armed guards' dogs.
Then, nothing at all. Then nothing at all. Then nothing at all.
  Then come the peasants. And that's all.

In Manhattan, they were still less welcome. Though useful, insofar as they did dirty jobs that earlier immigrants now thought of as beneath them, Italians from the southern provinces were regarded with hostility by many New Yorkers. Their dark complexions, lack of English, and devotion to an alien food were all regarded as distasteful. They were much more volatile than northern Europeans, it was commonly supposed, and prone to deadly knife fights and vendettas. Worse, only a minority embraced American institutions with the fervor expected of immigrants. Few Italians mixed with men of other nationalities, and well under half actually applied for U.S. citizenship. For many Sicilians and Neapolitans, the United States was a place to work hard, spend little, and save ferociously; many planned to return home with their savings. These were habits many Americans regarded as ungrateful and insulting.

Opinion hardened further at about the time the Terranova family first came to Manhattan. There was concern at the number of anarchists and socialists pouring into the country to preach revolution. There was concern at the number of criminals. Nineteen Italians in every twenty of those passing through Ellis Island were found to be carrying weapons, either knives or revolvers, and there was nothing in American law to stop them from taking this arsenal into the city. The Sicilian police were said to be issuing passports to known murderers in order to get them out of the country—a calumny, it transpired, but there were still real reasons to take such problems seriously. So many Italians were passing through Ellis Island every day that it was not possible to check their statements properly. But when the 1,400 passengers on board the SS *Belgravia* were subjected to a spot investigation, one in six was found to have given false information. "Statistics prove," the *Herald* trumpeted in one alarmist feature article, "that the scum of Southern Europe is dumped on the nation's door in rapacious, conscienceless, lawbreaking hordes."

SO FAR AS THE members of the Morello-Terranova family were concerned, though, New York was a welcome haven. They were safe there from the Italian authorities. Cooperation between Sicily and the United States was all but nonexistent at the time; certainly the police in Palermo and Corleone made no effort to discover if any of their wanted men were hiding in the United States. And only when an Italian became so notorious that the American government wanted to expel him would the New York police trouble to discover if the man had a criminal record in Italy. Any immigrant who had been in the United States for three years or more became, in any case, immune from deportation. All Giuseppe Morello and his stepfather had to do was steer clear of trouble for that long. Then they could put their difficulties in Sicily behind them.

Where Terranova and his family went when they disembarked from the Ellis Island ferry remains unknown; nor do we know exactly when they were reunited with Morello. In all likelihood, however, the clan took lodgings in the main Italian quarter of Manhattan. Speaking no English and already pining, like most immigrants, for the familiar staples of the old country, they would have made straight for Little Italy.

The Italian district of New York, centered around Mulberry Street, was still in its infancy in 1893. It had been predominantly Irish as late as 1890, when Mulberry Bend, a kink in the road a few blocks north of City Hall, was the most reviled slum in the city: rife with disease, thick with litter, and home to communities of the desperate and destitute with names such as Bandit's Roost and Bottle Alley. "There is not a foot of ground in the Bend that has not witnessed some deed of violence," wrote the reformer Jacob Riis, whose after-hours visits to the rotting lodging houses and drinking dens of Mulberry Street produced some of the most memorable images of old New York. Among the horrors Riis described were homes so caked in filth they would not burn when set afire and "stale beer dives" in windowless, earth-floored cellars, where patrons desperate for oblivion sank rotgut whiskey and the flat dregs of empty beer barrels discarded by saloons.

It was largely thanks to Riis's eloquent campaigning that the worst excesses of Mulberry Street were swept away in 1890, leaving the district to the next great wave of immigrants from southern Europe. Three years later there were already tens of thousands of men, women, and children crammed into the seething streets around the Bend, a population larger than that of most Italian towns.

Conditions in the tenements of Little Italy were grim, though certainly no worse than they had been at home. Most of these dilapidated premises had been built before new zoning laws improved the standards of New York housing. They typically sprawled over almost the entire lot, so there was little light and no room for recreation; in the absence of gardens and public parks, children played on rooftops or in the streets. Almost every building was cold and damp in winter, when walls became so saturated with damp that they steamed whenever fires were lit. In summer the same apartments baked, so much so that even Sicilians, well used to infernal heat, preferred to sleep out on the rooftops or the fire escapes.

Privacy was nonexistent in the district. Bedrooms doubled as parlors and kitchens as bedrooms; every toilet, down the hall, was shared by fifty or sixty people. There were no bathing facilities; washing meant a visit to the public bath. There was no central heating; the only source of warmth in some apartments was the kitchen stove. Those lucky enough to have fireplaces in their rooms stockpiled coal on the floor, in corners, under beds, making it impossible to keep things clean. Every tenement, in any case, was infested with cockroaches and bedbugs. All had rats.

"More than anything I remember the smells of the old neighborhood," said one old Corleone Mafioso of the Little Italy of his youth.

You can't believe how many people lived together in those old houses. There were six or seven tenements on Elizabeth Street where we lived and in those buildings, which were maybe five or six stories high, there must have been fifteen or sixteen hundred people living. And everybody took in boarders, too. A lot of the guys who came over from Sicily were not married or had left their families in Italy. They were only there at night since they were out working all day, and at night there must have been another seven or eight hundred guys sleeping in the building. We had it pretty good because there were only four of us in three rooms, but in some other apartments you had seven or eight adults and maybe ten kids living in an apartment the same size.

Some of the smells were good. I can remember, for example, that early in the morning, say five o'clock, you could smell peppers and eggs frying when the women got lunches ready for their sons and husbands. But more than anything else I remember the smells of human bodies and the garbage. There was no such thing as garbage collection in those days and everybody just threw it out in the street or put it out in the hallways. Christ, how it stank!

Poverty was an everyday reality for most of the families of Elizabeth Street, just as it had been at home in Italy. Higher incomes in New York, where it was possible for even an unskilled laborer to earn $1.50 a day— a sum thirty times the five-cent wage typical in Sicily—were offset by the higher cost of living, and many families willingly endured privation in order to remit larger sums to relatives at home. Pasta and vegetables formed the staple diet, purchased from the innumerable street cart peddlers who thronged the streets of Little Italy, and meat remained a luxury for most. Delivery vehicles inched along the pulsing thoroughfares pursued by a procession of small children who scavenged for anything that fell—or could be made to fall—from them. Few people owned more than the clothes on their backs and perhaps a single item of Sunday best. Even sheets and blankets were scarce commodities. Joe Valachi, born to Italian parents in New York a few years after the Terranova family arrived from Sicily, remembered that "for sheets my mother used old cement bags that she sewed together, so you can imagine how rough they were."

Simply finding accommodation in the overcrowded tenements of Little Italy was hard enough. Work, good work with decent conditions and some prospects, proved a good deal more elusive. Many emigrants, hundreds of thousands of them, had been lured across the Atlantic by tales of the immense wealth of the United States and so arrived in New York filled with the hope that they, too, would accumulate an easy fortune. The reality proved very different. The only jobs available to unskilled Italians were the filthy, menial ones that Americans thought were beneath them. Rag picking—sorting through heaps of stinking rubbish in search of bottles, bones, and cloth that could be resold for a cent or two—was one source of casual employment for the men. Others labored on sewer repairs, did construction work on the new subway, or manned the city's garbage scows. Women worked in dimly lit sweatshops, ruining their eyes by staring at the fast-moving needle of a sewing machine for nine hours at a stretch, or labored stripping feathers for mattresses and pillows in workshops that brought on lung disease.

This sort of casual work was monotonous and poorly paid. It was also frighteningly insecure. Men were hired by the day to labor on contracts that might last for a week or two, rarely longer. Women did piecework, perhaps gluing envelopes at the rate of three cents for every thousand, and lived with the threat that any dip in productivity would result in dismissal. The endless stream of immigrants pouring through Ellis Island meant that there was competition for even the basest work, and for many Italians of Bernardo Terranova's generation the solution was to go to work for a *padrone,* an overseer who spoke some English and who contracted to supply cheap labor to a variety of businesses. The more fortunate—those with some wealth, some skill, or some connections—got help from friends and relatives who had already settled in the United States. This is almost certainly what Terranova and Morello did. Small colonies of Corleonesi already existed in the New York of 1893, one in Little Italy and another in East Harlem, where a second Italian quarter was taking root in the blocks around East 107th Street. Terranova had some skill as an ornamental plasterer, and he and his stepson most likely got at least a little temporary employment in this way.

Whatever the men of the family tried, though, it soon became apparent that it was not enough. The American economy was stalling. Fewer and fewer were able to find even temporary jobs; by summer there was almost no work to be had anywhere in New York. The American economy, foundering since 1890, was sliding into full-blown depression. It was the worst economic crisis yet experienced by the United States. The great crash of 1893 was under way.

THE CRASH OF 1893 was a slump as bad in almost all respects to the Great Depression of the 1930s. There was a run on gold; the value of stocks and shares plummeted; thousands of companies went bankrupt; and at least five hundred banks failed. It was no time to be an impoverished immigrant in a frightened New York. By December, fully a quarter of the working population had no job.

Morello and the Terranova family spent that terrible year living in Manhattan. How they survived there is unknown, but their position must have been precarious. Even with the help of fellow Corleonesi, Terranova and Morello had two wives and seven children to support; none of the family spoke English; and only one of their offspring was old enough to earn—Lucia, Terranova's eldest daughter, turned seventeen that year. Their savings and even the sale of their personal possessions would have stretched only so far. When it became clear that the economy would not recover quickly, the only realistic solution was to search for work outside New York.

Ciro Terranova, the second youngest of Bernardo's sons, was the only member of the family who ever spoke about these early years. Five years old in 1893, just old enough to grasp something of the problems that his parents faced, he recalled his half brother Giuseppe leaving New York to hunt for work soon after their arrival. Morello traveled south, to Louisiana, a well-worn route for Italian migrants in those days. Severe labor shortages in the Deep South, where the cotton fields and sugar plantations had never recovered from the emancipation of their slaves a quarter of a century earlier, made the landowners of the state eternally anxious to hire immigrants. Sicilian laborers were particularly highly valued; they worked hard, were inured to backbreaking toil, and were often skilled farmers, too—plantation managers never ceased to be amazed at the variety and quantity of food that their Italians conjured from the little kitchen gardens they were allowed to tend. Italians, Southern gentlemen discovered, worked willingly at even the dirtiest jobs, and unlike Chinese laborers, who were readily tempted by offers of better jobs, they generally fulfilled their contracts.

According to Ciro Terranova, Morello worked at first as a fruit peddler, "selling lemons with a bag on his back." In two months he accumulated sufficient money to send for the rest of the family, and, when they arrived, he and his stepfather went to work on a plantation. It must have been early in 1894 by then, at the time that the seed cane was planted, and there was plenty of work in the fields. Afterward, in spring, laborers were needed to pull weeds and clear drainage channels. In August and September, the growing cane was thinned, and in the autumn it was harvested.

October marked the beginning of the *zuccarata*—the grinding season—in the sugar parishes of Louisiana. Gangs of Sicilian laborers spread out through the fields armed with machetes with which to hack down the giant canes, then hauled them to nearby wagons and transported them to mills where they were washed, cut into pieces, ground, and clarified. Sugar crystals, mixed in with molasses, went from the mill to enormous centrifuges, where they were separated; from there the sugar was loaded into wagons and shipped to a refinery.

It was hard, physical, unrelenting work, a test for any able-bodied man, much less one as crippled as Morello. Work began at sunrise and went on until dusk, sometimes considerably later. In that time, a good man could harvest three or four tons of cane, but, in order to maximize production, plantation owners would hire entire families and give work not only to women but to children as young as five. Probably all of the Terranova children cut and stacked cane together from October until the harvest season ended in January 1895.

The work did not pay badly by the standards of the time. Men could expect to receive sixty-five cents a day outside the grinding season and as much as $1.50 for working an eighteen-hour day during the *zuccarata* itself. Women and children got less, perhaps $1 and ten cents respectively. But rough accommodation was provided free, and even if only by stinting themselves, eating nothing but bread and the vegetables they grew themselves, a thrifty family could save as much as $2.50 a day for the duration of the season. This must have seemed a fortune to men and women used to the sort of wages paid in Sicily, and it even compared favorably to the $200 a year that unskilled workers earned in New York at this time, from which the costs of rent and food would have to be deducted.

Louisiana had other attractions for Italian immigrants. Temperatures during the winter months were close to what Sicilians were used to and were far more comfortable than chilly New York. And for the duration of the harvest season, anyway, a large Italian community flourished in the sugar fields. More than two thousand Sicilians came to Louisiana in 1893—some direct from their homeland, in boats that sailed between Palermo and New Orleans, depositing the workers that they carried directly into the fields—and others from distant parts of the United States.

It is legitimate to wonder whether Terranova and Morello took advantage of this fact to extort from and to terrorize their fellow workers, as the Mafia had done in Corleone, and whether either found his way to New Orleans, where there was a fast-growing community of Sicilian criminals. A decade or so later, certainly, Morello would travel frequently to the Crescent City, where a cousin lived and he apparently had numerous acquaintances. There is no evidence, however, that any member of the family took part in such activities when they were working in the sugar parishes, and when Morello and the Terranovas left Louisiana after a year, it was to go not to New Orleans or New York but to an agricultural community in Texas where the Mafia held no sway.

The family went, Ciro recalled, to Bryan in Brazos County, a farming community south of Dallas, tempted by the offer of a house, the loan of a team of horses, access to a doctor, and the guarantee of work in the Texas cotton fields. Almost certainly they settled on the east bank of the Brazos River at a spot where another group of men from Corleone had erected a shanty township in the 1870s. On the far bank, opposite, was another crude Italian settlement, this one consisting of people from the Sicilian town of Poggioreale. The two communities spoke different dialects, were rivals, and looked upon each other with mutual distrust.

Morello and the Terranova family spent two years farming outside Bryan. According to Ciro's recollections, his father and half brother worked as sharecroppers, renting a parcel of land—available in those days at the rate of five dollars an acre—on which they planted and harvested their own cotton. The family was free to sell its crop, paying a portion of the proceeds to the landlord, and conditions seem to have been better than they had been in the sugar parishes; according to Ciro, only his father and Morello had to work full-time.

Life in Brazos had a Sicilian simplicity. The menfolk labored in the fields. The Italian women of the colony, including Angela Terranova and Maria Marvelesi, cooked for their families, rolling pasta by hand and leaving it in the sun to dry, baking bread in outdoor ovens, and sending their children off into the fields with their husbands' dinners. They sewed their families' shirts, trousers, and dresses, made their own soap from lye and grease, and washed their clothes by hand in iron pots over a fire. Their children weeded the crops, chopped wood, and "helped around."

For all this, wresting a living from the Texan soil was difficult, even for Italians with experience of farming. The land baked in the summer and the soil was poor. Crops had to be watered by hand during the dry season, from buckets heaved up from the river, but when it rained the only way for men and mules to cross the fields was by strapping broad planks of wood to their feet. Few pesticides were sold in the Bryan district; instead Italian farmers planted garlic, sunflowers, and marigolds to ward off insects, put up birdhouses and drinking basins to attract birds, and embedded stones in shady corners to encourage toads. "Farming wasn't that good in those days," the grandson of one of the pioneer Sicilians remembered decades later. "They made just enough to eat and sleep and buy a few clothes."

This harsh life can hardly have appealed to a man like Giuseppe Morello. Farming in Brazos County was a grinding business for ordinary Sicilians. For criminals, for Mafiosi who had grown used to much easier lives, it must have appeared doubly frustrating. By the beginning of the Terranova family's second year in the cotton fields, it had already become clear that there was no quick fortune to be made from cotton: The dry soil of the Brazos River watershed required considerable improvement if it was to yield a decent crop. Morello was not willing to make this effort. In any case, there was no real incentive for tenant farmers to invest such Herculean efforts in someone else's land.

The decision to return north was taken in the autumn of 1896. The family's time in the South had already been tinged with tragedy; soon after the Terranovas' departure from New York, Morello's one-year-old baby, Calogero, died. A second boy, born probably in the Louisiana sugar fields, was given the same name, but by the end of Morello's second year in Texas he and every other member of the family were sick with malaria, a disease then rife along the Brazos River, an area that had been ignored by earlier waves of German and Czech settlers because it was so prone to frequent flooding. Illness made the decision to abandon sharecropping an easy one to take, and so did the reports filtering down from the north of a New York that was at last recovering from the crash of 1893. By the first months of 1897, two years after the family had arrived in Texas and three after they had left Manhattan, Morello and the Terranovas were back on the raucous streets of Little Italy. This time they were there to stay.

NEW YORK'S ITALIAN neighborhoods had changed considerably in the brief time that Morello and his family had been away. The number of

Italians in the city tripled between 1890 and 1900, and the Little Italy centered on Elizabeth and Mulberry streets had grown so considerably that it now ran well over half a mile along the Bowery. Sister colonies in Greenwich Village and East Harlem had also multiplied many times in size, and overcrowding had become an even greater problem; there were so many people in so many apartments in some districts that the population density was worse than in Bombay. On the other hand, the economy of the Italian quarter was flourishing again. Demand for familiar staples ensured that there was a growing trade in imports of lemons, olive oil, and wine. Artichokes, an ingredient of minestrone, were shipped into the city by rail all the way from California. There were Italian grocers, cobblers, bootblacks, and bankers, Italian newspapers and clothes. In 1897, according to one estimate, the inhabitants of Little Italy were making so much money that $30 million a year was being wired or carried back to friends and relatives at home. A much larger sum, this news implied, was being earned and spent on the streets of New York.

With money came the prospect of a better life. An honest laborer might secure a permanent position; a petty businessman a handcart or a shoeshine stand to call his own. But for the criminals of the Italian districts, the burgeoning wealth of many immigrants meant more and better opportunities to prey on their fellow men. In the course of the 1890s, the sort of incidents that had characterized Little Italy in earlier years— mugging, petty theft, and knife fights—began to give way to new and more sophisticated forms of crime. The first protection rackets had begun to flourish on the streets of the Italian quarter by the last years of the decade. Then came determined attempts to target the wealthiest of the district's immigrants: extortion, backed by threats of violence, and the seizure and ransoming of children. As early as 1899, there was a "kidnapping craze" among the Italians of Brooklyn.

Crime was certainly no less prevalent in Little Italy than it was elsewhere in Manhattan. Joseph Petrosino, who knew as much about the immigrant community as anyone, contended that only a minuscule proportion—3 or 4 percent, he thought—were actually criminals. But there were 200,000 Italians in New York by 1900, and even a small percentage of that total was still a lot of men: well over 5,000, if the detective's estimate was correct. Nor was there much chance that Italian crooks might be deterred by the prospect of punishment. "At that time," confided Giovanni Branchi, the Italian consul general in New York, whole parts of the town, whole streets, were inhabited by Italians only, with their shops, cafes, etc. All these places were virtually without police supervision with the exception of the regular Irish policeman at the corner of the street, who did not care a rap what Italians did among themselves so long as they did not interfere with other people. At the time there were only two or three policemen who spoke or understood Italian . . . so that in nine cases out of ten any Italian committing a crime was nearly sure of going unpunished if he only escaped a few days from arrest.

According to various figures that were bandied about at the time, in fact, only one out of every 250 crimes committed in the Italian quarter was reported to the police; of these, only one case in every five yielded arrests; and of the cases that did come to court, as few as one in three hundred resulted in a conviction. Small wonder that, for many immigrants, justice was something a man had to obtain for himself. And small wonder that for Morello and others like him, the prospects of a successful criminal career began to seem as bright in the United States as they had ever been in Sicily.

It did not take long for Italian crooks to demonstrate just how lucrative organized crime could be in several American cities. Extortion rings, which had been commonplace in Sicily and sprang up in the Italian quarter of New Orleans as early as the 1850s, appeared in New York during the last years of the nineteenth century and in Chicago—home to another large and growing Italian community—after 1901. The methods adopted by the men responsible were very similar. The victims, generally storekeepers or bankers or other wealthy immigrants, would receive a letter demanding a substantial sum of money. They would be directed to take an envelope of money to a lonely meeting point or hand the cash over to a man who would call on them at their place of business. Failure to comply, they were warned, would result in the destruction of their premises and perhaps in their own deaths.

The letters, which were always anonymous, were often phrased in bizarrely courteous Old World language, but the underlying threat of violence was ever present. "I beg you warmly," one such missive concluded, "to put them [the notes] on your door within four days. But if not, I swear this week's time not even the dust of your family will exist." Another, even blunter, letter warned:

You got some cash. I need $1000.00. You place the $100.00 bills in an envelope and place it under a board at the northeast corner of 69th Street at eleven o'clock tonight. If you place the money there, you will live. If you don't, you die. If you report this to the police, I'll kill you when I get out. They may save your money but they won't save your life.

Sinister communications of this sort—received unexpectedly by victims who knew all about the impotence of the police—usually had the desired effect. Most of the extortionists' targets were terrified, and unknown hundreds handed over sums that they could barely afford. Not everyone complied, of course, but the brave and the stubborn few who ignored the letters could expect to get a visit from the gang, and though it was not unheard of for a victim to shrug off even their threats and remain unmolested or to negotiate the payment of a smaller sum, everyone in Little Italy had heard of stores destroyed by dynamite, children kidnapped and sometimes murdered, and rich men shot or knifed to death for failing to hand over cash.

Bombs were the favored tool of the extortionists. They were anonymous, created a terrifying effect, and were easily assembled—so many Italians were employed in the construction trade that it was a simple matter to steal dynamite. They could even be used outside the streets of Little Italy; a New Jersey justice of the peace, who had convicted several members of one gang, was "literally blown to pieces" by a parcel bomb delivered to his office. Even in high-profile cases of this sort, however, arrests were few and far between, and it was widely known that many of the most famous and influential Italians in the city had caved in to the extortionists' demands. The best-known of these victims was the opera star Enrico Caruso, who met one demand for $2,000 and, when this fact became public knowledge, was rewarded for his capitulation with "a stack of threatening letters a foot high," including another from the same gang for $15,000.

To many New Yorkers, including the reporters of the English-language press, the most compelling feature of these cases was the bizarre decorations that adorned the extortion letters. Demands were accentuated with crude drawings of skulls, revolvers, and knives dripping with blood or piercing human hearts. Many also featured pictures of hands, in thick black ink, held up in the universal gesture of warning. It was this last feature that inspired a journalist writing for *The New York Herald* to refer to the communications as "Black Hand" letters—a name that stuck, and, indeed, soon became synonymous with crime in Little Italy.

From there it was but a short step to the idea of the Black Hand as a distinct organization, with its own leaders and hundreds, if not thousands, of members scattered through the country. The notion of a powerful, professional criminal conspiracy did seem to answer many questions, not least explaining why the authorities found it so very difficult to make arrests. The police, led by Petrosino, did what they could to ridicule the idea, but without success. Conviction that a Black Hand society actually existed soon took root. By 1905 the San Francisco *Call* was reporting that the organization had thirty thousand members and chapters in a dozen cities across the United States. In 1907, Black Handers were blamed for as many as three hundred killings in Manhattan alone, and the number of their outrages was said to be increasing at the rate of four a day.

From the perspective of most New Yorkers, the Black Hand was at once a thrilling source of entertainment and a symbol of just how desperately uncivilized Italian immigrants could be. For the men and women of the Sicilian quarter, who lived with the threats of the extortionists every day, it was a reminder of how little had really changed since they had crossed the ocean, to be preyed upon in the United States as they had been preyed upon at home. For Giuseppe Morello, though, the success of Little Italy's extortionists was if anything an inspiration. For if unorganized amateurs, lacking skills and experience, could make a success of such illegal enterprises, what opportunities must there be for real criminals, men who would not scruple at raining far greater destruction down upon their victims and enemies? How much money was waiting to be made by the ruthless? What, in short, were the prospects for an American Mafia?

CHAPTER 4

"THE MOST SECRET AND TERRIBLE
ORGANIZATION IN THE WORLD"

=

THERE WAS NO MAFIA WHEN MORELLO ARRIVED IN THE UNITED States, no network of families such as existed in Sicily, no American "boss of bosses"—perhaps no *cosche* operating on the far side of the Atlantic at all. But there were emigrant Mafiosi living in several states, and these men were in communication with the families that they had left behind in Italy, both actual and criminal.

Men of respect had been crossing the ocean ever since the 1870s, when emigrants first began to flood from Sicily. Some left the island because they were poor and went to America because the booming of the citrus business meant there were flourishing trade routes between Palermo and several U.S. ports; others emigrated to join their families. America also became a place of refuge for Mafiosi fleeing problems at home. Morello was one, but there were others who, like him, were in trouble with the law or escaping some murderous internecine feud. Tunisia, which had long been the favorite refuge of exiled Mafiosi, was closer to Sicily—a mere few hours by sea from Palermo. But the United States offered much that a sojourn in Tunis did not: prospects for work, a fast-growing Italian community, and, crucially, better chances to make money.

The Mafia initiates who did cross the Atlantic in the nineteenth century were small fry, nonetheless. The bosses of the richest families enjoyed far too much influence at home to have any need to leave their island, and on the handful of occasions when they and their immediate lieutenants thought it wise to leave Sicily for a while, they were more likely to go to the mainland under the protection of influential friends, as Giuseppe Valenza, the brutal landowner from Prizzi, had done in 1877.

The same bosses also did so well out of their Sicilian rackets that they had no particular incentive to test new markets on another continent. One thing that can be said for certain about the first Mafiosi to arrive in the United States—Morello and his family included—was that they were not sent there by their superiors as part of any worked-out plan to expand the influence of the fraternity. They traveled as private citizens, and if they did continue to pursue a life of crime, it was because the *mala vita* offered them the best prospect of a good living.

No more than a few scant traces of Mafia activity date to the years before Morello's arrival in the United States; most come from ports, and all from towns that were home to large Italian communities. There may well have been more going on in these places than we realize; *cosche* kept no lists of membership, and there is almost never any way of knowing which of the hundreds of Sicilian criminals who arrived in the United States over the years were Mafia initiates, nor how many of the several dozen men named in the American press as Mafiosi actually were men of respect. Newspaper coverage can be misleading; at times, particularly in the middle 1870s, the early 1890s, and after the Barrel Murder in 1903, the word *Mafia* was deployed as a form of shorthand to describe all manner of Italian criminals. Only a handful of personal testimonies survive. Often the sole indication that this man or that really was a Mafioso comes from tracing the events of later life—the arrests, convictions, and associates that he acquired in the course of his criminal career.

For all this, even the most conservative analysis suggests that, by the turn of the century, men with Mafia connections could be found in Boston, San Francisco, Pittsburgh, St. Louis, and Chicago and in the rough-and-tumble mining towns of Pennsylvania. Outside Philadelphia, for instance, members of several Sicilian Mafia families began settling in Scranton, Pittston, and Wilkes-Barre during the late 1800s. The first to appear were the Sciaccatani—men from Sciacca, on the south coast of the island, a known stronghold of the fraternity—who arrived in Luzerne County during the 1880s and found work in the local pits. They were followed by families from Montedoro, who built homes in the Brandy Patch area of Pittston; their gang, known locally as the Men of Montedoro, extorted protection money from Italian miners. So did the Mafia of Hillsville, near New Castle, led by a man named Rocco Racco, who in 1906 unwisely drew attention to himself by murdering a local game warden in a dispute over a dog. And, more than a decade before Racco was arrested, tried, and hanged, the first members of the DiGiovanni family, from Palermo, arrived in Montgomery County. The Secret Service began uncovering evidence of counterfeiting in the latter district as early as 1896 and linked the business to the Sciaccatani. The ring was circulating forged currency in several Pennsylvania coal towns and as far away as Baltimore.

None of these little pockets of Mafia criminality attracted much attention from the press; even the Racco trial, a nine days' wonder in its time, was only scantily reported beyond the eastern seaboard. But one Sicilian murder did cause a sensation throughout the United States before Morello's arrival in the country. It was a killing that took place in New Orleans, at the American end of one of the most important trade routes to Palermo. It began with a dispute between two armed gangs of Sicilians, resulted in the death of a controversial police chief, and ended with one of the most notorious mass lynchings ever to occur in the United States. It also convinced several million Americans that the Mafia existed.

DAVID HENNESSY SWALLOWED the last of his oysters, washed down his supper with a glass of milk, and glanced out onto Rampart Street. It was close to midnight on October 15, 1890, and an inch of rain had fallen in the streets of New Orleans that evening, turning the city's manure-strewn, unpaved roads into a filthy slurry and forcing the handful of pedestrians braving the weather to take off their boots and socks and roll their trousers to their knees to cross between the sodden sidewalks. So he was pleased to see the storm had eased, leaving behind it little but a thick, damp delta mist that swirled through the streets of the French Quarter and drifted down toward the Mississippi.

Hennessy, at thirty-two, was the youngest chief of police in the United States, and one of the most famous. He was a good-looking officer—"pretty Dave," the New Orleans newspapers called him—and brave as well as shrewd, a teetotaler in a city of hard drinkers and a man who had survived the corrupt morass of New Orleans politics with his personal integrity more or less intact. Yet Hennessy had his dark side, too. He made arrests without worrying too much about using proper procedure. He played a full part in the squalid factionalism that undermined his city's police department. And he had favorites—friends, relatives, and allies whom he met at a private members club known as the Red Light—and no shortage of enemies. A few years earlier he had put a bullet through the brain of one of them, the then chief of detectives, and won himself a disputed acquittal at his murder trial by claiming self-defense.

More recently, in the spring of 1890, Hennessy had found himself embroiled in another dangerous dispute, a bitter wrangle between two groups of Sicilians in the city docks. In those days the New Orleans waterfront was almost entirely controlled by gangs of black and Irish longshoremen, who competed for the most lucrative contracts and kept the best jobs for themselves. The handful of Italian stevedores were left to squabble over minor bits of business, the most important of which were contracts to handle the unloading of Italian-owned fruit boats sailing from Central America. A large proportion of this business was in the hands of the Macheca Brothers shipping line, and, for the best part of a decade, Joseph Macheca had awarded his contracts to a company run by the four Provenzano brothers: Peter, Vincent, George, and Joe. In 1886, however, a rival firm named Matranga & Locascio had appeared on the waterfront. Tony and Charles Matranga won several contracts by bidding low and two years later secured a monopoly over the entire Italian fruit business.

Hennessy knew Joe Provenzano, who ran the Provenzano company; both men were members of the Red Light club. He had less to do with the Matranga brothers, who had come to New Orleans years earlier from western Sicily. As police chief, he certainly knew that the Matrangas were widely hated on the waterfront—they paid miserably, less than half the wages offered by the Provenzanos—and that relations between the rival firms of longshoremen had been deteriorating sharply. He knew that Charles Matranga blamed the Provenzanos for three recent murders in the Italian quarter, among them the unsolved killing of a man named Giuseppe Mattiani; he also knew that Mattiani's torso had been found in an attic room on the corner of Bienville Street, smeared over with coal oil and stuffed into a greasy sack, its legs removed and the head cut off and burned beyond recognition. Hennessy had heard rumors that Joe Provenzano had vowed to "soak the levee in blood" if he did not get his contracts back. But Hennessy worried more about the Matrangas. In the last few months the chief had uncovered evidence that both brothers were members of the Mafia, a society whose existence had been rumored in

New Orleans for almost a decade. He may also have known that the family maintained links to the *cosca* in their hometown of Monreale.

It was the Italian authorities, oddly enough, who had gathered the first real evidence of a Mafia in New Orleans. More than a decade earlier, at the tail end of the 1870s, the Monreale police had been hunting a man named Salvatore Marino, a leading member of the Stoppaglieri—the "Stoppered Mouths" or "new Mafia" of that town. Marino had been arrested for murder in 1875 and held in jail pending a trial, only to be released when, thanks to his influential Mafia friends, a court official had stolen and burned the prosecution files. The same shadowy allies had then obtained a passport for Marino and arranged for him to flee to New Orleans, where he changed his name and, by his own admission, established a branch of the Stoppaglieri in the city, a task made considerably easier by the presence of a large community of emigrant Monrealesi along the Mississippi. When in an expansive mood, Marino was prone to brag to friends of the enormous influence he wielded. He told one man who worked for his grocery business that he was the capo of an association numbering forty-five thousand men.

Marino's boastful indiscretions eventually reached the ears of Sicily's police, and a spy by the name of Rosario La Mantia was dispatched to the United States to find him. La Mantia succeeded in his mission, but Marino died of yellow fever soon afterward, leaving the agent to return to Italy late in 1878 with several compromising letters he had recovered from the dead man's house. One of these documents was a note from a member of the Monreale Mafia addressed to Tony Matranga in New Orleans. The state prosecutor in Palermo later identified both Matranga and Marino as "members of the association of the Stoppaglieri."

How Tony and Charles Matranga and the New Orleans Stoppaglieri fared during the 1880s is not known, but the gang apparently grew stronger after Marino's death. Certainly Joe Provenzano—although by no means an unbiased source—claimed to have had heard a great deal about the fraternity that he called the "Stopiglieri." "They're people that work for the Matrangas," he told several reporters.

> There are about twenty leaders of them. They are the committee, and there are about 300 greenhorns who have got to do anything the leaders say. . . . They pay them $10, $20, or $100 to get a man out of the way, and if the man they order to kill some one

won't do it they have him killed, so he can't tell anything to the police.

They've got the Mafia Society everywhere . . . in San Francisco, St. Louis, Chicago, New-York, and here.

The Matrangas flatly denied that a word of this was true, telling the New Orleans *Daily Picayune* that Provenzano had spoken out to hide the fact that he himself was a Mafia boss. But the Matrangas had no proof, and it was their rival who supplied the most intriguing details of the Stoppaglieri's influence and methods. According to Provenzano—who explained he had his information from a former Matranga ally who had come to work for him—it was Mafia power that lay behind the brothers' fast-growing business on the waterfront. The man had described his initiation into the secret society: "They brought him into the room and he saw [Charles] Matranga dressed in a black domino [a loose cloak incorporating a mask], and others were dressed in dominoes, and they made him swear on a skull with a dirk [knife] in it. He said he was willing to rob people, but he didn't want to have to kill anybody, so he got out of it."

No one in New Orleans paid much attention to stories of this sort at first, and it was not until May 1890 that David Hennessy himself was drawn into the struggle between the rival groups of longshoremen. In that month the violent dispute between the two finally burst the bounds of the Italian quarter when a crew of Matranga stevedores was ambushed after midnight in the streets above the docks. Three men were badly wounded in a fusillade of gunfire, and Tony Matranga, hit in the knee, lost most of his right leg. Hennessy investigated, and when his men uncovered evidence that the Provenzanos were involved, he locked up Joe and his three brothers and announced that he would send to Italy for the records of both families. The police chief also sent letters seeking information about Joseph Macheca, the shipping magnate who had given the Matrangas their contracts. Macheca had been orphaned in childhood and adopted into a Maltese family, but he, too, came from a Sicilian family.

That was in the summer. Now, in October 1890, Hennessy's investigation was complete and he was expected to give evidence at the Provenzanos' trial for the docks ambush. According to two men who knew the police chief well, he had marshaled fresh information against the

Matranga brothers in the form of a packet of incriminating transcripts from Italy and "a great deal of dark evidence about Joe Macheca, whom he considered to be a troublemaker." George Vandervoort, Hennessy's secretary, heard that the chief had confronted Macheca with some of this information and threatened him with the state prison. According to Vandervoort, Macheca and the Matrangas were terrified by Hennessy's investigation and likely to respond violently. "He dug deeper into the order than any outsider had ever dared," the secretary said, "and when he was up to see me he said he had evidence to uproot the Mafia in this country. He had ascertained facts that would have uncloaked their band of assassins and would have sent a great crowd to the penitentiary for perjurers." There was sufficient fear for the police chief's safety for a private detective agency to be assigned to watch his home.

Hennessy himself appeared as unperturbed as ever. With the Provenzano trial a mere two days away, he had attended the New Orleans Police Board as usual, then sprawled in his office talking with a policeman friend named Billy O'Connor. At eleven, the two men went for their late supper, sharing a plate of oysters.

Hennessy said good night to O'Connor at the door, then turned uphill and trudged through the mist on Girod Street toward the small frame house that he shared with his mother. It was almost midnight on October 15. Hunched behind his open umbrella, the police chief did not see a group of five roughly dressed men skulking beneath the awning of a cobbler's shop on the far side of the road. The men watched as Hennessy approached, pressing themselves into the shadows as he strode by. When he had passed, they stepped onto the sidewalk, leveled their guns, and opened fire.

The boom of two heavily charged shotguns and the sharper crack of several pistols rumbled through the mist. Even the police chief, famous for his quick reactions, had no prospect of avoiding the attack. A large-caliber revolver bullet tore into his chest, passed through a lung, and came to rest against the membrane of his heart. A second round struck an elbow; a third broke a bone in his right leg. The whole of his right side was raked with buckshot.

Knocked backward by the force of the impact, Hennessy slumped to the sidewalk for a second, gasping with shock and pain. Then, as if to prove his legendary toughness, he hauled himself to his feet, drew his own gun from his waistcoat, and began to limp after his fleeing assailants. Terribly injured though he was, he discharged two futile shots into the gun smoke before tripping over a doorstep and collapsing for a second time.

Billy O'Connor had walked no more than a few hundred yards toward his own home when the sound of shooting rang along the street. He turned and sprinted through the mud until he came upon his wounded friend propped against a step. Even in the semidarkness, O'Connor could see the ragged holes torn by the shotgun pellets and feel the sticky warmth of blood on his companion's clothing. Hennessy's lips were forming almost silent words. O'Connor, kneeling in a pool of liquid mud and gore, pressed an ear close to his face.

"They gave it to me," hissed the dying man. "And I gave it them back as best I could."

"Who gave it to you, Dave?" O'Connor asked, and the answer came so quietly that he barely caught it above the rasp of labored breath.

"Dagoes," Hennessy mumbled to his friend. "The dagoes did it."

WHEN THE CHIEF'S WORDS reached the ears of New Orleans's police and press, they unleashed a sensation.

Hennessy's men had passed a miserable night dredging the muddy gutters along Girod Street in search of the murder weapons; by dawn they were all for picking up some suspects first and worrying about their stories later. Their views were shared by Joseph Shakspeare, New Orleans's mayor. Shakspeare, like most members of the ruling class, had no love for the city's "dagoes," with their different customs, strange food and religion, and incomprehensible language. He shared the casual racism that prevailed in the United States during its Gilded Age. "We find them," he once remarked when pressed for an opinion of Italians, "the most idle, vicious and worthless people among us. . . . They are filthy in their persons and homes and our epidemics nearly always break out in their quarter. They are without courage, honor, truth, pride, religion or any quality that goes to make the good citizen." Certainly Shakspeare saw no reason to protect such people simply because there were no witnesses to the Hennessy shooting and no one who could identify the murderers. The mayor's orders, when they came, were unequivocal: "Scour the whole neighborhood! Arrest every Italian you come across, if necessary, and scour it again tomorrow morning."

Whipped up by the mayor and the press—which reported sightings of suspicious-looking Sicilians in the most inflammatory terms—the police descended on the Italian quarter of the city. They were joined in their endeavors by the Committee of 50, a group of vigilantes led by a prominent lawyer named William Parkerson. In the absence of firm evidence against any of their suspects, the authorities followed the mayor's edict to the letter, rounding up suspects on a whim. Almost 250 Italians found themselves in custody.

The least suspicion was enough to get a man charged. A pushcart peddler who had failed to turn up at his usual pitch was summarily arraigned. A boy only twelve years old, thought to have been a lookout for the ambush gang, was also hauled before the courts. But so were five members of the Matranga family and the man widely regarded as the most powerful Italian in the city: Macheca.

The case against all the prisoners was inconclusive. The authorities did contrive to place two undercover Italian-speaking detectives in the jails where the suspects were being held, and one of them, a young Pinkerton operative named Frank Dimeo, spent three months in a stinking cell, courting dysentery or worse in his efforts to build a case against the defendants. But no actual confessions were obtained, and when the Hennessy murder trial opened at the end of February 1891, all but nineteen of the arrested men had been released, among them Tony Matranga. The case against the remaining prisoners was far from conclusive and rested chiefly on a series of disputed identifications. The principal defendants, Macheca and Charles Matranga, were both rich enough to lavish substantial sums on high-class lawyers, and neither man expected to take chances in the trial. Down on the waterfront it was said that they had plans in place to bribe the jury.

To keep proceedings as simple as possible, the defendants were to be tried in two groups, beginning with Macheca, Matranga, and seven others. Their trial proved sensational—not least because one of the accused, an unstable laborer named Emanuele Polizzi, broke down in the dock and openly charged Macheca and Matranga with being joint leaders of the New Orleans Mafia. Fortunately for the two defendants, the value of this evidence was diminished by the fact that Polizzi was clearly mad. Having delivered his evidence, the prisoner spent the remainder of the proceedings slumped glassily in a chair, rousing himself intermittently to attempt to bite passing court officials; Macheca and Matranga, meanwhile, produced a dozen witnesses to show that they had been at the opera at the time of the shooting—an alibi the prosecution averred was so convenient that it had probably been carefully arranged.

Most of New Orleans's citizens, certainly, considered the defendants to be guilty, and the verdicts, when they came, stunned the city. The jury pronounced itself split over the guilt or innocence of three of the Sicilians, each of whom had been placed by at least one witness on the street where Hennessy was shot; the presiding judge ordered that this trio be tried again. The remainder of the defendants, Matranga and Macheca among them, were found not guilty on the grounds of insufficient evidence. Crucially, though, none of the men were immediately released. There were additional charges, of "lying await with intent to commit murder," still to be faced.

Had the defendants in the Hennessy case been found guilty, it seems safe to say, vastly less would have been heard about the case. As it was, the acquittals led directly to an outbreak of violence so savage and uncontrollable that it would be remembered vividly for years, and not only in New Orleans. The whole town pulsed with anger at the notion that a group of murderous Sicilians was escaping justice, and next morning, March 14, 1891, the local *Times-Herald* carried an advertisement so laden with menace that it frightened the entire Italian community:

MASS MEETING

ALL GOOD CITIZENS ARE INVITED TO ATTEND A MASS MEETING
AT 10 O'CLOCK A.M., TO TAKE STEPS TO REMEDY THE FAILURE OF
JUSTICE IN THE HENNESSY CASE. COME PREPARED FOR ACTION.

Among the fifty-one signatures appended to the appeal were those of William Parkerson and several local politicians.

Word spread fast throughout the city, and a crowd guessed to be eight thousand strong gathered next morning at the appointed time. Many had armed themselves with guns, knives, clubs, or staves. The vigilante leader, Parkerson—his eyes "snapping fire"—delivered an inflammatory speech, denouncing the acquittal of the "Mafia Society" and ending with a rousing call for his audience to "follow me, and see the murder of Hennessy vindicated." The mob, a watching newspaperman reported, "went mad, shouting, 'Yes, yes, hang the dagoes!'" and began marching on the parish jail. Arriving at the prison, the vigilantes were still more incensed to find that, in an attempt to save lives, the warden had released all nineteen Italians in his custody from their cells and had urged them to find hiding places in their cell blocks.

The mob would not be denied. A rear gate was promptly broken down, and members of the crowd stationed themselves as guards at all the exits while a well-armed execution squad—sixty men strong and handpicked by Parkerson—combed purposefully through the prison buildings in search of anyone Sicilian. Six prisoners, betrayed by other convicts who pointed out their hiding places, were herded against a wall and killed with shotguns; at least a hundred blasts were fired, tearing their bodies into pieces. Macheca, cornered with his back against the bars of his cell, picked up an Indian club in a vain attempt to defend himself but suffered the same fate, and Polizzi, the madman, was seized alive and handed over to the thousands milling about outside; they wasted little time in stringing the boy up from a nearby streetlamp, half hanging him, then sending more than thirty bullets into his body. When Parkerson emerged to announce that the killing was over, he was carried off in triumph on the shoulders of his men. "Mob violence," the lawyer piously remarked as the crowd dispersed, "is the most terrible thing on the face of the earth. You have performed your duty. Now go to your homes, and if I need you, I will call you."

Eleven men were killed in Orleans Parish Prison, the single largest lynching in the history of the United States, and most Americans believed that justice had been done. In truth, though, there was strong reason to doubt this. Five of the dead were members of the group of prisoners still awaiting trial; they had never even been brought before a court for Hennessy's death. On the other hand, several of the most notorious of those arraigned for the Hennessy murder escaped, and among the eight survivors was Charles Matranga, who had found a secure hiding place under the floorboards of a rubbish closet in the women's section of the jail. Passions in the city cooled so quickly after the lynchings that he was able to go back to his old job as boss stevedore without apparent hindrance and to continue working, seemingly peaceably, until his retirement in 1918.

Whether Matranga retained any active involvement with crime on the waterfront remains obscure; certainly he was never convicted of any offense. Nor was much more heard for several decades of the New Orleans Mafia, although dark rumors still swirled out of the bayous from time to time: word of an Italian plot to murder all the officials in New Orleans in 1890, concern over a spate of eleven unsolved murders of Italians five years later. It may be that the lynchings disrupted the Stoppaglieri's operations, or at least made the gang more cautious. Whatever the truth, though, the United States had received its first glimpse of the Honored Society at work.

THE HENNESSY MURDER sparked the biggest Mafia scare of the century and by far the most influential. It cemented belief in the society's existence among thousands of Americans. It also greatly increased hatred and fear of Sicilians throughout the country. In the coming decade, a large proportion of all the violent crimes committed by Italians in the United States would be routinely attributed to the Mafia, and as a result there was more violence and discrimination against Italians. Eight Sicilians were lynched in Louisiana in the 1890s, another three in 1896, and five more three years later. There were minor scares in Denver in 1892, in Milwaukee in 1897, and in San Francisco in 1898.

In Boston, two Italian policemen received threats from a "Mafia" that claimed to have forty-five members in the city. Lieutenant John Wheeler of the Chicago police said he was certain, from personal experience, that "a branch of the Mafia society" existed in his city—an opinion that was echoed by A. L. Drummond, the storied former head of the Secret Service. There were still plenty of policemen, judges, and reporters who took a different view, and evidence that proved the existence of a "Mafia society," rather than merely suggesting it, was difficult to find. In Chicago, Lieutenant Wheeler's boss, Inspector Michael Lewis, insisted that he had not "the slightest reason to suspect the existence of the Mafia in Chicago," and Oscar Durante, who edited the local Italian American daily, went further. "This is all sheer nonsense, stupidity, imbecility," the newspaperman exploded. "Every time a drunken row among Italians occurs, the people and the press cry 'Mafia.' There is no such organization and never was."

Only in New York was there persuasive evidence for the existence of what *The New York Times* described a few years later as "the most secret and terrible organization in the world"; only in New York were the police disposed, for a while at least, to believe that there were Mafiosi in the city. Evidence that members of at least one Sicilian Mafia family were active in New York dated back a good way, too—to the spring of 1884, in fact, when both the Police Department and the Secret Service were alerted to the activities of two brothers named Farach.

Raymond and Carmelo Farach had come to New York from Palermo, though at such an early date (the summer of 1853) that they were probably not themselves Mafiosi. But the police in Brooklyn, where they lived, were sure that the pair had some secret source of income. Raymond Farach was an impressive-looking, educated man who spoke excellent English, stood six feet tall, and was immaculately groomed and dressed, from his cultivated side whiskers to his shoes—more than would be expected of a man who owned and ran a little photographic studio. His younger brother, Carmelo, was similarly well turned out, despite earning his living as a barber and co-owner of a failing cigar store. Raymond undoubtedly had criminal connections. But it was Carmelo Farach who came to the notice of the police first when, early in April, his body was discovered in a remote field on Staten Island. He had been stabbed through the heart.

Farach's death was certainly peculiar, as the *Brooklyn Daily Eagle* did not hesitate to point out. For one thing, it was written off as a suicide at first, even though the surgeon who examined the corpse determined that Farach had cuts to his face and had been stabbed from behind. For another, the body was found with a sword cane by its right hand, though Farach was left-handed. Finally, when detectives went to talk to the dead man's business partner, Antonio Flaccomio, they discovered, by inspecting his handful of possessions, that he had recently scoured and cleaned his clothes with acid. The police took much more interest in Flaccomio thereafter, and in time they located a witness on Staten Island who had seen Farach talking with a man who answered his partner's description only a minute or two before his death. Several more testified to the perilous state of Farach's cigar business and to having observed him fighting with Flaccomio over money. Another man had seen Farach and Flaccomio board the Staten Island ferry on the morning of the stabbing.

Much of this information was hard-won. A Brooklyn barber who was one of the last to see the dead man alive refused to say a word to reporters, stating: "I don't want my name to be put in the papers because those Sicilians are a bad, treacherous lot, and my life would not be safe for a moment if it were known I had said anything either way." (The newsmen, who had little time for Italians, printed his name anyway.)

Raymond Farach was also reticent. "Italians that come from Palermo are, as a rule, the worst men in Italy," he told the police. "They will knife a person as soon as look at him." Few were surprised when, at the inquest into Farach's death, the coroner's jury called the case murder but said there was too little evidence for any formal charges to be brought.

That was the last that was heard of Antonio Flaccomio for more than two years. The chief suspect in the Farach case left New York soon after the inquest and traveled widely through the United States—to Buffalo, Louisville, Chicago, and New Orleans.

Flaccomio did not return to Brooklyn until July 1886, when he paid an unexpected call on Raymond Farach—who later said Flaccomio had confessed and begged permission to return to New York, an odd thing for anyone to ask of a moderately prosperous small businessman. According to the *Daily Eagle,* Raymond told his visitor he could not live in Brooklyn ("If he does, and I again encounter him, I will kill him!"), and Flaccomio had gone instead to Little Italy. Certainly it was in Manhattan, outside Cooper Union on St. Mark's Place, that Carmelo Farach's murderer met his own death two years later.

Flaccomio had spent the evening of October 14, 1888, playing cards with a group of friends. Walking home, he was suddenly attacked: Two men rushed up to him on a street corner, and while his companions grappled with one, the other pulled out a wicked-looking bread knife and stabbed him in the chest. Flaccomio had just sufficient time to mutter, "I am killed" before he crumpled to the pavement. In the ensuing confusion, his murderers escaped. They had been recognized, however, and—between themselves—the dead man's friends agreed they were Italians.

The Cooper Union stabbing was not the sort of case New York's police would normally have solved. It was a purely Sicilian affair, and the NYPD had a poor record of tackling Italian crime. Only two of its detectives spoke the language—Joseph Petrosino was still seven years from his promotion at this point—and the half-dozen witnesses, all of whom were friends of the victim, had sworn a solemn vow to deal with the matter themselves rather than divulge the murderers' identity to the authorities. Yet the Flaccomio killing was rapidly investigated and, to the surprise of most of Little Italy, apparently just as quickly solved.

The man responsible for this unexpected turn of events was Inspector Thomas Byrnes. Irish, forty-six years old, with thinning hair, a shaggy mustache, and eyes that glinted like steel knitting needles, Byrnes was the head of New York's Detective Bureau. Renowned as the most brilliant policeman in the city, Byrnes was an innovator who reformed the department's record department, introduced the Rogues' Gallery, which collected crooks' mug shots, and perfected the brutal but productive methods of the third degree. He was also rich, having, with the help of stock tips provided by Wall Street insiders, assembled a portfolio of property and shares worth seventy times his five-thousand-dollar salary.

Byrnes had taken an interest in the Cooper Union case for a couple of reasons. The first was official: Flaccomio—quite unknown to his friends—had been a police informer, one of the few the NYPD possessed in Little Italy. He had recently provided the Detective Bureau with evidence against a fellow Sicilian and apparently provided information about the Mafia as well. Byrnes's second reason was personal. He had built much of his reputation for exceptional police work on well-timed disclosures to the press and saw, in Flaccomio's murder, the prospect of further headlines, not least because he thought that he could crack the case.

Byrnes's first move was to arrest the witnesses. He had three of the men who had been with Flaccomio when he was killed locked up in New York's grimmest prison, the Tombs, on Centre Street in lower Manhattan. Three days' confinement in the jail's tiny, dripping cell blocks yielded names. The killers, Byrnes informed the press a few days later, had been two brothers from Palermo named Carlo and Vincenzo Quarteraro. It was too late to capture Carlo, who had had slipped out of the country disguised as a priest, but Vincenzo Quarteraro was arrested and then sent for trial.

Byrnes felt sure he had his man—so sure that he supplied New York's newspapers with the details of his case. He had been struck, he said, by the intelligence and criminal abilities of the men whom he had locked up in the Tombs, but more so by the details of the ruthless fraternity that they described. "They are rather intelligent and have received some education," Byrnes told *The New York Times*.

They are fugitives from their native country, having been engaged there in various crimes and offenses. The criminal classes in Sicily are banded together in a secret society known as "The Maffia," all the members of which are pledged to protect each other against the officers of the law. If one of the society commits a crime, all the other members are bound to shield and keep the crime secret under pain of death. The members of this society are chiefly forgers, counterfeiters and assassins. Murder with some of these men is simply a pastime. They have no pity, and think nothing of killing any one who stands in their way or betrays their secrets.

How much of this intelligence had been wrung from Byrnes's interviews is difficult to say. The inspector may have had some of his details from other sources, perhaps even from newspaper accounts of Sicily. But his knowledge of contemporary Mafia activities in the United States was detailed enough to suggest a firsthand source of information. There were, he explained to the *Times*'s reporter, "two principal headquarters of this society in this country—one in this city and the other in New Orleans." The two groups were connected, so that "members of the society who commit a serious crime in this city find refuge among friends in the South, and vice versa." New York's Mafiosi were also well enough organized to deal with unreliable associates. Flaccomio had been marked for death when it was discovered he had passed information to the authorities, and the dead man had known all about the danger he was in—a few days before his murder he had sat down to talk with his thirteen-year-old son, explained that he would inherit the family fruit store if he, Flaccomio, died, and asked the boy to take good care of his sister.

Coming from a policeman of Thomas Byrnes's stature, these disclosures were significant. The newspapers that reported the interview saw no reason to doubt them, and when Vincenzo Quarteraro came to trial at the end of March 1889, the same papers ran stories under the headline THE "MAFIA" MURDER. Unfortunately for the police, however, the publicity given Byrnes's statements had concealed essential weaknesses in their case, the most important of which was that there was no real evidence against Quarteraro other than the statements of the victim's friends, all of whom were criminals themselves. Even John Goff, the assistant district attorney charged with prosecuting the case, admitted that it would be difficult to secure a conviction. "He says that if the charge was larceny he would recommend the dismissal of the indictment on the evidence, but as it is murder he does not care to take the responsibility," the *Times* observed.

Goff had found one witness to testify to the Mafia's existence: "an Italian whose death was ordered for having given information to the Government . . . A scarred cheek shows that an effort was made to carry the Mafia's decree into execution." Against that, though, Quarteraro mustered a formidable array of testimony, American as well as Italian, to prove that he had been miles away at the time of the killing. Goff's evidence, on the other had, was supplied by a succession of lowlifes—"the scum of Sicilian society"—who failed to impress either judge or jury. Quarteraro's attorney openly accused the three men Byrnes had locked up in the Tombs of having committed the murder themselves.

The Sicilian's eventual acquittal seems to have come as no surprise to those who had actually watched the trial, but it was certainly an unwelcome blow to Byrnes. The inspector had staked a small part of his immense credibility on Quarteraro's guilt, and the jury's verdict left him scrambling to distance himself from his earlier statements. "As a class," the inspector told the *New York Tribune*, "Italians do not seem to be dangerous to the public of this city." Most were actually law-abiding; there were "no portraits of Italian thieves in the Rogues' Gallery." When the Hennessy shooting brought the Mafia back into the news a year later, Byrnes declared that while Sicilian killers could certainly wreak havoc in the distant South, "no band of assassins such as the Mafia could be allowed to perpetrate murders in New-York."

Inspector Byrnes's volte-face was an important milestone in Mafia history. The great detective possessed the prestige to sway New York's newsmen and New York public opinion. Had Vincenzo Quarteraro been convicted, the papers would have reported Byrnes's triumph and approved his verdict on the Mafia. The idea that members of the fraternity were living in New York might easily have been commonly accepted a year or more before Giuseppe Morello so much as set foot in the United States, and the police, particularly the Detective Bureau, would almost certainly have taken a much tougher stance against Sicilian crime and perhaps even have recruited more Italian detectives. Courts, too, would likely have been more willing to convict suspected Mafiosi than they were after the Quarteraro verdict.

As it was, however, the consequences of New York's first and least-remembered Mafia trial were very different. The police grew more wary of Italian crime. Newspapers grew more skeptical. Most important of all, Byrnes—the most famous, the most celebrated, the most powerful detective in the country—more or less washed his hands of Little Italy and its inscrutable inhabitants. "Let them go ahead and kill each other," the inspector was reported to have said—and whether he did say it or not, it was a view widely held in the NYPD. Thenceforth, for several decades, the police would pay far less attention to crimes committed in the Italian quarter than they would to similar offenses reported from elsewhere in the city. Murders, bombings, public outrages—all these were still investigated, naturally, though it was relatively seldom they were solved. But more minor crimes, even crimes of violence, received short shrift, and Italian criminals who preyed solely on Italians went unmolested much of the time.

The Hennessy and Flaccomio trials, between them, shaped America's view of the Mafia for more than a decade—the former more than the latter, for Quarteraro's trial attracted only a tiny fraction of the coverage accorded to the events in New Orleans. But if Vincenzo Quarteraro's acquittal went largely unremarked on in the country as a whole, it did have important consequences in New York itself, and one was to make it easier for the earliest Mafiosi in the city to operate unhindered.

For Morello, that was very welcome news, because—for Morello— crime was about to pay.

CHAPTER 5

THE CLUTCH HAND

=

GIUSEPPE MORELLO HAD RETURNED TO NEW YORK FLUSH WITH the money saved from a year in the sugar fields of Louisiana and two more of sharecropping in Texas. It probably amounted to a good sum for the day—five hundred dollars would be a reasonable estimate. That would have been enough to pay for a decent apartment in the Italian quarter and keep the whole family for a year, or it might have provided the seed capital for a small business. That Morello and the Terranovas did not possess sufficient cash for both purposes is suggested by their choice of residence; as late as 1900, Bernardo Terranova still lived at 123 East 4th Street, in a small apartment in a poor tenement district, and Morello in a room at the foot of Second Avenue at East Houston Street, one of the most densely populated slums in all Manhattan. Most of the family's savings were poured instead into an ornamental plastering business that Terranova opened in the Italian quarter. For the next few months, Morello helped his stepfather when he could—as did Vincenzo, Nicola, and Ciro, after school. At the same time, Morello began to plow what remained of the family's money into business ventures of his own.

Whether the man who had played such a prominent part in the affairs of the Corleone Fratuzzi really meant to live an honest life in the United States remains something of a mystery, but the available evidence suggests he did, at least at first. There was, after all, the lingering threat posed by Morello's 1894 conviction in Messina, and the six-year sentence waiting to be served should he ever be deported to Sicily; then there were the attempts, apparently sincere, to wrest a living from the land in Texas and Louisiana. There was never any suggestion of criminal activities in those years, though there may well have been some after the family returned to New York—even five hundred dollars did not go all that far in Manhattan in those days. Certainly, if Morello really meant to start fresh in the United States, that ambition did not survive the failure of four successive attempts to make his mark as a legitimate businessman.

The Clutch Hand's first acquisition, in the spring of 1897, was a coal store in Little Italy. It lasted only a year. After that, Morello ran an Italian saloon on 13th Street and another on Stanton Street that had to be closed only six months after it opened "on account of no business." Business wasn't much better up on 13th Street, and the second bar was also sold. His most ambitious venture was a date factory that employed fifteen or twenty people, but this too swiftly failed. Morello, Ciro Terranova said, "kept this factory for about six or eight months, but used to lose on it." By the spring of 1899, the money was mostly gone, and the bars and factories—Terranova's plaster contracting company excepted— were sold or closed.

It must have been then, sometime in 1898 or early 1899, that Morello returned to his old trade as a counterfeiter. There was, after all, something irresistible in solving money problems simply by printing money, and the Clutch Hand had the right sort of acquaintances among the criminals of the Sicilian community; he maintained a wide correspondence with exiled Corleonesi in every part of the country, exchanging letters with men as far away as Kansas City, New Orleans, Belle Rose in Louisiana, and even distant Seattle. In New York, on the streets of Little Italy, there were hundreds more men who had the necessary skills.

For the New York office of the Secret Service, led then by a hugely experienced veteran by the name of William P. Hazen, the first faint whiff of trouble came as early as the spring of 1899. Agents in Boston tracking the activities of another Italian counterfeiting gang, the Mastropoles, had begun intercepting letters sent between its members. That March they found one postmarked New York, which, when opened, proved to have been sent by Morello. There was nothing especially incriminating in the letter itself, but when dealing with Italian gangs it was standard practice to forward this sort of information to the agency's headquarters in Washington, D.C. There it was entered, checked, cross-referenced against existing lists of suspects, and then forwarded to sister offices for further investigation.

John Wilkie, the director of the Secret Service, took care of the last part of the job himself, dictating a note to Hazen requesting that an agent be sent down to Second Avenue to search the new suspect out. Hazen assigned the task to Special Operative Frank Brown, and Brown caught a streetcar to the East Side the same afternoon. The agent located Morello's address but could find no trace of the Clutch Hand, nor anyone who would admit to knowing him. The matter did not seem especially important at the time; Morello was just another name, and there were always dozens to be checked. Brown reported his failure to Hazen, who filed a two-line report to Wilkie and then rapidly forgot about it.

It was an error he and several other people would live to regret.

SEVERAL MILES UPTOWN, in a small apartment on the first floor of 329 East 106th Street, Giuseppe Morello was busy installing a small printing press in an empty room. It was an old, unsophisticated machine, certainly not one capable of producing exact copies of Treasury bills, but it was the best he had been able to obtain. Perfect reproductions were unnecessary anyway. The Clutch Hand's counterfeits would be passed at night in busy places—saloons, gambling houses, oyster bars—where they would be subjected to no more than a cursory examination. They would not fool a bank or a policeman, but they were never meant to.

Morello had moved to the Italian enclave in East Harlem just in time, apparently more by luck than judgment, and probably because he needed a larger base. The press had to be positioned where the sound of forged notes being struck would not easily be overheard, and there were printing plates and sundry other items of equipment that were far too precious to be left unguarded. All had to be stored in the apartment, which would also act as a home and the headquarters of several members of the gang.

The counterfeiters were an odd, mixed bunch. Morello had located an Italian from New Jersey who knew how to make printing plates, and a young Sicilian named Calogero Maggiore to take charge of disposing of the notes. Maggiore, who looked younger than his twenty years, had a job ironing shirts in a laundry and no criminal record, a decided advantage in Morello's eyes. He would seek out buyers with a more experienced Italian, a street hustler known as "Lingo Bingo" around 106th Street, and there were at least two other Sicilian members of the gang. But the remainder of Morello's men were Irish, led by a Brooklyn oyster bar proprietor known as the Commodore and a streetwise crook named

Henry Thompson. Thompson, who was nicknamed "Dude" for his natty taste in clothes, recruited another eight or ten queer-pushers, all of whom were told they could purchase as many of the forged notes as they wished at a discount of 60 percent. Since the plates Morello had commissioned from his printer friend turned out five-dollar "General Thomas head" bills of a type first printed in 1891, the pushers would have to find two dollars in good currency for every five-dollar fake they bought.

The Clutch Hand was very careful. Maggiore and the other Italians knew where the counterfeiting operation was based, but the less trustworthy Irish queer-pushers, even the Commodore, were kept in ignorance of this essential detail; they met and talked to Maggiore or to Lingo Bingo on the streets. Most of the bad currency would be passed well away from 106th Street, too; Dude Thompson's most reliable men— three down-on-their-luck Irish petty crooks—were told to work the beach resorts out on Long Island, where the stores and restaurants opened late and the counter staff were often far too busy to check for forgeries.

The one other potential source of trouble was the maid Morello had hired to cook and clean for him. She was an Irish girl named Mollie Callahan, the daughter of Dude Thompson's lady friend. Mollie's sweetheart, Jack Gleason, was another minor member of the gang, and Morello must have concluded that she could be trusted. Just to be certain, though, the girl was told to stay away from the room in the apartment where the press, the plates, and other counterfeiting gear were stored.

For several months all went well with the Clutch Hand's preparations. Two copper plates were etched, and paper resembling the sort used to print the five-dollar notes was purchased. Test sheets were run off on the press, and inks mixed until the colors more or less matched. Morello seemed satisfied; distribution of the counterfeit bills would begin in the New Year, he said.

Then, one day in late December 1899, Mollie Callahan's inquiring mind got the better of her common sense at last. She had glimpsed the press while she was cleaning. Exactly what was being printed, though, remained a mystery to her—one that neither her mother nor her lover would explain. Unable to restrain her curiosity, the girl waited until she thought the place was empty, then crept into the forbidden room.

A bundle concealed the printing plates, and Callahan picked it open. A gleam of copper caught her eye, then a neatly etched five-dollar symbol. Then a movement to one side, by the door.

Whirling round and stifling a scream, Mollie found herself staring deep into the blackest eyes that she had ever seen.

THE DISAPPEARANCE OF MORELLO'S servant girl on the cusp of the new century went unnoticed by all but her closest relatives; there were always thousands of runaways on the streets of New York. Callahan's mother, fearing the worst, reported her daughter's absence to the precinct house on East 104th Street, where the police launched a routine investigation. No one they spoke to seemed to have any idea where the maid had gone—no one, that is, but Jack Gleason, to whom Mollie had confided some of her suspicions concerning her mysterious employer. Gleason felt sure his girlfriend had been murdered, but he was far too frightened of the Clutch Hand to say as much, and the Italians the policemen questioned shrugged their shoulders expressively and regretted that they could not help. The apartment on 106th Street was checked, but there was nothing to be found there, and the press was gone.

Morello had the counterfeiting operation under way again by March. It was still a small-scale business—about two hundred five-dollar bills were printed and the forged notes, wrapped individually in newspaper, were sold to the queer-pushers in batches of three or four at a time. Five dollars was double the daily wage of a workman at the time, however, and at a profit of nearly two dollars each, even two hundred bills would generate a decent income.

On good days, dealing forged notes was not a high-risk business. The stores and bars where the bills were passed rarely examined them, and when a counterfeit was detected it was often enough for the pusher to apologize, say he had no idea how he had gotten the note, and replace it with some genuine currency. There were narrow escapes, however. Edward Kelly, one of Thompson's men, was picked up on May 23 when he was caught trying to pass a Morello bill on East 46th Street in earshot of a beat patrolman. Mary Hoffman, the proprietor of the clothing store Kelly had entered, screamed for the police, and Officer Bachmann, of the local precinct, appeared before the Irishman could bolt. Kelly, who had been attempting to purchase a pair of drawers, was arrested but kept quiet. Taken to the nearest station house, he insisted he had won the bogus note playing craps and said nothing to implicate his confederates.

Kelly was released on bail a few days later and went straight back to passing bills, and it was not until May 31, 1900, that things went seriously wrong for the Morello gang. It was a warm and pleasant early summer evening, and the resorts on the Queens side of the East River were crowded with revelers, ideal conditions for passing counterfeits. Three of Dude Thompson's men—Kelly, Charles Brown, and John Duffy—were working the resort in North Beach, palming off bills in sideshows and restaurants. To minimize their risk, each carried only a single Morello note, mixed in with genuine currency. A fourth member of the gang, Tom Smith, a black-mustached night watchman, hung around on a nearby street. His job was to be the pushers' "boodle carrier"—the man who held a roll of notes but did not attempt to pass them. The theory was a good one: If any one of Thompson's men was captured, he would be holding only a single forgery, and the ambitious scale of Morello's operation would be hidden from the police.

It was shortly before 10 P.M. when a North Beach restaurant owner took a second look at a five-dollar bill and recognized it as a forgery. Kelly, who had presented the note in payment for a plate of oysters worth five cents, tried to talk his way out of the situation, without success. Instead the proprietor summoned several policemen to detain him, and when someone pointed out that Kelly had entered in company with John Duffy, Duffy was arrested, too.

Tom Smith, the boodle carrier, escaped, but a sweep of all the shops and shows on the waterfront dredged up Charles Brown, the third member of Dude Thompson's group. All three of the queer-pushers were taken to the 74th Precinct building, booked, and held in the cells overnight. The next morning the police called Hazen's office, and the prisoners were taken to the U.S. marshal's office in Brooklyn. By the time Assistant Operative Tyrrell, one of Hazen's men, got there at lunchtime on the first of June, the three had all been questioned and were each being held on bail of three thousand dollars.

Left solely in the hands of the police, the investigation into Morello's counterfeiting ring might have ended there, but the Secret Service did things differently. Hazen had little interest in getting men as insignificant as Kelly off the streets. The important thing, he knew, was to trace the notes back to the men who had printed them and to seize their press.

The first thing was to persuade one of the arrested men to talk. Tyrrell accomplished this quite neatly by checking over the men's records and then taking Charles Brown aside. Brown had a prior conviction for larceny—he had served four years in Sing Sing prison—and was not keen to return to jail. By dangling the lure that the Secret Service would go easy on him, Tyrrell obtained a full confession. Brown named names and, thanks to his information, agents began tailing Dude Thompson around his haunts on the East Side.

It did not take Hazen's operatives long to gain the confidence of Dude and his confederates. Two Secret Service men posing as potential buyers of counterfeit notes eavesdropped as the Irish members of Morello's gang talked over the North Beach incident, blaming the arrests on the carelessness of Brown and his confederates; the three men had gotten steaming drunk before leaving New York. Thompson, who still had six Morello notes to dispose of, sold one to the agents, and a few days later Hazen's men went to see Kelly in prison and got from him some idea of the location of the printing press.

Penetrating the depths of the Morello gang took time, nonetheless. The agents spent a week identifying Calogero Maggiore, and they were still not sure who stood behind the young Sicilian when Hazen gave the order to round up as many of the gang as possible. On the morning of June 9, a Saturday, four operatives picked up Dude Thompson, Jack Gleason, and several of their confederates. Gleason talked immediately, apparently glad to confide his suspicions concerning the disappearance of Mollie Callahan. Knowing that word of the arrests would soon spread through the district, Operative Burke went straight to Maggiore's favorite saloon on East 106th Street. Hoping to entrap the young Sicilian, he offered to buy twenty dollars' worth of counterfeits. Maggiore left the bar to fetch the notes and was arrested on the corner.

It was only now, at the last moment, that the Secret Service men found out about Morello, and the Clutch Hand's arrest that early summer afternoon owed more to luck than it did to the agents' judgment. Jack Gleason was standing outside the 106th Street saloon telling Hazen's operatives the little he knew about Morello when the Irishman spotted his employer hurrying across the road. The Clutch Hand had been lurking in a dark recess of the bar, watching Maggiore do his business, and made off when he realized that his man had been arrested.

Agents Burke and Griffin seized him on the corner of Second Avenue and East 108th Street at 2:15 P.M.

Morello was escorted to the police station house on 104th Street to be booked. It was the same building in which Margaret Callahan had reported her daughter missing six months earlier, and the first time that the Clutch Hand had been arrested since his arrival in the United States. Morello proved to have $26.39 in genuine currency on him and no counterfeits, and Hazen and his agents quickly realized that they had little firm evidence against him. Gleason was the only member of the gang to identify their leader. The other counterfeiters refused to betray him— inspired by either loyalty or fear—and without the press and the printing plates, none of which were ever found, it was impossible to prove that Morello had produced the General Thomas notes. Fortunately for the Clutch Hand's prospects, American law also prohibited the conviction of criminals based solely on the testimony of accomplices.

Morello's cunning in distancing himself from his criminal activities, a practice he would follow throughout his career, was clearly shown when he and the other members of the gang were brought before Judge Thomas in the U.S. Circuit Court. Calogero Maggiore, little more than a boy, was singled out as the ringleader of the gang and sentenced to six years in Sing Sing. Brown got three years and Kelly two. Morello was discharged and walked free. He had enjoyed a narrow escape, and he knew it.

The way forward was plain enough. There was no security in working alone, no certainty in relying on confederates from unknown backgrounds, or on men who lacked the steadfastness and loyalty that came from swearing binding oaths. Those qualities could be found only in Sicilians—in other Mafiosi. The Clutch Hand would have to build a family of his own in New York City.

BETWEEN THE SUMMER of 1900, when he so nearly went to prison, and the spring of 1903, when he was arrested for ordering the Barrel Murder, Giuseppe Morello assembled the first Mafia gang in Manhattan. It was only a small group of men at first, but they were all utterly loyal to him, and if the branch of the Stoppaglieri in New Orleans led by Charles Matranga had claim to be the first *cosca* in the country, Morello's family boasted a vastly more significant distinction: It survived. It grew and changed over the years, fighting and merging with other groups until the outward traces of its early days were lost. But its history can be traced all the way to the introduction of Prohibition, then through the 1920s and the great Mafia war that followed, up until the present day. In that respect, as in others, the Morellos were the first family of organized crime in the United States.

The most important quality that Morello sought in his new associates was absolute reliability. His lieutenants were related to him by blood or marriage or were recruited from Corleone. These were men the Clutch Hand had known and trusted in Sicily, and who knew and trusted him in turn. Morello was proud of this fact. Letters written by the boss and his closest advisers were signed not only with their names but also with the salutation "All of Corleone."

The same exclusivity did not apply to the rank-and-file members of the gang, who came from all over western Sicily—a purely practical decision, in all likelihood, since there were still only a handful of Corleonesi in New York. In any case, the petty rivalries that poisoned relations between neighboring communities in Italy mattered scarcely at all in New York; no matter where a Sicilian might hail from, he would have more in common with someone born elsewhere on the island than he ever would with the Neapolitans—with whom there was considerable rivalry—let alone with native Americans. There were strict limits to this policy; to gain acceptance to Morello's gang, a potential member first had to be vouched for by a man from Corleone. But by 1903, the first family was thirty strong and included men who hailed from a number of small towns in the Sicilian interior, among them Carini, Villabate, and Lercara Friddi.

Morello's position as the head of the family was not challenged by anybody. There is no record that Bernardo Terranova, still working full-time as an ornamental plasterer, had any involvement in his stepson's criminal activities; if he did, it was most likely to proffer advice based on long experience. Morello's stepbrothers, meanwhile, were still too young to take much responsibility. Vincenzo, the eldest, was seventeen in 1903, Ciro fourteen, Nicola a year younger than that. Ciro had recently begun working as a waiter in Morello's spaghetti restaurant. The other brothers seem to have assisted in the plastering business; as they became older, all three became gradually more involved in the family's criminal activities without ever challenging their leader. At the time of the Barrel Murder, Morello's most prominent lieutenant was Vito Laduca, who came from Carini, just outside Palermo, and had spent some years in the Italian navy before turning to a life of crime.

Laduca had served a five-year prison sentence in Sicily before emigrating to the United States in February 1902. He was older than most other members of the gang and possessed a strength and ruthlessness Morello admired. As well as taking a very active role in the family's counterfeiting business—Laduca traveled widely to sell the Clutch Hand's forged notes and was arrested in Pittsburgh on a charge of possessing counterfeit five-dollar bills in January 1903—he was a brutally effective extortionist, referred to in the New York press as the "dread bulwark of the Black Hand." Laduca's criminal activities also extended to kidnapping. Concealing his true identity behind the alias "Longo," he was the chief suspect in the abduction of Antonio Mannino, the eight-year-old son of a wealthy Italian contractor, for whom a fifty-thousand-dollar ransom was demanded. Mannino was released after a week for what was widely believed to have been a far lower payment, but Laduca was nonetheless able to send large sums of money home to Carini, where he was thought of as a wealthy man.

The ease with which men such as Vito Laduca moved from Sicily to New York and gained admittance to Morello's family suggests strong links existed between the Mafiosi of the old and new worlds at this comparatively early date. Others made the same journey (among them Giuseppe Fontana, chief suspect in the murder of Marquis Emanuele Notarbartolo, who appeared in the United States in the autumn of 1901) and, when they did, became members of the Clutch Hand's circle so rapidly that their arrival must have been expected and planned for. Giuseppe Lalamia and the brothers Lorenzo and Vito Loboido were seen with Morello by Flynn's Secret Service men less than two weeks after stepping ashore at Ellis Island. From a few scraps of surviving evidence, it appears that once the first family had been established, Mafiosi leaving their homeland for America would obtain letters of recommendation from their bosses in Sicily that had to be presented to the leaders of the fledgling *cosca* in New York. As other Mafia gangs emerged elsewhere, the same credentials, sent by mail or telegram, were also required if a man wished to move between cities in the United States. There were plainly advantages in being able to guarantee the reliability of a man born in an unfamiliar part of Sicily who was not known personally to the existing members of a family.

Welcomes could be far more elaborate than those accorded to Mafiosi of no consequence. Men who had established a reputation in Sicily would be received in New York with elaborate courtesy. One of the most eminent bosses to make the trans-Atlantic crossing, Vito Cascio Ferro, of Bisaquino in the Sicilian interior, had been in Manhattan for only three days when he received a letter addressing him by the honorific "Don Vito" and inviting him to "eat a plate of macaroni" with Morello, Giuseppe Fontana, and four other New York men of respect. It was most likely through Morello that Cascio Ferro was introduced to another band of Sicilian counterfeiters, led by Salvatore Clemente and a notorious female forger by the name of Stella Fraute. Cascio Ferro became involved with Fraute's gang and narrowly escaped conviction when the Secret Service rounded up her associates in 1902. In return for this respectful welcome, the Sicilian boss—at least according to tradition—offered Morello and his family advice on the best means of improving the profitability and efficiency of their operations.

BY FAR THE MOST IMPORTANT of the men who joined the Clutch Hand's *cosca* in the first years of the new century was Ignazio Lupo, who had been born in Palermo and who first arrived in the United States in 1898. A decade younger than Morello and vastly less experienced, with a moon face that he kept generally clean shaven, Lupo nonetheless brought brains, imagination, and even sophistication of a sort to the Clutch Hand's gang of thugs. He was "extremely intelligent," William Flynn discovered, and "by all means the best looking of the bunch," not to mention so emotional that he could easily be moved to tears. But Lupo was also just as ruthless as Morello, and so predatory that he would be known to generations of New Yorkers as "the Wolf." He spoke quietly in a high-pitched, almost feminine voice that perfectly conveyed his silky menace, and could be unpredictable and violent. "I give you my word," said Flynn. "Lupo had only to touch you to give you the feeling that you had been poisoned."

Ignazio Lupo had been born in 1877 to a family that possessed some influence in its native city, thanks in part to its links with the Palermo Mafia. When the Wolf reached the age of eighteen, his father set him up

in his own store on the Via Matarazza, where he sold high-quality clothing and dry goods. According to the records of the New York police, he
was already an active criminal by this time and had joined a "Black
Mailing gang" that was probably an offshoot of one of the city's families;
a relative, a man named Francesco Manciamelli, would rise to take the
leadership of one of the half-dozen Palermo *cosche* around 1912.

Lupo might well have stayed in Sicily and forged a career there had it
not been for an incident that occurred one day early in 1898. He was
serving in his dry goods store when a business rival named Salvatore
Morello came in to demand that Lupo stop undercutting his prices. The
Wolf refused, and at least in his telling of the story, the argument got out
of hand. The dispute became a fight, and when Morello pulled a knife,
Lupo drew his revolver, with fatal results.

The Wolf hid in Palermo for about five days, time enough to discover
that he would probably be prosecuted. Advised by his anxious family to
flee, he sailed for Liverpool and then to Montreal, eventually entering the
United States illegally via Buffalo. By the time Lupo reached New York,
he had been found guilty in absentia by the Italian courts and was
wanted in Palermo to serve a twenty-one-year sentence for murder.

The Lupo family had money—enough to set Ignazio up in his
Palermo store, and enough to get him out of Sicily at short notice—and
the Wolf had no apparent difficulty in finding his feet in New York. He
set up a store on East 72nd Street in partnership with a cousin named
Saitta; then, after a falling-out, he moved to Brooklyn and imported olive
oil, cheese, and wine from Italy. By 1901 Lupo was back in Manhattan,
running a prosperous grocery shop at 210–214 Mott Street, in the heart
of Little Italy. Over the next few years, the business grew, until he was the
owner of a large wholesale operation at 231 East 97th Street and at least
half a dozen retail stores. His Mott Street flagship, which stood seven
stories high, boasted quality foodstuffs, sumptuous new delivery wagons, and an inventory running to well over one hundred thousand dollars' worth of goods. It was generally regarded as the most prestigious
grocery store in the Italian quarter: "easily the most pretentious mercan-
tile establishment in that section of the city," *The New York Times* observed, "with a stock of goods over which the neighborhood marveled."

Lupo liked to present his success as something he worked hard for,
and indeed he did labor long into the evenings at his Mott Street office,
where, according to a contemporary, another early Mafioso known as Zia

Trestelle, he shuttled ceaselessly between a reception room and his private inner sanctum, alternately barking orders and receiving a succession of mysterious visitors. The truth, though, was that Lupo's increasing affluence owed at least as much to his association with Morello, which allowed him to call on all the growing strength of the Clutch Hand's criminal family. In return Lupo provided the Morellos with a base of operations eminently suitable for preying on weak, frightened, and friendless immigrants, the grocery trade being a favorite cover for Italian criminals at this time. As Morello well knew, the most feared, most efficient gang then based in Little Italy—a group run by a Calabrian named Giuseppe D'Agostino—identified likely victims through its own chain of corner grocery stores. There, as Petrosino would eventually discover, they "wormed information as to the financial standing of Italians living thereabout until they had the rating of nearly every man of their nationality then dwelling in the city. The rest was easy. Demands, accompanied by dire threats, were sent to the ones marked for plucking." The Clutch Hand, Petrosino thought, set out to imitate D'Agostino's operation, with such conspicuous success that his Sicilians pushed the rival Calabrians out of the Italian quarter within a few years.

If nothing else, Morello's interest in the grocery trade helps to explain the startling rapidity with which Lupo rose in the first family—the Wolf and the Clutch Hand having, on the face of it, as little in common as Palermo had with backwater Corleone. The Sicilian capital was the most cultured place south of Naples, a city frequently praised for its graceful proportions and noble architecture, and Lupo had picked up something of his hometown's swagger. He dressed well, favoring tailored clothes, and could be seen parading through Little Italy in a buggy drawn by a white horse, his hat tilted rakishly to one side. Morello, on the other hand, detested such displays, preferring a life lived in shadows. The contrast between his police mug shot and Lupo's is striking. The Clutch Hand, frozen in time soon after his arrest in the summer of 1900, wears a vest, a rough scarf, a cheap waistcoat, and an ill-fitting jacket. His chin and cheeks are unshaven and his mustache untrimmed. Lupo, pictured three years later, sports a superior air and a fashionable hat. His face has been expertly shaved, though he affects a neat mustache, and he is well turned out in an expensive jacket.

For all this, Morello certainly respected Lupo. First noticed in the company of the first family in 1902, the Wolf had joined the innermost councils of the gang nine months later, and the two Mafiosi, Flynn would write, made a formidable team:

> Lupo was the business man of the two. Morello had in his make-up more of the cunning of the born criminal. He was cautious like the fox and ferocious like a maddened bull. Lupo was always suggesting new ways for the investing of the money.

From this perspective, it is not surprising that the alliance between the pair was formalized that Christmas when the Wolf married Morello's twenty-two-year-old stepsister, Salvatrice Terranova. The wedding took place in St. Lucia's church in Italian Harlem, up on East 104th Street, the Clutch Hand attending and signing as a witness.

Lupo's union with Terranova may have been a marriage of convenience, a way of tying a man of obvious ability to the Morello family and perhaps even of sealing some sort of pact between the Mafiosi of Palermo and Corleone. If so, that did not prevent the marriage from being a success. Ignazio and Salvatrice would have five children—four girls, beginning with Onofria in 1906, and a boy, Rocco, who would eventually follow his father into the family business—and they remained wed for more than forty years. Salvatrice had nothing but praise for her husband. He was "very considerate of me, and always attempted to provide the necessities of life for myself and our children," the Terranova girl would write. "He has been kind to us all and I would consider him and excellent father and husband."

Marriage must have been in the air in Little Italy that year, for Lupo was not the only member of the Morello gang who wed. In the early months of 1903 the Clutch Hand, too, decided to seek a bride, though in his case it would be for a second time.

MORELLO HAD LIVED a largely solitary existence for half a decade, ever since his first wife had died in 1898. Maria Marvelesi's passing, at the age of only twenty-nine, perhaps as a result of malaria contracted during the family's sojourn in Texas, had left the Mafioso with a two-year-old son, Calogero, but the boy did not live with his father and was almost certainly raised by Morello's mother and unmarried sisters. Freed of this encumbrance, the boss preferred to flit between cheap tenement apartments in the poorest districts of the city, most of them, apparently, little more than places to sleep. He was living in East Harlem in 1900, and in a squalid, cluttered attic room downtown at 178 Chrystie Street three years later, but he was seldom to be found at any of his various addresses. When he was, he worked at night, got home late, slept in. Neighbors either did not know him or pretended not to.

Morello did feel some need for female companionship. By 1900 he was seeing another Sicilian woman, with whom he had another child, a daughter born, probably, early in 1901, and so far as the police and Secret Service were concerned, the couple lived as man and wife. But Angela Terranova did not see things that way. The Clutch Hand's mother disapproved of his relationship, and shortly before the Barrel Murder, she and her daughters decided it was time to find her son a second wife. They wanted a woman from a family that they approved of, and one who came from Corleone.

Morello seems to have agreed—"I have a notion to get married," he confided to one female acquaintance, asking her help in breaking off his earlier relationship—but the task of locating a suitable bride fell to his eldest sister, Marietta Morello, who was dispatched to Sicily to make the necessary arrangements. Having called for advice on relatives who still lived in Corleone, Marietta settled on a pair of sisters named Salemi. She procured photos of them and returned to New York. Morello examined the portraits, then chose the younger of the sisters, a striking twenty-year-old named Nicolina—Lina to the family. The necessary arrangements were swiftly made, and that summer Marietta Morello sailed again for Sicily, taking Lucia Terranova with her and returning in September with Lina and a substantial dowry, amounting to nearly four hundred dollars. Sailing with the Clutch Hand's bride-to-be were her elder sister and a brother, Vincenzo Salemi. Vincenzo would marry Lucia that December, four days after Lupo the Wolf and Salvatrice were wed.

The Salemi family was clearly sealing an alliance with the Morello-Terranova clan; the Salemis were also obviously aware of their new in-laws' criminal activities and may even have had ties of their own to the Corleone Mafia, since Lucia Terranova's new husband, Vincenzo, became involved in New York organized crime. But Lina's marriage to Morello, like Salvatrice's union with Lupo, was no mere marriage of convenience. Lina would bear her husband three daughters and a son, the first in 1908, and be his staunchest supporter, too. Dark-haired, passionate, and possessed of a sharp temper, Lina could read and write—unusual accomplishments in a Sicilian woman of her time, though like Morello she spoke no English and would not learn to do so for a decade or more. She also possessed a strong sense of her own worth. There would be no more contact between Morello and his Sicilian mistress, nor even with the couple's infant child—who died, in any case, before she reached the age of two. Nor would there be more living in cramped, decrepit rooms. Soon the Clutch Hand was established in a larger and more comfortable apartment on East 107th Street, close to his parents, sisters, and brothers. The family was still not affluent—not then, and not for several years, their rapidly increasing income being diverted into investments or offset by the sharply rising costs of running their numerous illicit businesses. But, thanks in large part to Lina, Morello was at last living in a style more suited to a man of respect.

THE FAMILY BUSINESS was still booming, and by 1903, Lupo's grocery empire was growing fastest of all, spreading from Little Italy to include outposts in Italian Harlem and Brooklyn. The opportunities, both commercial and criminal, seemed endless. Well-off customers were targeted with Black Hand letters. Lupo's wholesale operation, which underpinned the retail business and supplied Italian food and wine throughout the city, was used to extort money from dozens of independent grocers who were forced to pay premium prices and who quickly learned how dangerous it was to contemplate transferring their business to a cheaper rival. Veiled threats soon gave way to violence—beginning, often, with the poisoning of the expensive and vulnerable teams of dray horses every grocer needed to make deliveries, and progressing from there to the bombing of stores and even homes. One shopkeeper, Gaetano Costa, a Brooklyn butcher, was shot dead in his own store for refusing to pay a demand for a thousand dollars, and Salvatore Manzella, who dealt in Italian wines and foods from premises on Elizabeth Street, was reduced to bankruptcy by four years of unceasing extortion. Manzella at least survived long enough to testify that he had been visited regularly by Lupo, who had forced him to sign a series of blank receipts and delivery notes. The Wolf filled these in and discounted them as he pleased. "My life was at stake," Manzella said, asked why he did it, and in all he was bled for several thousand dollars over the years, including one sum of $1,075 in cash, which was every cent he happened to have in his store when Lupo called.

Counterfeiting, too, remained central to the Morellos' business, though the family was by now highly wary of the Secret Service and alert to the dangers of printing its currency in Manhattan. It was safer by far, Morello calculated, to send printing plates to Italy, where forged currency could safely be run off far from the prying eyes of the new head of the New York bureau, William Flynn. The problem of smuggling the counterfeits back into the United States remained, but the success of Lupo's wholesale business suggested a solution. By 1902 the Wolf was importing thousands of dollars' worth of wines, olive oil, and foodstuffs from Italy, and his consignments, off-loaded at Manhattan piers, received no more than cursory inspections from customs agents. Morello arranged for his crudely printed dollars to be sealed inside gallon olive oil cans. The new operation was an immediate success; in all, considerably more than ten thousand dollars of forged notes were brought into New York under the noses of U.S. customs agents and distributed in New York, Pittsburgh, Yonkers, and perhaps half a dozen other cities.

Flynn was aware by the first days of 1903 that Morello notes were circulating in Manhattan. The Italian printers' work was scarcely hard to spot (the notes contained no fewer than ten spelling errors, the Chief explained), but the Secret Service made little headway despite expending considerable resources in the fruitless search for the counterfeiters' plant. A handful of queer-pushers were arrested, but none could be made to talk. Discipline in the first family was fierce—fiercer by far in 1902–3 than it had been two years earlier, and with good reason considering the jail terms handed down to Calogero Maggiore and Dude Thompson's Irishmen.

The Clutch Hand had learned the lessons of 1900 well. His gang was now entirely Sicilian, from the queer-pushers on the street to the boodle carriers and on up to the senior Mafiosi who actually arranged for the money to be distributed. Morello and Lupo had as little to do with the business as possible; there was to be no incriminating trail of evidence to lead the police or the federal authorities to them. And the system worked well. The most important members of Morello's family all evaded detection, and when Vito Laduca was captured in Pittsburgh with two pushers and a quantity of the boss's five-dollar bills, he obtained his release within a week, while the pushers were both held for trial.

A handful of leaks and potential leaks were plugged, and with such decisive ruthlessness that only the weak or the extremely foolhardy would have considered betraying Morello. The most dramatic example of the Clutch Hand's determination to protect himself came in the summer of 1902, when the appallingly mutilated remains of a Brooklyn grocer were discovered on the shore of the East River at a spot named Dead Man's Cove. Giuseppe Catania, a strapping, muscular Sicilian, commonly thought to have the strength of two men, or even three, had run a store at 165 Columbia Street through which Mafia counterfeits were passed. Catania, who had probably been introduced to the Morello gang by Lupo during the Wolf's brief sojourn in Brooklyn in 1901, had been missing from home for two days when a group of boys swimming in the river uncovered a pair of large potato sacks in undergrowth above the waterline. Curious, and hoping that the contents of the sacks might possibly be worth something, the boys sliced them open with their pocketknives. One contained a set of gore-saturated clothes. The other held the missing grocer's naked body, securely trussed with a length of rope, the ankles forced up tight against the lower back and the torso all but drained of blood. The dead man's throat had been cut, and his head dangled from his neck by a solitary tendon; he "must have bled a gallon from the horrible wound," the *Brooklyn Daily Eagle* speculated, adding that it would have taken several determined attackers to overcome so strong a man.

The police investigation into Catania's murder got nowhere, quickly foundering amid speculation about vendettas formed long ago in Italy and fallings-out with friends. The dead man's wife and six children swore that he had had no enemies, and the story, front-page news at first, faded from the newspapers after a week. The police did eventually conclude that the Mafia lay behind the killing, but there was no firm evidence and no arrests, and it was left to the dogged William Flynn to uncover the true motive for the murder. The murdered grocer, the Chief learned a year later from informants in Little Italy, had liked to drink, and, drunk, tended to talk as well. Word of his indiscretions had reached the Clutch Hand, who decided that no mere warning was sufficient. When the doomed man had last been seen, in Manhattan just before his murder, he had been in the company of Lupo the Wolf. Catania's gruesome death, his near decapitation, the sealing of his body in sacks that were intended to be found—all were products of Morello's determination to convey a message to the members of his family: Weakness and lack of discipline meant inevitable death.

THE CATANIA MURDER plugged one potential leak in the Mafia's counterfeiting operation, and Morello would have no more trouble with men talking when drunk or spilling secrets. That much was proved at the end of 1902, when several members of his ring were caught in Yonkers, just to the north of New York, while passing the Clutch Hand's bills.

The pushers, Isadore Crocevera and Giuseppe Di Priemo, Madonia's brother-in-law, were typical minor members of the Morello gang. Both came from western Sicily—Di Priemo from the small town of Santa Margherita in the province of Agrigento, and Crocevera probably from Palermo—and both had only recently arrived in the United States.

Accompanied by a boodle carrier named Giuseppe Giallombardo, the two Sicilians spent the evenings of December 29 and 31 passing Morello's five-dollar notes in exchange for drinks, cigarettes, and food. They tendered one bill at Rafael Barbarita's saloon and another at John Rossi's butcher's shop, where it was presented in payment for a packet of kidneys and pork chops—butchers were favored targets among counterfeiters because the grease that accumulated on their hands made it harder for them to detect forged currency, which also tended to be greasy.

Nothing untoward occurred on December 29, but the three Sicilians were less fortunate on New Year's Eve. One of the storekeepers who had been handed a counterfeit bill took a second look at it when the pushers left his premises, then summoned a passing patrolman. Di Priemo and Crocevera were unlucky. The officer spotted the pair huddled in conversation just along the street, and both men were arrested.

Morello would have been grimly satisfied to know how well his pushers stood up under questioning. Flynn made a series of determined efforts to wring information from the prisoners, but neither Crocevera nor Di Priemo would utter an incriminating word. Several separate interrogations failed to drag a shred of useful detail out of either man, and even Chief Flynn, who had grown used to Sicilian recalcitrance after eight months in New York, was convinced that this mulishness was based on something more than ingrained hatred of authority. "I knew that none of these men would talk," the Secret Service man would write. "If any one of them did, and was released, his body would doubtless be found, broken and mutilated, within 24 hours."

Flynn tried one last subterfuge to get his prisoners to talk—a clever effort to set the two Sicilians at each other's throats the next time they were questioned. "With a great show of secrecy" (he explained his tactics some years later),

> I kept Di Priemo locked up with me in an inner office for more than an hour. Crocevera, of course, knew that he was in there, and my scheme was to make him think that Di Priemo had confessed, thus leading the other prisoner, in a spirit of spite, to incriminate his companion, and perhaps divulge many secrets of the band.
>
> After I thought Crocevera had had time to think things over, I dismissed Di Priemo. As he left my office I went to the door with him, and in sight and hearing of Crocevera shook him cordially by the hand and bade him goodnight heartily, as if I was much gratified by what he had told me. As a matter of fact, he had told me next to nothing, but I wanted to strengthen Crocevera's suspicions against him.

It was an elaborate charade, and one that might have worked in different circumstances, but not with two members of the Morello family. So far as Flynn could see, his efforts had no effect. Crocevera glowered fiercely as Di Priemo left. But when he was marched into Flynn's office moments later, he was as unforthcoming as ever.

Morello's queer-pushers went to prison three months later without betraying their superiors—Giallombardo for six years, Di Priemo for four years, Crocevera for three—and leaving the Secret Service without leads to the inner councils of the gang. But Flynn's efforts had not been in vain. As he would not discover until later, the Chief's subterfuge had indeed convinced Crocevera that the family had been betrayed, and if the counterfeiter had nothing to say to Flynn, he had plenty to tell the other members of Morello's gang. Word of Di Priemo's supposed betrayal reached the Clutch Hand's ears, and the queer-pusher's willingness to deal with Flynn was soon common knowledge in Little Italy.

How much Di Priemo knew of this is hard to say, though it would be surprising if he was unaware of his associates' suspicions. Whatever the truth, the pusher was safe for the time being, his prison cell in Sing Sing being beyond the reach of Mafia justice. The same could not be said, however, of Di Priemo's brother-in-law, Benedetto Madonia of Buffalo, who occupied a more senior position in the Morello family and had likely introduced Di Priemo to the gang. That had been a serious miscalculation, as it now appeared, and it was followed by further errors. In March, Morello had asked Madonia to go to Pittsburgh and arrange for the release of the two queer-pushers who had been arrested there with Vito Laduca. Madonia failed and, worse, wrote to New York to request money with which to grease the wheels of Pittsburgh justice. When Morello replied that there was none available, the Buffalo man responded with an angry note, full of abuse, in which he accused the Clutch Hand of caring nothing for the men who worked for him. There was bad blood between the two thereafter, which explained why Morello seized the thousand dollars that Madonia raised in Buffalo and sent to Little Italy to pay for his brother-in-law Di Priemo's defense.

It was only a few days after this, in the first week of April 1903, that the Clutch Hand received another letter from Madonia. This time the Buffalo man wrote to announce his imminent arrival in New York. He wanted an audience with Morello, and help in arranging for Di Priemo to be moved to a prison nearer Buffalo. Above all, he wanted his money back.

Few things were more likely to anger the Clutch Hand than a demand for money, particularly one from a man he thought had let his family down. Morello sent back word agreeing to the meeting, but scarcely for the reason that his lieutenant hoped. Then he set about preparing a reception. Madonia could come to New York if he wished to. But if he did, he would not leave alive.

CHAPTER 6

VENGEANCE

=

"CLEAR THE COURT OF ALL PERSONS HAVING NO BUSINESS HERE!"

Peter Barlow leaned forward on the magistrate's dais at Jefferson Market police court, a Gothic monstrosity that rose in gaudy red-brick tiers over 10th Street at Sixth Avenue. He was annoyed that he had to shout to make himself heard above the rising hubbub in his crowded courtroom. It was bad enough that he was hearing cases on a Sunday, worse that he had been given charge of the arraignment of Giuseppe Morello and twelve of his associates, all held since their arrest three days earlier on suspicion of involvement in the Barrel Murder. And it was certainly intolerable that, with the prisoners marshaled just outside the door, all waiting for the hearing to begin, his courtroom was filled to overflowing with a throng of incomprehensible Sicilians, most of them fierce-looking men in frayed second-best suits, and all of them talking at once.

"Clear the court!"

Barlow was new to Jefferson Market. He had been a magistrate for less than a year. But he had heard about the Black Hand and the Mafia, and knew that Italian gangsters habitually packed courtrooms with their intimidating friends. These men would sit in the front rows of the public seating and glare menacingly at the prosecution witnesses as they took the stand. Shushing, hissing, threatening gestures—all were used to cow their adversaries into silence. Faced with a fierce-looking row of hoodlums, and all too uncomfortably aware that the names and addresses of those who offered testimony were routinely published in the press, many a witness stuttered and lost his chain of thought, or retracted every word of the statement he had sworn to give. Barlow had little doubt that the Morello gang hoped to dissuade as many of Chesty George McClusky's witnesses as they could from giving evidence.

"Clear the court!"

The first few people in the public seats began to move at last, but it took Barlow's ushers several minutes to eject the last of the unwanted spectators—most still protesting in their native language—and to escort in the prisoners. Morello stood flanked by Vito Laduca (whose knife, the police revealed, had been smeared with a rust-red substance that they believed was human blood) and Messina Genova, also a butcher, who Petrosino now believed had struck Madonia's deathblow. Bail on these three had been set high, at $5,000 a man. Most of the remaining prisoners had their bails fixed at a more modest $1,000, including Ignazio Lupo, who had been the last of the thirteen men to be arrested. A few minor members of the gang, including three who had been in the United States for only a month, were held on bonds of a mere $100.

It was April 19, 1903, the first day of the first hearing into the barrel killing, and the day before Joseph Petrosino would finally confirm the victim's identity. For men who claimed to work at menial jobs, the Sicilians had secured first-rate representation. Morello and Lupo had retained Charles Le Barbier, one of the half-dozen most celebrated lawyers in Manhattan; five lesser attorneys from Le Barbier's firm had charge of the other members of the gang. According to the police, the legal fees had been met by a compulsory levy raised in Little Italy by other members of Morello's family, the total collected being as much as ten thousand dollars. Over the next few weeks, word would filter in that similar collections had been made in other cities on the eastern seaboard, a startling testimony to the boss's growing influence. In Boston, seven Sicilians appeared at police headquarters to beg for protection against the Mafia, "by which," a local paper noted,

> they claimed to have been ordered to contribute to the defense fund in the barrel murder case. Each of the foreigners showed a letter from New York. They were thoroughly frightened even when they were in the secure shelter of [the chief of police's] private office. The letters told them that everywhere they went they were marked men; that the eye of the Mafia was on them always; [and] that they were as good as dead if they did not send the required money immediately.

Le Barbier and his associates set about earning their fat fees as soon as Barlow opened the proceedings. "I ask that the weeding out process begin today," Le Barbier began. "There are a great many prisoners, and as this was a secret murder, all these men could not have had a share in it." A "bunch" of his clients should be dismissed at once, the advocate continued. When Barlow rejected his request, Le Barbier fired back by highlighting the single greatest weakness in the prosecution case:

I am sure the police are on the wrong track. They have made a great mistake. The proof of this error is apparent when, from day to day, they have failed to establish the identity of the victim of these murders. I ask that the Assistant District Attorney point out one among the prisoners against whom there is some ground for the belief that he is guilty.

Le Barbier's interjection set the tone. Hamstrung by Inspector McClusky's insistence on premature arrests, Assistant District Attorney Francis Garvan had no real answer to him, nothing but hope that an identification would be made and some prospect that he could at least prove that the gang had been engaged in a conspiracy. To make matters worse, Morello himself gave away nothing on the stand; the Clutch Hand denied so much as knowing the dead man, and answered most questions with a shrug of the shoulders and "I don't remember." Lupo, called next, struck the reporters in the courtroom as suave and unruffled. He "perjured himself again and again," one newsman thought, but there was little that even McClusky could do about such lies other than to vow to waiting reporters that "the prisoners will be given the third degree to the limit in the hope that one of them will break down."

It was not until the hearing's second morning that Garvan got his stroke of luck. The assistant DA was halfway through another unproductive examination when a clerk from his office crept into the courtroom with a piece of paper on which was scribbled information just phoned in from Buffalo: a name, and the details of the dead man's home and circumstances. It took Garvan a moment to digest the news. Then he smiled, put down the note, and started to recall the prisoners, beginning with Morello. Had they ever met a Benedetto Madonia? The result was the closest thing to a sensation the newsmen covering the hearing had yet witnessed. "Each denied knowing the man," a reporter from the *Sun* observed, "but the first time the question was asked, there was a great babbling in Italian among the prisoners and they were apparently very much excited."

Garvan got in a few more good blows after that. His best moment came the next day, when he produced the ledger Flynn had found in Morello's apartment, with its entries relating to Madonia, and with it a letter Petrosino had recovered from the dead man's family. The letter, addressed to Buffalo, had been scrawled in red ink in the same crabbed Sicilian script as the ledger entry, and Garvan forced the Clutch Hand to admit that he had written it. It was proof that Morello knew the barrel victim. The letter was also, at least in the eyes of the police, the dead man's death warrant. "In the Mafia," one officer explained to the *Evening Journal,*

> it is not customary to threaten. The leader does not communicate to a suspected member that his acts have rendered him subject to the death penalty. Their method of procedure is more subtle.
>
> To the offending member of the Mafia a letter written with red ink, in lieu of blood, is sent. . . . Compliance with the contents, or the contrary, will not affect the doom of the recipient. To an Italian versed in the ways of the Mafia, the receipt of such a letter is equivalent to a sentence of death.

The press made a good deal of this revelation, and the prosecution could now prove, by way of the letter and the ledger, that Morello had lied under oath in swearing that he did not know Madonia. But neither the written evidence nor anything that the ADA pried out of the prisoners proved that any one of them had participated in the Barrel Murder. Madonia had last been seen by Flynn's operatives walking off down Prince Street at eight in the evening with several of Morello's men. But what had happened to him after that remained a mystery. Speculation, circumstantial evidence, tips from several informers—all had helped the police to reconstruct those last few hours. But none of it was admissible in court. There was insufficient information, Barlow concluded on the fourth day of the hearing, to hold any one of the prisoners on a charge of murder. That meant that all thirteen would have to be discharged.

Word of the prisoners' impending release spread quickly to the crowd of friends and relatives waiting outside the courtroom. But Morello and his men got no farther than the courthouse steps before McClusky rearrested them, this time on charges of perjury—each man having denied on the witness stand that he so much as knew Madonia.

Lupo was held on a separate counterfeiting charge; correspondence that Flynn had taken from his room showed that he had been mailing forged notes to Italian laborers in Canada.

So far as most New Yorkers were concerned, all this legal maneuvering meant little. Morello was still under arrest in the House of Detention with his men. The police were searching for more evidence. There was still time for them to make a case, and Petrosino had brought Salvatore Madonia, the dead man's son, to New York to give statements. The young Madonia indeed proved to be a font of useful information: He gave the police details of his father's thoughts, his movements, and the belongings he had taken with him on his travels. At times Salvatore amplified or contradicted the information Petrosino had obtained from the young man's mother. She had described her husband's pocket watch as a valuable gold one, for example, but Salvatore said Benedetto had actually taken his son's cheap tin watch when he left for New York. It was easily identified, Madonia added, being stamped with an image of a locomotive on its cover.

Salvatore had little doubt about the murder. "I believe my father was killed by the Mafia because he threatened to reveal secrets which had come into his possession," he told Petrosino. "He knew a great deal about the members of Morello's gang, and I believe that through fear or revenge they murdered him." His statement was so persuasive that even the usually cautious sergeant made a bullish statement of his own when cornered by a reporter from the *Evening Journal*. ("This murder," the Italian detective said, "has done more to reveal the extent to which the Mafia flourishes in New York than anything else that ever happened before. Heretofore the name 'Mafia' has been associated with the Italians of New Orleans. It is now made clear to every one that the largest and most dangerous branch of the society in existence has its headquarters right here in New York.") But there was plenty more that Petrosino wanted from his witness, not least his statement in an open court. The inquest into the barrel victim's death had just been scheduled for the first of May, and that would give the police another opportunity to interrogate Morello under oath. That evening the detective booked Madonia into a hotel on Bleecker Street and left him there under the protection of a Sergeant Illich.

Petrosino planned to return next morning, but he was not the only person in Manhattan who saw the young man as a vital witness, and something took place that evening to shatter his informant's fragile confidence. Madonia begged Illich to stay the night with him and double-locked his door. Rising early the next morning, the young man then declared that he would not stay in New York any longer. "If I remain here they will kill me," he informed his bodyguard. "I shall have to go away from Buffalo and hide somewhere where I am not known. Even then I am afraid they will find me. Their vengeance never rests."

There was nothing that Sergeant Illich or anybody else could say to dissuade the boy, and an hour or two later Madonia was on board a fast train back to Buffalo. With a week to go until the inquest, the police had just lost their most important witness.

WILLIAM FLYNN HAD barely thought about the barrel case for several days. There had been so little time; the demands of his heavy caseload had confined him to the collection of scraps of extra information that he had forwarded to Washington. He and his men had played no part in McClusky's laborious and unproductive questioning of the thirteen Sicilians or in the proceedings at Jefferson Market. Nor had Flynn looked in any detail at the exhibits and evidence the police had gathered.

Barlow's hearing changed all that. The public might feel reassured that Morello remained in custody, and be taken in by optimistic statements that the barrel mystery was close to a solution; Flynn knew better. The evidence against the counterfeiters was so weak that it seemed likely that the entire gang would escape conviction. Irritated though the Chief still was by McClusky's handling of the case, he felt that he should try to help.

McClusky made no objection when Flynn called at headquarters on April 25 and asked if he could see the evidence; after Barlow's ruling, even the police inspector was willing to admit that he would welcome some assistance. Flynn was shown into an empty room, and, a few minutes later, several boxes were brought in and piled against a desk for him. Most contained the personal possessions of the thirteen prisoners, seized from their homes or taken from their pockets ten days earlier.

Flynn spent some time going through the containers, finding nothing of special interest until he reached the box that held the items taken from Morello's bodyguard, Petto the Ox. The Secret Service man tipped the contents over the desk and let his eyes wander over the detritus of the

Ox's life: a motley assembly of cigar butts, handkerchiefs, loose change, and junk. Toward the bottom of the pile he noticed a scrap of paper. Flynn spread it open on the desk and saw it was a pawn ticket issued by Fry's Capital Loan Company, a store at 276 Bowery. The ticket was dated April 14, the day after the Barrel Murder. Capital Loan had advanced Petto the sum of one dollar in exchange for a pocket watch.

Flynn thought back to the day of the murder and recalled that Madonia's waistcoat had sported a watch chain but no watch. He called Detective Sergeant Carey. Had the ticket been redeemed? he asked. No, Carey said; Madonia's wife had stated that her husband was carrying a large gold timepiece—an item worth far more than a dollar, even to a pawnbroker. The police believed the old watch must be Petto's.

Flynn knew nothing of Salvatore Madonia's statement, nothing of the cheap tin watch the boy had loaned his father, but the pawn ticket intrigued him. Check it, he urged Sergeant Carey. Just to be certain.

IT WAS NOT UNTIL the next day that Carey got around to visiting the Capital Loan Company, and by then the sergeant had read Petrosino's dossier. He asked a clerk to redeem Petto's pledge and waited while the man looked over the ticket, rummaged under the counter, and produced a battered timepiece with the outline of a locomotive punched into its cover.

Carey recognized the watch at once. Its description matched Salvatore Madonia's, right down to a mass of scratches on the neck where the boy had once tried to pry the casing open. It seemed unlikely that the barrel victim would have given away a watch belonging to his son, and since young Madonia's father had not been short of money, it followed that the timepiece had almost certainly been stolen by his murderer. The sergeant hastened back to Mulberry Street to find McClusky.

Carey, as he most likely knew, was only just in time. No one had imagined, until now, that Petto was a man of any importance in Morello's gang, or guessed that the Ox might have played more than a minor part in the Barrel Murder. Indeed, the police had thought so little of him that Petto was still being held on a bail of just five hundred dollars, a figure so low that he had by now found a bail bondsman willing to supply it. The police had uncovered the one piece of evidence tying the Morellos to Madonia's murder on the very morning Petto was due to be released.

McClusky recognized the importance of Carey's find at once and wasted no time in placing a phone call to the House of Detention. Then, having instructed the warden not to release Petto under any circumstances, the inspector hurried over to the Criminal Courts building on Centre Street to speak to the district attorney. The upshot of all this activity was the best news the police had had in weeks: Petto's bondsman was turned away from the House of Detention, and, shortly afterward, the Ox was arraigned and charged with murder.

Word of these developments did much to restore morale at police headquarters, where McClusky made several more bullish statements to the press. Sergeants Carey and Petrosino resumed the questioning of Morello's men with extra vigor—as promised, several of the prisoners were subjected to the physical interrogation methods of the third degree—and the two detectives began to think for the first time that they were making progress. Pietro Inzerillo and Joseph Fanaro both showed signs of talking, Carey said, and when Fanaro, who had been seen in the murdered man's company more often than any other member of the gang, spent several hours closeted with Assistant District Attorney Garvan, word spread that the Sicilian was prepared to testify. To Carey, even Morello

> seemed to be weakening; I thought that he might talk. It had not been unusual to find that gang leaders like him would talk, for the tradition prevails among this type of criminal organization that the king can do no wrong, and Morello was a king.

So far as Petrosino was concerned, however, this was wishful thinking. Morello was too stubborn and too well aware of the weaknesses of the police case to break as easily as that, and Fanaro and Inzerillo were both too frightened of their leader to risk turning against him. If the NYPD wanted more arraignments and convictions, it would have to prove its case against a stone wall of Sicilian obstruction, starting with a strong performance at the coming inquest. The effort would be worthwhile; the right verdict would open the way for charges to be brought against the other members of the gang.

A week remained before the inquest opened, long enough for Petrosino to make the necessary arrangements. First Salvatore Madonia and his mother were ordered back to Manhattan to give evidence. Then Giuseppe Di Priemo was brought down from Sing Sing to be examined as to his part in the Madonia affair. The witnesses were plainly reluctant, Salvatore perhaps most of all. Among them, however, or so Petrosino hoped, the three could do much to explain Madonia's death and illuminate his relations with Morello.

Before any of that could happen, though, the Manhattan coroner would need to find a dozen men willing to serve as a jury.

FOR GEORGE LEBRUN, the Barrel Murder inquest was turning rapidly into a nightmare.

LeBrun was Manhattan's assistant coroner, and one of his innumerable duties at Coroner Gustav Scholer's court was to empanel inquest juries. He had years of experience of this, and never had he found a routine task so difficult to organize. Newspaper coverage of the "Mafia murder case" had left the readers of the New York press in little doubt as to the ruthlessness and brutality of the killers, and the majority of the jurors summoned would not sit, citing various excuses. "Even with the formal arrests," LeBrun confessed, "I had difficulty getting enough men to serve," and the assistant coroner was left in no doubt why. Several potential jurors, the man from the *Herald* wrote, "made no secret of the fact that if it could be avoided they would be most loath to sit on a jury and have to bring in a verdict of guilty against a member of the Mafia, even if the weight of evidence was conclusive, and it was evident that in the minds of several of them the prospect of Mafia vengeance in such an event was extremely vivid." When, after a delay of almost a day, a jury was finally assembled and the jurors' names were read, not one among the dozen was Italian. Most were stolid men with German names who lived far from Little Italy.

Interest in the case was great; every public seat was filled, and a line stretched down the corridor outside. Most of those who did gain entry to the courtroom were Sicilian, and though these spectators sat impassively through most of the proceedings, there were ominous stirrings on the public benches whenever critical pieces of evidence were heard. Scholer, unlike Peter Barlow, never ordered that his court be cleared.

Assistant District Attorney Garvan again took charge of questioning the witnesses. The most dramatic moment of the morning came when Petto the Ox was on the stand. The prisoner, who had sat sullenly through Garvan's interrogation and refused to look at the array of stilettos and other "gruesome objects" brandished by the ADA, was stonewalling more questions

> when a photograph of the murdered man showing him as he appeared after death, was suddenly thrust by Detective Sergeant Petrosino beneath the eyes of Petto, who is directly charged with the murder. The man gave a start of surprise, his eyes rolled, and he clasped his hands convulsively, but it was only a moment . . . he recovered his self control and, shrugging his shoulders, refused to look again at the photograph, although it remained in front of him for fifteen minutes.

Mostly, though, Garvan and Petrosino struggled to make an impression on their witnesses. Newspaper reporters made much of the admissions of Nicola Testa, who was the butcher's boy at Vito Laduca's Stanton Street store and who startled the press bench by agreeing that he was the nephew of the murdered Brooklyn grocer Giuseppe Catania—but that was merely circumstantial evidence. Giovanni Zacconi, a Sicilian with a stake in the same store, was named in court as the owner of the wagon that had carried Madonia's corpse away, and a warrant was issued for his arrest. But Joseph Fanaro, of whom much had been expected, had plainly reconsidered his position since his meeting with the district attorney. Placed on the witness stand, he remained determinedly mute, denying absolutely that he knew Madonia even though he had made a lengthy statement on the subject only two days earlier. It was "a remarkable exhibition of an apparent loss of memory," the *Herald* caustically remarked.

Fanaro's mulishness was the first clear sign that Garvan and Petrosino's case was not going according to plan, but the remainder of Garvan's witnesses fared even worse under the defendants' steely gaze. Lucy and Salvatore Madonia had both given statements identifying the tin watch that Carey had retrieved from Capital Loan, but, once on the witness stand, Salvatore began to speak with "evident misgivings," terror etched on his face. Carey was there to see the youth give evidence. "The watch," he said, was handed to the lad. He looked at it and was about to speak when there was a shuffling of feet and a hissing in the courtroom, which was filled with swarthy-faced men. One of these jumped up and put his fingers to his lips. Young Madonia was now not so sure it was his father's watch.

"It looks like mine," the boy stammered at last in answer to Garvan's question, "but there may be many watches like it in the world, and I cannot say it is."

Lucy Madonia, the dead man's wife, was just as equivocal. She, too, was handed the timepiece, and she, too, started as the same stirring of bodies and rustling of feet swept through the courtroom. The same dark-skinned man half rose for a second time, and "Mrs. Madonia," Carey said, "positive the day before that the watch was her husband's, now suffered a lapse of memory." The Madonias' useless testimony was a huge blow to the police, shattering the one firm link between Petto the Ox and the Barrel Murder, and what was left of the police case crumbled when Pietro Inzerillo took the stand. The confectioner, "who had been prepared, among other things, to admit the presence of the sugar barrels in the rear room of his shop," blanched at the same sinister shuffling of feet and refused to talk.

The final witness called to the stand on that first afternoon was Giuseppe Di Priemo, Madonia's imprisoned brother-in-law. The squat Sicilian was the last of the witnesses whose evidence might have indicted the Morello gang. Knowing that Di Priemo had every reason to loathe the Clutch Hand, Petrosino had done what he could to persuade the queer-pusher to give evidence, promising full protection from Morello's family. Apparently reassured by that guarantee, Di Priemo had spent nearly two hours two days earlier giving a statement to Francis Garvan, but once in court, he took the oath and promptly withdrew every word. The counterfeiter "laughed on the stand," a bitter Sergeant Carey would recall, "and said that Petto was his very good friend and surely would not have killed his brother-in-law. Yet we knew he hated the bull-necked man." This once, Carey thought, his witness was not particularly intimidated by the massed ranks of Sicilians in the courtroom. So far as the detective sergeant was concerned, Di Priemo had an altogether different motive for his silence: He planned to exact his own revenge for the murder of his sister's husband.

The inquest ran for seven more days after that, but the verdict had been decided long before it staggered to a close. Madonia, the jury ruled, had certainly been murdered—but by "a person or persons unknown." There would be no more indictments; even Petto was eventually released from his damp cell in the Tombs. Morello was never heard to utter another word upon the subject. But it was not long before events elsewhere brought the Barrel Murder back to the attention of New York's papers. When they did, the city and the city's police got a longer, deeper, cooler look at the dangers of angering the Mafia.

GIUSEPPE MORELLO LEFT few clues to his true character beyond the little that can be deduced from his crimes, which were intelligently planned and resolutely executed. He was in many respects conventionally Sicilian: a man who took his duties both as son and as the head of his own family seriously, and was so determined to honor his father's memory that three of his own sons, in succession, were christened "Calogero." More than that, though, Morello was a man of dominant personality and steely determination, both attributes that were most likely products of the struggle he was forced to wage to overcome his disability. His exceptional qualities—for a murderer, at least—are evident in his achievements, for though there had been Mafiosi in the United States long before the Clutch Hand arrived there, none was ever regarded with so much awe by his fellow criminals.

There was, even so, little that was attractive in Morello's makeup. True, he was an innovative boss, one who rarely felt bound by other people's rules, and he created, in the first family, a criminal organization of considerable effectiveness. The gang was, moreover, very much his own creation; it bore only a passing resemblance to a Sicilian Mafia family, and not the least of the Clutch Hand's talents was an ability to weld together a disparate group of Mafiosi from different towns and backgrounds and make them so formidable that they gained an ascendancy over all the other gangs in New York's Italian district. But Morello was also treacherous and unforgiving, an autocrat who suppressed all dissent and rarely sought advice from even his closest lieutenants. Only Lupo the Wolf, of all his numerous associates, seems not to have feared him; the remaining members of the family acted as much from terror as from loyalty. Chief Flynn, who mulled over the puzzle of Morello's personality for years, concluded that the boss was interested chiefly in power, not money, which explained why he lived modestly and why he never made as much as he might have done from his murderous career. For Flynn, the Clutch Hand's actions were really not hard to explain. Morello, he wrote, was simply "bad—thoroughly, conscientiously and zealously bad. . . . There are few men of whom you may truthfully say that they enjoyed being criminals. Old Giuseppe was one of them."

It was Morello's obsession with power, the Chief was sure, that made him such an implacable enemy, determined to exterminate the weakness within the ranks of his own gang that the barrel case exposed and perfectly willing to kill even his most loyal followers if it suited his purpose. Certainly it did not take a man of the Clutch Hand's cunning to deduce that the Secret Service knew far more about his family's doings than he had realized, and that the gang's brush with the authorities owed much to the incompetence of his own men—not least that of Petto the Ox, whose decision to relieve Madonia of a one-dollar watch could easily have cost the boss and several other men their lives. Morello's own analysis of events soon convinced him that he had at least one traitor in his ranks, and he apparently also grew determined to rid himself of a number of men who knew too much about the Barrel Murder. The thirst for vengeance against all those who he believed had wronged him was one of the Clutch Hand's most pronounced traits. In the autumn of 1903, he began to plot against them all.

The first man to die in the aftermath of the Barrel Murder was Salvatore Especiale, a New York Sicilian of some education who was found dead, with two bullets in his chest, on a street corner in Brooklyn that December. According to the local police, Especiale had known Giuseppe Catania and had some peripheral involvement in the Madonia affair as well. More significantly, as Captain Condon of Fulton Street station explained, he was rumored among his associates to have been "used as a 'stool pigeon' by the Secret Service men." Especiale, it was said, had been responsible for supplying information that led to the arrest of several Italian counterfeiters. There is nothing in William Flynn's files to suggest that this was actually true; what mattered, though, was that his fellow Sicilians believed it was. Especiale certainly knew he was in danger. He had purchased a steamship ticket to Naples a few days before his death, and "the dread penalty," so one newspaper observed, was widely understood to have been exacted by the Mafia and "was now believed to be the tragic sequel to the ghastly barrel murder mystery." Morello, in other words, had ordered the murder of a man who he believed to have been Flynn's informant inside his counterfeiting ring.

The next in the series of killings linked to the Madonia affair did not take place until October 1905, and it occurred far from New York, in the mining town of Wilkes-Barre, Pennsylvania—itself a noted stronghold of the Mafia and the Black Hand. The victim on this occasion was Tommaso Petto, who had fled Manhattan soon after his release from jail in January 1904 and had been living in the town under his real name, Luciano Perrini. Petto had continued his criminal career after leaving New York; he had amassed several arrests, and the other Sicilians of the district were, a Wilkes-Barre newspaper reported, "often afraid of him. It is alleged that he was a member of the Black Hand and Mafia clans [and] he was what is known as a boss or king among his countrymen." Whatever Petto's reputation, though, it was not sufficient to save him from assassination. A few days before his murder, the Ox's pretty wife had noticed a stranger hanging around their house, and when she informed her husband, he had taken her sufficiently seriously to begin carrying a large-caliber revolver in his waistband. This gun was discovered lying by the body after Petto was found sprawled dead in the road close to his home on the evening of October 21. He had been ambushed on his return from work and given no chance to return his assassins' fire. Five rifle bullets had smashed into his chest from a short range. From the size of several of the wounds—"large enough to admit a teacup," one local journalist reported after speaking to the town's police—it appeared that the Ox's killers had used explosive bullets to make sure of killing their man.

News of Petto's death reached New York days later, and it was immediately supposed that he had been killed by Giuseppe Di Priemo in revenge for his involvement in the Barrel Murder. The *Sun* even reported that the imprisoned counterfeiter had been seen by several people in Manhattan, "on a hunt for 'The Ox,' and that he had gone to Pennsylvania in search of him." Flynn, though, was adamant that Di Priemo could not have been Petto's killer; in October 1905, the Secret Service man observed, Benedetto Madonia's brother-in-law was still locked up in Sing Sing. The Chief was correct. Di Priemo's surviving prison records show that the earliest date he could have been paroled was April 14, 1906.

So far as Flynn was concerned, the most likely solution to the Petto murder mystery was that the Ox had been murdered by another of Madonia's relatives. "To my mind," he wrote, "there was no doubt that the slaying was an act of vengeance." It was not long, though, before the police began to formulate a rival theory. Petto, it was speculated, had been a victim of Morello himself, shot dead as a punishment for the idiocy he had displayed in pawning Madonia's watch and because he knew too much about the barrel mystery.

The notion of Morello as the killer, wreaking vengeance on the members of his own gang, and perhaps using his own Mafia connections to have the murder carried out, was an idea that gained greater currency over the next few years as several other members of his family met equally violent deaths, in several cases far from Manhattan. Vito Laduca was the next to die, shot dead in Carini, Sicily, in February 1908; then Messina Genova was murdered in Ohio. A year after that, in the summer of 1909, Giovanni Zacconi—the Stanton Street butcher thought by Petrosino to have driven the covered "death wagon" that took Madonia's body, in its barrel, to its resting place on East 11th Street—was also killed. Zacconi had abandoned New York for a new life as a fruit farmer in Danbury, Connecticut. On July 28 he was ambushed by a group of seven killers who attacked him with shotguns in a country lane. At least a dozen shells were fired, and the Mafioso was found by his son lying by a ditch with half his face blown away. "He was," one Washington newspaper reported, "arrested in connection with the famous 'barrel murder,' [and] it is believed he incurred the enmity of the organization and was slain for revenge." The *Chicago Tribune* said much the same, adding: "The police explain the four killings [of Petto, Laduca, Genova, and Zacconi] on the theory that the real murderers of Benedetto have been killing the men who knew the details of the crime."

SOMEHOW, FEW PEOPLE seemed at all surprised at the collapse of the Barrel Murder investigation. New Yorkers had grown used to seeing Italian crimes going unsolved, almost always for lack of conclusive evidence. But a yearlong Secret Service operation lay in ruins, along with all the lonely, boring, dangerous hours of observation that it had entailed. Worse, Morello and his confederates had been thoroughly alerted to the fact that they were under continuous surveillance.

The Clutch Hand had always been a careful man; now, the Secret Servicemen assigned to watch him observed, he had grown almost pathologically cautious. His movements became ever more unpredictable, and when he did emerge from one of his haunts, he walked rapidly, frequently glancing over his shoulder to see if he was being followed, and developed the unnerving habit of turning a corner and vanishing by darting into a nearby building before the man tailing him could catch up. Arrangements were also made by the Morello family for mail to be delivered covertly to an unknown address, probably a bar or store owned by one of the boss's friends. The Secret Service, which had obtained more firm evidence of wrongdoing by intercepting the gang's correspondence than from any other source, spent months attempting to discover where the missing mail was going, but without success.

Flynn was extremely perturbed by this turn of events. Lupo and Morello were among "the most dangerous foreign criminals in the country," he had concluded, and he had warned McClusky that his arrests were premature. "Too many policemen," the Chief complained, "make the mistake of viewing an arrest as their most important function. The most vital task of a policeman is not an arrest—but a *conviction*. An arrest without the necessary evidence for a jury is not only wasted labor, but in its final analysis a confession of weakness."

What made the failure to prosecute the gang the more galling in Flynn's eyes was the inability of the police to learn from their mistakes. The NYPD made no real attempt to keep the Morello family under surveillance after May 1903, let alone to investigate the sources of its income or obtain fresh intelligence about its members. Petrosino, who might have played a central role in such an effort, found himself swept off almost immediately to check the rising tide of Black Hand crime; he had little time to spare for longer-term investigations over the next two years. McClusky and his Detective Bureau were relieved to drop the case. That meant that the job of keeping an eye on Morello and his men fell by default to the ordinary patrolmen of the first family's local precinct, the 104th Street station, who were woefully ill equipped to deal with such well-organized criminals. Rather than concentrating, as Flynn urged, on quietly amassing fragments of intelligence, the police instead indulged themselves in a campaign of petty harassment. "The detectives," Ciro Terranova said, "used to come around very often and search everybody.

Since the time of Morello's arrest, each and every member of my family, including my brother, have been searched on average twice a week."

The Morellos had some reason to resent the attentions of the 104th Street men; on one occasion, several officers seized Ciro and his brother Vincenzo while they were out searching for a doctor to tend Morello's son and, ignoring their protests, dragged them off to the station house for interrogation. But the Sicilians had more reason to be grateful. The crude efforts of the Harlem precinct barely hindered the family's activities, the police felt they were "doing something," and their regular harassment made the Morellos more careful and so more effective. For Flynn, the 104th Street campaign amounted to rank incompetence.

What was really needed, it seemed clear to almost everybody, was a police squad dedicated to Italian crime. There was reason enough to set one up; the number of Black Hand bombings, shootings, and stabbings rose fourfold between 1903 and 1907, by which time *The New York Times* alone was reporting in excess of three hundred incidents a year—a figure that implied that a far greater number of similar offenses were going unremarked. And while at this same time the number of Italian-speaking policemen on the force was gradually rising, Petrosino was the only man devoted to tackling crime in Little Italy. Detective Sergeant Antonio Vachris, a Genoese who was Petrosino's opposite number in Brooklyn, complained that he spent more of his time dealing with saloon license violations than he did with the Black Handers of his own borough, and of course that meant that the officers who were assigned to investigate murder and extortion in Italian Brooklyn had no chance of grasping the intricacies of such cases, nor even of making themselves understood to their witnesses.

It was not until January 1905 that a new police commissioner solved this conundrum, partially at least. Worried by the rising tide of violence in Little Italy, William McAdoo, a reform-minded New Jersey lawyer, brought together a small group of Italian-born officers to tackle the problem. Petrosino, still a detective sergeant then, was the obvious choice to lead this new Italian Squad, but McAdoo scoured the ranks of the NYPD for other speakers of the language, eventually unearthing eight more men, among the four thousand then on the force, who possessed the necessary linguistic skills. There were so few Italian policemen in New York, in fact, that Petrosino's deputy, Maurice Bonsoil, was half

Irish and half French, but Bonsoil had grown up in a Sicilian quarter of the city and spoke the dialect better than he did English. There were other surprises, too: The addition of an Irish-sounding patrolman, Hugh Cassidy, to the ranks of the squad baffled newspaper reporters until it was discovered that the man had been born Ugo Cassidi and had Anglicized his name.

Petrosino's nomination to lead the new Italian Squad was well received throughout the city, not least in Little Italy itself, where word of the appointment helped assuage growing concern among the great majority of honest immigrant families that the spate of bombings and kidnappings for ransom was getting out of hand. Early successes, including the solution of an especially bloody murder in the Bronx, helped to burnish the detective's reputation further. Petrosino also scored a signal victory in arresting and having deported to Italy an important Neapolitan criminal named Enrico Alfano, who was one of the heads of the Camorra, an extended, organized criminal band that terrorized Naples in much the same way as the Mafia did Sicily. Alfano had fled to the United States after the murder of a rival boss and was widely considered untouchable. His deportation caused a sensation in Italy, where it resulted in an eleven-month trial and, eventually, in thirty convictions—the fiercest blow struck against the Camorra in a generation. Petrosino's exploits also made a deep impression on the Italians of New York, many of whom had viewed Alfano with a superstitious dread. The Neapolitan crime boss had been seen, *The New York Times* reported, "in the light of a demi-god; he was thought to be invulnerable to bullets and able at all times to escape his pursuers." Yet the Italian detective had defeated him.

By the time the Alfano affair reached its conclusion, Joe Petrosino was unquestionably one of the two or three most famous policemen in the city, and arguably in the entire United States. He was certainly influential enough to browbeat his superiors into increasing the size of the Italian Squad, which grew to number thirty men by 1908, with ten more stationed across the East River in Brooklyn. "The personality and the mentality of the chief of the Italian squad are striking," wrote one reporter who returned impressed from interviewing Petrosino.

He is short in stature, but stoutly built. He is clean-shaven and shows a strong but determined jaw. The mouth is firm, the lips are set in a straight line, suggesting purpose rather than severity. The eyes are not the searching eyes of the inquisitive prodder, but the intelligent eyes of a student. There is generally a kindly light in them, a light that makes one feel easy in mind. They invite you to be confidential, and when the straight line of the lips breaks into a smile, you can readily imagine that you are talking to some gentle and thoughtful person who has your interests at heart.

Petrosino is suave, but this is never discovered until too late, and the Italian criminal who has been chatting with him over a wicker-jacketed Chianti bottle, finds a strong hand clasping his wrist and the information is given to him that he is under arrest.

But for all this, the same writer warned, the Italian Squad was hard pressed to keep up with the demands placed on it: "Petrosino and his men seldom know what it is like to get eight hours of sleep in twenty-four."

Petrosino was promoted to lieutenant in 1907, and most of the press coverage that he generated in abundance was positive; his name was so well known and well regarded by this time that he even became the un-witting star of a whole series of dime novels, published in Italy, which portrayed him as a sort of New York Sherlock Holmes. But the larger question of whether any detective was truly up to such a task was seldom asked. Certainly it was expecting too much of even forty officers to suppress crime in a community that by now numbered well over two hundred thousand people, and it did not help that the men of the Italian Squad were provided with the bare minimum of resources. The squad was given a little office of its own on Elm Street, a short distance from police headquarters, and had its own Rogues' Gallery and files, but no effort was made to integrate this intelligence with the main NYPD files, let alone to share information with Flynn's Secret Service, and the squad remained almost entirely reactive, attempting to solve crimes that had already been committed rather than mounting the sort of long-term surveillance Flynn advocated in the hope of preventing those that were still being planned. To make matters worse, Petrosino still kept much of his own invaluable experience in his head—he boasted to one newsman of being able to identify three thousand Italian criminals by sight—and while this made him a formidable adversary in person, it was a dangerous habit, and one that worried his superiors, who realized how much would be lost if the lieutenant decided to retire or was actually killed.

For his handful of critics, indeed, Joe Petrosino was a good deal less effective than his press coverage suggested—a Victorian policeman who kept the peace in Little Italy in a Victorian way. Having joined the NYPD as long ago as 1883, and having served more than half a dozen years as a beat patrolman before rising to the rank of plainclothesman, Petrosino had always relied as much upon his muscles as his brains—a Brooklyn alderman had once accused him of punching "more teeth than a dentist" from the mouths of criminals. Nor would anyone who knew both men have said that he was in Flynn's class as a detective. Petrosino was more of a plodder, a stolid, careful, conscientious man who got results by sheer hard work, solid experience, and the occasional distraction of a modest disguise.

"As a story book detective," a critical reporter from the New York *Sun* once observed,

> Petrosino would have been a lamentable failure. His devices were simple. But his commonplace appearance and the fact that he had to deal with a class of criminals not particularly intelligent obviated the necessity for unusual cleverness in his methods. . . . He impressed most people as a short fat man, rather dull than otherwise, certainly not to be feared by a malefactor with a mind above a pig's, [and] he looked as unlike a detective as you could imagine. He loafed about the wine shops of the lower East Side, the West Side and Harlem; he worked for a day or two sometimes in trenches with laborers; he passed himself off as an immigration official or as an employee of the Board of Health. A big cap, the brilliant red bandana, boots or a long overcoat were about all the properties he needed.

It was true, another newsman added, that Petrosino's men did get a few of their results with the help of clever tricks and innovations such as fingerprinting. But, like their boss, they often seemed more comfortable practicing old-fashioned police work of a sort poorly suited to tackling newfangled crimes. The nightstick, the third degree, the stool pigeon, and the telephone tip-off to a friendly journalist when a newsworthy arrest was about to be made: These were the tools of the Italian Squad.

———

ON WALL STREET a mile from Petrosino's Elm Street office, William Flynn was also calculating how best to keep watch over the first family.

Had Flynn worked for the Police Department, he might have left Morello alone. The Chief's sole duty was to catch counterfeiters, and the Barrel Murder case had brought the gang's efforts to distribute bogus notes to a hurried stop. The family had burned ten thousand dollars of counterfeit bills on the boss's orders immediately after his arrest, and the realization that the operation had been exposed by the Secret Service was sufficient to persuade Morello's Sicilians to seek less risky ways of making money. The men of the New York bureau found no evidence that the gang was involved in counterfeiting in the months that followed the Clutch Hand's release from jail in the summer of 1903.

Flynn's instinct, though, was that Morello was still dangerous. The Mafia had already turned to counterfeiting twice; it struck him that there was every prospect that it would do so again. And there were still the loose ends of the Yonkers counterfeiting case to be followed through, investigations that led to the uncovering of the Canadian end of the Morellos' distribution operation and with it traces of a more extensive mail fraud—the gang had been sending small quantities of notes by mail to agents in Italian communities all over the country. Then, that October, three other Morello agents went on trial, with the upshot that each received a sentence of six years. All in all, Flynn felt certain that his surveillance of the Clutch Hand ought to be resumed. If there were any signs that the Sicilians were making preparations to resume their counterfeiting schemes, the Chief wanted to hear about them long before they were a serious concern.

Aside from all that, there was also Morello, who Flynn knew had gotten away with murder, and for whom the Secret Service man had begun to feel considerable loathing. "He has become enveloped in mystery," Flynn once observed in notes about his enemy,

[and] ultimately he will be looked upon as a big bad man, but he wasn't and isn't. He was a little bad man. He was vicious and vindictive and dangerous generally . . . treacherous but yellow. His mob was, like all mobs, a fluctuating quality. He enlarged it or decreased it to suit his own immediate purposes, [but] his staff was

composed of as sinister an aggregation of cut-throats as I have ever surveyed, arrested and sent to prison.

There was more to Flynn's determination to put a stop to the Clutch Hand's activities than mere dislike, of course. By 1906, the Mafia was evidently a significant threat to law and order in New York.

As the Chief pointed out, convicting Morello would put one of the most murderous men in the city behind bars. "I'm of the opinion that 50 murders could be traced to the Morello-Lupo outfit," he wrote.

Actually putting this decision into action was more easily said than done, of course. More so even than the Italian Squad, Flynn's Secret Service bureau—indeed, the agency as a whole—was desperately short of men. Between the years 1890 and 1910, the number of Secret Service agents assigned to offices across the United States was never more than forty; the average was only twenty-seven men. Nine of those, plus Flynn, were assigned to the New York bureau, which made the Wall Street office the only one of any size outside Washington. But the city was home to so many forgers and counterfeit bills that every agent in the city was kept busy. In most years, more than a fifth of all the counterfeiting cases in the country meant work for the Manhattan office.

Both Flynn and his predecessor, William Hazen, had been aware for years they had a problem. As early as the summer of 1900, Hazen had written pleadingly to Washington, informing headquarters that the New York bureau required, at a minimum, a stenographer, a typist, and more agents. Little had changed by 1903, when, during the Barrel Murder investigation, Flynn's men had worked sixteen-hour shifts, slept four hours on a sofa in their office, and then gone back out on the streets again. Now, that same autumn, the Chief was able to spare no more than one or two men to watch over Lupo's grocery store and Inzerillo's café, and that merely on an intermittent basis. As the months passed without any sign of a resumption of counterfeiting activity, even that watch was wound down and discontinued.

All this did not mean, however, that Flynn abandoned all attempts to monitor the New York Mafia. Informants recruited in Little Italy kept his office supplied with fragments of intelligence, and, unlike the minor street thugs favored as stool pigeons by the Italian Squad, the Chief's recruits were generally former forgers with a good knowledge of serious crime. Tony Brancatto, Flynn's top man in the Italian Quarter, was a

Sicilian tailor who had once run a large-scale counterfeiting ring. Since his release from prison shortly before the Barrel Murder, Brancatto had—so Flynn believed—reformed, and the Sicilian now supplied the Secret Service with a stream of useful information, much of it gleaned from criminals' gossip in Italian bars.

Italian-speaking agents supplemented such informants on the streets. In 1903 the New York bureau employed one such man, Larry Richey (born Ricci), a Philadelphian who had joined the Secret Service at sixteen as a result of a dime novel adventure—he had chased a ball down into a basement that turned out to be the lair of a counterfeiting gang. A few years later, Flynn added a second Italian speaker to his staff. Peter Rubano, an older and more experienced operative, became the Secret Service's chief undercover man in the Italian quarter, assimilating so well into the life of the district that eventually, so Flynn recorded, he wormed his way into the outer circles of the Morello family itself. Over the years, both Richey and Rubano succeeded in producing large quantities of useful information.

The task of recruiting able agents of such auspicious quality was made easier by the fact that the Secret Service was regarded as a glamorous employer. The name, the lure of exciting detective work, and the relatively handsome pay of four to seven dollars a day (half as much again as a policeman's) combined to encourage large numbers of well-qualified potential agents to apply for the handful of posts available. There were seldom fewer than three thousand men on Director Wilkie's waiting list, and this meant that it was possible to select honest operatives of high attainment who possessed specific qualities; even Flynn had had to wait a decade for his chance. "In the Secret Service," the Chief once explained to a curious journalist, "are specialists in dealing with certain callings. There are, for instance, the 'lawyer,' and 'doctor,' and the 'engineer.' They can pass themselves off as doctors, lawyers or mechanics as the case requires." At Flynn's instigation, the bureau even brought in female agents on occasion, a remarkable and forward-looking policy never dreamed of by New York's Police Department. Nor was there ever any problem with corrupt, dishonest agents—this at a time when the Police Department was entirely awash with graft and almost every officer on the force took bribes.

The back office staff responsible for maintaining the Secret Service records in Washington were of the same high quality, and their files, a well-maintained and well-indexed collection, together formed an invaluable resource. The bureau's headquarters in Washington boasted a Rogues' Gallery, in Room 35 of the U.S. Treasury Building, that featured displays of 250 active counterfeiters and photographs and records of ten thousand more. Files bulged with samples of counterfeits, and clerks labored over ledgers containing the criminal records and exact physical descriptions of every forger and queer-pusher ever arrested by the bureau. The volume of fresh intelligence processed each morning was considerable. Each Secret Service agent was required to submit a daily report summarizing his activities in minute detail, and the names and the information these reports contained were carefully indexed and cross-referenced, providing Flynn and his colleagues in other bureaus with access to a formidable quantity of information on counterfeiting and counterfeiters throughout the country.

All these resources, all this information, gave Flynn a large advantage when it came to watching the Morellos. When the Chief discovered that the gang had begun to meet in a room at Lupo's wholesale store, he rented a room across the street. He also arranged to have mail dropped into a local box recovered, opened, and read. His agents followed Morello and his men when they left New York, sometimes trailing their targets as far as New Orleans. And long months of dogged detective work—hours standing on street corners observing, weeks spent piecing together the details of the gang's movements, actions, and acquaintances—ensured that Flynn generally had a shrewd idea of where Morello was and what he was doing.

When the Mafia moved, he would be ready.

CHAPTER 7

FAMILY BUSINESS

=

THE BODY LYING IN THE BROOKLYN MORGUE HAD BEEN REDUCED to little more than packages of meat. Its arms and legs lay piled on one side of the slab, sawn clean through at the shoulders and thighs and still clad in the fragments of a suit. The torso and the head lay on the other, the throat cut and the trunk expertly drained of blood—"almost complete sanguination," in the grim phrase of the medical examiner. The face had been so hacked up with a straight razor that it no longer appeared human. Even Antonio Vachris, who had fifteen years of service with New York's police, had never seen such awful mutilations.

The injuries themselves, though, were familiar enough. The dead man's nose, lips, and tongue had all been roughly cut away, and all were missing—punishments typically inflicted by Sicilians on traitors. The remainder of the mutilations—the slashed throat and the dismemberment—were warnings to anyone who might think of doing likewise. That explained why the body had been dumped where it was likely to be found: wrapped in two oilcloth bundles and thrown onto a stinking dump in Pigtown, a dilapidated Brooklyn neighborhood populated largely by Italians.

The victim had been young and strong, of middling height, though poorly dressed and showing little sign of wealth. Putting a name to the remains would usually have been a lengthy task, but when Vachris slid his fingers into a jacket pocket, they closed around an envelope that held a folded square of paper. It was a letter postmarked Carini, Sicily, a few weeks earlier, and addressed by one Antonio Marchiani to his son Salvatore in New York. Unfolding the paper, Vachris read an urgent scribble in Sicilian: "I hear from a number of people who have returned from America that you are constantly in company of a lot of bad Palermo people," the elder Marchiani had written. "It is the express wish of your father and mother that you cut loose from them, as you cannot come to any good end with them. If you have not the money to return, we will send it to you. Never mind how poor you are: Come home."

Vachris replaced the letter in its envelope. The butchered remains lying in front of him now had a name. But clearly Salvatore Marchiani had had no time to heed his father's warning. His expertly dismembered body was the plainest evidence imaginable that someone powerful and vengeful had wanted him dead.

Marchiani was only twenty-two years old at the time of his death in February 1908, but, as the Brooklyn police discovered over the next few days, he had an interesting background. He had lived three years in the United States but was a frequent visitor to Sicily. He had extensive criminal connections. And he was widely believed around Palermo to have been a member of the Mafia. More intriguing still, the young man had links with Giuseppe Fontana—the Mafioso tried for murdering the former governor of the Bank of Sicily—and with Joseph Fanaro, the red-bearded Palermo man who had been arrested, with a dozen others, at the time of the barrel killing. He and Fanaro had, indeed, spent his last night on earth playing cards. So far as the police could tell, Fanaro had been the last person to see the murdered man alive.

As Joe Petrosino would point out, both Fontana and Fanaro had ties to the Morello family. Whatever it was that Marchiani had done to get himself killed—and the Brooklyn police had several theories to account for that—there was little doubt who was responsible. All the evidence suggested that the murder was Morello's work.

NO ONE WAS EVER charged with the Pigtown killing, there being no witnesses and so no firm proof to back up Petrosino's strong suspicions. But if the body on the Brooklyn dump proved anything, it was how inexorably Morello's Mafia family had consolidated its strength in the years between the Barrel Murder and this new killing. In 1903, Morello's power had stretched no farther than a few blocks of Little Italy. By February 1908, when Marchiani died, it reached across the five boroughs of New York, even to the remote part of south Brooklyn where the body was discovered.

That power could be exerted only in the Italian districts of the city, of course. And rival gangs continued to exist, even within the tight confines of Little Italy. They ranged from small groups of amateur extortionists all the way up to the notorious Five Points gang led by Paul Kelly—an Italian who took an Irish name—which at its peak was said to number twelve hundred men. As early as 1903, however, sprawling but ill-disciplined gangs such as the Five Pointers had begun to lose ground to tighter, smaller, better-organized bands of criminals, and with good reason. The Five Points gang boasted a competent leader, Kelly, but few other men of marked ability. Their strength consisted largely of an undifferentiated mass of slow-thinking, poorly educated, violent street thugs, and their income was minuscule in relation to their numbers, consisting almost entirely of the proceeds of muggings and petty thefts. The Morello family, on the other hand, was better disciplined and more ruthless and made money more efficiently from its vastly more ambitious crimes. The eclipse of the Five Pointers by the Mafia was complete by 1905, when Kelly, with his gang rapidly disintegrating, was forced to flee north to Harlem and seek Morello's protection. The Clutch Hand welcomed the old gangster to East 116th Street and rented him an apartment in a building owned by the Morellos.

The root of the Morello family's effectiveness lay chiefly in its leadership and discipline. Morello himself stood unchallenged at the head of the gang, his orders obeyed without question, and Lupo made an effective deputy. Their power rested on their willingness to have men murdered, and over the years the New York police attributed a lengthy list of killings to Morello, starting, Petrosino thought, with the death of Meyer Weisbard, a jewelry peddler whose body was found stuffed into a trunk at the New York docks in January 1901. Weisbard had had his teeth knocked out and his throat cut—seemingly for being overly impudent in demanding payment from his Italian customers, since three hundred dollars' worth of his stock was found in the blood-saturated trunk with him. A year later, an Italian banker by the name of Louis Troja, widely believed to be the richest man in Harlem, met a similarly violent end, bludgeoned to death in his business premises, and the list went on from there. Nor were Lupo and Morello the only members of the Mafia to resort to killing, at least in Petrosino's view. Vincenzo Terranova, the eldest of the Clutch Hand's stepbrothers, was the principal suspect in the murder of "Diamond Sam" Sica, a barber-cum-gambler shot dead on a Harlem street early in 1908. And Nick and Ciro Terranova did not scruple at killing women, plotting to strangle another gangster's former girl-friend when they discovered she had learned the details of one of the Morello family's assassinations.

Few of these murders were committed by the men who ordered them, of course. Instructions were passed down from the boss to lower-ranking members of the Mafia, who were expected to plan and execute the killings and take all the risks. Men brought into the Morello family, or initiated into rival groups such as the Camorra, were told that unques-tioning obedience would be required, and that included committing murder if so ordered. "Sometimes," explained a Neapolitan named Ralph Daniello, one of the tiny handful of men who actually testified in court as to the methods of the earliest Italian American gangs,

> the system does not run smoothly. Then there is trouble—and death. Sometimes the leaders of one district look with envious eyes on the wealth made in the others; sometimes an outsider tries to squeeze in. Sometimes one of the leaders tries to depose his fellow boss and get a larger share of the spoils for himself. Sometimes a gambling house owner forgets to give over a share of his winnings. Then one of the leaders would call one of us into his house. "This man is in the way," the boss would say, naming someone. "He interferes. Go *get* him."
>
> We went. We did not dare protest. It was the other man's life or ours. For the murder, we did not get a cent, but we knew that if we returned to headquarters without finishing it, that same day would see our end. We lived in constant terror.

Lowlife thugs of Daniello's type were scarcely specialists in murder. They were retained, on weekly pay that amounted to as little as ten dol-lars, to carry out all the miscellaneous tasks of gangland, from running card games and gambling houses to collecting extortion payments. There were plenty of examples of men of this dubious caliber botching the killings they had been assigned to commit. Mike Fetto and Johnny Esposito, ordered by Ciro Terranova to shoot dead the owner of a suc-cessful gambling joint, both failed miserably to complete their assign-ment. Fetto, the first man to attempt the job, went to the club in question but could not find the man he had come to murder. When he returned the next day with Esposito, his partner shot the wrong man by mistake.

Fortunately for the two gangsters, Fetto made amends by shooting dead the gambler whom the pair were actually supposed to kill.

Morello, more than other leaders, did take steps to improve his men's murderous efficiency. He provided them with guns and encouraged them to become proficient with them. At first Morello's men worked on their aim in the shooting galleries that then proliferated in Manhattan, but places of this sort were dangerous—the police might be watching them—and alternative arrangements were promptly made. "There is a wood on the outskirts of New York," the *Herald* reported a while later in an article bemoaning the fast-rising tide of murder in the Italian quarter,

> where certain trees are almost cut in twain by the leaden slugs which have been fired into targets nailed to them. It is there that they become proficient with the revolver and the shotgun with the barrels sawn off short.
>
> When a man is marked for death his assassins learn the street which he passes through most frequently on his way home at night. Then an apartment or a stable with a window facing this street is selected. . . . Some night when the victim is strolling homeward the ugly snub-nosed barrels are thrust through the window, which has been kept open just wide enough day and night. There is a squeeze on the trigger, the roar of the explosion to which Harlem's "Little Italy" is becoming accustomed, and by the time the police enter the building from which the shot was fired there is nothing but a few empty bottles, a table and a chair, and the smell of stale tobacco smoke.

The real solution to the problem of killing efficiently was to leave the business to professional assassins, the first of whom were certainly in business as early as 1912. The Morello family passed many of its trickier problems to a killer named Lulu Vicari, a short, prematurely gray-haired man of thirty, so dark complexioned he was often mistaken for a Cuban, and identified by one of Flynn's informants as "one of the most dangerous of the Morello gang. It is said that he does most of the shooting for the Terranovas." Rival gangs had their own specialists, patient and methodically ruthless men who often were equally lethal. One freelance Italian holdup man, foolhardy enough to make a living by robbing gangsters on the street, purchased a chain-mail vest to protect himself against attack. A pair of assassins trailed him for a week, waiting patiently for the day that he appeared without his armor; when he did, they quickly shot him dead. Similarly meticulous planning went into the murder of a known enemy of the Morellos, Giuliano Sperlozza, a Black Hander who so feared being shot that he took to hiding in a windowless room deep inside his tenement. His killers entered the building while he was absent one day and placed a chalk O mark halfway up the door leading to his hideaway. Sperlozza was killed by a sniper who fired through the window, through the O, and into the extortionist as he sat in his chair on the far side of the door.

Most work of this sort was done on the direct order of a boss, either to maintain discipline and exert control over the members of his own family, or as part of a war with rival gangs. But organized crime had grown sufficiently sophisticated by the second decade of the century to hire out killers to third parties. The most notorious incident of this sort—notorious because the police eventually broke the case, setting off a lengthy series of trials and appeals—occurred in downtown Manhattan in 1914 when an independent poultry dealer by the name of Barnet Baff began selling his stock at prices well below those set by the Jewish-run cartel that controlled the chicken racket in West Washington Market. When dire threats failed to weaken Baff's determination, the poultry dealers turned to the Morellos for help. A Mafia man by the name of Ippolito Greco agreed to hire out four gangsters to "take care" of Baff, who was shot through the head soon afterward. The four murderers, who were each paid a hundred dollars, were tracked down after an investigation that lasted nearly a year; it took four more to establish to the satisfaction of a jury who had hired the gunmen and why.

Murder, of course, remained a last resort, even for Mafiosi, but it was the threat of it that underpinned discipline within the Morello family and ensured that the members of the gang stuck strictly to the Clutch Hand's rules, which were clearly set out and astonishingly bureaucratic. Morello's Mafia was governed by a set of nine regulations, which apparently were issued to each man upon initiation; one copy, discovered in "a small black book closely written in the nebulous dialect of Sicily," turned up among the possessions of a man arrested by Flynn and carefully set out the rights and role of both the boss and his associates. Insulting another member of the family or leaving New York without Morello's explicit permission could both be punished with a twenty-dollar fine.

Lying or drawing a weapon on an associate merited expulsion from the family. Another article shed light on the finances of the gang, explaining that its members were expected to turn over four-fifths of their earnings to the "society"—meaning, in effect, Morello. Several more dealt with the plainly important topic of gang meetings, which the boss possessed the sole right to call, which had to be announced at least a day in advance, and which members of the family were required to attend on pain of being cut out of "the next division of funds."

Morello was not alone in issuing formal sets of rules. A few earlier New York gangsters had done so, and another set of gang regulations would turn up a few years later in Ohio, the work of a Mafia-like Italian group known as the Society of the Banana. Nor was the Clutch Hand's evident ambition remotely unfamiliar to New York's underworld. What was unusual about Morello was the speed with which he was able to expand his influence, first through the city and then beyond its boundaries, at a time when long-distance communication still involved telegrams and letters, and when crossing the United States from top to bottom, side to side, meant journeys lasting several days. Morello had been in the country only since 1893, resumed his counterfeiting career in 1899, and formed his criminal family in 1900. By 1903, though, he was the uncrowned king of Little Italy. And three years after that, he was acclaimed as boss of bosses of the entire American Mafia.

IT WAS NICOLA GENTILE who revealed the Clutch Hand as the most senior, most powerful Mafioso in the country, and probably no one in the Italian underworld was better placed to know the truth.

Gentile, too, was a Sicilian, born in the province of Agrigento in 1885. According to his own account, given decades later when he was in his seventies and no longer had a lot to fear, he emigrated to the United States in 1903, lived and worked in Kansas City, Missouri, and was initiated into what he called the *onorata società*—the Honored Society, the Mafia—in Philadelphia two years later. Later Gentile moved to Pittsburgh, where he joined another Mafia family, and he spent time in San Francisco and Chicago, too. In his youth, the Agrigento man was arrogant and tough—"the classic raw material of the Mafioso"—and he soon built a reputation as a killer, ingratiating himself with his fellow Sicilians in Pittsburgh by violently subduing the local Neapolitans. ("You cannot become a *capomafia* without being ferocious," he explained.) But Gentile was something of a diplomat as well, with contacts among members of the Mafia in many cities, and one of the Mafiosi with whom he was acquainted was Giuseppe Morello. There is no reason to doubt a man of his seniority and experience when he described the Clutch Hand as "boss of the bosses of the honorable society when I first entered it."

It would be easy to read too much into this title. The Mafia of 1906 was a loosely organized collection of families in eight or ten large cities that rarely acted in concert, and there is certainly no proof that Morello tried, or even wanted, to exercise direct control over families in far-flung parts of the United States. What the Clutch Hand did do was act as an adviser and an arbitrator—and arrange matters, on occasion, to benefit New York. Where he governed, he seems to have governed by consensus. But the fact that his authority was recognized at all by men living thousands of miles from Manhattan is testament to the respect in which the Corleone boss was held.

How large and how powerful the American Mafia had become by 1906 cannot be said with any certainty. Only a handful of fragmentary records survive. Taken together, though, these scraps paint a picture of a more complex organization than almost anyone suspected at the time— one in which *cosche* were springing up in a growing number of towns, wherever there were large Sicilian populations. It was a fraternity that maintained links with its compatriots in Italy and whose bosses in the United States were also in regular communication. And, while still fatally prone to the sort of murderous internecine disputes that soured relations between families in Sicily, the American Mafia was also evolving mechanisms to resolve disputes and so maximize the money it was making— profit, as Flynn once pointedly observed, being "all these people were concerned with."

Nicola Gentile, with his ceaseless wanderings, makes a fine guide to the Mafia as it existed in the first decade of the century. His memoirs describe families in New York, Philadelphia, and New Orleans, in Pittsburgh and Chicago—where Anthony D'Andrea, a turn-of-the-century counterfeiter, had emerged much as Morello had, and was now the leader of the city's Mafia. (The D'Andrea whom Gentile described—"so savage and so fierce" and "greatly feared in all the United States"—became an influential politician in Chicago's Italian wards and flourished until his murder there in 1921.) Kansas City and San Francisco were also mentioned; Boston, Baltimore, Detroit, and Wilkes-Barre were not, though there is independent evidence of Mafiosi operating in these districts from the first years of the century. In another decade families would be established in several other large cities—Cleveland, St. Louis, Los Angeles, and Buffalo—and some of these groups probably had their roots in the prewar period as well.

There had been hints, dating to the last decade of the nineteenth century, that Mafiosi were in touch with one another across the continent, and that men of respect sometimes traveled from town to town on business. A Sicilian arrested in Philadelphia on a charge of sending Black Hand letters testified "that he and his companions were members of the Mafia and that they were in communication with similar branches in New York, Baltimore and Pittsburg." That was in the winter of 1903, and channels of communication apparently existed through the American interior by that date as well. Francesco Di Franchi, said by the police in California to be "an agent of the murderous la Mafia society," had been in New Orleans at the time of the Hennessy shooting, was thrown out of Denver a few years later, and was finally shot dead in San Francisco in December 1898. Di Franchi had appeared in the Bay Area only a few days before his death, having arrived there from New Orleans in pursuit of yet another Italian, whom he planned to kill. In Chicago, meanwhile, Carlo Battista—found standing over the body of a dead Sicilian on Grand Avenue in February 1901—had just come to the city from New York; stranger still, a police search of the dead man's pockets turned up evidence that the victim, in turn, had been a witness to a murder in Manhattan. And some years later, on the West Coast, a gunman by the name of Mike Marino ("who according to the police," the *Los Angeles Times* reported, "is one of the head gunmen for the Mafia in this country and abroad") shot dead at least two more Sicilians with a rifle from a moving car. Marino, the police disclosed, was an experienced killer, already wanted for murder in New York, Chicago, San Diego, and Seattle.

Morello, too, was an occasional traveler, one whose influence was clearly felt across large swaths of the United States. The earliest indications of the Clutch Hand's growing importance were discovered among the collection of five hundred letters seized from his Chrystie Street attic room at the time of th Barrel Murder. These communications, the *Herald* reported after a briefing from Flynn, "were received from Sicily and from nearly every city of importance in this country," but the most revealing among them had been mailed from New Orleans—still home to the second-largest Italian community in America—and came from one Francesco Genova, whom the Secret Service believed to be the brother of Messina Genova, a member of the Barrel Murder gang. This letter discussed a young killer named Francesco Marchese, who had recently escaped from Sicily after receiving a thirty-year sentence for murder. Marchese had made his way to Louisiana and established contact with Genova, who was now recommending him to Morello, explaining that he was held in high regard in New Orleans and Palermo. Morello did find him a job; Genova's letter was apparently an example of a system, later described by Flynn, that enabled members of various Mafia families who were not personally known to one another to transfer from one city to another with the help of letters of recommendation from their bosses.

Morello's influence in New Orleans was not confined merely to matters of administration. A few years later, probably in 1908, several of Flynn's operatives tracked the boss on a visit to Louisiana, this time to deal with an Italian hotelier who had, the Secret Service heard, grown so angry at the Mafia's rapaciousness that he had threatened to reveal everything he knew to the police. Morello arrived in the city, held meetings with some Sicilians there, and after a stay of three or four days was observed by Flynn's men parading through the Italian quarter of the city, "wearing on his head a red handkerchief knotted at the four corners." It was a Mafia death sign, the Chief explained, and a visible display of the Clutch Hand's authority in New Orleans. That afternoon, Morello caught a train back to New York; that evening,

> the offending Italian was found dead in his [hotel] with a score of knife thrusts in his breast very like those received by the victim of the "barrel murder." The direct evidence was again lacking on which to convict the dreaded visitor. Yet the Italians of all the country took this stabbing as they had the "barrel murder," as a warning not to defy the authority of the big chief.

The New Orleans incident seems to have been unique. Ostentatious assertions of authority were not generally Morello's style, and though he very likely ordered other murders, for the most part the Clutch Hand advised and governed by letter or, more formally, through a central Mafia "council" that was established some time before 1909. The creation of a ruling body of this sort—known among Mafiosi as "the Commission" and said to meet every five years—is known from later testimony, dating to the 1930s and beyond, but its existence some two decades earlier suggests an organization of unexpected sophistication, given the difficulty and expense of travel at the time. Gentile and Morello both discussed the council, though, Gentile explaining that it consisted of no more than a handful of the most powerful bosses from around the country and was responsible for broad strategy. A much larger "general assembly," numbering as many as 150 delegates, also met and had a wider brief, electing capos in cases of dispute and giving its approval to proposals to silence troublesome or recalcitrant Mafiosi. According to another Morello letter seized by Flynn, the two assemblies were separate, and membership in the council did not entitle even a powerful boss to speak at meetings in the assembly: "He can come but only to hear and then has no right to the floor, neither right to an opinion or right to vote," the Clutch Hand wrote.

Whether or not either the Mafia council or the general assembly had real influence is not known, but it seems doubtful. The council, as Gentile pointed out, often did little more than rubber-stamp decisions of the boss of bosses, who would settle matters in advance after consulting his advisers. Gentile was still more scornful of the general assembly, which was, he said, "made up of men who were almost illiterate. Eloquence was the skill that most impressed the hall. The better someone knew how to talk, the more he was listened to, and the more he was able to drag that mass of yokels the way he wanted." If anything, mention of councils, debates, and votes underlines the difficulty of persuading any group of criminals to agree on anything, not least when each boss and each family are engaged in a ceaseless quest to expand their influence, broaden their business, and improve their profits, often at the expense of their fellow Mafiosi. From this perspective, the assemblies described by Gentile and Morello were safety valves as much as anything else—mechanisms for heading off disputes between rival gangs before they could turn into all-out wars. And there certainly was a need for institutions of this sort. By the middle of the first decade of the century, the Mafia had begun to make serious money.

THE RAPIDITY WITH WHICH the Morello family grew in strength and in sophistication was startling. The Morellos substantially improved upon the crude methods of the Black Hand, preferring more enduring, far more profitable protection rackets, which meant that rather than extorting enormous one time payments from their victims, the Mafia levied weekly payments from a variety of businesses, from wealthy storekeepers down to the poorest peddlers. Individually, the sums involved were often small, scarcely worth bothering with, but they mounted up over time, and few in Little Italy escaped the gang's attentions. East Harlem was "pretty rough in those days," recalled Joe Valachi, the son of an impoverished vegetable seller from Naples who was born in the district in 1904. "You could hardly walk around without catching a bullet. I remember my father had to pay a dollar a week for 'protection,' or else his pushcart would be wrecked."

"Protection" amounted, in effect, to a form of tax: pay it and be left alone, or refuse to pay and accept the consequences. "Dipping the beak," the Mafia called it, and it was already commonplace in Sicily; according to Mafia lore, the idea was introduced to the Italian quarter of New York by Vito Cascio Ferro when he arrived in the city in 1902. As Cascio Ferro explained the technique, it was a matter of expediency, mere common sense. "You have to skim the cream off the milk without breaking the bottle," Don Vito once said. "Offer people your protection, help to make their businesses profitable, and not only will they be happy to pay, they'll kiss your hand in gratitude."

Whether Cascio Ferro was actually responsible for the idea—and it seems unlikely that no such scheme had existed before—protection did mean something when two or more rival gangs were competing for the same territory, and most Sicilians grudgingly accepted the necessity of paying it. "With the Mafia . . . at least they gave you somethin'," one shopkeeper observed. "The other gangsters gave you nothin' each time you paid them somethin'." But the idea that Mafiosi were somehow benefactors, even defenders of the poor, was laughable, though it was something that the gangsters themselves claimed and perhaps believed; so was the notion that their criminal activities, from murder to extortion, were the only way that immigrant Sicilians could secure justice and respect. The truth was that Morello and his henchmen were parasites who terrorized their fellow countrymen, exploited the weak, and dealt in fear. Before 1920, when Prohibition opened up opportunities that earlier generations of racketeers had scarcely dreamed of, Italian criminals preyed only on Italians. There was nothing remotely heroic about the things they did.

Morello himself certainly felt no compunction in extorting from other Sicilians. The Clutch Hand understood instinctively how to go about obtaining cash, masking the threat of violence behind a veneer of bonhomie and adding refinements of his own. William Flynn noted a telling vignette of the boss on his rounds, which, judging from the circumstances, must date to 1902:

> "Good morning, Carlo Pelestrina," Morello would say, entering a countryman's shop on the East Side. "Your wife is well? And the children—ah the children—they are well? It gladdens me to behold you so happy, so prosperous, so successful. People fight to enter your excellent shop, Carlo Pelestrina." "Good morning, *padrone* Morello," would be the reply of the uncomfortable Carlo, for the sight of Morello in one's shop had the effect of denaturing any existing cheerfulness. "Thank you, I am well, and my wife and children too. . . . But is there anything I can do for the good *padrone*?" "A mere trifle. I desire silver for this small bill." And Giuseppe would lay down the worst imitation of a $2 or $5 bill poor Carlo ever beheld. Did Carlo protest? He did not. He produced the silver and expressed his vast gratification at being able to offer so insignificant a service to *padrone* Morello.

Subtly varied techniques of extortion followed in due course. By 1903 the Clutch Hand was using bogus Black Hand letters to obtain expensive services for free, as a young Sicilian doctor named Salvatore Romano would testify. According to Romano, Morello's scheme was cunning in its simplicity. He began by mailing threatening letters to Romano's family, then offered his own services as an intermediary to deal with the "Black Hand gang" responsible. Carefully retrieving the notes he had sent—supposedly in order to examine their handwriting, but in reality to dispose of any evidence—the boss reported a few days later that the "threat" had been dealt with and that he had settled with the blackmailers by paying them one hundred dollars, a sum that he would easily recover when the Black Handers "found out who he was." Romano and his family were effusive in their thanks, as Morello had anticipated—so much so that when the son qualified and opened his own practice in East Harlem, he gladly accepted the Clutch Hand as a patient free of charge.

Matters ran swiftly out of control, as many of those who encountered Morello discovered to their cost. "He began to call on me," Romano said.

> And then the brothers-in-law, and then the cousin called. . . . I treated all their relatives, and all free of charge. . . . The whole number of relatives, babies and patients amounted to about sixty. They would call me; I would examine them, prescribe them, but I got no pay, on account of the obligations, also the familiarity. Right from the start I thought I was doing a wise thing not to ask money for my services.

Again, a few small sums soon multiplied. After a year, Dr. Romano was treating so many members of the Morello family that the remainder of his practice was suffering. Eventually he was forced to relocate to Rochester, 250 miles upstate, simply to make a living.

THE MANHATTAN IN WHICH Morello flourished after his discharge from prison late in June 1903 was growing faster than it had ever done before. The number of immigrants pouring through Ellis Island grew larger every year, reaching three thousand a day—more than a million a year—in the spring of 1906. One in five of this vast mass of naïve, eager, sometimes friendless future citizens remained in the city and became New Yorkers, and there were months when very nearly half of that great total was Italian. Little Italy burst its bounds. East Harlem, too, grew rapidly, north and south, until New York threatened to overtake Naples as the largest Italian city on earth. And though most of these immigrants were poor and some were destitute, the Italian quarter as a whole grew rapidly in wealth. The number of Italian businesses more than doubled. Incomes increased sharply, too; remittances sent home to Italy rose by more than a third between 1900 and 1906. More disposable income meant more people with jobs, more people with savings, and more people worth terrorizing. For Morello and his criminal family, this was a happy time—years in which the Mafia's revenues increased rapidly in tandem with its influence.

Opportunities to make money were to all intents and purposes limitless, which was just as well, since the gang had to make up for the loss of income from its counterfeiting business while also warding off potential rivals, and there seems to have been little that Morello would not sanction in his relentless drive for profit. The Clutch Hand's gang stole horses and wagons and resold them—an important criminal trade at a time when automobiles were rare and expensive, and one so common in New York that more animals were reported stolen in the city every year than in the largest western states. Experienced horse thieves could change an animal's appearance so completely it was rendered unrecognizable; manes were trimmed, hooves clipped, tails docked, and wagons repainted before the stolen rigs were resold through crooked livery stables. Kidnapping, too, enjoyed a vogue in the Italian quarter in the first decade of the century, and according to the NYPD the Morello gang was involved in a number of important cases. The Clutch Hand's police record notes that he was arrested in connection with several incidents, among them, almost certainly, the 1906 kidnapping of Antonio Bozzuffi. Bozzuffi was the fourteen-year-old son of one of the wealthiest private bankers in Little Italy, a man Morello certainly knew since he had helped to charter a front corporation for the Mafia a few years earlier. The boy was held captive for three days while a ransom said by the newspapers to amount to twenty thousand dollars was negotiated. After his release, young Antonio described being tied to a bed and tortured with stilettos by a group of masked Sicilians.

The Morellos operated many other rackets, too, and it appears that these subsidiary businesses were controlled by individual members of the family, who were given free rein to run them much as they wished so long as the appropriate tithes were paid. A good deal was little more than petty crime—one junior member of the gang described the theft of fifteen watches as a good evening's work—but much was not. One favorite way of making money was to lodge fraudulent insurance claims. Members of the gang encouraged frightened shopkeepers to purchase expensive fire insurance policies; then, when the insurance was in place, Morello's men would set the property ablaze and collect a substantial portion of the settlement.

Insurance fraud was the province of Antonio Cecala, a relative of Lupo's, who came from Corleone and claimed to be a barber but in reality made his living as the head of a "band of incendiaries" whose members specialized in burning down heavily insured properties. According to Cecala—a burly, balding, thuggish man in his mid-thirties—the business was actually one of the least lucrative that the Morellos were involved with ("I am poor because I did not soon enough learn the way to profit in the society," he said), but it still required a fair degree of expertise and daring.

"How do you do that?" the incendiary was once asked by a novice member of the gang.

"For instance," he replied,

> you own a store of some kind. You have insured it against fire. You have paid your insurance from time to time and do not wish to pay any more. Now to realize on the money paid you must burn. You do not wish to do it yourself as it is too risky. So you send for me. I in my own way will plan and start a fire that will never be questioned. When the insurance company pays you, you pay me a percentage.

Cecala claimed to be an expert in this line of work. "I use glycerine," he explained, "mixed with other matters. It does not smell at all and leaves no traces of its own burning. It takes three or four men. I direct them and they bring the material. I pay them five dollars each a night for the time they work." He was dismissive of the efforts of amateurs who had little understanding of how to set a fire without leaving telltale traces for an investigator to discover. Accused of starting a blaze in a dry goods store on Mulberry Street in which several innocent people had died, Cecala waxed indignant:

> That is not my line. I do not set fires to cover murders. That fire was started by a Neapolitan band that were in with the proprietor of the dry goods store. . . . They made a mess of it because they did not start the fire right. They started it in the side of the store and afterwards put explosives on the stairs so that traces of how it started would be lost. After setting fire to it they ran away over the roofs. If I had had that job, it would have been different. All traces

ould have been lost from the store door and there would not
have been many accidents to the families above. They could
have run out in the yard.

Crimes of such magnitude inevitably attracted the attentions of the
police, but problems, the Sicilian added, could generally be smoothed
over in the United States. A large part of the secret of the Clutch Hand's
apparent invulnerability, so Cecala patiently explained, could be attributed to the Mafia's carefully maintained relationship with the local police
precinct:

> Morello knows how much money he has given to detectives,
> when and where it was given, and the names of those who have
> taken it. He has always gotten out of everything in which he was
> implicated. Only recently in the "barrel murder" he got out. They
> watch him all the time. Even now he is being watched. They do
> not like to because he knows he has paid them money. But they
> are ordered to and have to. When the order is given to the police
> to arrest Morello, policemen whom he has fed always will warn
> him and he will hide. When they go to his house to arrest him
> they can never find him. Simple, isn't it?

The notion that the police protected criminals was hardly news in
turn-of-the-century New York, where endemic corruption was a fact of
life. Several exhaustive judicial inquiries had shown that the police were
tools of the city's ruling politicians, who kept firm control over all ap-
pointments to the NYPD. Novice patrolmen paid as much as three hundred dollars for a position on the force, a substantial sum that could be
recovered only by their agreeing to help channel bribes paid by Manhattan's brothels and illegal gambling houses upward to the city's ruling
class. Vice was thus tolerated, licensed, and controlled, creating a hugely
profitable, wholly illicit criminal economy that turned over an estimated
$3 million a year by 1900. Revelation of the existence of "the System"
made the entire city cynical; in Cecala's opinion, laws prohibiting various crimes existed not to protect citizens, or even because the authorities
were puritan, but to provide politicians with opportunities to make vast,
almost entirely risk-free profits. "In this country, money counts and
nothing else," the Sicilian explained. "Sooner or later it all goes into the

one pocket. Give money to the police and the detectives and they will leave you in peace. Kill someone and if you have money you will get out of it. The American newspapers prove that every day. But if you are poor and cannot buy your way out, they will kill you for it."

The ease with which the police could be bribed and the political authorities corrupted made possible far larger and more profitable rackets than Cecala's insurance frauds. Prices in virtually all of New York's major industries were set artificially high as a result of gangsters extorting large sums in "protection," and the most profitable of these illicit businesses were those involving goods that all consumers simply had to buy. The coal racket, the ice racket, and the "wet wash"—that is, laundry—racket all brought in substantial sums, and, most important of all, there were also numerous food rackets involving milk, fruit, vegetables, fish, and meat. Run efficiently, with all the major wholesalers fixing prices and paying a percentage to the racketeers, the latter could be astoundingly lucrative. The chicken racket in West Washington Market, which cost Barnet Baff his life, was estimated to be worth at least one hundred thousand dollars a year, and a few years later the artichoke racket—a major source of income for Italian gangs, since artichokes were an indispensable ingredient of minestrone—was estimated to be worth twice that, the Morellos levying assessments of up to fifty dollars per truck of vegetables entering the city. Enforcement was vicious and uncompromising, as Baff discovered to his cost. Anyone trying to evade the cartel that controlled the markets was liable to find his transport damaged or his stock adulterated, and as usual it was all but impossible for the police to trace such acts of terrorism to their source. In time, the Morello family and their rivals refined their operations further by moving into labor racketeering, infiltrating and increasingly controlling the powerful trade unions in the markets. With the workforce doing the gangsters' bidding, it was a relatively simple matter to inflict intense pressure on recalcitrant dealers by calling strikes or ordering persistent minor acts of sabotage.

The scale of all these operations was substantial. The Manhattan wet-wash racket was controlled by three large corporations, which agreed among themselves to charge no less than $1.50 a bundle for laundry. Investigation of the Baff murder revealed that the Washington Market "poultry trust"—a cartel of more than twenty wholesalers—collected ten dollars from every dealer in the market for each railroad carload of birds to reach New York. The trust protected its position by doing business solely with unionized shippers and butchers, and its enforcers meted out blackjackings and beatings to those who refused to cooperate. Dealers who resisted or complained were further punished by being made to pay a 6 percent surcharge on their purchases, and that for poultry of an inferior standard.

The importance of rackets to the Morellos increased considerably over time. The first family's earliest involvement in such schemes probably dated to about 1905, and for perhaps half a dozen years they made up only a part of the family's business, though an increasingly lucrative one. So important were the rackets to the Morellos that the Terranova brothers became increasingly involved. Vincenzo, the eldest of the three, became an iceman, with his own company, Morello & Barbero. In the years before the advent of refrigeration, ice was among the most vital of commodities and the only way of preserving both foodstuffs and medicines. Ciro, meanwhile, became gradually more powerful in the vegetable rackets while still supposedly employed by Bernardo Terranova's plastering business. Only Nick, the youngest brother but also the most natural leader among the three, played no recorded part in this side of the family's activities. He certainly was involved in the theft and resale of horses and wagons, but his real role in the Morello gang made him far more influential than that. Increasingly, as the years went by, the youngest Terranova began to oversee the whole of the family's businesses. While he did that, his stepbrother, Morello, was devoting more and more of his attention to the problem of how to handle all the cash his family was making.

HOW MUCH GIUSEPPE MORELLO earned over the years from extortion, counterfeiting, and his numerous rackets cannot be known with any certainty, but it was plainly a great deal of money. William Flynn, who knew more about the first family's businesses than most, believed that Lupo and Morello between them turned over somewhere in excess of two hundred thousand dollars "in a few years," a figure that apparently did not include the profits of several legitimate businesses acquired with funds generated by their criminal empire. Morello began making investments of this sort at an early date—by 1903, his assets already included the spaghetti restaurant on Prince Street where Madonia was murdered, a barbershop and a cobbler's on Tenth Avenue, and two houses that were leased to tenants—and this portfolio was regularly augmented. "As fast as Morello got money," Flynn explained, "he would farm it out by acquiring a barber shop or set up a man in a shoe repairing shop," and at much the same time, Lupo the Wolf was developing his grocery business into the envy of Little Italy. At a time when a family could live in New York on three hundred dollars a year, the Clutch Hand and his brother-in-law were wealthy. The truth, so far as anyone can gauge it, is that Morello was probably worth some thousands of dollars in 1903, some tens of thousands four years later.

It was Lupo, so Flynn explained, who came up with the idea of capitalizing on the booming construction market in a city struggling to accommodate a million new immigrants each year. A six-story tenement block, the most common and most profitable variety of housing in New York, could be put up for about $25,000 and when completed contained twenty-four small apartments, each of which could be rented at a rate of about $130 a year. Developers could thus recover their investment over an eight-year period, while retaining a highly salable asset in the tenement itself.

Since not even the Morello family's illegal enterprises generated the sort of funds required to pay for the construction of entire tenement blocks, Lupo arranged to sell shares in a newly incorporated construction company and then obtain mortgages on suitable lots. The upshot was the formation of the Ignatz Florio Co-Operative Association Among Corleonesi, a company chartered on December 31, 1902, and named in honor of the most prominent Sicilian businessman of the day. The real Ignatz Florio, a shipping magnate from Palermo, was one of the wealthiest patricians in Italy and came from a family known for doing business with the Mafia. In all likelihood, however, Florio remained entirely ignorant of the Ignatz Florio Co-Operative and never discovered that the Morellos were trading on his good name on the far side of the Atlantic.

As chartered, the association had a modest capital of $1,200, and Lupo did not feature on the list of the company's directors. The company's president was another Corleone man, Antonio Milone; Morello was listed as treasurer, and four other directors, all prominent figures in the Sicilian community in Little Italy, rounded out the board. Shares in the company were offered at two dollars and five dollars, and there seems to have been no need to coerce anybody into buying stock. Grudging respect for the Clutch Hand's business sense was sufficient to persuade several hundred small investors to purchase a share or two apiece.

Most of the Co-Operative properties were built in the outer reaches of the city, where land could still be purchased relatively cheaply. "The main purpose of the association," Flynn explained, "was to accumulate sufficient funds to erect two rows of Italian tenements in One Hundred and Thirty-seventh Street and One Hundred and Thirty-eighth Street and Cypress Avenue, in the Bronx," and these properties were completed by 1906. There were several other projects too. The Co-Operative purchased lots on 80th Street, 109th Street, and Beach Avenue. The largest of its developments was a row of tenements built at 140th Street and Lenox Avenue, for which mortgages totaling $120,000 were issued at the tail end of 1905.

Some details of the Florio Co-Operative's methods are known because four of its shares were purchased by the Romano family, and Salvatore Romano, the doctor whose services the family plundered at will, later gave evidence at a grand jury hearing regarding this part of Morello's crooked business empire. Romano's mother was the first of her family to invest; she acquired four shares in 1903 for five dollars down and made a gift of two to her son and daughter. Some years later, probably in 1906, when shareholders voted to increase the company's share capital nearly two hundredfold, to $200,000, Mrs Romano added further to this holding. Whether she ever saw a cash return from her investment seems doubtful. "The shareholders," her son explained, "received dividends each time a building was completed. They could withdraw these funds or roll them over to be invested in the Association's next project. Most chose the latter course." Mrs. Romano was among those who simply let their investment in the Ignatz Florio Co-Operative ride—and with good reason, since for the first four years of its existence the association was a great success.

The buildings constructed by the association were sold as soon as they were finished; neither Morello nor Lupo had any interest in becoming a slum landlord. They sold three six-story buildings on 138th Street to a company named Harris & Trimble in February 1907, and a trio of 140th Street properties went to a well-known landlord, Therese Kummel. Both transactions generated good returns; the figures show profits of $15,000 on 138th Street and $9,000 on 140th Street.

The Florio Co-Operative was big business now. In 1905–6 alone,

Lupo and Morello took out mortgages totaling $336,000 to fund a dozen construction projects, and this in turn meant there was considerable pressure to make the new share issue a success. With nearly $198,000 worth of stock to sell, at a new price of a hundred dollars a share, it was no longer sufficient to tout the shares around in Little Italy. New investors had to be sought, and large quantities of the newly issued stock were disposed of outside New York, a significant portion of it purchased by the Morello family's criminal associates. By 1907, according to Flynn, "there were stockholders all over the country, as far west as the Mississippi valley and south to the Gulf of Mexico," many of whom were important Mafiosi.

The new shareholders were far wealthier than the impoverished Corleonesi who had bought up the association's first stock issue in penny parcels; they could well afford the $100-a-share price. But, as time would tell, they were also a good deal less patient than Morello's earliest investors.

Less patient, and more dangerous.

THE IGNATZ FLORIO CO-OPERATIVE had been neatly positioned to flourish while the economic times were good, but the business was poorly placed to survive even a modest economic downturn. Land had been purchased while prices were high, on the assumption that values would continue to soar and finished buildings would always command good prices. Three, and sometimes four, construction projects had been put under way at once, which meant that there were rarely any cash reserves. And—so Flynn reported, anyway—Morello soon developed the dangerous habit of dipping into what remained of the association's funds, further depleting the sums available to run the business on sound lines.

The depression of 1907, which laid waste to the American economy more completely than any financial panic since the slump of 1893, thus hit the Ignatz Florio Co-Operative hard. This crisis, sparked by a failed attempt by one financier to corner the market in copper, spread rapidly, thanks largely to the catastrophic underlying weakness of most large corporations, and by late summer share prices were falling more sharply than they had ever done before. As stock tumbled, finance houses all along Wall Street found themselves with insufficient assets to cover their exposure, and one by one they failed. So severe were the financial shock waves generated by what had been a purely American disaster that its effects were felt around the world. Thus 1907 marked the beginning of one of the world's earliest global recessions.

Thanks in part to the firmness of J. P. Morgan, the greatest financial titan of the day, the worst of the panic had run its course by October 1907. But even Morgan at the height of his powers could not stop the financial crisis from tipping over into a general slump. New York's immigrant communities were among the worst affected by the deepening crisis. Twenty-five banks failed in Little Italy alone, and their collapse cost twelve thousand customers their life savings. Hundreds of small businesses went to the wall. Only those that were well established, well run, and well managed had much chance of survival.

The Ignatz Florio Co-Operative was not well run, and it felt the full force of the recession. The price of land and property both plummeted, exposing Lupo and Morello to large losses on several projects, and by the summer of 1908 the association had exhausted its remaining funds and began to default on its obligations. At least three suppliers began legal actions against the company in an attempt to recover their losses. Morello was able to settle one by paying the $895 that was owed, but another case, a suit brought by the building firm John Philbrick & Brother over the much larger sum of $5,000, rumbled along for the best part of three years, evidence—if any were needed—that the fledgling Mafia could not yet challenge or intimidate American-owned companies and that it still had little influence outside the Italian community. Work on new projects ceased. The Co-Operative itself staggered on until 1913, but it never succeeded in recovering its losses, nor regained even a fraction of its old eminence.

The recession hit other parts of the first family's business empire, too, and among the most prominent casualties was Lupo's chain of grocery stores. Fewer and fewer Italians could afford the Wolf's high prices, and to make matters worse, he, too, had acquired the habit of draining his businesses of cash to fund his high-class way of life. With economic conditions still worsening, even the flagship Mott Street store was teetering on the brink of closure by the autumn of 1908. According to *The New York Times*, Lupo's property portfolio was worth about $110,000 at this time. The Wolf, however, had mortgages totaling $72,000 and had just remortgaged for a further $13,000.

Lupo's problems, like Morello's, mostly involved unpaid suppliers. The most significant requirement for any strong grocery business was cash flow; creditors typically demanded payment within thirty days, and failure to move stock in that time led swiftly to missed payments and suspended accounts. Lupo's solution to this problem seems to have been to sell in bulk to whoever could be cajoled or browbeaten into paying even a fraction of what the unsold goods were worth. By the time auditors appointed by several of his most pressing creditors arrived at Mott Street to pick over the accounts, the entire chain of stores had assets, including stock, of only $1,500, and debts in excess of $100,000.

The Wolf's humiliation was completed that October when he received a highly public visit from Joe Petrosino. The police had received word that Lupo, desperate for cash, had begun resorting once again to crude extortion, backed by a series of bloodcurdling threats. What happened next soon entered the folklore of the Italian quarter. "According to those who witnessed what occurred," *The New York Times* reported some time later, "Petrosino walked up to Lupo and said something in a low voice. Then the detective's fist shot out and Lupo fell to the floor. Petrosino—according to the story of the eyewitnesses—gave Lupo a severe beating."

It was a story destined to lose nothing in the retelling, and the Wolf's already dangerous temper was not improved by the exaggerated versions of events that soon began to circulate. The most lurid and suggestive of these stories had the detective dumping Lupo's beaten and unconscious body in a barrel in the middle of the street.

THE NEW INVESTORS in the Ignatz Florio Co-Operative were the next to see their money disappearing. The trickle of judgments lodged against the association was becoming a flood: $125 in March 1908, $529 in April, another $123 in June, all to individual contractors. A further $474 was claimed by the New York Cornice & Skylight Works, and $700 by the Ericsson Engine Company. Next came New York Supreme Court hearings brought by larger, more disgruntled creditors, one that September and another the next May, the latter ending with judgment in the plaintiff's favor to the tune of $8,032.

The need for more funds became pressing, then urgent. When Ignazio Lupo vanished from New York, hotly pursued by his creditors, his final snarling act of defiance was to order $50,000 of groceries on credit and have the goods shipped to a dockside warehouse in Hoboken, New Jersey—from which they were to have been sent to Sicily for sale by old associates in Palermo. But Petrosino, following the paper trail, tracked down the missing consignments and had them impounded, closing off another hoped-for channel of illicit cash.

Recession and the failure of Lupo's stratagem left the first family in serious financial difficulty. By the autumn of 1908 Morello had been forced to return cap in hand to his shareholders, explain that they would not be receiving any dividends on their investment, and ask them to consider bailing out the Co-Operative with an additional injection of funds. As might be expected, the news went down badly, not least among the Mafia bosses the Clutch Hand had talked into buying up the shares issued in 1906. "Some of the members who had lost their money began to crowd Morello," one of the boss's principal lieutenants recalled to Flynn a few years later. "[They] threatened to kill him."

The Clutch Hand knew these men meant what they said, and he took the threats seriously—seriously enough to turn back to the one sure way he knew of making very large sums of money very quickly.

It was the end of October 1908. The Morello family was back in the counterfeiting business.

CHAPTER 8

GREEN GOODS

=

ANTONIO COMITO HAD DECIDED THAT HE LOATHED NEW YORK.
Comito was a slight man in his early thirties: black-haired, clean-shaven, five feet four. Born in Catanzaro in Calabria, a dirt-poor region in the toe of Italy, he was ambitious and bright and spoke four languages—two of them, Spanish and Portuguese, picked up during seven years spent in South America, where he had worked as a teacher, a printer, and an assistant to the Italian consul in Rio de Janeiro. Yet things had gone badly wrong for him ever since he'd come home from Brazil. There were no jobs to be had in Catanzaro, and when, growing increasingly desperate, he sailed for New York in the summer of 1907, it was only to discover that there was no work there, either.

Alone and all but friendless in Manhattan, Comito took a room with his brother's family and secured short-term positions in two print shops. By the spring of 1908, his fortunes had reached their nadir. He was unhappy at home, where his brother had become increasingly overbearing, and the plummeting American economy was making it harder than ever to scrape a living. He lost his first job, which had earned him ten dollars a week, in March 1908, and took two months to find another, which paid less. By August he was out of work again, and this time there were no positions to be had at any salary.

Manhattan that autumn was no place for a man without friends or savings, and Comito would have been destitute had it not been for two small pieces of good fortune. He contrived to maintain the memberships he held in two fraternal societies, the Foresters and the Sons of Italy, and these offered him a social life and the chance to earn a few dollars in commission, touting among other members for printing work that he passed on to a former employer. He also met an Italian woman in her early thirties who was alone in the United States and looking for a man as a "protector." Katrina Pascuzzo was no beauty, but she was hardworking and sensible, and she earned a few dollars a week from cleaning work. By the end of October, Comito had moved out of his brother's flat and into rented rooms on James Street with her. The couple "lived together agreeably," as the Calabrian recalled, dividing all that they earned equally. The fact that Comito was already married, to a wife whom he had left at home in Italy, seems to have troubled him not at all.

Even with Katrina's modest earnings, money remained a problem, and work was still impossible to find. Then, unexpectedly, at a meeting of the Sons of Italy held on November 5, 1908, an opportunity presented itself in the form of a tall, sandy-haired stranger who pulled Comito aside as he started for home. As the pair strolled along the street outside the meeting hall, the stranger made an offer that seemed—at the time as much as in retrospect—very nearly too good to be true. There is no work to be had in New York, the man observed in Sicilian-accented Italian. You should come to Philadelphia. I have friends there who will make you the master of your own print shop. They will pay you twenty dollars a week, and the work will not be onerous. Come to Philadelphia and your worries will be over.

Comito had never made a secret of his profession—the fact that he was a printer was generally known among the Sons of Italy—so he was not especially surprised that a man whom he had never met before knew so much about him. And the chance of regular work at a decent salary was sufficient to blind him to at least two warning signs. The sandy-haired stranger, he would recall, stared intently as they talked, "searching my eyes for something he expected but did not see," and "often spoke as if he were on the verge of saying something more than he did . . . [and] just as he was apparently about to say something he would check himself and smile vaguely in an indifferent way." None of this appeared to matter at the time, however, and though Comito had only the haziest notion of where Philadelphia was, he did not even bother to ask his new friend's full name. "The truth is that, all in all, I took him to be a good man," he wrote, and he readily agreed to meet again in a few days, to be introduced to the Sicilian's companions. His only real concern was that he would lack the experience to operate unfamiliar machinery and might lose the chance of a good job in consequence.

Comito's friends and family urged caution. An uncle warned him of the Black Hand and urged his nephew to "be careful not to acquire bad habits or companions. He said that affable strangers would lay traps for my down fall, that I must always be on the look-out." Katrina, more pointedly, observed that they lacked the cash to go to Philadelphia. She let herself be persuaded, though, and two days later, at ten o'clock on a dreary Sunday morning, Comito's new acquaintance materialized as promised on his doorstep. A second stranger—shorter, stronger, more forbidding—hovered at his shoulder. This man's hair was receding, his face lined; his razor slash of a mouth turned down at the corners. He looked to be about forty years old. "Mr. Comito," the man from the Sons of Italy announced, "I present to you my friend, the gentleman of whom I spoke, owner of a printing shop in Philadelphia. His name is Antonio Cecala."

COMITO KNEW NOTHING of Giuseppe Morello, nothing of the Clutch Hand's decision to begin counterfeiting once again, nor of the Morello family's urgent need to find a competent Italian printer to do the work; nor of Antonia Cecala's particular expertise in the field of insurance fraud; nothing, in fact, of the Mafia at all, if his own account can be believed. But Cecala, he sensed, was a dangerous man to be involved with. The squat Sicilian was brutal and sarcastic, and his teeth were yellow and stained, which turned even his smile into an evil leer. He was also prone to fits of violent temper, as Comito discovered when they toured the town to buy a secondhand, foot-driven printing press and Cecala nearly came to blows with the seller. Afterward the two men called at a photographic store in the shadow of Brooklyn Bridge, where Cecala purchased a camera and chemicals. When Comito asked what the camera was for, his companion brushed away the question with an angry shrug, and he was equally evasive when asked about the print shop in Philadelphia. Cecala's chief concern was to get Comito out of New York as quickly as possible and to ensure that Katrina accompanied them. Katrina, when she heard this, felt nervous, urging Comito that "things are not clear—all is not as they say." But avarice and wishful thinking, together with a touch of fear, persuaded him to overrule her.

The next morning, November 11, Cecala reappeared at ten with two companions. The first he introduced as Nick Sylvester, a slight Italian

American, not much more than a boy, whose job it was to pack the goods and load them onto a wagon. The second, Cecala continued, was his "godfather," a man in his mid-thirties named Salvatore Cina. Taller, thinner, balding, and roughly dressed, with a crushing grip and a thick Sicilian accent, Cina was, so Cecala explained, "very rich, has businesses of his own in Philadelphia." Noticing the printer's appraising look, he added: "Do not regard his poor clothes as representing his wealth. It is his choice to be one of us."

That, Comito thought, was an odd remark. "What do you mean by 'one of us'?" he asked.

"That you may know sometime in the future," Cecala replied. "How can we be sure now that it is well you should know? You must wait until we are satisfied." And with that, he and Cina climbed onto the loaded wagon. They pulled up Comito and Katrina after them and, with Nick Sylvester at the reins, set off for the New York docks.

"It was a strange answer to a natural question," the printer mused,

and I let it pass without further notice. But I took pains to watch and listen carefully to whatever [Cina] might say. I knew immediately that he was of a lower class and extremely uneducated. This was the first time that anything had occurred particularly which would have made me think that Katrina was right when she said, "All is not as they say."

Indeed, there were several reasons for concern, now that Comito's suspicions were aroused. The baggage, he noted, had been labeled not for Philadelphia but for "Highland, N.Y.," a discrepancy Cecala brushed away by explaining it was merely a stop on their journey. Then again, Comito and Katrina were never left alone long enough to talk. And when the party boarded a ferry for a journey up the Hudson River, it became clear that they would be traveling after dark.

"At what time will we be in Philadelphia?" I asked, still dissatisfied with the turn affairs were taking and his deliberately evasive answers.

"Tonight, about eight o'clock," [Cecala] answered, and looked me straight in the eye.

"Why do we arrive at night?"

"It is better for us because no one will see what we are doing and we will need to give an account to no one."

"Why do we need to fear giving an account to anyone," I asked boldly, determined to sift matters down. "We are doing nothing dishonest, are we?"

"That, Comito, I will not answer now," he whispered in a hissing way. "But listen to what I say. Do as you are bid from now on. Your life is forfeit." And he gave me that sign that struck horror to my soul. Quickly throwing a finger to the center of his forehead and drawing it straight across from left to right, he lowered it to his throat and drawing it across his windpipe, made a suggestive noise, like the slitting of a pig's throat.

Comito was left alone on deck for a short while after that, but Cecala soon reappeared, this time to baldly announce that he had insufficient money to pay all the party's fares. Comito had not a cent on him, but Pascuzzo had a five-dollar note that she had hidden in her stocking. Pressed by Cecala for cash, she retrieved the bill and offered it to him. Cecala snatched the note away. "I knew you had it, for I was told," he remarked in an icy tone. "But I wished to see if you would lie."

When Cecala had gone again, Comito remonstrated with his mistress. She ought not to have admitted she had money, he complained. But "with her usual foresight," Katrina said that she thought she had been watched in their apartment earlier when she had hitched up her skirts to hide the bill.

The loss of the five dollars was serious, both Comito and Katrina knew. They were traveling upriver into the approaching winter, heading for an unknown destination in the company of a vicious group of strangers, to carry out some unknown but no doubt illegal work—Comito thought it might be printing pornography. And now they were penniless, without the means to fend for themselves should they get an unexpected chance to run. "I remained like a stone," Comito recalled.

My courage oozed away and I asked no further questions. But a thousand and one evil thoughts surged through my mind. It flashed upon me that all these preparations had been but part of a scheme to trap me. I felt in my heart that . . . they were cunning and had led me so far it would be hard now to get back.

We reseated ourselves upon the lounge. . . . Soon with a million horrible thoughts crowding my tired head I was asleep.

CECALA HAD LIED AGAIN. It was nearly one in the morning by the time the ferry tied up to a jetty at a deserted spot far up the Hudson, and by then the weather had turned bitter. A crisp layer of frost covered the ground; the trees were bare; hills came crowding in on both sides of the river; and after a while the wind got up and began to blow fresh flurries of snow into their faces. Comito listened hard as a member of the crew called out the details of the place where they had landed. "I failed to hear the world 'Philadelphia,' " he commented.

In fact they were in Highland, a tiny farming village fifty miles up the Hudson, and had been heading north, away from Philadelphia, ever since setting out from New York. Comito and Katrina, no wiser still as to where they were actually being taken, allowed themselves to be driven on to Cina's farm, an hour away, to spend the night, and from there they were sent on to another property, this one owned by Cina's brother-in-law, a Tampa Mafioso named Vincenzo Giglio. Cecala soon vanished—back to New York, Comito was told—and there the couple waited for the best part of a month. It was not until December 8, 1908, that Cina and Giglio loaded up the cart again. With Cina at the reins, the printer and Katrina were driven deeper and deeper into the surrounding woods.

Both Comito and his mistress were well aware by now that they were not going to Philadelphia, but neither knew quite where they were. They had certainly not expected to be quite so isolated, and the desolate terrain and lack of human habitation were intimidating. "In half an hour of the coldest driving that I had ever experienced," Comito would recall months later, "we were so far in the country that there were no more houses, nothing but trees and the road we were on." They pressed on farther from there, driving for two more hours through a maze of bare, skeletal trees, the cart groaning all the while under the weight of their luggage and their horse stumbling and slipping on the ice, until at last they reached a desolate spot around a bend from which a small stone house could just be glimpsed between the trees. It was utterly isolated.

There was no other sign of houses, nor any traffic on the rough wood track—nobody and nothing, Cina roughly assured them, but a mail cart that passed once a day. The printer was prodded from his seat. "This is the place you are to live, friend Comito," Cina said.

The stone house was chilly and uncomfortable. It was a good-sized property, with three stories and six rooms: a kitchen and a storeroom on the ground floor, a workroom and two small bedrooms above, and finally a garret attic. But there was no heat, no light, no running water, and no tables, chairs, or food—nothing but two dilapidated beds, the printing press that Cecala had purchased in New York, and what they had brought with them on the cart. Giglio set up a small stove in the kitchen and did his best to fix the broken beds.

Comito thought of running off, getting away, and realized at once how difficult that would be. He still had no money, nor the sort of clothing he would need to hike across rough country. He did not know where he was, or how to get to the nearest town or village. And Cina had told him that he and Katrina would never be alone in the stone house. That promise had seemed a comfort once, but now he saw that it was not. The men assigned to provide company would be watching him as well.

Next morning, another man appeared with a cartload of provisions: kerosene for the stove, a hundred-pound sack of potatoes, flour, thick black bread, oil, smoked fish, tomato sauce, and macaroni for the kitchen. The food was of good quality and there was plenty of it, but that merely made Comito more despondent. Supplies sufficient for several months implied a long stay in the woods.

Still he had no idea what was required of him. He searched the workroom where the printing press now stood and found no type, no forms, no plates. Whatever it was that Cina and Cecala were working on, he thought, must still be in New York.

IN AN ANONYMOUS apartment in the north part of the Bronx, far from the eyes of the Secret Service, Antonio Milone sat in a small room he had converted into a makeshift photographic studio. He was carefully assembling a set of flimsy zinc sheets. To Milone's right was a shallow trough filled with nitric acid and alum; beside that sat a jug containing a careful mix of half a dozen other chemicals. It was time to etch the printing plates.

Milone was a secretive man who valued privacy. He rarely mixed with other members of the New York Mafia; most, indeed, had no idea he existed. Only Morello himself, and a handful of his most trusted associates, knew where the engraver lived, and few even of their number understood his true importance to the first family. Milone was Morello's moneyman. For several years, as president of the Ignatz Florio Co-Operative Association, he had overseen the laundering of the family's illegal income, managing its investment in a widening portfolio of legitimate businesses. Just as important, from Morello's perspective, his friend knew how to make money, literally. Milone was an experienced engraver and a competent printer who possessed the steady hand required to engrave counterfeits. He was the first person the Clutch Hand had turned to when he was forced back into the green goods business.

Milone had been asked to etch two separate sets of printing plates, from which two different sorts of currency would be made. His first commission was for a Canadian five-dollar note, to be printed in five colors, which meant that five different plates had to be engraved. His second was for a three-color U.S. two-dollar bill.

The two-dollar note was a common piece of currency, selected apparently because its face value was sufficient to make it worth the risk of forging but not so high as to excite much attention when it was passed in shops and bars. The five-dollar bill had been chosen, despite its additional complexity, because it would be easier to pass. For one thing, the Canadian note was unfamiliar to most Americans, and any imperfections in the engraving and printing would have a better chance of escaping notice. For another, Canadian currency lacked one of the chief security devices used in the United States. American bills were printed on a special grade of paper made with silk threads running down their length. These could easily be seen by anyone holding the note up to the light and were almost impossible to counterfeit. Canadian currency was silkless.

The technique that Milone used to etch the plates was called photoengraving. He began by obtaining a perfect example of a genuine note, then laid it absolutely flat and photographed it. Next, he dipped one of his zinc sheets into the trough of nitric acid, then spread the same plate with a coating from his jar of chemicals—a solution of ammonium, ammonium hydroxide, egg albumen, and water that was highly sensitive to light. This mixture was allowed to dry.

Milone's next task was to transfer his photographic negative to the plate. Working with great care, he placed the reversed image in position on the treated plate, pressed it down, and clamped the plate and the negative together. He then slid this assembly into a large box that looked much like a contact printer and closed the lid. The box contained a powerful arc light. Milone switched on the machine and waited. Inside, the arc blazed onto the negative, hardening the ammonium solution on the plate wherever it passed through the photographic film.

It took a minute or two to make the exposure. Switching the arc light off, Milone removed the plate, laid it flat on the table in front of him, and very gently spread a thin layer of ink across it. Next, he washed the whole plate several times with water. The water dissolved the unhardened ammonium solution wherever it had been shielded by the negative. Milone shook off the last few drops of liquid and tilted the plate so that it gleamed. The copper now bore a delicate negative image of a Canadian five-dollar bill, its lines hardened by the action of the arc light.

The last step in the platemaking process was the most difficult, calling on all of Milone's experience. The plate was returned to its acid bath so that the surfaces to be printed could be etched. To prevent the solution from eating its way under the lines of the image, however, Milone had to dust the surface of the plate carefully with a powder known as dragon's blood—a resin that slowed the action of the acid. The counterfeiter had to repeat the delicate process of removing the plate from its acid bath, washing it, reinking it, and dusting it with dragon's blood at least half a dozen times before the etching was complete. After that, using a magnifying glass, Milone examined every millimeter of the plate for errors. Lines that required deepening or correction had to be recut by hand.

By the time the counterfeiter had finished his work, it was the middle of December. Milone wrapped the eight plates carefully in cloth and newspaper. They were ready to be used.

SNOW BLANKETED THE WOODS west of Highland. It lay two feet deep around the stone house and piled up in drifts against the walls. Comito had abandoned all hope of escape. He had nothing to do—"those days seemed years"—and he was concerned about Katrina, who was doing all the cooking and the household work and who had come down with a fever. It was almost a relief when, on the morning of December 15, there was a knock on the door and Cecala and Cina entered just as yet another snowstorm broke. They had brought more food, and a cloth bundle protruded from one of Cecala's pockets.

"Don Antonio," Cecala said, "come upstairs. We must talk."

They went up to the room where the press was, and Cecala unwrapped Milone's printing plates. "Here is the work that we must execute," he said. "Here are the plates. Look at them. Without anyone knowing it we will all soon be rich."

Comito knew at once that this was counterfeiting and that he was in far worse trouble than he had imagined. "This is not my work," the printer protested helplessly. "It is very difficult work to execute. I do not even know how to prepare the press."

"You have to do it," Cecala rejoined, his voice hardening. "You must do it. Your life will be taken and none shall know why or when if you do not. You will never be found."

Comito did his best to remain calm. The plates were too small for the press, he explained. They could not be printed unless they were mounted on blocks, and there were no blocks in the house.

Cecala seemed to think that this was mere dissembling. "It is time we perhaps told you more of who we are and how we work," he replied.

There are twenty of us who have organized this affair. Others higher up in famous places know of it. They will receive their share. Should anything slip and we get into trouble there will be thousands of dollars for lawyers and we will be freed.

We will respect you as one of us, and Katrina shall have respect at all times. When we have made millions, she will be sent to Italy with money of her own. But you, Don Antonio, you will stay with us for life.

We are big, bigger than you know. . . . You will know perhaps, later on, about the many branches of our society, and how it is possible for us to do things in one part of the country or world and have the other half of the affair carried out so far away that no suspicion can possibly come to us. After you have obeyed and seen some inkling of our power, you will be glad to become one of us.

The printer listened miserably as Cecala went on. The Sicilian talked for about ten minutes, setting out what was required and how it should be done. A hundred thousand sheets of paper had already been purchased, in various qualities and different sizes. The correct inks had also been procured. He himself would help to mix them.

Comito could only sit and nod his head. He would do his best, he said.

IT TOOK FIVE MORE DAYS to fetch the blocks, and when Cecala returned to the stone house he had another stranger with him.

The newcomer was tall and muscular, with quartz-flecked hair: in his mid-forties, Comito guessed, and "apparently a Sicilian of high birth," since he dressed well and wore expensive jewelry. Cecala introduced him as Zu Vincenzo—"Uncle Vincent"—and explained that he had come to help with the printing of the notes. The newcomer had once run a small bank on Elizabeth Street. He was "very capable," Cecala added, and could be relied on for advice when he and Cina were not there. Zu Vincenzo brought the number of people living in the house to six.

The arrival of the blocks meant that there was no reason to delay the printing any longer, and the first proofs were struck off that night—though only after Comito had protested one last time and felt the full force of Cina's violent temper. The men worked steadily until dawn on Christmas Eve, and it was only when the sun came up that they at last found the correct shade of green for the Canadian five-dollar note. That afternoon, Cecala and Cina selected the best of the samples and departed for New York, where the notes were to be "shown to persons qualified to judge them," and three days later they were back, this time with orders to print new proofs in a darker color.

Work on test printings of the counterfeits continued throughout the first week of January 1909. To Comito's relief, Cecala and Cina stayed away from the stone house for much of the time, leaving Giglio and Zu Vincenzo to help him with the work. The three men soon settled into an unvarying routine—mixing inks, running proofs, adjusting the press—and the work proceeded largely in silence. The few conversations that Comito did overhear only encouraged him to say as little as possible. "They would tell me stories that made me shiver," the printer recalled, "laugh roughly and tell how much [money] they had frightened from someone, or how neatly they evaded the *carabinieri* in the old country, or the fool police here."

Comito knew by now that he had been brought to Highland by a well-organized group of criminals. He knew, from Cina's bragging and the stories Giglio and Zu Vincenzo told, that most of the men holding him had police records in Sicily. But he still had no clear idea of who exactly the men were or to which society or gang they owed allegiance. He guessed that they were members of the Black Hand, the group his uncle had warned him so adamantly against, and saw and heard nothing to change that opinion until one day in January when Giglio was absent and Zu Vincenzo told the printer more about the story of his life.

"While working," Comito would recall,

> Uncle Vincent told a thing that I shall never forget. He said that he had been a cattle raiser in his native town. That one day while in the country he had been approached by two men who stated that they desired to buy some oxen. He said that he wanted to see whether they had much money, so stated that he would not talk business unless he knew they meant business. One of them thereupon showed some money. Without a word of warning, Uncle Vincent stated that he threw his rifle to his shoulder and shot the man dead in his tracks. The companion had run when he had fired and he followed him, chasing him some distance. Upon catching up with him, as the man kneeled and cried for mercy, he swung his rifle by the barrel and "scattered the fool's brains all over the field." Having killed them both, he returned to his first victim and rifled his clothes, taking 250 lire from the body.

Having committed a double murder for such a paltry sum, Zu Vincenzo had little option but to flee his village. He wrote his family a letter, explaining what had happened and telling them not to worry about him, then took a train to Palermo. In the harbor, Vincenzo found a sailing boat skipper willing to take him to Tunis for one hundred of his 250 lire, and there he stole sufficient money to book a passage first to Tokyo, then to Liverpool.

It was, Zu Vincenzo told Comito, not until

> March 1902 [that] he sailed from there to New Orleans. He knew that on arriving here he would have no trouble, as he had so many friends who would help him because of what he knew about

them. In fact he explained that this was one of the greatest secrets of success: "Find out something about someone and then hold it over their heads and you need never work."

I was tremendously interested in this story and asked: "Have you worked while you have been in America these last six or seven years?"

"Never," he stated emphatically. "Nor do I ever expect to. It is too easy to live in this country without work. If I knew the man who invented 'work,' I would kill him with pleasure."

"Then how do you manage to live?" I asked, remembering my struggle for work in New York.

"You are too new among us to know certain things," he replied in a mysterious way. "When you have become so deeply interested in the affairs of our society that you cannot stop, you will then know how to live without work."

"Then you belong to some society?" I asked. "That gives you money?"

"Yes, but it is not like your Foresters or Sons of Italy. Nor is the money given to me in the way you think."

"How then?" I asked.

"When you know of our [society] and its powers and wonderful workings, how it protects its members at all times, and the many other things that make it so valuable, you will forget all about these others you call societies now."

"And what is the price of initiation?"

"Nothing."

"No money?" I asked, astonished.

"No," he replied, "no money, but there is a price."

"And what is it?"

"A courageous deed will be given you to do."

"For instance what?"

"Well, Don Antonio, you have heard of tyrannical people who oppress and make laws, of rich men who have so much wealth they cannot spend it, of children of such people or of traitors?"

"Yes," I replied, wondering what this had to do with courageous deeds.

"Well, it might be necessary to punish them for their greed or arrogance. . . . Perhaps they may have done something to hurt this society or one of its members, and you would be picked to punish them in secret."

"And what is this society called?"

"It has no name."

"Is it a mutual aid society?" I asked.

"No."

"Where are its headquarters?"

"There is no one place. In all parts of the world except Japan."

"In Italy?"

"Yes, in Italy."

"But the president and other officers, who are they?"

"Few of the members really know themselves. But that there are heads is certain. [Just] question an order once. [You] will be heard and punishment follows. Then too, when we are in sore need of funds, should the police become active, it is never hard to find money to protect the members."

"Perhaps," I ventured, "it is the Masons?"

"No, it is a society with no end to its power. It is bigger than the Masons and will last as long as man."

This talk of living without working plainly appealed to Comito, who said: "I must enter soon, for all here are members but me, is that not so?" Zu Vincenzo assured him that they were—"Yes, and all trusted members too, powerful in this country"—and explained that new members of the society could not be admitted until they had met its bosses and shown them "respect." Only then, he said, would they "christen you."

"Christen me?" [Comito] cried. "I have already been baptized in the Roman Catholic religion, and now you would baptize me again?"

"Certainly, but this would not be a matter of religion. That amounts to nothing. This is more serious. Something you shall never forget."

"More serious than religion?" I gasped. "That cannot be."

"Is that so?" he asked laughingly. "That is what you think."

Initiation into the mysterious society, Uncle Vincent went on, took time. First a prospective member would be tested. Next came the bestowal of "a title from us which you will bear in secret." But Comito was left in little doubt that the "test" of which Vincenzo spoke was murder:

It is so arranged that if you succeed in doing what we [set] as a test, that you cannot afford to do other than stick with us for the rest of your lifetime. It is protection for us and [means] an easy life. That is why there are so few traitors. All over the world you will find our work flourishes, and it is because of the way in which we christen you that it is so. Some fools who know nothing say there is no such organization, and they cannot be blamed. They know so little. There is one, and a big one, stronger than countries and police. Some day, Don Antonio, after this work at hand is done, you will be given a test. Then you can learn much. None of we members ever do know it all.

Comito was transfixed by these accounts, and Zu Vincenzo seemed inclined to explain further, but at that point in the conversation Katrina called out from the kitchen and the Mafioso fell silent. "I had heard enough," Comito concluded his recollection. "The papers are full every day of such tests and deeds, [though] they do not read as such." And, frightened though he was, the printer began to think that he should seek acceptance by the nameless society. He was terrified—at least, so he explained it later—that he and Katrina would be murdered when the work was finished if the Sicilians decided they could not be trusted.

ORDERS FOR THE COUNTERFEITS were coming in from all over the country. A Brooklyn banker wanted to purchase fifty thousand dollars' worth of currency, and Mafia families elsewhere in the United States had been advised that they could buy two- and five-dollar notes at the rate of fifty cents on the dollar. This was a substantial increase on the price that Morello's forgeries had commanded eight years earlier, and one that reflected the increasing professionalism of his counterfeiting operation. The gang now planned to run off twenty thousand of the Canadian bills and fifty thousand two-dollar notes in all—a total of two hundred thousand dollars in bad currency.

They printed the Canadian notes first. The zinc plates engraved by Antonio Milone for the five-dollar bills consisted of five pieces, corresponding to the colors needed for each bill: dark and light green, violet, red, and black. For all the forger's efforts, they were far from perfect; even with practice, Comito found it all but impossible to stop ink blotching between the finer lines. The first three thousand bills were run off, nonetheless—a long and tedious process, since each one had to pass through the press five times, after which the sheets were separated from their fellows and spread out on the floor to dry, a process that took longer in the cold. All in all, the job took Comito and his companions in the old stone house a month to finish, and by the time the last of the five-dollar notes had been cut, counted, and stacked in an empty macaroni box, it was the end of January.

Cecala appeared and took away the counterfeits a few days later. "There were seventeen thousand five hundred and forty five dollars," Comito remembered, "[and] I understood that [he] was to take them to the people with whom he had arranged for their distribution throughout the entire country. I heard it said also that their distribution had been so arranged that the whole lot would be put out on the public within an hour of a certain day to be set and arranged for beforehand"—a highly implausible suggestion, but one that certainly illustrated the soaring confidence within the Morello family.

The first proofs of the two-dollar bill were struck on the first of February. The American note was easier to print, at least in theory, since it had only three colors, but Comito soon discovered that the job was harder than it looked. The greens of the genuine note were particularly difficult to match. The next morning, after an entire night of fruitless experiment, the Sicilians conceded defeat. They needed the help of a specialist in printing inks, Cecala said, and Comito should go to New York to find one.

The counterfeiters had, it seems, correctly judged the shift in their companion's mood; Comito could now be trusted not to run straight to the police. Presented with five dollars to pay the fare, and driven to the nearest railway station two days later, the printer stepped off his train in Manhattan at noon. He was unaccompanied and could have gone directly to the nearest station house. Instead he took the El, the elevated railway, north to a rendezvous with Cecala at 630 East 138th Street. This building, though Comito did not know it, was one of the tenements

erected by the Ignatz Florio Co-Operative. It had been built by
Giuseppe Morello.

Two and a half months had passed since Comito had left New York,
and he had been given little reason, in that time, to suppose that Cecala
was not the leader of the counterfeiting gang. Now, though, he found his
adversary waiting on the first floor of the building, flustered and considerably concerned. There was someone else that he must meet, Cecala
said, as he ushered the printer up a second flight of stairs.

Comito had no idea who the man who stood waiting in the upstairs
room might be, nor what he wanted, but he was instantly struck by the
stranger's air of effortless authority. "He was wrapped up in a shawl of
brown color," the printer recalled, "oval face, high forehead, dark eyes,
aquiline nose, dark hair and mustache, about forty years old." The first
thing that Comito noticed "was that he had but one arm visible." The
second was Cecala's trembling deference as "with a great amount of ceremony and much display of importance," he introduced the printer to
Morello.

"I was surprised in the change in Cecala's manner when listening or
talking to this man," Comito said.

> He seemed to take the part of receiving orders from one with
> whom he was friendly but tremendously impressed with. He at
> times acted as though he feared at any moment he might cause the
> dislike of Morello. . . . The very air seemed charged with sup-
> pressed excitement. I saw from the way in which Morello acted
> and was treated that he was a leader, and the deference shown
> to him at all times was convincing of his high standing among
> these men.

The meeting was brief and to the point. Morello's interest, it transpired, lay solely in resolving the problems with the two-dollar notes. He
asked a number of searching questions about Comito's expertise, and
though he was plainly not impressed by all the answers—there was "a bit
of distrust" in his eyes, the printer realized with a jolt—he agreed that
they should find an expert in the art of mixing inks. Nothing seemed to
disconcert him. When Comito said that he was frightened of discovery,
the Clutch Hand promised to send arms and ammunition. "The first
stranger who is suspected will be killed before he is asked questions and

be buried in the wood where he will never be found," he added. "It is simple." Comito thought he spoke of murder "as though he were talking of lighting a cigar."

Morello seemed less than pleased with Cecala's performance. "Nino," he murmured as the meeting ended, "I wish that you would not have the professor come here any more. You know that I am followed night and day by the detectives, and when they see a new face they arrest him. They think much of me, but can prove nothing. So to be safe we had best have no one connect with me who might be picked up."

"I know that," Cecala said, stung by the reprimand. "But what suspicions can they have of Don Antonio? We certainly have taken him with us nicely."

"These detectives are very smart," Morello snapped. "Do I not take much time to plan to outwit them?" And with that he left the room through a rear exit and, with a piercing parting glance back at Comito, vanished in the direction of the 138th Street El.

WORK ON THE TWO-DOLLAR bills resumed on February 6 and continued for several weeks. The correct shade of green ink was obtained, after a good deal of experiment, by Antonio Milone, who added several chemicals to the inks and sent a technician up to Highland to explain the technique. The new arrival, Giuseppe Calicchio, was a sad-eyed man from the southern region of Puglia who was in his early fifties and had once been a manufacturer of counterfeits in Italy. Calicchio had worked before with the Morellos, who respectfully referred to him as "Don Giuseppe," but he had little to show for the association. "He was dressed poorly," Comito thought, "and had a suit that made him appear as a mechanic."

The counterfeiters settled back into an unvarying routine. Comito and Calicchio prepared the plates and mixed the inks; Giglio and Zu Vincenzo took the printed sheets from the press and dried them; the guards who still wandered through the woods outside would come indoors every few hours to clap and stamp their freezing hands and feet. To Comito's relief, Cecala and Cina were absent most of the time. The two Sicilians had set to work to sell Morello's five-dollar bills and spent several weeks traveling by rail throughout much of the United States to show samples to likely customers. The two men visited Chicago, Cleveland, Pittsburgh, Boston, and Kansas City, returning occasionally to inspect the two-dollar notes that Comito was producing. Cecala complained occasionally about their progress—the U.S. bills were still not difficult to spot as fakes. But aside from their infrequent appearances, the work proceeded without alarm or incident for some weeks, until February 12 or 13, when the occupants of the stone house were startled to be woken at two in the morning by a brisk knocking at the door.

No one was expected, and the counterfeiters feared the worst. Zu Vincenzo seized his rifle and Giglio a revolver, which he cocked as he stood waiting at the top of the stairs. It was Comito, still clad only in his underwear, who was sent downstairs to answer the knock—which he did very nervously, half expecting the door to be smashed down by the police. But the men waiting on the doorstep were friends: Ignazio Lupo, clad in a thick fur coat and radiating bonhomie, accompanied by Cecala and Cina, who dragged behind them a large bag crammed with the firearms and ammunition promised by Morello.

The guns that Lupo had brought consisted of several revolvers and a case of repeating rifles of the most modern design, each capable of firing fifteen shots a minute. The Wolf gave a brief demonstration of the weapons, to general acclaim; then, at his order, the rest of the gang settled down to modify the ammunition he had brought. Each slug was carefully scored crosswise across its tip, hollowing out the point to create dumdum bullets that, Lupo explained, "would spread out and tear nasty holes instead of neatly boring through." The idea was, Comito said, "accepted with much laughter," and the Wolf seemed pleased that any police who discovered the house would have "a pleasant visit."

By the time the bullets had been modified, Katrina had prepared a late supper for the gang. There were not enough chairs to go around, so she and Comito stood, "acting as waiters to these lords at the table," while Lupo, Cecala, and Zu Vincenzo gossiped and laughed with Giglio and Cina. The talk was of how the Wolf had evaded his numerous creditors and the New York police and spent the last three months hiding on a relative's farm not far away, and of Cecala's efforts to sell the forged Canadian bills.

"What news do you bring, Ignazio?" Zu Vincenzo asked at last. The meal was over and the Mafiosi were lounging around the stove sinking glasses of wine.

"You know all that I know," Lupo replied, "except perhaps that Petrosino has gone to Italy."

Comito had never heard of Petrosino, but he could scarcely mistake the bitter hatred that Morello's men felt for him. "He has ruined many," the Wolf spat. "Here's a drink to our success here, and a hope of death to him." And they all raised their glasses in a toast.

"It is a pity," Lupo added, "that it must be done stealthily—that he cannot first be made to suffer as he has made so many others suffer. But he guards his hide so well that it will have to be done quickly."

Comito thought of what Cecala and Uncle Vincent had told him of the many branches of their nameless society, of their boast that it was "possible for us to do things in one part of the world and have the other half of the affair carried out so far away that no suspicion can possibly come to us"—and of how confident they seemed to be that retribution was about to rain down on their enemy.

Whoever this Petrosino was, he thought, and whatever he was doing in Italy, he was clearly in the gravest danger.

CHAPTER 9

"SEE THE FINE PARSLEY"

=

ON THE AFTERNOON OF NOVEMBER 15, 1908, AT MUCH THE SAME time that Antonio Comito was boarding his ferry up the Hudson River to Highland, the men of Lieutenant Joseph Petrosino's Italian Squad raided a Black Hand bomb-making factory concealed in the rear of a tenement in Little Italy. The squad made five arrests and seized a total of nineteen evil-looking bombs of various designs, each of them tightly wrapped in cord or bandages and detonated by a twelve-inch fuse. Any one of these murderous devices would, the lieutenant remarked, be "fully capable of destroying a house." Three days later Petrosino was in the news again, announcing his solution to a kidnapping mystery in East Harlem, and over the next three months the Italian Squad was called in to investigate eight bombings, several dozen Black Hand extortion threats, and fully a score of murders in the immigrant districts, at least half of which were thought to be the work of various gangs.

The year was ending much as it had begun, with crime rates rising in Little Italy. The murder rate was up. The number of bombings was up, and so was the number of threats and Black Hand letters reported to the police—a total that scarcely reflected the incidence of extortion in the Italian districts in any case, as the members of Petrosino's squad knew perfectly well. Attempts at turning back the tide got nowhere. James March, a wealthy Italian American who lived on the East Side, set up a "White Hand" society, consisting of respectable men willing to take a stand against the criminals, but it collapsed in only a few months, as had a similar organization in Chicago. "I have tried," March said, slumped in defeat, "to get up a society among the Italians for the purpose of giving information against blackmailing Italians to the police, but nobody will join it. Some of them would rather pay blackmail and thus encourage the scoundrels, than give information against them."

Italian crime was increasingly businesslike, better organized, more ambitious. When Petrosino rounded up the Black Hand gang led by one Francesco Santori, he seized account books filled with meticulously detailed entries that recorded the criminals' associates and the names and addresses of the Italians who paid the gang protection money. "The list covered four pages," the detective wrote, "and showed that at least 60 men employed in labor camps in various parts of the state were paying to someone sums ranging from $1 to $3 a week." The greater sophistication of the gangs posed all sorts of problems. Petrosino himself found it increasingly difficult to employ his old methods of detection anywhere in Little Italy. Once it had been enough for him to adopt some rough disguise and mingle with the clientele in the right sort of saloons. Now he was swiftly recognized wherever he went. Crooks roped in small boys and street peddlers to warn them when the detective was spotted. The name Petrosino means "parsley" in the dialect of southern Italy, and petty criminals and toughened gangsters alike soon learned to be on their guard whenever vendors' cries of "I have some good parsley! See the fine parsley!" came ringing through the tenements.

Just as bad, in the detective's opinion, was the continuing problem of obtaining convictions in the courts. Even the relative handful of Italian criminals who were arrested, charged, and tried still all too often escaped justice because terrified witnesses would not testify against them. The only real solution, Petrosino believed, was to deport as many undesirables as possible back to Italy and stop any more like them from entering the United States.

Petrosino had been urging New York to consider deportation as a weapon for years, ever since 1905, when the Stanton Street store once owned by Vito Laduca was blown to pieces by a Black Hand bomb and the men of the Italian Squad were driven to the point of exasperation by the impossibility of pursuing their inquiry to a successful conclusion. Italian crime had become "an epidemic," the detective observed then, and "the only remedy [was] deportation." He could pick out a thousand Italians who deserved to be sent back home. Within three years, Petrosino had increased that estimate; there were now five thousand Italians with criminal records in their hometowns who ought to be deported, he remarked to *The New York Times*. As for stopping such men from emigrating to the United States, the solution was to persuade the Italian government to permit the New York police to operate a bureau on its territory. American policemen in Italy could examine the credentials of would-be immigrants and bar those with criminal records from entering the country.

There was, of course, no chance that the Italian government would let a foreign police force operate on its soil, and though the immigration laws were tightened somewhat in 1907—with the result that Petrosino received from Rome a list of fifty "notorious" criminals who could legally be deported back to Italy—the problems that the detective faced were scarcely lessened for several years. The new immigration legislation was loosely drafted, and as many as half of the men that Petrosino attempted to charge under it obtained their release before they could be hustled onto a ship back home. The only really positive change, in fact, was the appointment of a tough new police commissioner to succeed William McAdoo. Theodore Bingham, who took up the post in 1906, was the first head of the NYPD to publicly back Petrosino and vow to tackle the problem of crime in Little Italy.

General Bingham—he had served with the Army Corps of Engineers and came to New York from a long posting in Washington—was one of the more active and more controversial police commissioners in New York's long history. A brusque, inflexible character who had lost one leg and had strong views on the problem of ethnic crime, the general was soon courting outrage in an article that suggested that fully 85 percent of New York's criminals were "of exotic origin"—more than half of them Jews and a fifth Italians, he added. The latter, in Bingham's considered opinion, were "a riffraff of desperate scoundrels, ex-convicts and jail-birds," views that caused such outrage that the commissioner was forced to issue a public apology. But Bingham stuck to the promises he had made to Petrosino anyway. He was willing to provide the resources needed to strike at the roots of Italian crime.

Petrosino was invited to submit his views in a report soon after Bingham took up his new job. His recommendations were sweeping and almost entirely impractical. The detective wanted a regulation banning more than one family from living in an apartment, which would reduce overcrowding in Little Italy and help "break up the gangs." He wanted pushcarts banned as well, "because they are used to transport bombs," and much tighter controls on the sale of explosives to Italians. Above all, Petrosino said, criminal law in general should be made more severe, "more Italian," because legislation enshrining the rights of individuals merely encouraged Sicilians and Neapolitans, who were not used to it, "to let loose all their lowest instincts." The best place to start, he added, would be to tighten the existing regulations on deportation and then encourage the Italian government "to send us the record of every criminal who has moved to America."

It was a remarkable document, one that reflected Petrosino's years of frustration more than it did practical policy, and of course there was not the slightest prospect that most of its recommendations would ever be acted on. Bingham, after all, had no power to change the laws of the United States. In fact, the only one of the detective's recommendations that could easily be pursued was the suggestion that more effort be put into obtaining copies of Italian penal certificates, which were documents that detailed the criminal records of men who might seek to emigrate to the United States, and so highlighted who should be denied admission to the country.

Bingham decided to start with those.

IT WAS THE *Herald* that announced the news, on February 20, 1909.

Theodore Bingham had taken stock of the situation in Little Italy and decided on a radical solution, the New York newspaper reported. There would be no further expansion of the Italian Squad, no revisions to existing regulations. Instead, a brand-new squad had been created, a "secret service" branch of the Police Department, and Petrosino had been appointed to head it. The lieutenant had been given fourteen men and instructed to use them "to crush the Black Hand and anarchists of the city"—extortionists and political radicals alike being more than willing to use bombs in order to achieve their aims. That was not all, however, for the Secret Service branch was to have a far wider jurisdiction than the Italian Squad. Bingham reserved the right to deploy Petrosino and his men "for any purpose that [he] may see fit"—which, as the *Herald* noted in a worried aside, meant, at least in theory, that "New York now has a secret police service similar to those in Paris and other national capitals."

For the moment, though, the Secret Service branch was to be devoted to Italian crime, and it was to work covertly. Petrosino aside, none of its officers were named; nor were its men to be subject to scrutiny by the NYPD. Petrosino was to answer directly to the commissioner, and Bingham had secured thirty thousand dollars of private funding, almost certainly from the same rich Italians who had tried and failed to set up the White Hand society seeking to take a stand against Italian criminals. It was enough to keep his new squad running for at least a year without the need to account to New York's aldermen, or anybody else, as to what the cash was being spent on.

What persuaded Petrosino to accept a transfer to the Secret Service branch is not known. Quite probably he was persuaded by the commissioner's promise that the new squad would be better equipped to tackle Italian crime and that someone would be sent to Europe to obtain the longed-for penal certificates. If so, the lieutenant's enthusiasm failed to survive the general's next bombshell. Bingham wanted Petrosino himself to travel to Italy.

Going home as an important emissary, nearly forty years after arriving in the United States, ought to have appealed to the detective; it might have been seen as one of the great challenges of his career, perhaps even as an opportunity to recuperate from his exhausting round of work in Manhattan. As it was, though, the offer was not welcome. The mission demanded a diplomat, someone capable of establishing warm relations with the Italian police, which Petrosino assuredly was not. It might also be dangerous. Bingham's man knew perfectly well that plenty of his former adversaries were now at large in Italy, particularly Sicily, and that many would be only too pleased to renew acquaintance with an old enemy on their home ground.

In truth, though, the reason why the detective preferred to stay at home was more personal. At the age of almost fifty, after long decades of bachelorhood and lonely devotion to the force, Petrosino had married in December 1907. And on the last day of November 1908, his first child, a daughter, had been born. Traveling to Italy would mean leaving his wife and baby girl behind.

Most people were surprised at Petrosino's marriage, perhaps even the policeman himself. He was known among his colleagues as a determinedly solitary man, one who worked long hours and endless overtime and devoted his few moments of leisure chiefly to music. Petrosino was an inveterate operagoer, haunting the stalls and the standing areas of the Metropolitan Opera in his snatched hours away from work; at home, in his own small apartment, he liked to practice on the violin. In the autumn of 1906, though, at an Italian restaurant on Spring Street, his eye had fallen on the proprietor's daughter. Her name was Adelina Saulino, she was a widow, and she was thirty-seven years old, nine years the detective's junior.

The courtship was protracted, conducted in the few hours Petrosino was able to snatch away from the demands of the Italian Squad. Mostly it was conducted at the restaurant, under Adelina's mother's eye. It was two years before Petrosino proposed, and according to a family tradition, the betrothal was not especially romantic. "You too must be very lonely," the detective began the wished-for conversation. "We could get along well together."

The marriage was a happy one, however, and Petrosino began to spend less time at work and more at home, particularly after his first child was born. By February 1909, his old enthusiasm for police work had noticeably diminished. He felt tired, even dispirited, and that was hardly surprising, since he had served very nearly three decades with the NYPD, more than almost any other officer, and half of them as a detective, with all the long hours and the dangers that entailed. He was forty-nine years old, he was due a pension, and he hated the idea of being away from his new family. Bingham had told him that the round trip to Italy, traveling via Genoa, Rome, and Palermo, would take almost three months.

According to the faithful Sergeant Vachris, who came down to the pier to wave him off, Petrosino left New York in "the worst of moods." He knew that he would be taking risks traveling in Sicily. "Watch out, boss," Vachris would remember warning him. "Down there, everything's Mafia."

PETROSINO SAILED IN COMFORT on the liner *Duca di Genova,* traveling first-class with cash supplied from Bingham's secret service fund. He could hardly do so under his own name, however, and the confidential nature of his journey dictated that he adopt a false identity. Petrosino made the voyage under the alias Simone Velletri, supposedly a Jewish businessman. He carried with him two smart, brand-new yellow leather suitcases and spent the first days of the voyage sequestered in his stateroom, studiously avoiding other passengers. When he did eventually emerge on deck, he told those who asked that he was returning home to Italy in search of a cure for a digestive complaint.

Petrosino's caution was entirely justified. He was too well known in the Italian community, and far too recognizable, to pass undetected on a vessel filled with New Yorkers. And on board the ship, sailing in steerage, was at least one criminal whom he had personally arranged to have deported to Italy and who might welcome the chance to take revenge. As it happened, there was no trouble on the *Duca di Genova,* but Petrosino was certainly recognized by at least one member of the liner's crew: Carlo Longobardi, the purser, who had seen his photo in the papers and approached him so enthusiastically that Petrosino was emboldened to confide his true identity, even unbending to the point of spending several hours regaling his new acquaintance with memories of his most famous cases. Petrosino made another acquaintance on board, too: a younger man who went by the name of Francesco Delli Bovi and was so often seen in Petrosino's company that later the Italian police would take a special interest in him. When they discovered that Delli Bovi had disembarked with Petrosino at Genoa and then vanished—no trace of him was ever found—it would be suggested that the mysterious passenger had been a secret agent of some sort, sent to worm his way into the detective's confidence.

Whatever the truth, Petrosino left the *Duca di Geneva* keen to complete his mission as rapidly as possible. Boarding the first available train for Rome, and clutching a slip of paper on which his new friend Longobardi had recommended some hotels, he arrived in the Italian capital that same evening, registered at the Hotel Inghilterra under another assumed name, and was up early the next morning to call at the U.S. embassy. The ambassador, Lloyd Griscom, had already received a telegram from Washington about him and provided letters of introduction to the Ministry of the Interior and to the local police. Petrosino filed both in his yellow suitcases alongside the materials he had brought with him from New York: a list of two thousand Italian criminals whose penal certificates he wanted, notes on several possible informants in Palermo, and his .38-caliber revolver.

Lieutenant Petrosino apparently felt safer in Rome than he had aboard the *Duca di Genova*. He was a stranger in the city, and there seemed no reason why he should be recognized, nor why anyone should take the slightest interest in what a squat, balding "businessman" was doing. He called formally on the chief of police, seeking the necessary permissions to continue with his mission and adding letters of introduction to the authorities in Palermo to the contents of his suitcases. For the rest of his stay in the capital, however, the detective took care to retain his anonymity. Planning a quick visit to his family home in Padula, he warned his brother, who still lived there, "not to let anybody know anything, not even your wife."

Petrosino would have felt considerably less sanguine had he known that his absence had already been noticed in New York, and far worse had he realized that the Italian-American newspaper *L'Araldo Italiano*, reporting on Bingham's secret service plans days earlier, had printed the information that he would leave for Italy—a detail that the newspaper could have obtained only from someone inside the Police Department. The same story ran in several other dailies, most damagingly, from the lieutenant's point of view, in the *New York Herald*'s European edition, which was printed in Paris but widely circulated throughout the continent. The article in question was scarcely sensational; it was tucked away on page six of the newspaper, and it mentioned Petrosino only in passing. But it was enough. News of the detective's mission appeared in several Italian papers, and by the time he reached Rome, hundreds of people in Europe and the United States knew that he was making for the city and that he would travel on from there to Sicily.

Petrosino's first inkling that his secret was out came on the afternoon of his second day in the Italian capital. Pausing for a moment outside the Press Club on the Piazza San Silvestro, he was hailed by two Italian American newspapermen whom he knew from New York. Visibly annoyed at being recognized, the detective begged the men to tell no one he was in the city. The reporters agreed, even offering to show him around the sights, but it soon became clear that they were not the only people to have spotted Petrosino. That same afternoon, while walking through the city center, the lieutenant noticed a poorly dressed man staring at him. "I know him," the detective told his friends, though he could not remember where they had met. Afterward, when the man made off, Petrosino put his police skills to good use and followed at a distance. He trailed the stranger to a nearby post office and watched while he composed a telegram. When the man stepped to the counter to send it, the detective sidled closer and heard enough to realize that the cable was on its way to Sicily.

HOPING, APPARENTLY, TO CONFOUND anyone still following him, Petrosino decided not to travel to Palermo on any of the passenger ships that shuttled up and down the Italian coast. Instead he took a train to Naples, where he paid the skipper of a mail boat to take him on board. The little steamer sailed south overnight, reaching Sicily next morning, and the detective stepped ashore in a quiet corner of the Palermo docks at dawn on February 28. He was convinced that his arrival had gone unremarked.

Perhaps feeling he had left his enemies behind in Rome, Petrosino soon recovered most of his self-confidence. He continued to take elementary precautions, checking into his hotel under a false name and donning a rough disguise for several of the journeys that he took outside the city to gather penal certificates. But he also made a number of simple errors, creating a trail that any determined enemy might follow. He opened an account under his own name at the Banca Commerciale in Palermo and freely revealed his true identity to the waiters in the Café Oreto, a homely place on the Piazza Marina where he ate supper with dangerous regularity. After his first few days in the Sicilian capital, Petrosino also felt secure enough to walk around the town without his revolver. He left the gun in his hotel room, stowed inside one of his suitcases.

Everything about the detective's actions over the next few days suggests that he was anxious to finish his work in Sicily as rapidly as possible. He worked ferociously long hours, beginning on the morning of his arrival, when, having called briefly on the U.S. consul, William Bishop, he put in almost a full day's work in the Palermo courthouse. He spent the next three weeks either in the courthouse or in the records offices of half a dozen outlying towns, copying out hundreds of certificates by hand. On Sundays, Petrosino stayed in his hotel and typed up his notes.

By the end of the first week of March, Petrosino had accumulated more than three hundred penal certificates from all over western Sicily, each of which was enough to secure the deportation of an Italian criminal from New York. He had also gone a long way to fulfilling a second aim of his mission, disbursing almost two thousand lire from Bingham's secret service fund to establish a network of informants on the island. This was especially dangerous work, since the men whom he approached were mostly criminals. Several, almost certainly, were more likely to report Petrosino's appearance in Palermo to their friends in the underworld than they were to assist the hated police, no matter how much money there might be involved. The detective's presence in the Sicilian capital could not remain secret for much longer.

The one thing that Petrosino did not do—in fact, conspicuously avoided doing for days after his arrival in the city—was to advise his Italian counterparts that he was in Palermo. He seems to have concluded, for whatever reason, that he could not trust the local authorities, and it was not until March 6 that he at last went to call on Baldassare Ceola, the commissioner of police, to present his letters of introduction.

Petrosino had some reason to fear that the carabinieri were in league with local crooks and Mafiosi. Accommodations had existed for many years between gangsters and police in many Sicilian towns, to the mutual benefit of both. But Ceola was a northerner, sent to Palermo from Milan eighteen months previously in the express hope that he would stay free of the taint of corruption, and he felt very much offended—as much by Petrosino's evident suspicion as by his rudeness in not calling earlier. Meeting the renowned American detective in person, moreover, Ceola found himself underwhelmed. The commissioner was a gentleman, like most senior Italian police officers: urbane, well educated, and at ease in the highest of society. The short, scarred Petrosino, with his abrasive manners and New York–accented Italian, made a distinctly unfavorable impression. "I saw at once," Ceola wrote to the prefect of Palermo, "that Lieutenant Petrosino, to his disadvantage, was not a man of excessive education." An unwise one, too, Ceola thought. When he offered the services of a bodyguard, Petrosino refused point-blank to accept one.

It seemed for some time that the detective was right, that his presence in Palermo was still unknown, and that word of his arrival was, if anything, more likely to leak through the police than anyone else. He worked on steadily for another week without apparent interference, and on Thursday, March 11, he called again on Bishop to inform him that his work was nearly done, that he would be leaving for New York in a few days' time. Each time he left the consulate, however, Petrosino had to pass through a large crowd of Sicilians hanging around outside, mostly men waiting in line for visas, and this time he was recognized. Two Palermo criminals had joined the line. One of these men was Ernesto Militano, a young thug described by the police as "an incorrigible robber of prostitutes" who was renowned as the owner of "the finest pair of moustaches in Palermo." The other was Militano's friend Paolo

Palazzotto. Palazzotto had returned to Sicily less than a week earlier after spending several years in the United States. He too had been deported from New York by the Italian Squad.

The two men both caught sight of the detective, and Palazzotto jerked forward as though to confront him. He was restrained by Militano, and Petrosino emerged from the crowd unscathed, clambered into a waiting carriage, and clattered off. Palazzotto had to content himself by shouting out, loud enough for everybody in the crowd to hear: "There goes Petrosino, the enemy of the Sicilians. He's come to Palermo to get himself killed!"

IN FACT, HAD PETROSINO only known it, his presence in the capital was already all too well known, not only to Ceola and the police but to a number of his enemies as well.

The *Herald*'s article of February 20 was responsible for most of the damage. It had been picked up by *Il Mattino* of Naples and then run by several other Italian papers. Enrico Alfano, the powerful former head of the Neapolitan Camorra, seems to have learned of the mission in this way. So, too, according to one newspaper, did a group of Baltimore Black Handers that Petrosino had broken up and had deported the previous summer. Best informed of all, however, were the members of the New York Mafia. According to Antonio Comito's testimony, Giuseppe Morello and his men knew that the detective had sailed for Italy as early as February 12, a full week before the *Herald* published and only three days after the *Duca di Genova* sailed. Their intelligence, no doubt, had come from *L'Araldo Italiano,* which had broken the news of Petrosino's mission three days earlier.

Lupo and Morello had every reason to wish Petrosino dead, Lupo perhaps most of all after the humiliation of the beating he had taken, and the two men had long bemoaned the difficulty of killing the policeman in Manhattan. "Damned detective," the Wolf exploded once within Comito's hearing. "The devil guards himself too thoroughly. When he walks it is with a loaded revolver in his hand covered by a pocket, and two policemen without their blue coats walk near him eyeing everyone." In Palermo, though, things would be much easier. The family had plenty of friends in the city, and Petrosino had a good deal less protection.

The chance was far too good to miss, and within days of the detective's sailing a pair of Mafiosi left for Naples and Palermo, their fares paid by the Morello family. Both men sailed under aliases, but their real names were Carlo Costantino and Antonio Passananti, and they had been employed in Brooklyn as managers of two of Lupo's grocery stores. Arriving home, they explained that they had come to Italy to avoid some pressing creditors.

Costantino and Passananti spent a few days with their families. Then they traveled into the Sicilian hinterland to call upon the man they had come to Sicily to find. He had been with Morello in New York years earlier and was now the most powerful Mafioso on the island. His name was Don Vito Cascio Ferro.

FRIDAY DAWNED OVERCAST, threatening rain, and Petrosino took an early train out of Palermo. He spent the morning in the courthouse of the nearby town of Caltanissetta, copying penal certificates there, and was back in the Sicilian capital that same afternoon, keeping an appointment before retiring to his hotel room to type up his work. At some point he pulled out a small pocketbook he had brought with him from Manhattan, which contained his handwritten notes on Sicilian criminals. Reaching for a pen, the detective added a new name to the bottom of a list. "Vito Cascio Ferro," he scrawled in his spidery script, "born in Sambuca Zabut, resident of Bisaquino, Province of Palermo, dreaded criminal."

What prompted Petrosino to make this note on this day is an intriguing question that has no certain answer. Cascio Ferro had not lived in the United States for years—he had made his escape from New York on the morning after the Barrel Murder, the only member of Morello's gang to do so. Traveling from Manhattan to New Orleans, he had returned to Sicily in 1904 and steadily accumulated a great deal of power. Petrosino had probably been given his name by one of his informants, but when and for what reason is a mystery. As things turned out, however, the addition of Cascio Ferro's name to the policeman's notebook on this day of all days would seem especially significant.

Petrosino remained closeted in his hotel room until evening. As it grew dark, at about 6 P.M., a violent electric storm broke over Palermo, pelting the stones of the Piazza Marina with heavy rain. The deluge lasted for an hour and a half, and by the time it ceased at 7:30, most of the people of the town had sought the shelter of their homes. The square was empty when Petrosino grabbed his umbrella and overcoat and hurried to the Café Oreto for dinner.

The streets were slick with water and the clouds overhead were still so black it seemed likely the storm would resume. Petrosino did not linger over dinner. He took his usual table up against a wall, where he could keep an eye on everyone who entered the café, and ordered pasta with tomato sauce, fish, fried potatoes, and a half liter of wine, all for 2.70 lire.

According to the recollections of the café's waiters, the detective was just embarking on the cheese course when two men entered the restaurant, looked hurriedly around, and went over to his table. The conversation was brief, and the two men did not sit down; after a few moments Petrosino waved them away. But as the strangers exited the restaurant, Petrosino rose to follow them. He threw down three lire to pay for his supper and left without waiting for the change.

On other evenings, the detective had turned left out of the café to return to his hotel. But on this night he crossed the road and went straight ahead, making his way around the Piazza Marina and keeping to the fence enclosing the Garibaldi Garden. The police who retraced his movements the next day thought he had been heading for a spot he had agreed to for a meeting with the strangers from the restaurant.

He walked exactly 220 yards, almost to the northwest corner of the square. The time was 8:50 P.M.

Three shots rang out in rapid succession across the piazza, then, after a short pause, a fourth, which most likely was the coup de grâce. The square was almost deserted after the rain; the only people in the vicinity was a group of passengers waiting for a streetcar on the square, and of these, only one, a sailor named Alberto Cardella, was brave enough to investigate. Cardella ran the thirty yards to the corner of the Garibaldi Garden in a few seconds, quickly enough to see a small, squat man sway away from the fence and collapse and to watch two men as they burst from the shadows, crossed the road, and lost themselves in the courtyard of the Palazzo Partanna opposite. Several gates in the courtyard exited into nearby alleys, and a few moments later the sailor heard the sound of a carriage driving away. Almost immediately after that, the lights illuminating the square suddenly flickered and died. Someone had cut the flow of gas to the piazza, making it impossible to organize an effective pursuit.

By the time another of the streetcar passengers had hurried to the nearest shop for candles, almost a quarter of an hour had passed and Cardella had been joined by the medical officer from his ship. The doctor made only a cursory examination; even by candlelight it was clear that the stocky figure sprawled along the fence was dead. Petrosino had been hit three times at close range, in the right shoulder, the cheek, and the throat. The third wound had been the fatal one. He lay next to his umbrella, blood still oozing from his mouth; his derby hat—long a familiar sight in Little Italy—had rolled toward the gutter. A heavy Belgian revolver sat abandoned on the pavement a few feet away—one of the assassins', since the detective's gun was still in his suitcase at his hotel. Going through the dead man's pockets, Cardella found a police badge, a checkbook, a notebook, some cash, and an unstamped picture postcard, addressed to Petrosino's wife, which ended with the salutation "A kiss for you and my little girl, who has spent three months far from her daddy."

IT TOOK FIFTEEN MINUTES for the first policeman to reach the scene, and rather longer for Commissioner Ceola, summoned hastily from his box at the theater, to take command of the investigation.

Ceola knew the murder would be a sensation. Petrosino was a U.S. citizen, and no U.S. police officer had ever before been killed outside his country in the line of duty. The Americans were bound to be outraged at the murder and to wonder why their man had not been afforded better protection. And the killing itself—with the getaway carriage standing waiting and the perfectly timed extinguishing of the piazza's lights—had clearly been meticulously planned. There was also the mystery of the dead man's willingness to follow two strangers out into the Palermo night. For some reason, Petrosino had trusted the men who had killed him.

Ceola's men rounded up as many witnesses as they could to the events in the Piazza Marina, but to little effect. No one had heard much, and only Cardella would admit to having seen a thing. A mechanic named Luigi Schillaci, whose job it was to oil and lubricate the streetcars at the nearby terminus, said that he knew the men who had fled into the Palazzo Partanna, but by the time he reached police headquarters he had changed his mind. "I didn't see anything and I didn't hear anything," the engineer now insisted.

With Ceola to urge them on, the Palermo police were nothing if not energetic. They rounded up 140 suspects, among them Ernesto Militano and Paolo Palazzotto, the crooks Petrosino had encountered outside the American consulate. Both men excited a good deal of suspicion; they had been in the Café Oreto earlier that evening, and Militano had suddenly shaved off his famous mustache—"Because my woman likes me better without," he protested. In the end, though, Ceola and his men decided that the murder had been too well planned and too cleanly executed to have been the work of petty criminals. As the days went on, they became increasingly convinced that Petrosino had been murdered by the Mafia.

The most important targets of Ceola's roundup were Sicilians whom Petrosino had helped deport from the United States, and one of the first men held was Carlo Costantino. A porter who came from Costantino's hometown, Partinico, told the police he had seen Morello's man reclining on a bench in the Piazza Marina only a few hours before Petrosino was shot. Antonio Passananti had been sitting next to him, the witness added; he remembered the two men clearly because he had thought that both were in America. A report from the police in Partinico brought more incriminating evidence. Vito Cascio Ferro, Ceola learned, had turned up in the town a few weeks earlier, asking after Costantino and his partner and evidently well aware that they were due in from New York. There was also the peculiar matter of a pair of telegrams that Costantino had sent and received. The first, addressed to "Giuseppe Morello, New York," had been wired the day after the Mafiosi arrived in Sicily, and it was so peculiar—apparently in code—that the telegraph operator at Partinico had forwarded a copy to the local chief of public safety. "I Lo Baido work Fontana," the message said. Morello's equally inscrutable reply was found in Costantino's pocket. "Why cut his whiskers off?" this cable read.

Only Antonio Passananti and Cascio Ferro were not among the 140 suspects whom Ceola detained. Both men had disappeared from their usual haunts on the day of the murder, and neither could be found by the police.

AS SOON AS WORD of the Petrosino murder got out, the Sicilian authorities were deluged with letters and telephone calls offering theories, tips, and information. The correspondence came from all over Italy and from the United States, thousands of pieces in all, but though Ceola had his men review every page of every letter, he took only three of the items seriously. All came from New York, and two were, apparently, written by the same man—someone who possessed a remarkably close knowledge of the inner workings of the Morello gang. The third letter, postmarked Brooklyn, had been written in Sicilian dialect but was probably composed by a man who had been born in New York. All three communications were anonymous.

None of the letters made complete sense by itself, but by reading the three of them together it was possible to piece together what had happened. According to the first—sent from New York on March 13, only hours after news of Petrosino's murder reached Manhattan—the killing had been ordered by Morello, Lupo, the Terranova brothers, Giuseppe Fontana, and three or four other Mafiosi, who had banded together to send a pair of agents to Palermo. The second communication, mailed two days later, added the names of several other members of the Morello family and explained that the detailed planning of the killing had been turned over to Cascio Ferro. The third letter was the only one to mention Costantino and Passananti by name. According to this missive, the two Partinicans had actually murdered Petrosino.

Ceola included all three of the letters in the report he was preparing for the Criminal Court in the Sicilian capital. They deserved to be taken seriously, he said, in large part because they contained information that was known to the police but had never appeared in the newspapers— most especially the involvement of Costantino and Passananti and the fact that the two men had sailed from New York to Palermo. There was also a clear motive for the murder: if not, as Ceola believed, because Morello feared deportation back to Italy, then certainly because of the threat that Petrosino posed to his family's criminal activities. Cascio Ferro's involvement also made a good deal of sense, given the boss's influence in Sicily—more so when Don Vito was finally arrested three weeks later, stepping off a train at Bisaquino station. A police search of his home turned up several incriminating bits of information, among them a photograph, taken in New York, that showed Cascio Ferro with Morello, his wife, Lina, and Giuseppe Fontana.

"Lieutenant Petrosino's arrival in Palermo frightened too many people and threatened too many interests," Ceola concluded in his interim report.

For this reason an international coalition was organized against him. Furthermore, the fatal ambush, carefully set up by the murderers, with the assistance of false confidential agents who succeeded in convincing the ingenuous detective that he could manage without the co-operation of the police, clearly shows that the preparation of the crime must be laid to an association of criminals possessing substantial resources.

Who else could that be but the Mafia?

CEOLA'S CASE WAS compelling but it was not watertight. It made perfect sense, and the circumstantial evidence apparently confirmed it, but it was doubtful that it would convince a jury. It was not enough for Costantino and Passananti to have been seen in the Piazza Marina hours before the shooting when there were no witnesses to put them there at 8:50 P.M. The mysterious telegrams might mean nothing as well as something. And to nobody's surprise, Cascio Ferro, who had had nearly a month to prepare for his inevitable arrest, turned out to have the strongest alibi imaginable. On the night of the murder, he explained to the police, he had been staying with the Honorable Domenico De Michele Ferrantelli, a nobleman who also happened to be a member of the Italian parliament. Ferrantelli, for reasons best known to himself, had recently employed the Mafia boss as an agent and placed him in charge of the sale of produce from his landed estate.

Cascio Ferro's story was not enough to stop Ceola from obtaining a warrant for his arrest, nor from confining him in a Palermo prison pending further hearings—though the Mafioso made light of that restriction by paying for a comfortable private cell. It was, however, easily sufficient to damn any attempt to bring Don Vito to trial, particularly after Ferrantelli confirmed, on his honor, every word of his friend's statement concerning his whereabouts on the night of March 12. And as things turned out, the combined influence of the two men was also easily sufficient to cost Baldassare Ceola his job. On July 17, 1909, a little over three months after the Petrosino murder, Commissioner Ceola received notification that he was being recalled to Rome and compulsorily retired. Four months later, on November 16, Cascio Ferro and Costantino were quietly released from prison and the charges against them both were dropped.

The Petrosino murder continued to crop up in the American press from time to time for years to come; there were rumors that the detective's murderer was working in a Pennsylvania coal mine or hiding out in Mexico. But none ever amounted to much. The killing remains officially unsolved.

NEWS OF PETROSINO'S DEATH reached New York within hours. The *Herald,* with its network of European correspondents, was the first paper to receive the word; its man in Rome cabled an account shortly after midnight, New York time, less than eight hours after the shooting and in time to make the morning edition. The *Herald*'s story was on the streets by dawn, and it was exclusive. A few hours later, just before ten, the first official telegram arrived—

> PALERMO, ITALY
>
> PETROSINO SHOT. INSTANTLY KILLED IN HEART OF CITY THIS EVENING. ASSASSIN UNKNOWN. DIES A MARTYR.
>
> BISHOP, CONSUL

—and by noon, the evening papers were already hawking their first extras. The shooting was front-page news in every paper, and all in all the press coverage of the story was enormous, even greater than it had been when President McKinley had been murdered eight years earlier. Most New Yorkers felt a sense of outrage, mixed with shock. Adelina Petrosino, woken at 2 A.M. by one of the *Herald*'s men, broke down in tears at the news; she had just received a letter from her husband in which he spoke of the risks he faced and told her how much he was looking forward to coming home. Emotions in the Italian quarter, though, were mixed. "Not in years has there been as much excitement in Little Italy," the *Tribune* observed. "A stranger in one of the cafés last night was an unwelcome guest. . . . Italians discussed the murder on corners and in cafés, and while some showed sorrow there were others who gloated over the death of the Italian detective."

The police, the paper added, were "boiling with anger" at the news, and for weeks hundreds of ordinary immigrants were routinely abused and harassed in the streets. Privately, though, there were those at headquarters who conceded that Petrosino should bear some responsibility for his own death. The lieutenant had fatally underestimated the power of the Mafia, and the influence and ruthlessness of Morello in particular; stripped of the security and the support he had enjoyed in Manhattan, the detective had made himself an easy target in Palermo, a woeful misjudgment that he had further compounded by leaving his wife with practically nothing. Unlike the great majority of New York's policemen, Petrosino had been an honest man and had never banked a small fortune in graft. It took a public subscription, which raised $10,000, and the decision to grant the widow a $1,000-a-year city pension, to properly secure Adelina's future.

The one thing that almost everybody was agreed on was that Petrosino had died in the service of the city of New York and that the city should do right by him. Arrangements were made to have the body embalmed by a "professor," brought in specially from Naples, and returned to Manhattan for burial. When the casket was unloaded at the city piers on April 9, nearly a month after the murder, a large number of people were waiting for it.

The crowds were vastly greater at Petrosino's funeral on the twelfth. The day had been declared a public holiday, and a large assembly, well over twenty thousand strong, lined the streets as the murdered policeman was solemnly escorted on his final journey. Bells tolled; flags flew at half-mast on every public building. And when the last bars of Verdi's *Requiem* had faded in the interior of St. Patrick's Old Cathedral and the hearse set out for Calvary Cemetery in Queens, it was accompanied by a thousand policemen, two thousand schoolchildren, and representatives from sixty Italian associations, all in uniform.

Only one thing marred the dignity of the proceedings. Adelina's wish to have an open casket had had to be refused. Something had gone badly wrong with the embalming process, and when the coffin lid was lifted in the undertaker's parlor, Petrosino's corpse was black and swollen with decay. The only solution was for the casket to be sealed, and when the congregation filed slowly past the bier, a large photograph of Petrosino perched on top of the coffin did duty for the policeman's face itself.

CHAPTER 10

SHEEP AND WOLVES

=

THE NEWS OF PETROSINO'S DEATH, WHICH HAD REACHED NEW York on March 13, took only one more day to travel the fifty miles up the Hudson River to Highland.

Lupo brought it, early in the morning, when he arrived to inspect the latest batch of counterfeit notes manufactured in the woods. The spring thaws, which were at last melting the thick drifts of snow, had turned the grounds and unpaved roads to mud and made travel from the village to the old stone house more difficult, if possible, but the Wolf was in a buoyant mood. He pronounced the latest batch of two-dollar notes excellent and said Calicchio deserved a medal for his fine work with the inks. Then Lupo turned to Zu Vincenzo. "Petrosino has been killed," he said with a smile. "It was successful!"

"I knew it would be done successfully," Uncle Vincent replied, and Comito heard the triumph in his voice. Cecala wanted to know where the murder had been committed.

"In Palermo."

"Then it was surely well done," said Uncle Vincent.

"The way it was planned, it never could have missed in Palermo," said Lupo. "It is well he was fool enough to go there."

"Damn him," said Cecala, "it was a death too good for him. How many sons of mothers has he condemned for nothing!"

Zu Vincenzo thought the assassination would scare other policemen off the idea of going to Sicily in search of evidence to use against the Mafia. "No one will now dare to go to Palermo, for in going they will find death," he said. "But it is too bad that it could not have been done here. It would have helped us a great deal."

That thought did not bother Lupo unduly. The money used to send men after Petrosino had been raised in New York, he pointed out. "Some credit is due to us, though the Palermo crowd will get most." Cina opened a bottle, and Morello's men toasted their success in wine.

Production of the counterfeits continued at the same steady pace throughout March, The gang printed about five hundred notes a day, including $20,400 in American two-dollar bills, and the results improved significantly; Calicchio had painstakingly retouched the plates to tidy up the less convincing details. Cecala and Cina were delighted; the improved notes, they said, were easier to sell. Morello, in New York, also seemed pleased, since large additional supplies of paper began appearing in Highland every few weeks. According to Cina, the Clutch Hand had ordered that a total of $5 million in forged currency be produced, saying that work would cease only "when we were all rich."

Comito and Calicchio were less happy, Comito in large part because he had still barely been paid—only a few dollars here and there for five months' work, so little that he and Katrina could not even afford new shoes. But there was also the problem of the five-dollar bills. Morello's ambitious target would be almost unattainable without improvements in the Canadian notes, which, since they were being printed from photoengraved plates, were still blotchy and unlikely to convince anyone who took the time to study them. Cecala and Cina were having considerable trouble selling the fives; on one trip along the eastern seaboard, the pair had disposed of four thousand dollars' worth of U.S. two-dollar notes but found no takers at all for the foreign currency.

"That was not your fault," Lupo reassured Comito when the two Sicilians reported back to the stone house; "the plates are no good." But the other members of the gang were not so forgiving. When word of the problems with the five-dollar notes got out, even the most junior among them became abusive. Giglio, Sylvester, and the guard, a young farmer named Bernardo Perrone, told Comito that he was stupid, ate too much, "and should be fed to the hogs." Cina threatened the printer with a knife. And when another minor problem arose, several members of the gang lost what remained of their self-control:

> Bernardo grabbed me by the throat and forced me back against the wall, his fingers sinking in my throat until I thought that I was dying. Sylvester grabbed a revolver and cocked it, and, while

Bernardo held me, walked over and forced the muzzle into my mouth until the sight on the end cut my throat way back and I could feel its coldness against the back of my head inside. Giglio grabbed an axe and said he would dismember me. . . . They threatened to dig out my eyes and make my woman eat them raw.

It took Katrina's desperate intervention to make the men back off, and even then, Comito thought, "they desisted unwillingly, Bernardo saying: 'It is a shame to let such a good start go unfinished.'"

Comito took his companion's threats sufficiently seriously to fear for his life, and once, when they were left alone for a few minutes, he found one of Lupo's rifles and showed Katrina how to use it. "If people come with some excuse or other to get you," the printer told her, "it will be a sure sign that they have murdered me. Before they get you into a trap where they can kill you and hide your body, shoot them dead. Do not hesitate; they are devils and will likely enough come to you smiling to disarm your suspicions. Shoot, and shoot straight."

The real problem, as Comito knew, was that his position within the counterfeiting gang had been entirely undermined by Calicchio's presence. The master printer, with his greater experience and his engraving skills, was now the man to whom Cecala and Cina turned when there were problems to be solved; Comito had become a mere assistant, and a largely useless one at that. Even Lupo's mood underwent a change in time. When Cecala and Cina returned from another journey down the coast with alarming tales of angry customers and the news that a large number of five-dollar notes remained unsold, the Wolf exploded. Comito's shoddy work had cost the gang eight thousand dollars, he said, and the poor-quality bills would have to be destroyed. "What is his use here?" Lupo demanded of Zu Vincenzo as his temper flared. "This ugly Calabrian is not worth what he eats. He should have been tied up and his work burned on his head."

Only the risk of betrayal and, probably quite as important, the prospect of living in the woods without a woman to cook and clean for them seems to have prevented the gang from dispensing with Comito and Katrina, and both were acutely aware that the obvious solution, killing them, was unlikely to bother their companions for a moment. "What you are trying to do is get me to blow your damn brains out," snarled Cina when the printer begged to be allowed to return to New

York. "But that is too nice for a fool like you. You are dealing with gentlemen or long ago you would have been rotting in the farm here—you and the woman. Go on now and work before I stick you."

And Comito scurried away, "like a whipped dog, with my tail between my legs."

THE ONLY WAY TO fix the problem of the five-dollar bills was to engrave new plates. The job took a long time, two months, and it was not until the middle of June that Calicchio completed the work. The engraving was, Comito thought, "marvelously perfect," and the plates, for U.S. notes this time, produced fine proofs almost immediately. When Cecala took a few samples with him to show likely customers in New York and Hoboken, he returned with orders for more than $15,000 of currency.

As the pace of work increased, it became hard even for Comito to keep track of what had been produced. A stock of $10,000 worth of two-dollar notes and $14,700 of the Canadian fives was ready by the end of May, and they ran off $15,000 more in twos that month. A short while later, Cina returned from a trip through Boston, Buffalo, and Chicago demanding $13,500 more of the new twos, and Cecala had similar success in Philadelphia and Pittsburgh. In all, the total value of the forged bills printed in the Highland woods almost certainly approached $100,000, and the work took Comito and Calicchio until the middle of July to finish.

How much the Morellos made from this is very hard to calculate. Cecala and Cina did not often sell at the Clutch Hand's price of fifty cents in the dollar. The best they usually obtained was 35 cents, and often they were forced to accept as little as 20 or 25 cents—though even this was twice what other counterfeiters realized. The earliest batches of notes fetched so little that the operation was barely profitable when travel expenses had been deducted. Calicchio's notes, though, were of better quality, and tens of thousands of dollars' worth were printed; they alone could easily have earned $8,000 or more, which was an appreciable sum at the time. Whatever the real profits, the one certainty is that Morello kept the money for himself. Calicchio had been retained on a salary of $20 a week, which was not paid with any regularity. Comito, who had been promised $500 when the work was done, received no more than $40 for his services, and that over eight months. Katrina got nothing at all.

Work was finally suspended for the summer when the last of the two-dollar notes were printed, trimmed, and packed in bundles of a hundred. It would begin again in four months' time, Cina announced, when the first batch of notes had been disposed of. Until then, the press, the plates, and inks would be nailed up in boxes and hidden on his farm.

The next day, the dismantled press and plates were loaded onto Cina's wagon and hidden beneath a pile of hay. "Boys," the counterfeiter said, "the work is done. From tomorrow each man can attend to his own business." The gang dispersed. Comito was handed a single genuine five-dollar note and used it to take a train back to New York.

The enforced nine-month stay in Highland had had one beneficial consequence. Economic conditions had improved throughout the country while Comito was away, and there were jobs to be had in printing once again. It took only three days for the Calabrian to find work in an Italian-owned print shop in Brooklyn, and there, for the first time in nearly a year, he felt secure. Cina had promised to find him and pay the five hundred dollars he was owed, but Comito neither believed him nor even wanted the money. He was glad merely to have escaped Highland alive and vowed never again to risk his life for such a paltry reward. To keep the Morellos off his back, Comito wrote one last time to Cina, informing him that he planned to leave the United States for Italy. Then he went instead to live in Brooklyn, studiously avoiding places where he might encounter members of the gang.

And all went well for the best part of a month. Then, on August 12, 1909, Comito picked up one of New York's Italian-language newspapers and read of the arrest of a number of Sicilians. They had been charged with passing two- and five-dollar counterfeits. He checked the description of the bills: They were all forged Morello notes. Cecala and Cina were no longer the only people looking for him. Now he was wanted by the Secret Service, too.

CHIEF WILLIAM FLYNN had spent the six years since the Barrel Murder working hard to improve the Secret Service's efficiency. He had added several more agents to the strength of the New York bureau and assigned one of them, the Italian-speaking Peter Rubano, to undercover work in the immigrant quarter, where the latter spent time hanging around street corners and saloons. Rubano had started this work around 1905 and gradually became familiar with several members of the Morello family, most notably Lupo the Wolf. Lupo took Rubano into his confidence on several matters but never mentioned forgery to him; to compensate, Flynn also developed several new Italian informants, whose identities he kept strictly confidential.

Under Flynn's energetic leadership, the agency's New York bureau had become everything that the NYPD might have been but was not: efficient, discreet, and above all extraordinarily persistent. Known counterfeiters were subject to "life surveillance," not consistently, since the Secret Service lacked the manpower for such ambitious operations, but every few months at least, so that Flynn kept up to date with where the men lived and what they were doing. Thanks to this policy, Giuseppe Morello had been placed under intermittent observation ever since 1903, and over the years the service had come to know him fairly well, certainly well enough to have a firmer grasp than the police did as to how dramatically his power and his influence had spread. According to John Wilkie, Flynn's boss in Washington, the Morellos lay behind as much as "60 percent of the Black Hand extortion that has gone on in the United States for the past 10 years . . . as far west as Chicago and as far south as New Orleans." But Wilkie also knew that intermittent harassment by the detectives of his local police precinct didn't cause the Clutch Hand much concern:

> The oftener Morello was arrested, the more insolent he became. By this time he had come to sneer at the police and dictate whatever orders he saw fit; to the Italians he had come to dominate. . . . [His] maimed hand interfered with him as an outside man, so he did the thinking and ordered others to execute his plans.
>
> A rough and hard-faced scoundrel, he sat in his office and sent out orders.

Flynn, who had a love of personal publicity quite at odds with the professional discretion he maintained at work, would sometimes talk to newsmen about the tactics he employed to tackle counterfeiters, at least in general terms. The Chief stuck to two sensible but vital principles, a reporter from *The New York Times* explained ("First, hide your evidence-getting methods. Second, make the detection of crime not so much the result of one-man cleverness as a mosaic of information gained from many sources by specialists"), and both were plainly in evidence in the New York bureau's tracking of Morello. But the same journalist identified two other important reasons for the Chief's success: "His ideas are big. He shows it by the way he sweeps aside minor details and goes to the very heart of a subject. [He is] a man with suggestions of a bulldog's tenacity and words fewer than those of the average New Yorker."

For all that, though, for all the Secret Service's efficiency, Morello's care and cunning kept Flynn from discovering for the best part of a year that new counterfeits were being struck, and though counterfeiting in the old stone house had gotten under way in November 1908, it was not until the following May that the first forged bills appeared in circulation. These were the gang's first attempt at the Canadian bill, and thus were relatively easy to spot. They poured into Secret Service headquarters from bankers in Philadelphia and storekeepers in Pittsburgh, from Buffalo and Chicago, Boston and New York, and when it became clear that the bills were being passed in the Italian districts of each city, the order went out to mount surveillance of likely suspects. In New York, that meant Morello above all.

Flynn responded by ordering several of his men to recommence an intermittent watch, but there was nothing especially incriminating about the Clutch Hand's movements, at least not at first. Morello was too wary, too careful to fall into any of the obvious traps. He took pains never to be seen with known counterfeiters, nor to pass any forged bills. There were no more meetings with Comito, either, and for a while the Chief was uncertain whether the first family actually was behind the flood of counterfeits.

Deprived of any useful leads, Flynn turned instead to studying the phony bills. They were moderately good forgeries, he reported—of a far higher quality than the amateurish fives that the Clutch Hand had been manufacturing in 1900 or the greasy dollars he had had printed in Italy two years later, but still not fine enough to fool an experienced eye. The counterfeits were also suitable only for small-scale use in shops and taverns; because all the notes were printed from the same plates, they bore identical serial numbers, which meant it would be highly dangerous to pass more than one of them at once. Industrial though the Mafia's production was in scale, the operation remained at heart a minor fraud.

Thanks in large part to Morello's caution, it was not until summer that Flynn made his first real breakthrough, and it came not in New York but in Pittston, Pennsylvania: a grim, crime-ridden coal town with a large Italian population and a significant criminal presence. Forged bills began to surface there in June, and in sufficient quantity to persuade Flynn to venture south to carry out his own investigation. The decision was, in truth, one born of desperation, but it proved to be a good one nonetheless. Detailed questioning of local storekeepers led to a Sicilian of dubious reputation known locally as Sam Locino. Locino was put under surveillance. Once Flynn was certain that Locino really was passing the forged notes, he had the man arrested.

Locino proved to be an interesting character. He was scabrous, shifty, and untrustworthy, though possessed of a broad streak of self-interest that made him potentially useful to the Secret Service. In common with all the queer-pushers employed by the Morello gang, he worried about the prospect of a lengthy prison sentence but was vastly more frightened of betraying his suppliers. It took Flynn time to persuade his prisoner to talk, and when Locino did it was only after receiving ironclad assurances that he would be protected by the government, that he would not be forced to testify in open court, and that his name would be kept out of the press.

It was only when all three promises were made that Locino offered Flynn the thing he wanted most: the name of the man from whom he had acquired his counterfeits. The notes came from another Sicilian, the pusher whispered: a man from Corleone named Giuseppe Boscarini. Boscarini, he told the Chief, was a much older man, perhaps fifty-five, of middling height, with graying hair. He lived in New York but was a regular visitor to Pennsylvania. Better yet, Locino was confident that he would be willing to sell more counterfeits.

It was the news the Secret Service had been hoping for, and Locino's casual mention of Boscarini's hometown was a scrap of information filled with meaning for Flynn, whose years of painstaking surveillance had taught him that Giuseppe Morello always preferred to depend on other Corleonesi when he could. Still, much needed to be done to make even the beginnings of a proper case, and the next step was to obtain evidence in writing. Locino was ordered to send a letter to Boscarini inquiring about the availability of his counterfeits and asking for samples of the latest notes. His story was that he wanted to discover how easily the bills would pass in Pittston.

Flynn had experience of counterfeiting trials and knew that any attorney worth his fee would seek to prove that correspondence produced in evidence was bogus. Taking Locino's letter with him, he went to call on Pittston's mayor and then the local chief of police. Both men were asked to accompany the Chief to the local post office, where they witnessed him register the envelope addressed to Boscarini and mail it to New York. Registration, Flynn calculated, would force the counterfeiter to call at the post office to collect his mail. That in turn would give his operatives the chance they needed to identify him.

The plan worked precisely as the Chief hoped. Agents from the New York bureau stationed themselves inside the post office closest to Boscarini's home and identified the Sicilian when he came to collect his mail. Now armed with a detailed description of their suspect, Flynn's men followed him home and then kept watch on the premises until their target emerged the next morning and headed back to the post office. There Boscarini purchased a special delivery envelope, scribbled down Locino's details, added a false return address, and stamped the letter with two one-cent stamps placed upside down. Armed with that precise description, Flynn had no trouble intercepting the package at the Pittston post office the next day. It proved to contain two sample Morello notes: a two and a five. Now the Chief had the evidence he needed to arrest and convict Boscarini.

The investigation had reached a critical point, Flynn told his superiors in Washington. To swoop down on Boscarini would expose Locino to the vengeance of the Mafia, and that was something that the Chief was not prepared to do; aside from betraying a man he had promised to protect, the arrest would achieve little but drive the leaders of the gang into hiding. Flynn had a better idea, anyway. Instead of detailing men to pick up Boscarini, he gave Locino thirty-five dollars and sent his informant to Manhattan, an apparently satisfied customer eager to purchase a hundred dollars' worth of counterfeits. Locino located his supplier on a street corner in Little Italy and made the necessary arrangements, handing Boscarini the Secret Service money in exchange for a fresh batch of counterfeits. The exchange passed off without a hitch. Neither Sicilian was aware that Flynn had subtly marked each of the genuine bills, placing an extra dot of ink among Abraham Lincoln's shirt studs. By the time Locino had repeated the same procedure weekly for the better part of a month, it was September and the counterfeiters were holding well over one hundred dollars of the Chief's marked bills.

Flynn still needed to establish a connection between Boscarini and his superiors, the real leaders of the counterfeiting gang. It was not an easy one to make; the Corleone man was careful, and days of discreet surveillance produced no useful leads. Still, Boscarini could not run his business indefinitely without obtaining fresh supplies of counterfeits, and one afternoon in the early autumn the Secret Service operative assigned to tail him found himself taking a train up to Harlem, where the suspect hurried down a busy street and ducked into a doorway. The agent noted the address: 233 East 97th Street. It was a spot that Flynn knew well. Boscarini had disappeared into Lupo's old wholesale grocery store—a place now owned and operated by Morello.

The Chief felt certain that this was the spot where the counterfeiters gathered, but putting the store under observation was by no means a simple matter. Morello was certain to be wary, and East Harlem, in 1909, was more exclusively Italian than Little Italy had been six years earlier. Flynn's English-speaking agents could not hope to loiter on the street outside for weeks without being spotted, and arousing the least suspicion would likely ruin the entire operation. The solution was to use their Italian-speaking operative, Peter Rubano, who rented a vacant room across the street. The Secret Service's new base was sufficiently discreet to allow a succession of agents to maintain the watch; comfortably equipped, to enable them to do so constantly; and far enough above street level to shield the operatives from passersby. It also offered a first-rate view across the road into the windows of Morello's store.

The ruse worked well, and for several weeks agents noted all the comings and goings at the place. Flynn's men spotted Boscarini several times, then Antonio Cecala, and on one occasion even Lupo—who had not been seen in New York for nearly a year, not since the day he had fled his creditors. Better yet, the Clutch Hand himself paid several visits, and various other members of the Morello family flitted in and out. All this, of course, was merely circumstantial; there was no clear proof that any of these men were engaged in a conspiracy. The agents' logbooks, though, were certainly instructive. Boscarini and Cecala habitually entered the building separately, the operatives observed. But they were often on the premises together, and, when they were, they met in a third-floor room shielded behind "great boxes of macaroni and other Italian groceries piled high in the windows." These meetings were brisk and businesslike—none lasted longer than fifteen minutes. And afterward Boscarini always had fresh supplies of counterfeits.

The discovery that Antonio Cecala was implicated in the counterfeiting scheme was the biggest breakthrough yet in Flynn's expanding investigation. Another team of Secret Service men was drafted in to track the stocky arsonist, and, as their reports came in, the whole thrust of the inquiry changed. It was Cecala, the Chief realized, who was managing the distribution of the forged bills, and Cecala who could lead him to the shadowy Sicilians wholesaling notes from Chicago south to New Orleans. As more and more operatives were pulled from their duties across the country to assist with the surveillance, Flynn gradually uncovered the most ambitious counterfeiting scheme the Secret Service had encountered in its fifty-year history.

The network so painstakingly unraveled was a pyramidal distribution operation. Cecala, Flynn calculated, "made frequent trips to various cities, establishing agencies for the circulation of the bills," and there were six of these in all, each headed by a man who came from Corleone and was unswervingly loyal to the Morello family. These deputies in turn recruited half a dozen assistants to distribute forged currency in the various districts of their towns. Here, too, reliability was paramount. "It was," Flynn found, "necessary for these deputies to vouch for any person before Cecala would allow them to have any of the bogus money. . . . Thus the notes passed through at least three hands before they reached the purchaser, and sometimes the transaction was even more complicated."

The great virtue of this carefully designed system, from Morello's point of view at least, was that it insulated the Mafia leaders in New York from the distribution of the currency. It was Cecala's associates and their deputies who ran the greatest chance of discovery and the risk of arrest, but to arrest them would in no way help to secure Lupo or Morello. Cecala had issued each of his men dire threats regarding the violent consequences they and their families would face if anybody dared to talk, and "the prisoner, even if he had desired to testify against the counterfeiters, would not know who the leaders were."

It was all highly frustrating. "Like malignant spirits," Chief Flynn mused,

Lupo and Morello lurked in the dark and directed the movements of the pawns under them in the great counterfeiting scheme that was to make them wealthy and get them out of the difficulties into which the Ignatz Florio Association had plunged them. They took no chances—at least they thought they took none—and certainly they were not in the danger to which they exposed their aides.

It was they who pulled the strings, and their puppets responded. . . . Their system was mysterious, baffling, and almost perfect. But there were flaws in it, and the Secret Service found those flaws.

IT WAS LUPO WHO unwittingly supplied the final piece of evidence that Flynn required to bring his case to a conclusion.

The Secret Service never fully understood what prompted the Wolf to return to New York that autumn of 1909, with the creditors of his failed grocery business still not satisfied. Lupo told the few who dared to ask that his mind had been disturbed, that he had been working for his brother, a grocer, in Hoboken, and that he had been unable to discharge his debts only because he himself had been a victim of extortion—forced to hand over ten thousand dollars to a Black Hand group that had been threatening his chain of stores. Flynn believed that the more likely explanation was that Lupo had simply grown bored of hiding in the wilds of the surrounding countryside. Whatever the reason, the Wolf was soon a common sight in Little Italy again. He hired lawyers to fight his creditors on his behalf and took up many of his old activities, exuding much of his old self-confidence. Luckily for Flynn and his investigation, he also continued to make trips to Highland to inspect the latest batches of counterfeits.

The Secret Service operatives detailed to follow Lupo had strict orders not to risk discovery, and the first time they trailed the Wolf to Grand Central Terminal they found that he was taking extensive precautions against being spotted. First Lupo purchased a cigar and went into a smoking room, where he sat for some time watching the activity around him. Next he had his shoes polished, while he sat perched in a chair high on the bootblack's stand from which he carefully surveyed the crowd.

From there he left the station altogether, walking along West 44th Street until he reached a second entrance to the terminal. At that point he ducked back inside the station and hastened to the ticket office.

Flynn's men had dropped well back in order to avoid detection, and by the time they reached the ticket line Lupo was completing his purchase. The closest agent was too far away to hear the destination, but, as he watched, the Wolf proffered a two-dollar bill and received fifty cents in change. Wherever Lupo was headed, at that fare it had to be a spot no more than sixty miles outside New York.

Later that day, back in his office, Flynn ran through all the possibilities. "At first I thought it was Poughkeepsie," the Chief recalled. "Then I began to put two and two together, and, remembering that Lupo when he fled from New York went to Ardonia, a little town back of Highland, N.Y., I became convinced that the counterfeiting plant must be somewhere along the west bank of the Hudson River, not far from Highland. The country back of the hills that line the river is very wild and very lonesome, an ideal place for the plant of counterfeiters."

The more the Chief thought about it, the more certain he became that he was right, and by the end of September a team of Secret Service agents had arrived in Highland and begun to question the locals. Flynn's men soon discovered that Cecala owned a large farm outside the village—the local postmaster recalled receiving packages for him—and that he was often accompanied by Cina. Cina's close relationship with his brother-in-law and neighbor, Vincenzo Giglio, gave the agents another useful clue.

The old stone house in the woods evaded the operatives for a little longer, but in the end they found the Highland farmer who had leased it to Cecala.

The Chief was satisfied he had enough. It was time to move in on the Mafia.

FLYNN HAD ONE REMAINING concern: The size of the counterfeiting operation that was being uncovered was such that it would be difficult to arrest the whole group simultaneously, which meant there was a real risk that some of the gang would realize what was happening and get away. Aside from Morello and Lupo, Cecala and Cina, Boscarini and Nick Terranova, Flynn's list included several other influential Corleonesi: Domenico Milone, a director of the Ignatz Florio Co-Operative Association and now nominally the owner of the grocery store on 87th Street; Stefano LaSala, a power in the city's gambling underworld who had risen to become one of Morello's chief lieutenants; and two recent additions to the ranks of the first family, the Vasi brothers, Pasquale and Leoluca. Among them these men occupied twelve different addresses in New York, from Italian Harlem to Long Island City, Queens, and at least three more in Highland. Failure to secure the counterfeiters together was likely to have serious consequences, since any who received sufficient warning would certainly try to get away.

Flynn's great concern was that Morello himself would manage to escape. The Clutch Hand had always been a dangerously elusive man; weeks of careful surveillance in the Italian quarter had demonstrated that his movements were worryingly unpredictable, and to make matters worse there were a number of ways in and out of the tenement he occupied at 207 East 107th Street, and he appeared to use them all. The whole building, consisting of sixteen apartments, was occupied by members of Morello's family or their tenants, and Flynn could not even be certain which apartment the boss would be in on the day the raid was planned. The only way to be certain of locating Morello and covering every possible exit was to obtain exact, timely intelligence of the internal layout of the tenement. And that meant sending an agent into the building to investigate, with all the risk that that entailed.

Flynn decided to assign the task to the youngest and most anonymous of the Secret Service team: Thomas Callaghan, a seventeen-year-old so youthful-looking that he had been posing as a shoeshine boy along the street. It was a daunting assignment for an inexperienced agent, more so because the Chief wanted the job done late at night, when the Clutch Hand came home for the evening. Decades later, when he was the storied leader of the agency's Chicago bureau, Callaghan still recalled it as the most terrifying assignment he had ever undertaken.

"It was," the teenage operative said,

> a dangerous rookery in which to be trailing a killer. It was a four-story building with long hallways, closed stairways, and bare walls. When I finally saw Morello coming down the street around midnight, I noticed that he had his two brothers, Vincenzo and

Ciro, and another man with him. I ducked into the house and sneaked up to the second floor. It was pitch dark because the janitor had turned out all the lights at ten o'clock.

I knew Morello and his companions had entered the tenement, so when I heard them coming up the stairs, I tiptoed to the fourth floor. And then I thought, What'll I do if they keep going to the top?

Sure enough, they didn't stop at the third, but kept coming up. They were going to find me skulking there with no reason to be hanging around their place. I figured I was a squashed bug no matter what I did. Then suddenly—I don't know why—I decided to walk nonchalantly down the stairs.

I met them between the third and fourth floors, my heart thumping like a pile driver. When they heard me and when we came face to face, what do you suppose Morello said? "Scusa, please." I stepped aside and they kept going. I'll never know how I got down.

Gasping like a landed fish, Callaghan stumbled back out onto East 107th Street and glanced around. He had not been followed, and he had the information that Flynn needed: the building's layout and its exits, and above all the intelligence that Morello was spending the evening where the Secret Service wanted him, in an apartment on the highest floor.

It was a long night, the agents staking out the building would always recall—long because it was the middle of November, long because they were all so nervous, and long because Morello worked on until dawn. They waited and waited for the lights on the fourth floor to dim and for their man to fall asleep. It was not until nearly eleven the next morning, when Flynn calculated that he had to be in bed at last, that half a dozen agents and several detectives from the Italian Squad crept back into the tenement and up the creaking wooden stairs. The date was November 15, 1909.

Flynn had a key to the Clutch Hand's flat, either a copy requisitioned from the building's janitor or a skeleton key capable of opening a variety of doors. He turned it in the lock so gently that there was no click. The door swung open and the Secret Service men moved softly into the slumbering apartment. The detectives had their weapons drawn, but there was nobody about.

The second room that they tried was a bedroom. Morello lay sprawled out on his mattress, deep asleep. His half brother Nick Terranova dozed on a second bed alongside him. "We had virtually no desire to waken them," the Chief remarked, "until we were sitting on them."

A silent gesture, a flurry of movement, and the two Sicilians were roughly pinioned before they were properly awake. Flynn's caution was justified the moment that his men began to search the room. "Under Morello's pillow," he reported,

> we found four fully loaded revolvers; beneath Terranova's, five. That's bound to impress you. And two of Morello's guns were loaded with cartridges containing buckshot—three or four pellets in each cartridge. One might compare Giuseppe to a one-man war, and I frequently wondered whether he didn't fear himself at times.

The silence of the slumbering apartment had been well and truly shattered by this time, and the muffled sounds of the brief struggle roused the remainder of the household. Three or four half-dressed Sicilians emerged, all furious, all disputing the arrests; an Italian-speaking policeman supplied Flynn with a translation. Then Lina Morello herself appeared, an infant daughter in one arm and fury blazing white-hot on her face.

"The furore was spectacular," said Flynn.

> Morello's wife made herself extremely unpopular with us by drawing a wicked knife. It took two of us to get it away from her. Bereft of the knife she subsided into tears. She was to be murdered by the police. Her great, good husband was to be slain. And what was to become of these magnificent children of hers?
>
> Fatherless! Motherless! Ah, yes, she knew. They would be thrown into the river at night, like swine. Ah, but there was wickedness in the world when the police should break up this happy Christian home. The dogs of police. She would spit upon them.

The confusion in the packed apartment was indescribable. Morello and Terranova sat together on their beds, each clad only in his underclothes. The other members of the family milled around, shouting and arguing, creating the greatest possible confusion while another of their number took hurried advantage to conceal several pieces of incriminating evidence. A pack of half a dozen letters was thrust into a pocket in Lina's apron, which lay on the table. Lina herself scooped up her daughter Mary, who was only eight months old, "and it was more or less noticeable," said Flynn, "that she was stuffing something in to the child's clothes." Grasping her infant in one arm, Mrs. Morello made to leave the room, giving vent to another angry volley of Sicilian as she did so. The burden of this outburst, Flynn's detective friend explained, was that "she would go into the next room and put her beautiful children to sleep and then she would go to the prison and be mutilated by the dogs of police."

It took two large Secret Service men to part Lina from her daughter, and she resisted them with such determination that the agents "sustained 40 or 50 minor bruises" in the struggle. Then Operative Thomas Gallagher

suggested to Mrs. Morello that there might be something of interest to the government wrapped in the cloth that protected the little Morello, and instantly the mother became very emphatic in her native manner of making us understand that she "no understand."

Gallagher is a man of Irish extraction from the environs of Boston. In other words, he has a humorous instinct. So he suggested that maybe the poor baby needed a fresh diaper. There was a flash of volcanic fire in the mother's eyes and two strong arms held her secure while Gallagher removed the cloth from the infant's limbs.

Three notes, written by Morello to the heads of Mafia families elsewhere in the country, were found inside the infant's diaper. Lina's apron pocket contained several lurid Black Hand letters. All in all it was, Flynn thought, a first-rate morning's work.

Morello was allowed to dress and was led away. His half brother Terranova attempted to escape arrest by posing as "a crazy man . . . he just rolled his eyes, stuck out his tongue, and babbled incoherently," as the Chief recalled. "Still, he was brought in, and though he quit the crazy routine, he proved to be about as garrulous as a clam." And, up and down the city at much the same time, other operatives were raiding other addresses. Fourteen Sicilians were detained in all, and careful searches of their homes produced some incriminating finds. A bag containing $3,600 in counterfeit two-dollar bills was found under a bed in the Vasi brothers' flat, and the news from Antonio Cecala's home on East 4th Street was even more rewarding. Agents Burke and Henry seized $221 in genuine currency from the counterfeiter's wallet, and this, when carefully inspected, proved to include two of the subtly marked notes that Flynn had passed to Sam Locino. Another link between the counterfeits and their suppliers had been made.

The only member of the Morello gang to elude arrest was Lupo, who was then living incognito in Brooklyn. To Flynn's irritation, his men had lost track of the Wolf some days before, and he continued to evade pursuit for almost two months, only to be trapped when a characteristic piece of opportunism went badly wrong. Detectives from Hoboken had been investigating the theft of an upright piano and succeeded in tracing their suspect to a rented house in fashionable Bath Beach. The man they were after turned out to be Lupo. When the detectives recognized their quarry, they called the Secret Service bureau and invited Flynn to send an agent to assist in their planned raid. Flynn sent Peter Rubano, and Lupo was picked up without incident on the morning of January 8 as he strolled along the street outside his home. The Wolf was unarmed, and his pockets proved to contain nothing but a nail file and seven dollars in cash.

Lupo joined nine other prominent members of the Morello family in jail. Bail had been set at unheard-of levels: $10,000 for Morello, $7,500 for Cecala and Boscarini, and $5,000 apiece for the other members of the gang. None of the Mafiosi could raise such sums, so Morello and his men stayed in the cells while Flynn began preparing for his day in court.

THERE WAS STILL ONE yawning gap in the Secret Service case: the lack of a confession from a member of the Morello family. Flynn was not optimistic of obtaining it, nor was it strictly necessary; the Secret Service had obtained plenty of convictions in the past without the assistance of admissions from any of the defendants. A confession, though, would make it vastly easier to guarantee a guilty verdict, and though the Chief was certain none of Morello's men would talk, there was one member of the counterfeiting gang who might.

It's not certain when Flynn first heard Comito's name. He had not realized that the printer so much as existed when he raided the Morellos' tenement in mid-November. By the middle of December 1909, Flynn had discovered that two men working together had produced the Clutch Hand's counterfeits, and by Christmas, thanks to an informant, he knew about Calicchio. But as late as the first days of January, as his reports to Washington attest, the Chief was still referring to the second of Morello's printers as a mysterious "Calabrian," and he had no idea who he was or where he lived.

It was luck, pure chance, that led the Secret Service to Comito only a week or two before the gang was due in court. Charles Mazzei, one of the Italian informants so carefully cultivated by Flynn, knew Calicchio, and it was Mazzei who passed Flynn word that the master printer had been working for Morello. Through Calicchio, Mazzei then heard that there had been a second man printing notes at Highland. But though Flynn hung back in the hope of learning more, his new lead yielded little more than that until, one day early in January, Calicchio unexpectedly saw Comito scuttling toward him down a Brooklyn street. The two men exchanged wary greetings; they had not seen each other for six months. When Calicchio spoke critically of Cecala and Cina, though, Comito, suddenly emboldened, supplied his colleague with his new address. That crucial scrap of information, passed by Calicchio to Mazzei and by Mazzei to Flynn, led almost immediately to a raid.

The Chief, by his own admission, had no inkling that Comito was an unwilling accomplice, and he expected to discover evidence that his new suspect was heavily caught up in the counterfeiting scheme: "bundles of [forged notes] in his rooms," perhaps, "together with letters and other evidence connecting him with Lupo, Morello and the others." Certainly Flynn anticipated trouble; he sent nine men to make the arrest. It was a surprise when they found nothing. A careful search of the Calabrian's apartment revealed "not a single bogus note, nor any blackmail letters," and Flynn began to change his mind.

Comito, Mazzei had already told him, was an even-tempered little man derisively known to the Morellos as "the Sheep." That name, the Chief decided, appeared well deserved; his prisoner was simply too timorous to be a full-fledged member of the Mafia. Comito, he admitted, "had [not] profited at all by the counterfeiting scheme" and "was not at heart a criminal." This discovery was a surprise but also an opportunity.

If the Sheep had been coerced into working for Morello, there was a chance that he might talk.

Flynn, who had conducted hundreds of interrogations, realized instinctively that his prisoner would not respond to bullying or threats.

> Instead of placing him under arrest I sat down and had a long talk with him. . . . I soon learned that if I could get him to talk I would have a witness who could fasten guilt upon almost every man of the band.
>
> This strange character was influenced to a remarkable extent by kindness. There were tears in his eyes when I told him that neither he nor Katrina would be arrested. . . . The girl was spirited away and put under the protection of the government and Comito himself was under my own supervision. For days he was in the Custom House in New York, never leaving the building except disguised and with me.
>
> For days I worked over him, always treating him with the greatest kindness and striving to overcome the fear which at times got the better of him. . . . Each night I went with Comito to some Italian restaurant and dined on spaghetti with tomato sauce and onion soup, until I felt inside like a Sicilian and added inches to my girth. At first, Comito glanced fearfully about him and only played with his food. He knew the men with whom he had to deal, and he knew their methods, but gradually he came to look on me as [someone who] would protect him even against the secret vengeance of the men from Corleone.

Bolstered by Flynn's repeated reassurances, Comito's weak resistance crumbled. His apartment had been raided on the fourth of January. Within a week he had reached an agreement with his captors: testimony against the Morello family and, in return, protection, immunity from prosecution, and the money to make a fresh start somewhere other than New York.

With that the whole story came pouring out. Comito, Flynn discovered, had vivid, almost perfect recall. He remembered absolutely everything, it seemed: his visits to the Sons of Italy, the introduction to Cecala, the offer of a job in Philadelphia, the river voyage to Highland, and the remote house in the distant woods. More than that, Comito unpicked the mechanics of the counterfeiting operation, providing information sufficient to incriminate nearly a dozen members of the gang, and offered evidence against the gang's principals, Lupo and Morello, who would normally have been almost impossible to convict. He described the Wolf's visits to Highland, toting guns and giving frowning approval to a succession of proofs, and his fateful encounter with Morello, clearly the leader of the gang, a man who behaved as though the enormous defer-ence that the others showed him were simply his due.

Taken down in shorthand and typed up, Comito's testimony ran for well over a hundred pages, or nearly fifty thousand words. It was the most complete and most incriminating body of testimony that the serv-ice had obtained for years, and Flynn thought that it would be sufficient to convict every member of Morello's family. For the time being, though, it was plainly best to keep that knowledge to himself. The less that the Clutch Hand knew about Comito and his evidence, the better.

LUPO AND MORELLO, meanwhile, were not idle. There were the usual stiff compulsory levies among Italian businessmen in Little Italy, to pay the costs of a defense led by Mirabeau Towns, one of New York's best-known but most expensive trial lawyers. Orders went out for the de-struction of the Highland printing press, and the remaining stock of counterfeits was burned or buried. There were also attempts to con-struct alibis for the prisoners; Cecala, for example, made arrangements for two witnesses to claim that he had been ill in bed with pneumonia on several crucial dates.

To nobody's surprise, the most elaborate of these efforts were made on Morello's behalf. Marshaled by Nick Terranova, who had been reluc-tantly released by Flynn when no firm evidence could be found to prove his involvement in counterfeiting, the members of the Clutch Hand's family designed an elaborate alibi. Morello, they decided, should claim to have been ill for the preceding year. Unlike Cecala, though, whose wit-nesses were a daughter and a friend, the boss would call on solid, inde-pendent testimony to shore up his alibi: A pair of doctors, Salvatore Romano and Salvatore Brancatto, would swear on oath that he had been incapacitated.

Romano, of course, had helped the Morellos before. In January 1910 he was still practicing in Rochester, the town to which he had been obliged to flee in order to avoid the attentions of the Clutch Hand's family, and he knew nothing of Flynn's arrests until early in January 1910, when he unexpectedly received a letter from his mother in New York.

"This is the way it was done," he recalled a few months later.

> Mrs. Morello and the mother of Morello and the brothers of Morello went to my mother and began to talk to her. They [said] that he had got into very serious trouble. They also said that the only way that he could possibly be saved would be to produce an alibi. I was to say that he was not out at any time he was accused of being out. . . . I could then testify that I was treating Morello at the time and he was unable to get out when the charges alleged.

The boss, his relatives decided, would say he had been confined to bed with rheumatism throughout late 1908 and most of 1909. It was by no means an implausible claim; Morello, Romano said, was a hypochondriac, "always complaining," and though he was not genuinely ill, he apparently believed that he did suffer from the condition. To convince a jury that the boss could have taken no part in the counterfeiting scheme, however, Romano and Brancatto would have to testify that they had visited their patient regularly at home and had found him entirely immobile. That meant committing perjury in a federal court—something that Romano, for one, felt deeply apprehensive about.

Reluctant though he was to tangle with the Morellos again, the doctor knew he had no choice.

> My mother asked them not to call me, that it would be putting me into trouble, and that I would have to abandon the business I started. They told her that it was an absolute necessity that I come down from Rochester to testify. If I did not come, they said, Morello would be sentenced surely. . . . So my mother wrote to me. "This is the last proposition that they are going to give you," she said. "I think you cannot avoid coming down."

Romano agreed immediately. "I knew the character of the men I had to deal with," he said. "I knew that if I refused and Morello got a big sentence they would put the whole thing up to me. I thought of my mother down here [in Italian Harlem] going in and out at night, and I had something to fear."

Nothing happened for several weeks. Then, sometime in the middle of January, the doctor received an urgent telegram from Manhattan. Nick Terranova had sent it. "Be in New York tomorrow," the message said, and Romano obeyed.

"I am very sorry to trouble you," Terranova said when the two met.

"I know what you are losing. I know that you are doing this for us, but it is absolutely necessary. You are in no danger at all."

He said, "How many times a week do you want to say that you saw him?" I answered once a week. "I want to make my testimony as light as possible," I told him, "so as not to get into trouble with the Court." He said that once a week was probably too little; "Make it twice a week," he said.

Reluctantly, Romano agreed; in court, later, he would actually go further, testifying that he had called on his patient "two to three times a week" and diagnosed "articular rheumatism . . . which gave him severe pain and fever" in his legs. To make sure that all the stories were kept straight, Terranova took Romano to the holding cells to reacquaint him with Morello. "Don't worry," the Clutch Hand assured him. "There is no danger at all. Nobody saw me out of the house, and I was as pale as a ghost at the time."

Joe Petrosino had met his death eight months earlier by severely underestimating the power of the Mafia. Now Morello was making an equally serious mistake: By placing his faith in Dr. Romano, he was badly underestimating Flynn. The Clutch Hand plainly had no real idea how strong the government's case was, nor did he realize that Flynn had penetrated most of the protective layers in which he had cocooned himself. At trial the Secret Service would be able to call on statements from no fewer than eight operatives to prove that Morello had been out and about in the Italian quarter when he was supposed to be confined to bed. Flynn also had Comito's testimony. Against that weight of evidence, the word of two Sicilian doctors would prove to be of little consequence.

MORELLO'S TRIAL GOT UNDER way on January 26, 1910. It was held in New York, in the federal courthouse on Houston Street, a utilitarian building on a noisy thoroughfare ruled over by Judge George Ray. There were nine defendants. Aside from Lupo and Morello, Cecala and Cina were also standing trial, and Calicchio, the aging printer, too. Fourteen minor members of the gang had been convicted on charges of pushing counterfeits a few weeks earlier; a dozen others, including Giuseppe Boscarini, were to be prosecuted separately in the spring.

The members of Morello's family put on a show of strength on the first day. By order of the Terranova brothers, Ray's courtroom was "thronged with a rabble of Italians," and a large crowd of Sicilians who had arrived too late to find space on the public benches milled about in the corridors outside. Some of the latter broke into the empty U.S. marshal's office, where a razor-sharp stiletto was later found embedded to a depth of several inches in the wall. Further crude attempts at intimidation followed. A second knife turned up the next day on the jury benches as proceedings opened for the morning. It was removed before the jurors saw it, but word of the discovery got out, and the knife and its meaning was one of the chief topics of conversation in the courthouse that day. Efforts were made to silence witnesses as they took the stand as well; according to *The New York Times,* at least one Sicilian spectator made lurid "death signs" during the first week, "hissing and sweeping nails across his throat." Judge Ray, a pinched, humorless man of below-average height who had heard more counterfeiting cases than any other man on the East Coast, would stand for none of this. He had the hissing Sicilian ejected from the building and stationed extra ushers in his court, and there was no more trouble after that.

The trial itself had been scheduled to last a month. Morello and his codefendants faced a huge number of charges—an unheard-of 548 in total, all felonies and all carrying considerable sentences, but the real reason why so much time had been allotted to what appeared a relatively simple case was not made clear until the first full day in court. It was then, with a rustling along corridors and consternation rippling through the defense, that Antonio Comito took the stand and began to tell the jury of his experiences in Highland.

Morello had expected an acquittal until then. There was plenty of evidence, he knew, against his chief lieutenants: Cecala had been caught with Flynn's marked bills, and the Vasi brothers with a large quantity of counterfeits. But these men were expendable, and there was nothing, or at least so the Clutch Hand thought, to link him conclusively to the counterfeiting scheme.

The printing press lay at the bottom of the New Paltz River, north of Highland, tipped off a bridge by several members of the Cina family. There was no reason to suppose that its resting place would be discovered. The plates, meanwhile, had been retrieved by Salvatore Cina's wife and concealed eight miles to the east, in the hamlet of Ardonia. Mrs. Cina had buried them on a farm owned by another of Morello's associates—a Sicilian farmer who went by the Anglicized name of William Oddo. It had been Oddo who concealed Ignazio Lupo while he was on the run from his creditors in New York.

Word that the plates were hidden at the Oddo farm had been far less welcome to Morello. The farm made a decent hiding place, of course. It was remote and seldom visited, and the Clutch Hand had no reason to suppose that Flynn knew of any connection between Oddo and the Morellos. But quite unknown to Mrs. Cina, the farm was already being used by the first family for other purposes. Morello had long felt a need for some remote spot in which to dispose of the bodies of his victims— men whom he wished to see disappear for good, leaving no trace of their whereabouts and no clues for the police. The Oddo farm met his criteria. Beginning, it seems, in 1908 or 1909, a number of bodies had been buried there, among them the remains of several men who had found out more about counterfeiting in nearby Highland than was good for them. Flynn later would talk of the spot as "Morello's private burial ground," and though there is no way of knowing just how many corpses were interred on Oddo's land, one thing is certain: Mrs. Cina unknowingly had deposited her bundle so close to the graves that any search would be more likely to uncover a dead body than reveal the missing plates.

Even the news of Mrs. Cina's error, though, did not anger the Clutch Hand so much as the sight of Comito entering Ray's courtroom. The diminutive Calabrian cut a curious figure in the witness box—he was nothing but a "thin, nervous youth," one newspaper reporter thought, and the enormity of his decision to give testimony was plainly terrifying him. But though Comito dared not meet the gaze of the defendants (he delivered his evidence with his eyes fixed firmly on a spot on the opposite wall), he held nothing back. By the end of the first day of his testimony, most of the reporters present thought there was no hope for Morello.

The Clutch Hand and his followers, a newsman from the *Sun* observed, were shaken to the core by Comito's unexpected appearance in the witness box. They "had not heard of his falling into the hands of the Secret Service men, and when he was sworn in as a witness against them . . . the glares of the eight men in the prisoners' row were not calculated to lend him encouragement." As Flynn had planned, though, it was far too late by then to stop the printer from testifying. Desperate measures were certainly attempted—a price of $2,500 was placed on the Calabrian's head only hours after he began his testimony, and Mirabeau Towns, in cross-examination, did his best to portray Comito as a blood-thirsty outlaw, a Calabrian bandit of some infamy now heavily involved in the white slave trade whose sworn testimony could not be trusted. In the absence of a single witness to back up Towns, however, such sugges-tions had little chance of doing damage.

There were few bright spots in the case thereafter for the Morello family. The Clutch Hand himself chose not to give evidence, as did Antonio Cecala, and though Lupo did testify in his own defense, noth-ing he said disproved Comito's allegations. Romano and Brancatto both appeared, and both men gave their evidence as promised, but the massed statements of Flynn's operatives reduced the doctors' testimony to tatters. Detailed notes of dates and times, read carefully from note-books, weighed a good deal more heavily with judge and jury than the vague statements of two Italians, however qualified, and the alibi that Morello and Nick Terranova had constructed with such care was shat-tered. Both Romano and Brancatto would eventually be charged with perjury.

Well over sixty witnesses were called in all, and though most barely detained the court (Lupo's wife was on the stand for less than a minute), Comito's testimony alone took so long to give that it was not until February 19 that Judge Ray brought the proceedings to a close, formally delivering his charge and sending the jury out to consider its judgment. In complicated cases, as Morello realized, a lengthy sequestration fre-quently indicated a "not guilty" verdict, and when the jury filed back in after a mere forty-five minutes' deliberation, both the Clutch Hand and the Wolf wore the haunted look of criminals expecting a conviction. But there was still hope even then. Both men knew that the punishments for counterfeiting were seldom severe. Since Flynn had taken charge in New York, they had generally run to less than a year for a first offense and three to five years for the leaders of a gang. With time allowed for good behavior, even the harshest of those sentences would mean spending little more than three years in jail.

It became clear almost at once, though, that this case was to be quite different. Judge Ray had taken the precaution of having the court cleared of spectators while the jury was at lunch, leaving only officials and reporters present as a long series of guilty verdicts was read. Even so, shocked murmurs rippled through the room as the defendants came forward, one by one, to hear their sentences pronounced.

Giuseppe Morello, Ray intoned: twenty-five years' hard labor and a thousand-dollar fine.

Lupo, thirty years and the same fine as Morello.

The remaining sentences were just as harsh. Calicchio, the master printer, got seventeen years in jail, Cina a year more than that. Cecala, Giglio, and Nick Sylvester all received sentences of fifteen years. More than a century and a half of servitude in all, to be served in the forbidding fortress prison of Atlanta.

Flynn would claim, in later years, that Judge Ray had been made well aware of Morello's lengthy record—the arrests as well as the convictions, the murders as well as the nonviolent crimes—and that his judgment took into account the Mafioso's guilt in the matter of the Barrel Murder. Whether that was true or not—the terms imposed were all severe, though only Lupo and Morello had been involved in the Madonia affair—the sentences were by far the longest ever handed down for counterfeiting by a U.S. court. "The words of the judge," the *American* reported, "seemed to strike the prisoners down like pistol shots."

Calicchio, who was the first man called before Judge Ray, appeared to have aged well beyond his fifty-two years, and he listened in silence as the court interpreter explained his sentence. Then, as the verdict sank in, the old forger began to scream, loudly and unceasingly, drowning out every attempt to quiet him. After a few moments of this unearthly wailing, officials were forced to half lead, half carry the prisoner to the holding cells, his yells echoing back along the corridors as he was dragged away. Calicchio's bubbling wails could still be heard through several doors as Morello was summoned, and the Clutch Hand seemed unnerved by the printer's performance. He slid rather than walked to the bar, and trembled as his sentence was pronounced.

Morello's English was good enough for him to understand the

judge's words without the aid of an interpreter, and his response was just as dramatic as Calicchio's. As Ray set out his sentence, New York's most feared Mafia boss dropped to the floor in a faint, then, half reviving, went into convulsions. Whether or not his collapse was an act intended to wring sympathy from the court—most of the disgusted newsmen present thought it was—he too had to be helped up and hustled from the room. Lupo, for his part, began sobbing as he stood before the judge and, by the time he had finished pleading for mercy, had "used up one whole handkerchief with his tears." The Wolf then stood, seemingly catatonic, while his thirty-year punishment was explained.

The shock of the heavy sentences was just as severely felt in the corridor outside, where word of the record terms, and the sound of groans and sobbing from the courtroom, set off furious mutterings among the friends and relatives of the convicted Mafiosi. U.S. Marshal William Henkel, in charge of security in court, had mustered nearly seventy men—thirty-five of his own officers, a dozen Secret Service agents, fifteen detectives, and six uniformed policemen—and all of them were needed to keep order as the news emerged. Henkel had to order that the corridor be cleared four or five times before things quieted down sufficiently for the prisoners to be manacled and marched away, and the short walk to the holding cells in the Tombs prison on Centre Street was a nervous one. Fully expecting that they might become a target for the remaining members of Morello's family, marshals and Secret Service men alike flinched as the press photographers outside discharged blinding volleys of flashbulbs. A brief panic ensued when a weaving drunk blundered into the column and appeared intent on breaking through to reach the prisoners.

It was pitch dark and freezing by the time the massive prison gates were reached. Henkel's marshals stopped the traffic on the street, holding up two streetcars, three women with five babies, and a weeping crowd of relatives while the prisoners were ushered inside. Flynn stepped forward and answered a few questions, glad to reap the praise to which his years of unceasing effort had entitled him. "That will help some," the Chief remarked with a half smile as the gates thudded shut— just the sort of understated comment that the press loved hearing from a Secret Service man. His words made most of the next day's papers.

CHAPTER 11

MOB

=

THE PRISON THAT WAS TO HOUSE MORELLO AND LUPO FOR THE next twenty years or more rose behind imposing walls to the southeast of Atlanta. It was the most important federal prison in America, and suitably enormous—the biggest concrete structure in the world. From outside, it looked more like a medieval castle than a prison, but appearances, in this case, were deceptive. The jail was still more or less brand new—the first group of convicts had arrived only in 1902—and its warden liked to paint it as a model institution. It was certainly better appointed than the state prisons the Morello gang had left behind them in New York, and was not designed to grind down its inmates' wills or break their spirits, as Sing Sing had been and in some respects still was. Prisoners were spared the rock breaking that constituted hard labor in other penitentiaries, being set instead to "useful tasks." Morello was assigned to the tailors' shop. Even more remarkably, the men worked "union hours," which meant an eight-hour day rather than the back-breaking dawn-to-dusk routine followed on the chain gangs then commonplace elsewhere in Georgia. After work, they returned each night to blocks that held a total of just eight hundred prisoners, mostly one man to a cell—an unheard-of luxury to other jails.

Discipline was strict but rarely violent. Corporal punishment did not exist; troublemakers received spells of solitary confinement on a restricted diet. Even the food was good, though there were none of the Italian staples that Morello and his followers pined for—"no spaghetti or garlic," a sneering journalist informed his readers. Inmates received three square meals a day: perhaps fish cakes, bread, and coffee at breakfast time, beef stew for lunch, and doughnuts or fried potatoes in the evening. Conditions were so marvelous, a reporter from *The Washington*

Post was told, that one prisoner, recently released, had smashed open a mailbox just to get himself arrested and returned to jail.

It was not the jail itself, in fact, but the sheer length of the sentences confronting them that weighed on the Sicilians' minds. Allowing for time off for good behavior, the earliest date that Morello would be considered for release was December 4, 1926, nearly seventeen years away. For Lupo the Wolf it was more than three years later: April 3, 1930. The sentences, Morello complained in a letter to his wife, were "enough to drive a man crazy."

What kept the prisoners sane, for the first year at least, was the hope that their appeal would be allowed. The remaining members of the Morello family worked hard to make that possible, and their prospects of achieving something improved immeasurably when they retained Bourke Cockran, a celebrated litigator and one of the highest-paid defense attorneys in the country. They raised the money required to pay him through the usual "appropriations" in East Harlem—where pushcart peddlers, merchants, and petty bankers were terrorized into handing over contributions—and in gifts sent by other Mafia families from as far away as Tunis; at one point the fund raised in this way stood at fifty thousand dollars, a portion of which was set aside to bribe witnesses from the first trial to change their stories. The Terranovas did what they could to bring political pressure to bear at the same time, and their influence in Harlem was such that both Republicans and Democrats seemed ready to help. All those efforts, though, counted for little when the case actually reached the appeals court. Flynn's case was just too watertight. The appeal was heard and dismissed in June 1911, and Cockran's fees were so enormous that there was no money left afterward to mount another attempt.

Thwarted though they had been in the courts, the remaining members of Morello's gang did not altogether give up hope. John Lupo, the brother of the Wolf, cultivated contacts in the Catholic Church in the hope of obtaining a recommendation for mercy from New York's Cardinal Gibbons. Another scheme that the Terranovas seriously considered was to have Morello accept full responsibility for organizing the counterfeiting operation, in the hope that Lupo might then be freed; the brothers believed, Flynn noted, "that once Lupo is out, they would have a better chance to get Morello out." This plan was abandoned almost as soon as it was explained to the Clutch Hand during a family visit to the

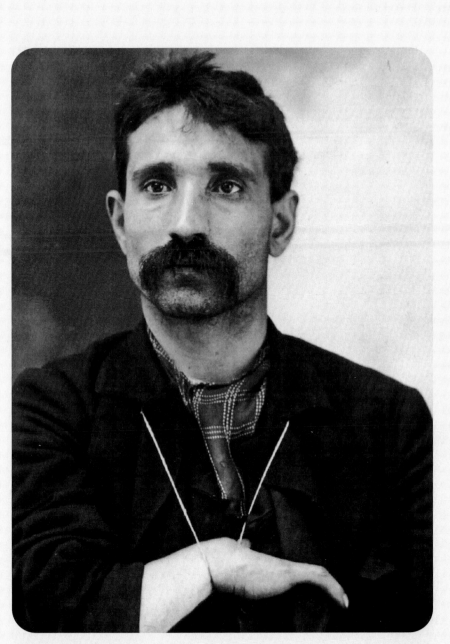

Giuseppe Morello, first "boss of bosses" of the American Mafia, is forced to display the deformed, one-fingered hand that earned him the nickname "the Clutch Hand" in this 1900 mugshot. According to Secret Service files, Morello personally committed two murders and ordered at least sixty more. Even the influential second-generation Mafia boss Joe Bonanno was terrified of him: "There was nothing of the buffoon about Morello. He had a parched, gaunt voice, a stone face and a claw."

A street scene in Corleone. The Sicilian town—notorious even in the nineteenth century—as one of the Mafia's great strongholds—was home to Morello and his brothers. The body lying facedown on the right with eleven bullets in it is that of Bernardino Verro, Corleone's mayor. Verro, who—to his lasting shame—was initiated into the Mafia by Morello's stepfather, paid the ultimate price for denouncing the society.

Below: Calogero Maggiore. A mere twenty years old, and a "shirt ironer" by trade, the young Sicilian was persuaded by Giuseppe Morello to front an early counterfeiting scheme. When the ring was broken up by the Secret Service in June 1900, Maggiore went to prison for six years; Morello walked free.

Above: Don Vito Cascio Ferro, Morello's ally in New York, became the greatest leader that the Sicilian Mafia ever produced. "Every mayor, dressed in his best clothes, awaited him at the entrance to his village, kissed his hands, and paid homage as if he were the king."

More Morello dupes: three of the Irish petty criminals picked up by the NYPD in the summer of 1900 for "queer pushing." They are (*left to right*) Chas Brown (alias Steve Sullivan), John "Red" Duffy, and Edward R. Kelly.

Bustling Little Italy in the early days of the century. The first Italian crime boss to gain control of the immigrant quarter was Giuseppe D'Agostino (*inset*), who used a chain of grocery stores as a front for a vast extortion ring. D'Agostino was forcibly "retired" by the Morello family in 1902 as the Mafia established itself, and the Sicilians promptly took control of his grocery rackets.

Giuseppe Catania. A giant of a man who worked with Morello as a counterfeiter, he talked when drunk—and was found nude, hacked to death, his head attached to his body by a single tendon, and trussed up in a potato sack on the Brooklyn riverfront.

Tommaso Petto, aka Petto the Ox. A Mafia strongman suspected of participation in the Barrel Murder, Petto died two years later in Pennsylvania, riddled with explosive bullets that had torn wounds "as big as teacups" in his body.

Benedetto Madonia (*above*) and Giuseppe Di Priemo (*inset*) both fell foul of the Mafia. Madonia, a senior member of Morello's gang, was the victim of the brutal Barrel Murder. His brother-in-law Di Priemo vowed vengeance but met his own death, violently, a few years later—another of Morello's victims, the police believed.

A reconstruction, from the *Evening Journal,* showing how Madonia's body was found stuffed in its barrel, the throat cut, the torso drained, and blood still oozing between the staves. The police were certain that the murder was intended as a warning—but for whom?

Benedetto Madonia in death. This morgue scene, hastily snatched by a photographer from William Randolph Hearst's sensational *Evening Journal,* shows Madonia after he had been stabbed more than a dozen times by members of the Morello gang, then all but decapitated with a single sweeping slash from a stiletto. The discovery of his body, stuffed into a barrel and abandoned on a lonely street, alerted New Yorkers to the existence of the Mafia.

Four pieces of evidence from the Barrel Murder case. *Above right:* the pawn ticket discovered by Flynn in a police evidence box that led the authorities to Madonia's tin watch, stamped with the image of a train. *Above and right:* four scrawled pages from Joe Petrosino's police notebook for April 1903. On the first spread (*above*), Pietro Inzerillo admits to selling empty barrels from his store, but says he "does not know what the Maffia is." On the second (*right*), Morello admits that "they say I am the chief of the Mafia" but denies any involvement in Madonia's killing.

Nine members of the Morello family

Vito Laduca, counterfeiter, kidnapper, and "dread bulwark of the Black Hand."

Giovanni Zacconi drove the "death wagon" that carried Madonia to East 11th Street.

Joseph Fanaro, the red-haired giant who lured at least two Morello victims to their deaths.

Carlo Costantino, who died riddled with syphilis—and still the lead suspect in the Petrosino murder.

Pietro Inzerillo, the confectioner who supplied the barrel in which Madonia's body was stuffed.

Antonio Cecala, murderous frontman for the family's green goods business.

Salvatore Cina: "You are trying to get me to blow your damn brains out."

Giuseppe Calicchio. "Professor" who printed $100,000 worth of forged bills.

Antonio Passananti headed the Morello grocery racket and killed himself at age ninety-four.

Joe Petrosino. "Short and heavy, with enormous shoulders and a bull neck, on which was placed a great round head like a summer squash," the pockmarked policeman was the greatest Italian detective in New York. The destroyer of dozens of Black Hand bands, and renowned for personally arresting the head of the Neapolitan Camorra, Petrosino met his match—and eventually his death—at the hands of Morello's Mafia.

Murdered by the Mafia in Sicily, Joe Petrosino was brought home to New York for burial. A crowd said to have been twenty thousand strong lined up to file past his bier; thousands more, most of them Italians, lined the city's streets as his coffin was driven to Calvary Cemetery for burial.

Two of the forged Morello notes that set Flynn on the trail of the first family and led eventually to the capture and conviction of Morello himself. The notes are (*top left*) a U.S. $2 bill and (*below*) a U.S. $5 bill, both engraved by Giuseppe Calicchio. The man coerced into printing the notes was Antonio Comito (*top right*), a timid Calabrian known to the Mafia as Comito the Sheep. Comito and his mistress, Katrina Pascuzzo (*below*), were held in a remote house deep in the woods of upstate New York for eight months in 1908–9 while the work was carried out.

William Flynn started his career as a Manhattan plumber but rose to become the most brilliant detective in the country. As head of the New York bureau of the Secret Service, his dogged perseverance over more than a decade resulted in the conviction of nearly two dozen members of the Morello family, including the boss himself.

Ignazio Lupo. Known to terrified members of the Italian community as Lupo the Wolf, Giuseppe Morello's moon-faced brother-in-law was a pitiless killer, noted extortionist—and the brains behind the Mafia's first moves into money laundering and real estate scams.

Dapper Salvatore Clemente, a notorious counterfeiter, emerged as Flynn's top informant inside the Morello family. It was Clemente who, at the risk of his own life, gave Flynn the location of the Mafia's grisly "private burial ground" on a farm upstate.

Calogero Morello, Giuseppe's eldest son, was murdered in a street brawl at the age of seventeen. Newspapers theorized that he died in a fight over the control of prostitution. It took Clemente to reveal the real—much more disturbing—truth.

Harlem's infamous Murder Stable. A ramshackle rabbit warren on East 108th Street, the stable lay—charged the *New York Herald*—at the center of a deadly vendetta that cost at least twenty-two lives, including those of several members of the Morello family. The stable was rumored to conceal a hidden Mafia torture chamber and killing rooms where victims were dispatched. Pasquale Greco (*inset*), brother of one of the stable's victims, told the *Herald*'s reporter that he fully expected to be the next to die.

Nick Terranova assumed leadership of the first family after Morello went to jail. He proved to be an able boss who tightened the Mafia's stranglehold on extortion rackets in the Italian districts. Receiving news of his nephew Calogero's murder, Terranova publicly vowed to "butcher every one" of the gangsters responsible—then hunted down and killed the first two of the men himself.

Giosue Gallucci. A politically well-connected Neapolitan, Gallucci ran the Italian lottery in East Harlem until his falling-out with the Morellos. Ten bodyguards were killed defending him, but not even the boss's habit of wearing a chain-mail vest could save him from assassination.

Ciro Terranova. The Artichoke King was the longest lived of the Terranova brothers, dominating Harlem's vegetable rackets during World War I and living on into the era of Prohibition and bootlegging. Forcibly retired by a new generation of gangsters, he died impoverished and all but forgotten in 1938.

The murder of Vincenzo Terranova, as reconstructed by one New York newspaper. The oldest of the three Terranova brothers was heavily involved in bootlegging when he was cut down by sawed-off shotguns fired by five men in a car who caught him outside an ice-cream parlor on East 116th Street, in the heart of the Morellos' territory.

The porcine Joe "the Boss" Masseria was "boss of bosses" during Prohibition. His attempts to dominate New York's families led to war within the Mafia. It was a war Masseria was winning until he lost his chief adviser—Giuseppe Morello. Morello's murder was swiftly followed by Masseria's own.

Ralph "the Barber" Daniello. A Camorra killer who took part in the Nick Terranova slaying, Ralph saved his skin by giving New York's police their first detailed look inside the city's Italian gangs. The Barber paid with his life for his betrayal, shot dead outside his Newark bar.

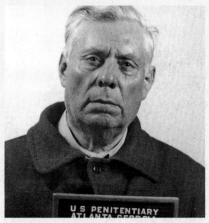

Giuseppe Morello's second wife, Nicolina Salemi, in middle age. A striking woman in her youth, Lina actively abetted her husband's Mafia career. She was possessed of a volcanic temper, said Flynn; during one raid she concealed incriminating evidence in her baby's diaper and attacked Secret Service agents with a knife.

Ignazio Lupo in old age. Returned to prison after resuming his career of murder and extortion, he served a total of twenty years, and by the time of his release in 1946 he was senile and had just days to live. "I should like to be a boy again in Sicily," he wrote, "and die young, very young, and never know all these years of struggle and evil."

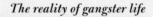

The remains of Gaspare Candella, found in a barrel on 45th Street in Brooklyn on November 8, 1918. The Morello family had introduced the notion of the "barrel murder" to New York fifteen years earlier; Candella's wounds were almost identical to those inflicted on Benedetto Madonia in 1903—indicating that he, too, had been a traitor to the Mafia.

penitentiary. According to William Moyer, Atlanta's warden, who had stationed guards and an interpreter within earshot, "it affected him so much that the Deputy Warden was obliged to relieve him from work and assign him to his cell, because he appeared to be mentally as well as physically in no condition to work, in other words this plan seemed to break Morello."

There remained the prospect of escape. Tentative plans for freeing the leaders of the Morello family were mulled over for at least two years. It was a nearly impossible task; no man had broken out of the Atlanta prison since it had opened its doors, and the Terranova brothers quickly abandoned any idea of blasting or shooting their men free. An escape, it was decided, would be possible only with the assistance of several guards, and these men would have to be heavily bribed. The scheme was enough of a reality for a concert to be organized in Harlem to raise funds; Flynn discovered that "a great number of tickets at $1.00 each had been sold." In the end, though, even this idea had to be rejected. The Secret Service chief tipped off Moyer to the Terranovas' schemes, the prison authorities took action, and Lupo and Morello were separated and forbidden to associate or talk. At the same time, the number of men guarding them was doubled. It was no wonder that Nick Terranova bitterly concluded that there was no prospect of getting Morello freed while Flynn remained with the Secret Service. He was just too powerful, Nick said, and had too great an influence in Washington.

THERE WERE OTHER WAYS of dealing with Flynn, of course. Ciro Terranova was overheard remarking that the Secret Service man "had a very big pull, and the only way to stop him would be by bullet," and the Chief's informants in Harlem brought word that other members of the Morello clan were debating the prospect of kidnapping his children, hoping to coerce him into supporting an appeal. At about the same time, two of Lupo's associates visited him in jail and received firm orders, Flynn was told, that he should be assassinated.

Had the Terranova brothers been determined to kill Flynn, they could probably have done so. The Chief lived in an isolated property in the far north of the city, and although he ordered his children never to venture more than a hundred feet from home, he felt unpleasantly exposed there. What saved the Secret Service man was Nick Terranova's prudence. The youngest of the brothers but also the most intelligent and the natural leader among the three, Terranova was certainly tempted by the prospect of striking back at Flynn. He realized, though, that any serious attempt would bring the authorities down on him—and, worse, would affect his brother's chances of parole. While there was any prospect of having Lupo and Morello freed by legal means, Nick decided, it would be foolhardy to kill their enemy. The endless series of appeals and legal efforts that the family launched after the men's conviction inoculated Flynn against attack.

The Terranovas felt no such compunction when it came to Antonio Comito. From the moment the Morello family learned that the printer was going to testify against their leaders, they became determined to murder him. The sum of $2,500 was offered to at least one crooked policeman in exchange for details of the Calabrian's whereabouts—the same figure that the Terranovas had put on the man's head. Soon afterward, Comito's worried uncle called Flynn to report that there were suspicious strangers hanging around outside his house, and a far worse panic erupted at the end of May 1910, when the hideously mutilated body of an Italian man in his thirties was dumped in the Paerdegat woods on the fringes of Brooklyn. The corpse was lying only a hundred yards from the spot where Salvatore Marchiani's dismembered remains had been hauled out of a rubbish dump in Pigtown, and it bore the characteristic marks of a Mafia killing. There were twenty-five knife wounds in all, seven of them in the abdomen and the rest to the face; the nose and one ear had been sliced off with a razor, and the remainder of the man's features were so ripped and torn that identification was impossible.

The first thought of the first policemen on the scene was that the dead man was Antonio Comito. Detectives hurried off to find the Terranova brothers and interrogated several members of their gang. Comito turned up, safe and well, soon afterward, but the NYPD continued to believe that the dead man—whom they never identified—had been a Mafia informant, and Flynn decided that it would be sensible to get his witness away from Manhattan. Within days, Comito found himself in a safe house near the Mexican border, and when he did return to New York after a year, it was only to collect $150 from Secret Service funds to pay for a steamship ticket home. Flynn was still sufficiently concerned to lend the printer a revolver for the duration of his short stay in the city, but Comito sensibly kept away from places where he might stumble across old acquaintances and sailed two weeks later, on July 1, 1911. Flynn heard sometime later that he had made it back to South America, where the Mafia held no sway, and had become a successful businessman. Whether he took Katrina Pascuzzo with him, or ever was reunited with his wife, remains unknown.

WITH THE FAILURE OF the appeal and their plans for escape, the reality of the sentences that stretched out before them struck both Lupo and Morello hard. Both men became morose, depressed. Disapproving comments in their prison files, noting that they laughed and joked with the other members of their gang, cease after 1911, to be replaced with worried correspondence from their families.

Morello, his loyal wife, Lina, observed in a letter that she wrote to Moyer, was "serving 25 undeserved years" and "has no comfort because he is buried alive." The boss suffered from indigestion and heart trouble, put on nearly thirty pounds, and grew increasingly angry, first at his family's failure to supply the constant drip of good news he needed to sustain his spirits, then at the failure of their efforts to produce results. "You are wrong," he told his wife in one letter, "and do harm to my health, for I am worrying all the time. . . . I alone know how much I am suffering." There were regular complaints about the lack of letters from his relatives and children.

Lina, though, was finding life no easier than her husband. Deprived of Mafia money, she and Lupo's wife, Salvatrice, were forced to take jobs in the feather business down on 105th Street, work that brought in so little income that they were reduced to visiting their reviled enemy, Flynn, to beg for the return of pawn tickets that had been in Morello's pockets at the time he was arrested. The three Terranova brothers supplied Lina with a pitiful allowance of $4.50 a week and no doubt made a similar contribution to Lupo family funds, but with five children to support between them the two women struggled to survive. As late as 1916, the Secret Service suspected both wives of passing counterfeit silver on their daily shopping expeditions in their attempts to make ends meet.

Living in such straitened circumstances, it is scarcely surprising that Morello's wife was upset by his surliness. "Listen, Giuseppe," she wrote at the beginning of July 1915, "I am somewhat convinced that you do not care for me, because I can see that you are not as you were at one time." Lina hoped that the fault might lie not with her husband but with the man who wrote his letters for him: "That he might not be able to explain well, as I see other letters that other wives get that are different to mine." In this, though, she was disappointed. Morello's real anger became clear when he scrawled a sharp letter to his brother Nick, criticizing the failings of each member of his family in turn. Lina was shown the correspondence, and she responded spiritedly:

> I remain somewhat surprised in reading your letter, especially that you are trying to forget the family. My feelings have been hurt, you are acting ungratefully.
>
> I have shed tears for two days, thinking of your unjust treatment. I thought of stopping writing to you, because my letters disturb you. On second thoughts, I decided to drop you these few lines, asking you whether or not you care for me to continue to write.

Morello must have hastened to apologize, for his wife's letters reverted to their usual affectionate tone thereafter; he was again "My always adored Giuseppe" and her letters closed with "many kisses from the heart, also from our children." But even so, the comfort the boss drew from his letters was not remotely enough to make incarceration bearable. Early release was all that he and his men craved, and, once their appeal had failed, the members of the gang were willing to do almost anything to get it.

One by one, the men began approaching William Flynn. It was time to talk.

FOR FLYNN, WHO HAD BEEN so frustrated for so long by the Mafiosi's veil of silence, it was a happy time. He had anticipated it, predicting to John Wilkie, on the day that the sentences were handed down, that Morello's men would barter information as soon as their situation appeared hopeless. He took satisfaction from being right.

Morello, to everyone's surprise but Flynn's, was the first of the men to crack. The Clutch Hand offered to make a statement in January 1911, before his appeal was even halfway done. "It was the privilege of a king," the Chief explained, for a Mafia boss to ignore whenever it suited him the vow of silence that he and his followers had sworn to uphold with their lives.

Morello's aim was to trade information for his freedom, and he had a shrewd idea of what the authorities wanted to know: "For weeks," a reporter from the *The New York Times* explained, "a story has been going the rounds of the cafes and restaurants of the Italian quarters that Morello was willing, in exchange for his liberty, to name the assassins of Lieutenant Petrosino." An Atlanta lawyer summoned to the penitentiary took down the boss's deposition, but the contents of his confession were never made public; when the statement was translated back into Italian for the boss to read, Morello appeared to take fright and refused point-blank to sign his name to it. According to at least two journalists, the unsigned document named Carlo Costantino as Petrosino's killer, and the Clutch Hand balked when he learned that other Mafiosi in New York had threatened members of his family.

Morello remained eternally tight-lipped thereafter, but it was not long before Lupo's lawyer indicated that he, too, might be willing to make statements. Then came Sylvester, then Cina. Calicchio would have talked if Flynn had asked him to, but the master printer had always been an employee, not a member of the gang, and he knew little. Cecala considered talking. Giglio did not get the chance; he dropped dead in the prison church, the first member of the group to die.

Flynn's interest in these lesser fry centered on the printing plates that had vanished when the Highland plant was broken up. The Chief wanted to locate them to forestall further appeals and also because he knew Nick Terranova hoped to resume the counterfeiting operation. The Secret Service was willing to trade a commutation for the plates, but not one of the men would talk about it. There was a savage irony, from the prisoners' perspective, that the one piece of information that could secure their release was the very scrap of knowledge that they dared not divulge. Disclosing the location of the plates in a corner of Morello's private graveyard meant signing their own death warrants. Any attempt on Flynn's part to excavate the burial site would risk the disinterral of the Clutch Hand's victims—and hence bring the likelihood of murder charges.

The men kept their mouths shut and stayed in prison.

IN TRUTH, AS EVEN Flynn conceded, any man connected to the Morello family had good reason to hold his tongue. The betrayal of Mafia secrets had long been an unforgivable sin—the most unforgivable sin, perhaps, one punishable by death—and with Morello scheming in Atlanta and the Terranova brothers thirsting for revenge, the Mafia's search for possible traitors was pursued with vigor and savagery from the moment the Clutch Hand was jailed.

Comito, the great betrayer, remained beyond their reach, but other informers were identified and hunted down, among them several whose identities Flynn had never revealed, even in court. The first to be found was Sam Locino, the Pennsylvania counterfeiter whose statements had given the Secret Service its break in the hunt for the Morello gang. Not long after the Clutch Hand's trial concluded, Locino was returning to his home in Pittston when he heard a rustling from some bushes as he crossed a vacant lot. Flynn's informant span around and was hit by two bullets fired by a man who had crawled out from the undergrowth. Locino was very lucky; the shots merely grazed his skull, and the killer ran rather than making sure his man was dead.

Others were less fortunate. Luigi Bono, a middle-aged Italian from Highland, fled back to New York for fear of the Morellos' vengeance and opened a small grocery store on Houston Street. Soon after his return to the city, Bono was badly frightened by some incident or warning and began returning home not along the street but across the rooftops to his tenement. This precaution was not enough to save him; on November 17, 1911, the grocer's body was found huddled against a fence on a nearby roof, a deep and ugly gash behind one ear. Bono had been struck down from behind by a man wielding an ax; one ear and his tongue had then been severed from his head, and what appeared to be ritual incisions were carved into his chest and legs. On his body, Flynn recorded, the police found a card that read: "This man was Morello's enemy."

It is not surprising, in such circumstances, that the Secret Service found it harder and harder to persuade its informers to talk. Even Nick Sylvester, who had been so desperate to cut his fifteen-year sentence that he quietly passed Flynn details of the location of the printing press, produced little or no worthwhile intelligence when he was finally released from jail. Flynn could still rely on his existing informants to a great extent; several, especially Charles Mazzei, continued to supply information from the fringes of the Morello family at great risk to themselves. But something more was needed, and it was not until October 1910 that Flynn found what he had been looking for: an informant who had access to the Morellos' innermost councils.

HIS NAME WAS Salvatore Clemente, and he had been known to the Secret Service ever since 1895, when he had earned an eight-year jail sentence for counterfeiting. Short but dapper, well turned out, with a handsome, open, smiling face that radiated bonhomie, Clemente was an ideal informant in almost every respect. He had a lengthy record, sufficient to establish his criminal credentials. He was also a Sicilian, born in 1866 and acquainted with practically every counterfeiter in New York. He was a close friend of the Terranova brothers, for whom he was a valued sounding board and confidant. And he had no wish to return to jail. A second lengthy prison sentence in the early 1900s had given Clemente his fill of life behind bars, and when the Secret Service picked him up again during the autumn of 1910, he was only too willing to deal with Flynn. The two men came to an agreement that October: Clemente's freedom and a small retainer, in return for reports from inside the Morello family.

Clemente began to prove his worth at once. It was his information that alerted the Chief to the existence of the Oddo farm and its grisly private graveyard. It was also he who warned Flynn that the Terranova brothers were making plans to snatch his children. But perhaps the most important details that the Chief's new man supplied were insights into the family's struggle to maintain its dominance in Little Italy. With Lupo and Morello locked away, potential rivals had begun to rear their heads. The Harlem Mafia had faced few threats on its home ground for years, not since the Barrel Murder showed just what the likely fate of any challenger would be; now, with the family seemingly leaderless, allies and old enemies alike began to circle. The next ten years would be bloodier by far than the preceding decade for every member of the first family.

The problem was lack of leadership at first, and for this Giuseppe Morello himself was chiefly responsible, since he refused to cede power without a struggle. For months the Clutch Hand tried to run his family from a prison cell, passing instructions to New York in elliptic Corleone slang that baffled even the Italian speakers assigned to read his letters and eavesdrop on his conversations. It was only in 1911, with the failure of the appeal—and with it the realization that there would be no swift return to Manhattan—that he yielded control to two lieutenants. His chosen successors were the Lomonte brothers, Tom and Fortunato, both Sicilians, both racketeers, and co-owners of a saloon on East 107th Street, which they ran with Morello's crooked brother-in-law, Gioacchino Lima.

Why Morello's choice fell on the Lomontes is not known. There was little to recommend them, superficially at least. They were not family. Both were still young, in their late twenties, and neither had been prominent in Harlem's underworld, nor had either ever been charged with any serious crime. The brothers may simply have been the last men standing after Flynn jailed the family's established leaders. Whatever the truth, they were at least well known to the Clutch Hand; he had first met them when they organized a plasterers' union years earlier, and he employed one of their cousins in his grocery business. Whether the brothers were the right men to lead the Morellos into a new and far more complex criminal era, though, was doubtful even at the time that they were given command of the first family.

The years from 1911 to 1916 are among the darkest in the history of New York's Mafia—dark, in that they were a period of bloodletting and turmoil, but dark, too, because they are so poorly chronicled. Personal testimony is absent, police records are lacking, and, since the Morello family steered well clear of counterfeiting after 1910, even Flynn, with all his bulldog's tenacity, could devote no more than a fraction of his scant resources to keeping an eye on events in Little Italy. Manhattan's newspapers, too, cut back their coverage of crime after 1914. With the Great War raging in Europe, the disputes of a few bloodthirsty gangsters began to seem more petty than thrilling.

For the Morellos, their enemies, and their allies, though, the years that followed the counterfeiting trial of 1910 were deadly—the most violent that they had ever known. The first family had lost its leaders and nearly half its men; Flynn, who had estimated the strength of the Clutch Hand's gang at 110 late in 1909, convicted 45 of them in 1910, this at a time when the rising tide of Italian immigrants was sweeping a flood of young, ambitious criminals into New York. Districts that the Morellos had dominated a decade earlier now seethed with likely competition.

The Lomontes responded to these threats as best they could. They rebuilt the strength of their family, initiating a number of new members. They also made deals and forged relationships with other gangs. By doing so, the brothers buttressed their position, but the protection they obtained through their alliances was gained at the expense of the family's clannishness and independence. Few of the newcomers who joined its ranks after 1910 were Corleonesi; some were not even Sicilian. And while the Lomontes' allies supplied extra strength, the Harlem Mafia was inevitably dragged into the disputes of its new friends.

A number of influential names make their first appearance in the Morellos' story at this time. One was Eugene Ubriaco from Cosenza, a Calabrian who had entered the United States in 1907 and became the first man from outside Sicily to rise to prominence within the Clutch Hand's family. Another was Joe DiMarco, an influential figure in the lucrative world of illegal gambling. DiMarco, his brother Salvatore, and another Sicilian, Giuseppe Verrazano (who ran card games downtown on Kenmare Street), gave the Morellos a larger stake in the criminal economy of southern Manhattan. The Morellos, in return, offered protection.

It was in Harlem, though, that the most unusual of the Lomontes' allies lived. She was a dumpy, mannish Neapolitan woman named Pasquarella Spinelli—square-faced, red-haired, and nearly sixty years old—and she was the owner of the largest livery stable for miles around: a tumbledown warren of corrugated iron hideaways that stood only a short walk from the brothers' feed store and stretched the width of a city block from its entrance at 334 East 108th Street. Though barely literate—she was well known in Harlem for keeping accounts scrawled with a lump of coal on whitewashed walls—Spinelli was rich, a successful businesswoman who lent money, leased tenements, and owned the Rex, the largest Italian vaudeville theater in Manhattan. To most of the population of East Harlem, she was also a sinister figure, and it was generally understood that most of her considerable fortune came from crime. The local police, for whom she acted as an occasional informant, knew Pasquarella as the head of a gang of horse thieves and extortionists, most of whom worked from her stable as grooms. She was worth three hundred thousand dollars, it was said.

The Lomonte brothers had good use for such an ally. For one thing, Spinelli was likely a valued customer of their feed store; for another, Nick Terranova, who ran the Morellos' horse theft racket, could use her stable to conceal his stolen animals—a service for which Pasquarella charged her customers the rate of five dollars a day. The closeness of the relationship between Spinelli and the Mafia was demonstrated in December 1911 when Nick opened a blacksmith's shop on her premises. What Pasquarella got from the arrangement is less clear, but it probably had much to do with her own need for protection in the Harlem underworld. Certainly a number of murders were committed on and around her property over the years (the *Herald,* in 1917, would put the total at more than twenty), so many that the place became infamous throughout the borough as the "Murder Stable." According to New York rumor—and it was rumor that was printed as fact by newspapers as august and as cautious as *The New York Times*—Spinelli's labyrinthine premises concealed makeshift torture chambers and murder rooms where the Morellos' enemies were questioned and killed, and the screams of their unfortunate victims could be heard drifting out across East Harlem late at night. In truth, accounts of this sort stemmed from error and imagination, but there is no question that Spinelli had many enemies and went in fear of her life.

If Pasquarella thought that the Lomontes and the Mafia could keep her safe, though, she was wrong. Only a few months later she was dead, shot through the head and neck by a pair of gunmen who had lurked outside the main doors to her stable and who had plainly waited some time for her to show herself. The murder was never solved; Spinelli's assassins escaped, and there were conflicting theories as to who had sent them. Some attributed the shooting to a vendetta Pasquarella and her daughter had been pursuing with some minor gangsters, while others, including the police, pointed to the machinations of her business partner, Luigi Lazzazzara.

In an underworld that was becoming more dangerous each day, no one could escape the consequences for long—not the owner of the Murder Stable, nor, as it soon became clear, even the Morellos themselves.

PASQUARELLA HAD BEEN one of Harlem's most prominent residents, but even her death made no difference to the smooth running of the Italian underworld. Lazzazzara took on the stable and the grooms, and the horse theft racket went on much as it had before. The same could not be said of the next murder to take place in the Sicilian quarter. That April, just three weeks after Spinelli was shot, Giuseppe Morello's only son was also killed. This time there were repercussions—for the boy's assassins, who were hunted down, and for the leaders of the Morello family themselves. By the time peace was restored a few months later, the Lomonte brothers had lost a good deal of their influence and a new boss had emerged from the ranks of the Harlem Mafia.

Morello's son was still young, only seventeen, when he was killed, and his death was all the more shocking for being unexpected. Calogero's death took place on a clear evening early in spring, a few blocks north of the Morellos' strongholds, as the boy was strolling up Third Avenue with his friend Joe Pulazzo. Just as they reached 120th Street, a group of men emerged from several doorways. Passersby heard voices raised, then several shots. The two groups had been grappling a moment earlier, and the shots were fired from point-blank range. Morello was hit once in the stomach, invariably a fatal wound at the time; Pulazzo took a bullet through a lung. Reeling back, the Mafiosi drew their own weapons and returned fire, mortally wounding one attacker. The two Sicilians were outnumbered, though, and so badly wounded that neither could get more than a few blocks from the scene of the ambush. Calogero, trailing smears of blood, staggered as far as Lexington Avenue before collapsing against some steps. An ambulance was summoned, and as the dying boy was stretchered aboard, a passing priest climbed in and gave the boy the last rites. Morello, Pulazzo, and their wounded assailant all died the next day in the hospital. None had said a word to the police.

Word of the triple shooting filtered down to Flynn next morning, and the Chief's inquiries soon revealed the basics of the story; Calogero's attacker had been "one Barlow, alias Kid Baker," a gang leader from the Upper East Side. The motive for the ambush, though, was harder to discern; Baker had no ties to the Mafia, and there was all sorts of speculation in East Harlem. One report suggested that Morello had been a police informant, killed on the orders of his family when his betrayal was unveiled. Another theory was that the ambush had had its roots in disputes over the control of prostitution in the Italian neighborhoods.

Salvatore Clemente would fill in the facts. Clemente's version of events differed considerably from the rumors that were circulating on the street. As it was, though, the counterfeiter's reports shone vital, unexpected light upon a little-known part of the Morellos' saga: the eclipse of the Lomonte brothers and the rise of Nick Terranova to the leadership of the first family.

It was at Calogero's funeral, Clemente said, that he first learned the truth about the murder. He was by then a favorite of the Terranova brothers—he had lent them the money to hire handsome carriages for young Morello's funeral procession—and they confided what had actually happened on 120th Street. Calogero, the Terranovas explained, was not merely the unlucky victim of a street brawl. He had been shot down as part of a vendetta: revenge, on the part of the Madonia family, for the murder of the barrel victim nine years earlier. The ambush had been carefully planned; Morello had been lured up Third Avenue by an urgent message sent not by Kid Baker but by Baker's lieutenant. The lieutenant, who was Madonia's nephew, had begun a scuffle to create a pretext for the shooting; afterward, according to the Terranova brothers, he had gone to Lucy Madonia in search of protection and begged her to use her influence to make peace. When Mrs. Madonia refused to intervene, the nephew was forced to flee New York for Italy.

The three Terranovas thirsted for revenge. Calogero was, after all, a Mafioso—even at seventeen, he had been "carrying a gun" for the first family. The brothers were also deeply concerned at the effect the news of the murder would have on the boy's father. "The family," Clemente said, "did not know what to tell Morello, as they fear when he hears of the death of his son it will perhaps kill him." They were also thoroughly disgusted by the Lomonte brothers' failure to seek vengeance. The Morello family's new leaders made no attempt to find Calogero's killers. Their unwillingness to avenge his death was a grave breach of Mafia custom, and at young Morello's funeral Nick Terranova publicly humiliated them, placing a hand upon his nephew's coffin and loudly swearing revenge. He would "butcher every one" of the Kid Baker gang, he vowed.

Nick wasted little time in making good on his promise. A week after Calogero's death, he vanished from East 116th Street one evening and reappeared the next morning with news that he had tracked down and killed the first member of the Baker gang. A few weeks later, the youngest of the Terranovas murdered again, this time shooting down the man who had sent his nephew the message that lured him to his death. Nick, clearly, was taking considerable risks; he and his brothers would undoubtedly be suspects if the killings were discovered. When Clemente called on them next day, he found his friends rehearsing alibis and "constantly sending out for papers and observing that there was nothing in them of it yet"—good news, of course, since it meant that the police knew nothing of the murder.

Terranova grew substantially in stature in these months. He was the youngest of three brothers, and only twenty-two years old in 1912; a year earlier, when Morello had been jailed, he had been thought too young and inexperienced to succeed as boss. Now, though, he revealed himself to be a natural leader, and by avenging Calogero's death he acquired an influence that matched and then eclipsed that of the two Lomontes. Other members of the Morello family began to ask him for advice and to depend on his decisions. The Lomontes, for their part, backed away. The brothers severed at least one of their ties with the Morellos at about this time, giving up their saloon on East 107th Street and opening another in its stead. The new tavern stood two blocks to the north, and they ran it in partnership with a man called Gagliano. Gagliano was the family name of another group of Mafiosi from across the East River in the Bronx.

It took time, of course, for the inexperienced Terranova to accumulate enough support to rival the Lomontes; Clemente was still referring to the first family as the "Lomonti gang" as late as 1913. What does seem indisputable is that the brothers' influence declined as Nick gained power. When that happened, the Lomontes turned to yet another ally for support. They turned to the King of Little Italy.

GIOSUE GALLUCCI, THE MAN who gloried in that title, was generally agreed to be the most influential Italian in New York. He had arrived in the United States in 1892 from Naples and gradually established himself as a power in East Harlem. By 1912 he had business interests throughout the district. He ran much of the ice trade in the summer and controlled the coal trade in the winter. He was also one of the biggest moneylenders in the Italian quarter, owned a string of cobbler's shops, dealt in olive oil, enjoyed a near monopoly on hay and feed sales to the district's livery stables, and was the owner of a popular bakery at 318 East 109th Street, where he lived in an apartment over the store. Everybody knew him; hundreds owed their living to him, and thousands more paid him in one way or another. "To Gallucci," said Salvatore Cotillo, who would rise from a middle-class home in Harlem to become the first Italian-born Supreme Court justice in New York, "all people were either hirelings or payers of tribute. It was a matter of concern in the neighborhood if you were looked down upon by Gallucci."

So far as the city's newspapers were concerned, the King was a legitimate businessman—the epitome, in fact, of the successful immigrant. He was a physically imposing man, large without being particularly tall, and always immaculately dressed in tailored suits. He sported magnificent waxed mustaches, and, at a time when New York's Mafia bosses still dressed in ordinary working clothes and only the dandified Lupo the Wolf had any pretensions to elegance, he flashed a $2,000 ring and fastened his shirts with diamond studs worth an additional $3,000, as he swaggered around Harlem swinging his loaded cane.

In Little Italy, however, Gallucci was generally understood to have made much of his immense fortune from crime—from racketeering, mostly, and extortion. Unlike the Morellos, though, he had taken the profits of his criminal enterprises and used them to insinuate himself into every aspect of life in the immigrant quarter. The King ran what purported to be the New York office of the Royal Italian Lottery but was in fact nothing more than a front for his own numbers racket, and he sold thousands of tickets every month throughout Harlem. More important, he was also heavily involved in politics. He was "certainly the most powerful Italian politically in the city," one newspaper remarked, "and during campaigns was exceptionally active."

Gallucci's ability to mobilize the vote in Harlem, to get immigrants registered and to make sure they cast their ballots as he told them to, allowed him to wield the sort of power that Morello never had: power that stretched beyond the confines of the Italian neighborhoods. Hundreds of thousands of immigrants meant hundreds of thousands of valuable votes cast, and, as a partisan of the all-powerful Democratic political machine, which ruled Manhattan from its headquarters at Tammany Hall, the King possessed influence that his rivals could only dream of. Tammany rarely lost an election, and that meant that it controlled the city's police, not to mention the huge army of bureaucrats responsible for handing out city construction contracts and licensing saloons. With Tammany at his back, Gallucci was all but immune from prosecution, and though he was occasionally arrested for minor crimes, the cases never seemed to come to court. The *Herald* observed in the spring of 1915 that the King was then "out on $10,000 bail on a charge of carrying a pistol, and so strong has been his political influence that it even reached Washington, and in two years he has not been tried on the charge."

Thanks to their interest in the feed store on 108th Street, the Lomonte brothers had known Gallucci for several years, and an alliance offered them security and influence. To other members of the Morello family, however, the friendship between the Lomontes and the King was deeply shameful. Gallucci, after all, was Neapolitan, and, in the Morellos' diminished state, he was also the Lomontes' superior, at least in the districts around his 109th Street base. It was a distinction so obvious that it was even noted by the New York newspapers. For the *Herald,* which followed Italian affairs more closely than the other English language dailies, the Sicilian brothers were actually nothing more than *mani forti*—strong men, bodyguards—in the retinue of the King.

THE LOMONTES' FALL had its beginnings in the weakness that they showed in failing to avenge Calogero Morello's death in 1912, but, bolstered by their alliance with Gallucci, it was not until two years later, in May 1914, that the elder of the brothers lost his life. Fortunato, then thirty years old, was murdered in the open, in broad daylight, by a gunman who approached to point-blank range and fired three shots. The boss died almost at once, hit in the neck, chest, and stomach only a few yards from the entrance to the Murder Stable and in the heart of "King" Gallucci's territory. His killer escaped in the confusion.

It was Salvatore Clemente who first drew attention to the oddness of Lomonte's murder. Few shootings in East Harlem were quite such public affairs, nor was there usually much mystery about the killer. Lomonte's death, though, might have been designed to demonstrate how powerless he was, and, asking around, Clemente discovered that the gunman's identity was a mystery even to the leaders of the Morello family. None of the witnesses had ever seen the man before. "No one appears to know who shot Lomonte," the informant said. "They think it was a stranger."

Fortunato's death left Tom Lomonte nominally the boss of the first family, but the younger of the brothers was by this time not much more than a figurehead. Certainly he lacked the power to offer any sort of aid to Giosue Gallucci, who now himself became the target of an unknown enemy. The King was well used to the ordinary feuds of Little Italy; he had survived several, and though there were inevitably casualties (his own brother, Gennaro, had been shot dead in 1909 in the depths of the Gallucci bakery), he had thus far always won his wars. As recently as 1912, the King had become enmeshed in a struggle for power with one of Harlem's most notorious Black Handers, Aniello Prisco—a murderous cripple who gloried in the lurid alias of Zopo the Gimp—and when the extortionist unwisely attempted to levy tribute on 109th Street, he was summarily executed by a Gallucci bodyguard. The gunman who killed Zopo was later charged with murder, but few who knew the King were surprised when the man obtained an acquittal on the grounds of self-defense.

This time, though, the boss was dealing with a more implacable enemy. Half a dozen determined attempts were made on his life—he was shot twice in the body in 1913, and again during a gun battle on First Avenue a year later. By then, bodyguarding Giosue Gallucci had become a spectacularly dangerous occupation. The King himself told a friend that ten men had died protecting him over the years, and by the spring of 1915 he was so concerned for his safety that he rarely ventured more than a few yards from his 109th Street bakery and took to wearing a lightweight chain-mail vest, a rare item then obtainable only from certain arms dealers in Chinatown. When yet another bodyguard was killed early in May, shot by a sniper who had been aiming at the boss, even the King grew fatalistic. Henceforth, he told a *Herald* reporter who called on him, he would go about his business without protection. "But they will get me," he added. "I know that they will get me yet."

Who "they" might have been, the *Herald*'s man did not suggest, but it was evident to all Harlem that Gallucci's enemies were well resourced, well organized, and astoundingly persistent. The assassins' chance came a few days later, at ten on the evening of May 17, when the King ventured briefly out of his bakery and hurried four doors down East 109th Street to a coffee shop owned by his teenage son Luca—"a place where men could gather, sip coffee, chat, and play pool, and the police said that if they were well enough known they could get something in that coffee." As the same reporter told it,

> as the two men entered the coffee house they saw several strangers there. Two more followed them in. Some one in the

rear opened the widows saying the place was too warm. Suddenly the lights went out and a man cried in Italian—

"We've got them at last!"

Then the shooting began. At least seven shots were fired. Luca threw his father back to the wall and held himself against him, crying "Shoot me! Shoot me!" They did.

Before the echoes of the shots had reached the street, the assassins, five or six of them, ran out, turned the corner of First Avenue, leaped into a waiting automobile, and were driven away. Neighbors and the police soon found Gallucci and his son, both mortally wounded. . . . [The killers had] sent a bullet through his stomach and another through his neck. At Bellevue Hospital it was said he could not possibly recover.

Gallucci and his son were both still conscious when they reached the hospital, but neither one would talk or help identify their killers. ("Both," another newsman recorded, "steadfastly refused to say how their wounds were inflicted, although assured death was imminent.") To the police, though, there were clues: Gallucci's killers had lain in wait for him, perhaps for days; there had been half a dozen of them; and they had taken the one chance they were offered swiftly and with savage determination. That narrowed down the list of suspects quite considerably.

The investigation proceeded only slowly, nonetheless. Then, on October 13, 1915, Tom Lomonte was murdered, too—in public. He was loitering on a street corner on 116th Street, talking to a female cousin, when a skinny youth crept up from behind and shot him three times in the back. A nearby policeman heard the shots, spotted the gunman, and pursued him as he made off down First Avenue. After a short chase, the youth darted into a tenement at 36 East 115th Street, scrambled up the stairs to the first floor, and hammered on the door of an apartment owned by a Mrs. Maria Pappio. By the time the pursuing officer reached the spot, he had thrown off his clothes, dived into a bed, pulled the covers up to his chin, and was pretending to be asleep. The policeman was not fooled; he dragged the boy out, searched under the bed, and there found a machine pistol. The gunman was dragged off to the nearest precinct house, where, under vigorous interrogation, he gave his name as Antonio Impoluzzo, admitted that he was nineteen years old, and said that he lived downtown, on East 39th Street, where he had only the most modest of criminal records.

There was no clear connection between Lomonte and the boy who killed him. So far as the police were able to establish, Impoluzzo had no friends, no family, and no business whatsoever on East 116th Street; nor did the detectives who investigated the Lomonte murder obtain a confession or anything but the feeblest of alibis from him. At the boy's trial, the same December, the jury heard a week of evidence but no mention of any motive, and he went to his death in the electric chair less than a year later without ever uttering a word about the murder.

Whether the killer kept silent out of loyalty or fear nobody knew, but the police were quietly convinced that he had been hired and sent uptown to kill Lomonte precisely because there was no chance he would be recognized in Harlem. The real question was who would need to take precautions of this sort, and the answer—as both Flynn and the police believed—was that Lomonte's death had probably been ordered by someone who lived in Harlem—the same person, in all likelihood, who had also ordered Fortunato's murder, and possibly Gallucci's, too. Someone whose own men would have been only too easily recognized on 107th Street.

Looking at the murders from a detective's point of view, the most likely killer was whoever benefited most from this series of bloody deaths. And, from that perspective, one suspect stood out. The deaths of the Lomonte brothers and Gallucci, after all, had one important thing in common: They might all have been designed to restore the Morello family to its old ascendancy.

CHAPTER 12

ARTICHOKE KINGS

=

Giosue Gallucci's death in May 1915 left the Morellos the dominant force in Harlem's underworld. Led now by Nick Terranova, the first family experienced little difficulty in seizing control of the lucrative Royal Lottery, as well as Gallucci's share of the coal, ice, and olive trades. There were other ways of making money, too, and if some were now in sharp decline (Black Hand crime became increasingly uncommon after 1912), others soon emerged to take their place. New forms of crime included labor racketeering—often involving the exploitation of workers via their unions—and, increasingly, narcotics, in which the police suspected the Morello family dabbled from around the middle of the decade. Gambling, too, became practically a Mafia monopoly. The family was richer than ever, probably earning tens of thousands of dollars in the twelve months after Gallucci's death.

Crime had become increasingly organized since the Clutch Hand's imprisonment in 1910. The Lower East Side was dominated by Jewish gangs engaged in much the same rackets as the Mafia, and at least as successfully. The West Side was partly Irish, and everywhere there were American criminals as well, involved in every form of business from illegal gaming houses to cocaine trafficking. The Italian underworld, meanwhile, remained as dangerous as ever, and even with Gallucci and Spinelli dead, the Terranova brothers were forced to deal with competitors based within a few blocks of their heartland on 116th Street. Most of these gangs, it is true, were weaker and less feared than the Morellos, but a handful were not, and of these the Terranova brothers' most dangerous rivals were other members of the Mafia. The first family was no longer alone. As early as 1912, New York was home to not one family but four.

WHILE OTHER CITIES, including large ones such as Boston, Chicago, and Los Angeles, never supported more than a single Mafia family, New York was too big and too much the focal point of Sicilian emigration for the same to hold true there. As hundreds of thousands of Italians continued to stream through Ellis Island each year, it was all but inevitable that the Morellos would eventually be challenged. Giuseppe Morello's open preference for Corleonesi was one reason for this; men from other Mafia towns in Sicily knew that they would find it difficult to rise to eminence within the ranks of his family. The city's sprawl was another; however strong the Morellos became, they could never dominate Brooklyn or the Bronx as they did Harlem, and it was in Brooklyn, sometime after 1902, that the second of New York's Mafia gangs was founded.

Its leader was Nicola Schiro—Cola Schiro, he was called—who had arrived in the United States from the small port town of Castellammare del Golfo around the year 1902. Castellammare had a strong criminal tradition, sending large numbers of emigrants to Chicago, Detroit, and Buffalo as well as to Brooklyn, and Schiro was thirty when he first appeared in the United States; between 1905 and 1910 he would find enough of his townsmen in New York to form a family. Like Schiro himself—who was an uninspiring leader, better at making money than he was at leading men—the Castellammare gang kept itself out of the news; the little that is known about the family survives in the words of Salvatore Clemente, who spoke of it to Flynn. Much the same can be said of the second of Brooklyn's families, this one organized by a Palermo Mafioso named Manfredi Mineo. Mineo, who also kept himself out of the public eye, was apparently an effective leader. His family, the smallest and newest of the city's four when Clemente described it early in 1912, would grow to be the largest in New York by 1930.

Both Brooklyn gangs seem to have acknowledged the Clutch Hand as boss of bosses before his imprisonment in 1910; both, certainly, attracted limited attention because they went about their business on the east side of the East River—where there were fewer newspapers and fewer nosy journalists—and because they steered well clear of Flynn by staying out of the trade in counterfeits. It was the third and last of New York's new Mafia families that caused the Morellos the most trouble, in part because the two gangs lived crammed uncomfortably cheek by jowl in Italian Harlem, but also because this gang's leader was a more formidable character than either Schiro or Mineo. Salvatore "Totò" D'Aquila was another Palermitano, which meant that he came from a city in which there were as many competing *cosche* as there were in New York. It also meant that he had been born in a town where the local Mafiosi considered themselves a cut above the yokels of the interior.

D'Aquila was less experienced than Schiro and Mineo. He was not quite thirty years old when he appeared in Manhattan, and though little is known of his first years in the United States, the first blot on his police record was a peculiar and fascinating one. In 1906, D'Aquila was arrested for working as a confidence man—an avocation that demands eloquence, quick thinking, and high intelligence of its practitioners, all useful attributes that were noticeably lacking in the majority of Mafiosi. D'Aquila was also, as he would soon prove, the toughest, strongest, and most aggressive of New York's rival bosses. It was the Morellos' misfortune that they shared the cramped and busy streets of Harlem with him.

Powerful new bosses such as Totò D'Aquila would almost certainly have risen to prominence whether or not Lupo and Morello had been jailed. It seems unlikely, though, that the first family would have faced quite so many threats so quickly had the Clutch Hand remained free. Morello's position as acknowledged boss of bosses would surely have prevented that; so, too, would the almost superstitious awe in which he was held. And the Morello who had—at least if the police were to be believed—half a dozen members of his own family shot or hacked to death as a precaution would surely have dealt with emerging rivals more ruthlessly than his half brothers felt able to. The truth was that no criminal organization, even one as well established as Morello's family, could survive unscathed the jailing of so many of its leaders. Nor could the Clutch Hand's successors simply demand the respect that the old boss had so laboriously earned. Mafiosi, whether Sicilian or American, have always had a keen appreciation of charisma and expect more than mere efficiency from the men who lead them. From that perspective, the appointment of the colorless Lomonte brothers to lead the Harlem family had been a terrible misjudgment on Morello's part. It permitted rival Mafiosi to rise in a manner that would have been unthinkable a few years earlier. It also meant that Nick Terranova had to face threats that the Clutch Hand never had.

According to Nicola Gentile, the well-traveled Pittsburgh Mafioso,

D'Aquila was a dangerous man: arrogant, ambitious, and feared rather than respected by his men. He was efficient, too, and with Lupo and Morello out of the way wasted no time in turning his own family into the strongest *cosca* in the city. D'Aquila achieved this feat in part by attracting defectors from New York's other Mafia gangs; most came from the Morellos. Among those who joined his family in search of greater power and larger spoils by 1912 were two well-known members of the first family: Giuseppe Fontana, the old Sicilian Mafioso notorious for his involvement in the murder of the head of the Bank of Sicily in 1893, and Joseph Fanaro, a suspect in the brutal killing of Salvatore Marchiani who had also been arrested at the time of the Barrel Murder.

The defection of a man of Fontana's experience and reputation was as good a sign as any of the shifting balance of power in Italian Harlem, and few of New York's Mafiosi can have been surprised when, with the Clutch Hand in prison, D'Aquila maneuvered to have himself acclaimed as boss of bosses. The title still conveyed no formal powers, apparently, and the new boss engineered his elevation in the approved way, by acclamation at a meeting of the Mafia's general assembly. According to Gentile, though, D'Aquila was ruthless in his determination to acquire influence, and Salvatore Clemente's evidence confirms as much. Through Clemente, Flynn learned that the Palermo man possessed and exercised the power to summon all New York Mafiosi to meetings. D'Aquila, moreover, closely controlled the admission of new members into all four families. "There are four gangs in this locality," the Chief's informant said, "and when a new member is proposed for any one of the four gangs, it is always brought up before [them all]."

By the autumn of 1913, in short, D'Aquila had established himself in a stronger position than Morello had ever claimed. His increasing dominance greatly worried the Schiro and Manfredi families of Brooklyn, as well as the Terranovas, and the strength of the D'Aquila family, which was by now equal to that of the other three Mafia gangs combined, posed such an obvious threat that for a time his subordinates combined their strength and openly opposed him. Clemente set all this out for Flynn, explaining that

> there are four gangs, that three of them are working together: the Manfredi gang, the gang headed by Nicola Schiro, both of Brooklyn, and the Lomonti gang of Harlem; that the fourth gang,

led by D'Aquila of Harlem, is opposed by the other three gangs; that [men have] been shot on account of the feud between these gangs in all probability; that no doubt there will be more shooting soon.

Clemente's predictions were soon proved correct when, taking advantage of D'Aquila's absence from New York on a trip home to Sicily, the Terranovas took revenge on both defectors from their ranks. In November, Fontana was ambushed on his way to work on 105th Street by gunmen from the Morello and Mineo families. Fanaro followed him into oblivion three weeks later.

Two deaths still amounted to a squabble, not a full-blown war, and D'Aquila's response, whatever it was (Clemente remained infuriatingly silent on the subject), did not include an escalation of hostilities. That left the Terranovas free to deal with another of their sometime allies, the most powerful of all the gambling lords in Little Italy. Still smarting from Fontana's and Fanaro's betrayals, Nick Terranova went gunning for the DiMarco brothers.

JOE DIMARCO HAD FEARED for his life for several years. Stocky, clever, smallpox-scarred, and twenty-eight years old, he owned a stake in the Lomontes' feed business and passed in the immigrant quarter as a restaurateur. DiMarco's real business, though, was running profitable card games throughout Italian Harlem, an avocation that required him to be nearly as well connected politically as Giosue Gallucci. He had been a Morello ally since at least 1910 but had fallen spectacularly from favor with the Lomontes' decline, not least because he would not give the Terranova brothers the larger share of gambling profits they believed to be their due. That had been uncomfortable, and over the next three years DiMarco had seen enough of Nick Terranova to recognize the murderous ambition in the rising boss. Word in the Italian underworld was that the two men cordially hated each other, that DiMarco had tried to have Nick shot, that the attempt had failed, and that the gambler's own life was now in danger.

The Terranova brothers first struck back at DiMarco in April 1913, when an assassin hidden behind a fence on East 112th Street opened fire as he walked past. The gunman knew his job; DiMarco was shot through the neck, leaving a deep and bloody wound. Taken to the hospital still conscious, he was told that he would die. It took several skillful surgeons and an "unusual operation" at Harlem Hospital to save him.

A year later, the Terranovas tried again. This time DiMarco was an even softer target: he was reclining, helpless, in a barber's chair on 106th Street when two men armed with sawed-off shotguns burst into the shop. This time the gambler was even luckier. Instead of closing to decisive range, his would-be killers opened fire from the doorway, turned, and ran. Lying there smothered in lather and blood, DiMarco felt cautiously about his body and found he had been wounded. A dozen pellets had struck home, but none had done serious damage. Again he survived.

Two narrow escapes would have been enough to persuade even an optimist to leave Harlem, and DiMarco was scarcely that. Late in 1914, he moved his operations more than a mile downtown, opening a large restaurant at 163 West 49th Street and hiring two gunmen to act as bodyguards. He rented an apartment above the premises and lived there with his brother Salvatore, seldom venturing out. These precautions were enough to keep him alive for another eighteen months, but they could not do so indefinitely, and in the summer of 1916 the Terranova brothers made a final effort to dispose of his elusive enemy and seize control of his gambling rackets. Everything was carefully arranged. There was to be no possibility, this time, of a mistake.

DiMarco, the *Herald*'s man in Little Italy reported,

> liked to play poker, and his enemies used that fact to lure him to his death. Some one guided him to a dark little room in the rear of a tenement down in James Street in the afternoon, where it was understood there was to be a poker game. DiMarco took one, or maybe two, of his bodyguards along. [One, Charles] Lombardi sat beside him at the poker table.
>
> How far the game had progressed, who was there in addition to DiMarco and Lombardi, and other incidents of the afternoon are blank to the detectives. They do know, however, that a "straight flush," a very unusual "hand," was dealt to DiMarco, for that "hand" was found under his bullet-riddled body. They believe that the dealing of that hand was the signal for the "gunmen" to open fire on DiMarco and his unsuspecting bodyguard. Twenty shots were fired, perhaps more. . . . DiMarco was shot ten times and Lombardi twice. Eight or ten men who had been in

the room and were a part of the murder plot escaped "clean," as the police say. That is, they got away before any one saw them and left only their hats as clews, and as ten straw hats were found the police are suspicious that they were left to mislead them.

There was a postscript to DiMarco's murder. The dead gambler's brother, Salvatore—long a force in the coal racket—was found dead two months later, sprawled in a clump of weeds on Washington Avenue. He had been struck hard across the forehead with some sort of club, perhaps a baseball bat, and lay with his skull turned to eggshell, his throat cut, and a large sum of money—the proceeds of the sale of his brother's restaurant—missing from his pockets. Salvatore's murder finished the DiMarcos as a force in the Italian underworld and made certain that there could be no feud with the Morello family. That, as it happened, was just as well, for by then the Terranova brothers were confronting a threat more serious than any they had faced. Over the East River in Brooklyn, a new power, hailing from Naples, was rising in the underworld—one as terrible and as murderous as the Mafia and no more willing to share the spoils of New York with others.

The Camorra had arrived in the United States. War was brewing.

THE CAMORRA, A CRIMINAL SOCIETY with roots deeper even than the Mafia's, had originated in Naples around the year 1820 as a mutual welfare fraternity for prisoners in the city's jail. It evolved outside of prison walls, moving first into extortion and then to the creation of a full-fledged gang of vicious crooks with bases throughout the city. The Camorra differed from its Sicilian rival in being far more hierarchical; among other things, it had a single recognized and formally anointed leader. In most respects, however, the Neapolitans worked in much the same way as the Mafia. There was a gang—a family—for each district of the city, led by a *capintrito* and consisting of anything up to a hundred men who were formally initiated into the fraternity and divided into four ranks. There was a central council, known as the Great Mother, which settled disputes and punished betrayals. And there were rackets, more or less identical to those run by the Sicilians: horse theft, blackmail, and the control of gambling. *Camorra* was, like *Mafia,* a word used by outsiders. Initiated members of the fraternity referred to it as the Società dell'Umiltà, the Society of Humility, or as the Bella Società Riformata, the Fine Reformed Society.

Since Naples was nearly as poor as Sicily, there were nearly as many Neapolitans in the United States as there were Sicilians, and most large American cities had their Neapolitan quarter and their Neapolitan criminals. When precisely the society first established itself in New York is obscure, though almost certainly it gained its first footholds later than the Mafia did. What can be said with confidence is that a number of prominent Camorrists entered the United States between 1900 and 1910, that most settled in across the East River from the Morellos' strongholds, and that they formed two distinct but allied gangs, one based on Navy Street in Brooklyn and the other farther out, in Coney Island. The former gang, based in a coffee shop at 133 Navy Street, was led by Alessandro Vollero, a youthful-looking thirty-year-old *capintrito* who had arrived in New York in 1907 with his wife and children. Vollero's boss, Pellegrino Marano, ran the Coney Islanders from a restaurant, the Santa Lucia, which stood close to the amusement parks.

Thanks in large part to the strength of the Mafia, the Camorra was significantly less powerful and less organized in New York than its Sicilian rivals as late as June 1916. There were fewer Camorrists than there were Mafiosi—one member of the Navy Street gang put their total strength, with that of the Coney Islanders, at no more than forty men—and they made their money from gambling and from dealing in cocaine; the far more lucrative vegetable, ice, and coal rackets were all controlled by Sicilians. Membership, too, was a privilege granted far more easily by the Camorra than it ever was by the Mafia. One low-level Neapolitan gunman spent years working more or less honestly in Buffalo before being suddenly summoned to New York and asked to join the gang, apparently simply because he had known another of the Coney Island leaders, Tony Paretti—Tony the Shoemaker, he was called—when they were young in Italy. The Camorra did resemble its Sicilian counterpart in some respects: Loosely linked Neapolitan gangs existed in a number of cities, from Boston to Chicago and from Buffalo to Pittsburgh, and the Neapolitans also organized their own initiation ceremonies, which closely resembled those of their Sicilian rivals. The same Camorra probationer described being handed a penknife and ordered to draw blood from his friend Paretti's arm. Marano then "went near the shoemaker's arm, and sucked the blood, and a little more blood came out. He said to me, 'You have gained.'" For all this, though, and ambitious though its leaders were, the Neapolitan gangs remained less influential than the Mafia even after Giosue Gallucci's death.

Relations between the Sicilians on one side and the Camorra leaders on the other were peaceful enough at first. The rival gangs stuck to their own territories, sharing the spoils of New York's rackets, and their leaders attended an annual "smoker" in Brooklyn, arranged to encourage amity between the two organizations. All this changed, however, after the year 1915, as the Camorrists, sensing weakness, became determined to expand into Manhattan, and the Terranova brothers attempted to resist their advances. The outcome was the first of many modern "wars" between rival factions of criminals.

One flash point was the Neapolitans' first appearance in Manhattan, when the Coney Island gang's Marano opened up a gambling house on Hester Street after Joe DiMarco was killed. Another was a budding feud between Vollero and Nick Terranova, whom the Navy Street gang boss blamed for the death of a close friend. It was only on the orders of Marano that Vollero agreed to keep the peace, at least until a conference between the two sides due to be held at the Santa Lucia late in June 1916.

Marano's plan was to bring the Mafia and the Camorra closer together, to ease friction between the gangs, tighten their joint control over the Italian underworld, and formally parcel out the New York rackets. The Neapolitans knew what they wanted from this arrangement—they were greedy for more money and more power, and Vollero particularly envied the Morellos' stranglehold over the artichoke trade. Motives were less clear on the Sicilian side, though the Terranovas were certainly anxious to avert the threat of fighting a war on two fronts—against the Camorra on one side and the even more grasping Totò D'Aquila on the other. If the Neapolitans read the first family's agreement to discuss concessions as a sign of weakness, though, they were sorely disappointed. When Marano announced that he wanted to discuss not just the vegetable racket but gambling, cocaine, and extortion, too, the Terranova brothers decided that they had heard enough. Unwilling to surrender their hard-fought-for dominance over any racket, Nick, Ciro, and Vincenzo stonewalled until the talks broke down. So far as Vollero was concerned, that was a declaration of war.

Cooperation between the gangs did not cease immediately; it was Vollero who supplied the gunmen who killed Joe DiMarco, and soon after the gambler's murder the Terranovas came down to Navy Street with fifty dollars, a gift for the assassins. By August 1916, Vollero was actively plotting his enemies' destruction.

In the end, though, it was not Vollero but Marano who decided that the time was right to dispose of the Morellos. The Coney Island boss's motives were clear enough—he wanted to seize control of the Mafia's rackets and in particular the three most valuable: the artichoke trade, the lottery, and gambling. The Morellos' dominance of the lottery particularly incensed him. "Yes," one of Marano's men would remember him raging, "it is true that these semen want to keep that game uptown, but they will have to figure it with me. I will show them who Don Pellegrino Marano is. I will have them all killed."

Tony the Shoemaker agreed. "All the Neapolitans are semen," he chipped in, "because if we could all get together and agree, after this job is done, we would all be wearing diamond rings; and we would get all the graft."

Marano's first task was to persuade the Navy Street gang to back his plan. This was by no means an easy matter; for all Vollero's scheming, most of the Navy Streeters, who were based just over the East River in Brooklyn, had long been just as friendly with the Morellos as they were with the Coney Island gang. The Morellos had even saved the life of one of Vollero's closest friends, Andrea Ricci, in some otherwise unrecorded incident a short time earlier, and it took Marano quite some time to persuade his fellow Neapolitans to agree to his scheme. Even then there were dissenters; Vollero's chief lieutenant, Leopoldo Lauritano, frankly told other members of the gang that he found the Sicilians more trustworthy than the Coney Islanders. In the end, though, greed won out. As Marano's right-hand man explained matters to the reluctant Ricci, "You must consent to the killing of the Morellos, because you know that up in Harlem there is quite some money to be made. You and I have been there. If we open up a saloon, you know that we can make money with the ice and coal."

"Andrea, you must consent," Vollero added. "You see, there is the graft on the artichokes, the policy [lottery] graft and the *zicchinetta* [card games], and the ice and coal. We had DiMarco killed to satisfy them. Now we can kill the Morellos to get this graft."

The Brooklyn Camorra of 1916 was nowhere as fearsome as the Morello family. It was far less well organized—both the Navy Street and the Coney Island gangs had existed for no more than a year or two—and not so well resourced. There was, for instance, little of the cooperation that stood the Sicilians in such good stead; both Vollero and Marano closely guarded important portions of their operations, the Navy Street boss refusing to share the cash he made peddling cocaine "to theatrical people and waiters," and Marano keeping the profits of his Harlem lottery for himself. Because of this, the Neapolitans agreed, it would be wildly dangerous to allow themselves to be dragged into a lengthy war. Their best and perhaps only hope was to remove the entire Morello leadership in a single stroke. Dispose of the Terranova brothers and their aides, Marano and Vollero thought, and their Harlem rackets would fall naturally, like ripened fruit.

It took the Camorra bosses a little less than a month to plot the Morellos' deaths. Six Mafia leaders were invited to Navy Street early in September, ostensibly to discuss the division of the New York rackets: the three Terranova brothers, Stefano "Steve" La Salle, Eugene Ubriaco, and lastly Giuseppe Verrazano, who had taken over from DiMarco as head of the Morellos' gambling interests. With those men dead, Vollero thought, what remained of the first family would flounder, leaderless. The foot soldiers of the Morello gang would either be reduced to petty crime or be forced to join forces with the Neapolitans of Navy Street.

A dozen members of Vollero's gang gathered on Navy Street the day before the meeting in order to go over the arrangements for the planned murders one last time. Three men had been chosen to do the killing, and arrangements were made for their guns to be loaded with special ammunition—bullets smeared with garlic juice and pepper, which were believed to cause infection in a wound and would, it was hoped, account for any Morellos who might be only injured in the ambush. The pistols themselves were concealed in a special cupboard hidden in the wall, and various other Camorrists were assigned lesser tasks: greeting the visitors, making them drinks, and escorting them to the Navy Street café.

The ambush had been planned for the afternoon of September 7, a warm early autumn Thursday, and the Camorra assassins made sure they were ready in plenty of time, carefully concealing themselves in doorways that looked out onto a corner of Johnson Street. To Vollero's dismay and disappointment, though, only two of the six Morello bosses appeared for the meeting: Nick Terranova and his friend Eugene Ubriaco. The reason for the others' absence was never known; Terranova's willingness to travel to Brooklyn without bodyguards suggests he was unaware of the Camorrists' treachery, and most likely the decision to leave the other four members of the gang behind was nothing more than ordinary caution. Whatever the truth, Nick's usually well-tuned sense of menace failed him now. Noticing that the Camorrist who served his glass of Moxie looked drawn and had turned white with stress, Terranova looked him up and down and said, "What is the matter? You are kind of pale. Don't you feel well?" "I don't," the man replied, and the Mafia boss shrugged the matter off. "Why don't you have someone examine you?" he said; then, when it was time to go, he and Ubriaco strolled off arm in arm down Johnson Street to their bloody deaths.

Vollero's gunmen held their fire until the men were close. Then, emerging from their doorways, they unleashed a hail of bullets, catching their targets from several angles. Terranova was the first to die; the Morello boss had no time to do more than half draw a revolver from his pocket before he crumpled in the nearest gutter, shot six times. Ubriaco lasted a few seconds longer, pulling his gun and backing off along the street as he tried to pick off his attackers. The Camorrists proved to have the better aim, however; Ubriaco was shot through the heart after discharging five of his six bullets. He collapsed on the pavement, his body lying amid shards of glass from windows shattered in the fight. By the time the last echoes of the fight had died away, Vollero's men had fired some twenty times. They had also disposed of the Morellos' most effective leader.

There was a long police investigation, naturally; the deaths had been too violent and too public, too close to children playing in the streets, to be brushed aside as gangland killings often were. The Camorrists, though, were unconcerned; they made regular protection payments to the local Italian detective, Michael Mealli, who was one of the first policemen on the scene and who conspicuously failed to turn in much in the way of evidence. They also felt safe on their own territory. "The police cannot get any witnesses down there," Vollero was heard to boast of Navy Street. "We can take care of the witnesses, we can get witnesses to prove anything we want. . . . They dare not come forward to testify against me."

Nick Terranova's death shook the Morellos to their core. Caught unawares by the sudden outbreak of hostilities, the Harlem Mafia was reduced to something close to disarray and soon lost another half dozen of its members. Four Morello associates were shot dead in Philadelphia; a gambler named Joe Nazarro was taken up to Yonkers, shot, and thrown under a streetcar simply for talking to the Mafia. Then, a month after Terranova's murder, Vollero managed to corner another Mafia leader,

Giuseppe Verrazano. Verrazano met his end in a restaurant on the Bowery, shot down by two more Camorra gunmen. After that, Ciro and Vincenzo Terranova felt vulnerable even on East 116th Street. The Terranovas stuck close to their headquarters, and their confidence was further shaken when neighbors reported that a group of Neapolitans had been attempting to hire rooms that overlooked the entrance to their apartment block.

In fact, Vollero's and Marano's efforts to dispose of the Morellos were even more determined than the Mafia realized. There was a plan to smuggle an enormous bomb into the cellar of the Terranovas' tenement and blow up the building with everyone in it. When this proved to be impossible, the Coney Islanders schemed to have poison slipped into the brothers' food. The Camorra had no choice but to end matters, Marano said; if they did not, the Terranovas would. Morello gunmen were spotted on Johnson Street, and in January 1917 Vollero himself only narrowly survived an attempted Mafia ambush. The Camorra boss spent several weeks in the hospital, recovering from shotgun wounds, and another member of the Navy Street group summed the position up succinctly: "We have to leave this game, because this game will be the cause of the death of all of us, [and] because after this game is given up, we are able to work and we will remove each and every one of them from our presence."

The Camorra never did account for Vincenzo and Ciro Terranova, but fear of imminent assassination certainly did gravely disrupt the Sicilian brothers' criminal businesses. With its leader dead and his successors scattering for cover, the first family was in no position to maintain its usual firm grip on its rackets, and Vollero and Marano wasted no time in moving in on the Morellos' operations. Gamblers who had paid tribute to DiMarco and Verrazano found themselves forced to make weekly journeys over to Brooklyn with their books.

The Camorra's dominance of the New York rackets lasted only a few months, roughly from November 1916 to the spring of the following year. Vegetable wholesalers were informed that they would henceforth pay dues of $50 a railroad car to Navy Street on all the artichokes arriving in the city, and similar efforts were made to wrest the coal and ice trades from the Mafia. The wholesalers, though, proved unexpectedly resistant, and to Vollero's fury, results were mixed; in some cases the Camorra's demands were so high that their intended victims could not afford to pay; in others, men who had been dealing with the Morellos for years resisted because they nursed suspicions that the Sicilians would soon strike back.

The Camorrists had had great expectations for the Italian artichoke trade, and their plans had beem ambitious. Marano's original idea was for his men to open their own store at Wallabout Market and use that as a base to drive rival dealers out of business. He was soon disabused of that notion by one Gaetano Migliaccio, an outspoken veteran of the vegetable wholesale trade who flatly declined to sell solely to the Camorra and who gave the Neapolitans a sharp lesson on the realities of his business. "Are you crazy?" Migliaccio demanded. "To begin with, you need a capital of ten or eleven thousand dollars, and then the persons will go to the police and have each and every one of you arrested. Leave it to me—if you want to sell artichokes, I will give you the oppportunity. I know what I am doing." The dealer eventually calculated that he could supply the gangs' Wallabout Market store with a maximum of forty boxes of artichokes—an offer that Vollero meekly accepted.

Marano and his men had little more luck with the other vegetable wholesalers of the district. Brooklyn's artichoke dealers bravely clubbed together and simply refused to pay Vollero's "tax" of $50 a car; the Camorrists responded with a counteroffer of $15, and the two sides eventually settled on a compromise of only $25. Marano had even less luck with the policy bosses who ran Italian lotteries and turned out to be "pretty hard characters themselves." The Coney Island gangster's first demand was for $1,000 a week. The gamblers flatly refused to make any such concession, bluntly stating that they would sooner close their games down than hand over such enormous sums; in the end Marano had to settle for a verbal agreement that his gang would cream a 60 percent share in the profits—a sum that came, apparently, to far less than the $1,000 he had originally demanded. In practice, even that proved to be a crippling amount; a few weeks later, after further negotiation, the Coney Islanders settled for a paltry $150 a week. Only in a single game in Harlem was the Camorra able to extort an 80 percent share of the winnings, and by early 1917, when Vollero found himself short of cash, he was glad to hand control of the Harlem lottery back to the gamblers who ran it in exchange for a mere two hundred dollars. As for the coal and ice merchants of Manhattan, many of whom were based in Italian Harlem, they proved even less easy to coerce, and the Camorra made practically no headway with them. In the end, for all their bluster and all their threats, the Navy Street and Coney Island gangs were bitterly disappointed by the income that they squeezed from the Morellos' rackets. They had anticipated giant profits.

There was, also, another problem: A man named Ralph Daniello had taken his teenage mistress and run off with her to Reno to get married.

ALFONSO PEPE, ALIAS RALPH DANIELLO, better known as Ralph the Barber, was a Neapolitan thug of little consequence right up to the moment that he vanished from New York after Nick Terranova's murder. Daniello was nothing special to look at—of medium height and stocky build, with a squared-off face, blank eyes, and an eight-inch scar that ran right across one cheek—and he was nothing special as a criminal. In his years as a member of the Navy Street gang, he had never risen above the lowest rung of the Camorra's rigid hierarchy, a station so far below Vollero and Marano that he was practically beneath their notice. Now, though, in the autumn of 1917, Ralph had his bosses' full attention. In Reno, and in trouble, he was threatening to reveal enough about their operations to get half the members of the gang locked up for life.

Daniello's problems had their roots in a murder he had committed eighteen months earlier. It was May 1916, and he was working in the lucrative narcotics trade, selling quantities of the new wonder drug, cocaine, that had arrived on the scene. Business had been good, but not long before the DiMarco shooting the Barber had been involved in a violent argument over a drug deal. Ralph's contact drew a weapon. Ralph fired first.

Prudence dictated that Daniello leave the city, which he did—though only when he was certain that the police were onto him, and then only in the company of his sixteen-year-old mistress, Amelia Valve. Exiled to the dusty streets of Reno, the Barber soon ran out of cash. It was at that point that Ralph wrote to his boss, Vollero, asking for money to be wired to him and for further payments to be made to his parents in Italy. That, he thought, was no more than his due recompense for years of faithful service. When Vollero failed to respond to any of Daniello's letters, Daniello grew bitter—so bitter, in fact, that the next time he picked up a pen it was to write instead to the New York police. The men of the Brooklyn Italian Squad recognized the Barber's value better than Vollero did. By the last week of November 1917, Ralph had been brought back to Brooklyn, telling the detectives everything he knew.

No Italian gangster had ever talked in such great detail. Even Comito's damning confession, seven years earlier, had lacked the range and the authority of the Barber's testimony. The information that Ralph gave cleared up twenty-three unsolved murders—among them Nick Terranova's—and supplied leads for hundreds of lesser crimes. Then there were the gangster's detailed recollections of day-to-day life in the Camorra, laying bare what it actually meant to serve a master like Vollero.

There was, at least according to Daniello, not much glamour in a Camorrist's life. He himself had lived for several years on a fixed wage of around fifteen dollars a week, and, in exchange for this paltry sum, he was expected to collect protection money and commit whatever assaults or murders his bosses might deem necessary. Married gang members earned a little more, some twenty dollars, but for many others the pay was less. "Members of the gang who just did odd jobs, and did not work regularly . . . would get seven dollars a week," the Barber said.

Amid this welter of extraordinary testimony, several facts stood out. Murder had played a large part in Vollero's strategy. Gamblers who refused to pay tribute to the Camorra might receive a single warning ("A rebel is first slashed with a stiletto on the cheek"), but any further failure to comply meant death. "Different methods were used," Daniello added, describing how he and his associates carried out their murderous instructions. "One man was caught in an ambush. More often, one of us started a quarrel over a game of cards so that the other could 'do the trick' in the confusion." In part, this willingness to use violence was almost certainly a function of the gang's small size. Among them, the Volleros, the Maranos, and the Morellos numbered no more than about fifty men, according to the Barber. This, in turn, suggested to District Attorney Edward Swann that the Camorra might be crippled by even a handful of convictions.

Daniello's confessions were certainly almost sufficient in themselves to doom both the Navy Street gang and their friends in Coney Island. Swann's star witness named names, identifying Vollero and Marano as the leaders of the Camorra and gunmen such as Tony Notaro and Tony the Shoemaker as the killers of Nick Terranova and Giuseppe Verrazano; all four men were soon picked up, as was Alphonse Sgroia, who had four murders to his name and went by the name of "the Butcher." The Barber's richly detailed testimony, which took the best part of two months to give, not only utterly disrupted the operations of both

Camorra gangs but shone a penetrating light into other murky aspects of the Brooklyn underworld. Most of the borough's Italian police officers were taking bribes, Daniello revealed, and he named names—implicating not only Mike Mealli, the precinct detective firmly in Vollero's pocket, but even such storied officers as Charles Carrao (the subject of a recent and admiring profile in *The New York Times*) in efforts to protect the Neapolitans from retribution. This part of the Barber's testimony caused a small sensation, and though Carrao escaped apparently unscathed, the same could not be said of the unfortunate Mealli, who was reduced to the ranks and put back on the streets as a beat patrolman.

The arrests of so many members of the Navy Street and Coney Island gangs severely disrupted the Camorra, and the Harlem Mafia was affected, too; Daniello's careful account of the part that he and his fellow Navy Streeters had played in arranging Joe DiMarco's murder made it clear that the killing had been committed to please the Terranova brothers. When that bit of underworld cooperation was exposed, Vincenzo and Ciro were arrested, too, along with several of their followers.

Most of the Mafiosi detained for the DiMarco shooting were eventually released, including Vincenzo. The district attorney's office muttered darkly that the first family "possessed influence" of a substantial and helpful kind. Ciro, though, actually stood trial—twice—for ordering the gambler's murder, making him the first of the Morello family's leaders to face a capital charge in court. The middle Terranova brother stayed in prison for more than half a year, and the case dragged on long after the initial hearing in February 1918—the first trial was halted when the judge fell ill, and the retrial could not be heard until the summer. Ciro was very fortunate in his choice of advocate; he was represented by Martin Littleton, a wizard from Texas who, despite having a mere nine months of formal schooling to his name, had somehow turned himself into the greatest American jury lawyer of his generation. It was Littleton who spotted the great flaw in the DA's case. Under American law as it then stood, no man could be convicted solely on the evidence of an accomplice, and, placing Ralph Daniello on the witness stand, the smooth-tongued Texan soon tied the hapless Barber in such knots that he was able to convince both judge and jury that Ralph and Terranova belonged to the same gang. With that admission on the record, Littleton moved for the whole case to be dismissed, and even his counterpart in the district attorney's office was forced to admit that "it was entirely hopeless to go to the jury" with an argument so heavily dependent on an informant's evidence. Ciro was discharged from custody on June 6, a relieved man, and returned to a rapturous welcome on East 116th Street.

The Camorrists who had been betrayed by the Barber enjoyed no such luck. Andrea Ricci died in 1917, shot dead by his own friends for fear he would betray them, and the cases against Pellegrino Marano, Alessandro Vollero, and their followers would occupy the Brooklyn district attorney's office and the courts for much of 1918 and drag on well into the 1920s; the last in this protracted series of prosecutions took place as late as 1926, when Tony the Shoemaker unwisely returned to the United States from Italy, where he had fled after the murder. Ralph Daniello was the chief prosecution witness in almost all of these trials, supported in several cases by a fellow Camorrist named Tony Notaro, who drew reams of press coverage by describing in some detail the Society's elaborate initiation rituals.

The Barber's detailed revelations of his career in the Camorra proved decisive. Alessandro Vollero was sentenced to death, a verdict he managed to get reduced on appeal to life imprisonment. The Coney Island boss, Marano, got twenty years to life for murder in the second degree; three other members of the gang were convicted of manslaughter and sentenced to terms of six to twelve years in Sing Sing. Others fled. Without its leaders, the remnants of the Navy Street gang dispersed and the Morellos, to their delighted astonishment, were able to reclaim almost all of the business they had lost after Nick Terranova's murder, from the *zicchinetta* games to the artichoke racket in the Brooklyn vegetable markets. Seen from this perspective, Ralph Daniello's testimony had greater impact than almost any ever given in a New York court. Without the Barber, the Neapolitans would almost certainly have won their war with the Sicilians and reduced the Harlem Mafia to a criminal irrelevance, with incalculable consequences for the history of crime.

As it was, the Camorra would never again be a force in New York's underworld. Nor, of course, would Giosue Gallucci. Ciro and Vincenzo Terranova were, in effect, the last men standing in the Italian underworld, and with the prisoners of Atlanta at last nearing the dates set for their parole, the Mafia's grip over Little Italy was as strong in 1919 as it had been a decade earlier.

All of which was just as well, since opportunities of unparalleled magnificence would soon present themselves.

CHAPTER 13

THE EIGHTEENTH AMENDMENT

=

GIUSEPPE MORELLO WALKED OUT OF THE FEDERAL PRISON AT Atlanta on February 1, 1920, paroled ten years from the day he had started his sentence. The world had changed significantly since he had gone away. New York was more crowded than ever; the city had added nearly another million people to its population, more than a hundred thousand of them Italians. Cars, a rarity in 1910, were commonplace in 1920. So too were subway trains. The country had emerged from isolation to fight in the Great War (Vincenzo and Ciro Terranova had both been issued with draft cards, though neither man was actually called up) and ended up richer and more powerful than ever. Crime, meanwhile, had grown steadily more profitable and complex. A hedonistic generation—men desperate to forget the war, women emboldened by flapper fashions and the vote—was sending the demand for illicit pleasures of all sorts soaring, with a concomitant rise in the competition for power and money. Even within the Mafia itself, new bosses had emerged to challenge the old order.

But Morello would not slide easily back into his role as boss of bosses, or even boss for that matter. Totò D'Aquila, who had taken on Morello's mantle after the Clutch Hand's conviction, had a stranglehold on the leadership of the fraternity. The ruthless Palermo man still controlled the most fearsome of New York's criminal families, and, arbitrary though his rule could be, none of the city's Mafiosi were disposed to oppose him. There were by now five families operating within the city limits, among them numbering as many as two thousand men of respect and their associates. Many would have been well known to Morello; a number of the bosses whose careers had begun before 1910 were still as active as ever, among them Cola Schiro in the Bronx and Manfredi Mineo in Brooklyn. But there were newer faces among the ranks of New York's Mafiosi, too. Several of them were friends of the Morello-Terranova clan, among them Joe Masseria, from Marsala in western Sicily, whose criminal record stretched back to 1907. The most influential of the new powers, though, was Umberto Valenti, a fast-rising thug known, according to Nicola Gentile, "as 'the Ghost' for his cruelty and his way of disappearing after an action." Valenti made a natural ally for the Morellos; he had based himself in a burgeoning new Italian quarter in Manhattan's East Village. But there were new rivals to be confronted, too, and the entire Italian underworld, whether friend or foe, was ready to fight for its share in the profits to be made in the immigrant districts.

The first family thus faced more competition and greater threats to its old dominance than ever before, this at a time when a good number of its old leaders were dead. Grievous losses had been incurred; the Morellos' battles against Gallucci and the Camorra war had stripped the Harlem Mafia of several of its best men and left the surviving Terranova brothers, Ciro and Vincenzo, as heads of the family. Ciro, the younger of the two, was the more active and influential; his artichoke racket continued to produce good profits, and he and Vincenzo had also become heavily involved in some equally lucrative criminal businesses. The murder of the DiMarco brothers had given the Terranovas a firm grip over much, perhaps most, of Italian gambling in Manhattan. But the DiMarcos' deaths also demonstrated the failings of Ciro Terranova's leadership. Morello had always been able to control his chief lieutenants; New York's Mafiosi may have feared the Clutch Hand, but they had always grudgingly respected him. Nick Terranova, too, had made an effective boss. But Ciro and Vincenzo commanded only a fraction of the regard that had buttressed both their predecessors. In the wake of the Camorra war, they had been compelled to retain their tenuous grip on power through violence.

It says a great deal for Morello's abilities and reputation that his reappearance in New York—accompanied, from the summer of 1920, by the almost equally influential Lupo—so unsettled Totò D'Aquila that the city's all-powerful boss of bosses was panicked into ordering just such drastic measures against the Clutch Hand and the Wolf. No firsthand evidence has survived of what happened in Manhattan that summer; Flynn, promoted to a post in Washington, had been taken off the case, and the Chief's intricate network of informants had fallen into disuse during the First World War. What seems to have occurred, however, was that Morello and Lupo were accorded a rapturous reception in Harlem—welcomed, feted, and restored, at least in part, to their old eminence. Word of their reemergence reached D'Aquila, and D'Aquila just as quickly sensed a threat. The boss of bosses took his time, ensuring that he retained the necessary support. Then, at the next meeting of the Mafia's general assembly, held sometime between June and September 1921, he saw to it that both his rivals were denounced. The two New Yorkers were labeled dangerous traitors to the established order, tried in their absence, and sentenced to death.

What precisely Lupo and Morello had done to deserve this fate remains unclear. The Clutch Hand had been working to reestablish his position in East Harlem. That much would have been expected, and no doubt tolerated, too. But it had soon become clear that Morello posed a much more direct threat to the new boss's rule. It is not unlikely that the Clutch Hand really had been plotting to usurp Totò D'Aquila's power and so regain his old eminence, and almost certain that he had struck up a dangerous friendship with Umberto Valenti, who was rapidly developing his power base in the East Village. It was this combination of north and south Manhattan, of an old leader noted for his cunning and a new one renowned for his viciousness, that D'Aquila feared. The death sentences passed by the Mafia assembly applied not only to Morello and Lupo but to Valenti and several of his followers as well.

Flynn and Nicola Gentile help to explain what happened next. Thanks, no doubt, to friends in the council, the three condemned leaders heard of their sentences before D'Aquila could put them into effect. Acting hurriedly, they fled the country, leaving by ship from Newport News, a small port in Virginia. It was the first time that Morello had left the United States since 1892, and though it was highly unlikely that the Italian authorities were still seeking him in connection with his counterfeiting conviction, now twenty-six years old, the decision does suggest that he was desperate.

The fleeing Mafiosi were next seen in Sicily, where they arrived around October 1921 in search of sanctuary and assistance. The men spent the better part of six months hiding around Palermo. It was during that time that Morello, Lupo, and Valenti called on Nicola Gentile in the hope that he could help resolve their problems.

The exiled Mafiosi had chosen their man well. Gentile was an established power in both the American and the Sicilian arms of their fraternity, a known conciliator who had helped resolve several similar disputes. But he was also a formidable boss in his own right, with "strong authority and relations within the Mafia all over the United States," as he put it himself, and by no means a mere diplomat. "You cannot be a *capomafia* without being ferocious," Gentile said, and he had first made his name in the society as a man of action rather than words. Arriving in Pittsburgh in 1915, Gentile had been shocked to discover that the local Mafia was cowed by the more powerful Camorra—Pittsburgh's Mafia capo even collected protection money in the Sicilian community on the Neapolitans' behalf. He responded by recruiting his own gang of violent street toughs (*picciotti* in Mafia slang) and using them to assassinate a number of Camorra leaders. The murderous efficiency of Gentile's gang soon brought the Neapolitans to the negotiating table, and there Gentile emphasized his superiority by humiliating his opponents. The Camorrists were threatened "with all-out war if they so much as offended another Sicilian," and, when they submitted, Gentile became the most powerful figure in Pittsburgh's Italian underworld. Soon afterward, he regularized arrangements by having the ineffectual capo shot and "sent back to Sicily in a luxury coffin," taking over as his city's Mafia boss.

It was thus fortunate for Morello and his companions that the Pittsburgh boss was disposed to help. Valenti, whom D'Aquila "considered the number one enemy and the first to be eliminated," was a "dear friend," the *capomafia* wrote, and Morello a respected former boss of bosses. Gentile himself was sufficiently influential in America to have another general assembly convened, and there, sometime early in 1922, a compromise was reached. Morello, in all likelihood, renounced all claims not only to his old position but also to the leadership of his own family; he must also have formally acknowledged D'Aquila as boss. At the same time the alliance between the Morellos and Valenti was somehow broken, almost certainly by Totò D'Aquila, who seems to have accepted Valenti back into his organization in exchange for his promise to help tackle the first family. When next glimpsed in the public records, the two were sworn enemies. The death sentences on the men were then revoked, and Morello, Lupo, and Valenti returned from Sicily that spring.

They arrived to find the city changing once again. The fragile peace that had long existed between its four Mafia families was coming to an end. D'Aquila's dominating ways explain part of the rising tension, but there many other reasons why the gangs of New York might come to blows. There was simply more to fight for in postwar Manhattan than there had ever been before, and the reason why this was so could be summed up in one word: *Prohibition.*

ALCOHOL HAD BEEN outlawed in the United States in 1919 with the passage of the Volstead Act. As later codified in the Eighteenth Amendment to the Constitution, the new law outlawed the manufacture, distribution, and sale of any alcoholic drinks. It also created the means to enforce the regulations: a new federal agency named the Prohibition Bureau, spread thinly across the country with a total of fewer than two thousand agents. A quarter of a million, one government official said, was closer to the number that would be needed to properly enforce the law.

Prohibition's proponents, chief among them religious leaders, firmly believed that they were saving the nation from itself, and to some extent they had a point. Drunkenness and alcoholism was responsible for several thousand deaths a year by 1919, not to mention a fast-rising tide of failed marriages and many more thefts, assaults, and petty crimes. "The insidious effects of alcohol are responsible for more misery than the late war," pronounced the bishop of Rochester, a firm supporter of the notion of a "dry" America, and millions of his countrymen agreed with him. Unfortunately for the authorities, however, tens of millions did not. Laws that lack public support are notoriously impossible to enforce, and the advent of Prohibition had no measurable effect on the demand for beer, wine, and spirits—not least in New York, where it was estimated that the 16,000 saloons that had existed in the city before the passage of the Volstead Act were replaced by 32,000 speakeasies. Thus, while it was relatively easy for the government to close down the country's large breweries and distilleries, new sources of supply were quickly found. Ale and liquor were imported from Canada and the Caribbean, smuggled in by boat all along the Atlantic shoreline. British exports of alcohol to Canada sextupled between 1918 and 1922, with virtually all the surplus finding its way south. Liquor was manufactured in the United States as well, in such quantities that the seizure of neither 173,000 illicit stills in 1925 nor forty million gallons of beer and wine five years later had any noticeable effect on the available supply.

Before 1919, even the best-organized and most efficient of the nation's criminals had controlled rackets worth no more than some thousands of dollars. Now control of a vastly profitable industry had passed to the underworld, and it had done so not merely without a struggle but with the active support of practically every drinker in the country. New York juries habitually returned not-guilty verdicts in even the clearest cut of Prohibition cases, and large-scale breweries operated virtually unchecked in busy city centers despite their telltale smells and smoke. Prices, meanwhile, increased so rapidly that a humble beer cost anywhere from twice to ten times what it had before the passage of the Prohibition laws.

There was, in short, a huge amount of business to fight for, and the streets of America's great cities soon turned into battlegrounds as rival gangs began to shoot and gouge their way to dominance over their local markets. Prohibition would lead directly to the emergence of a number of the greatest names in crime: Dutch Schultz, Waxey Gordon, and the Italian Frankie Uale in Brooklyn and Manhattan, and, in Chicago, Al Capone—born in Brooklyn to immigrant parents from Naples, at one time a minor member of a Brooklyn street gang, but by the end of the decade the most notorious boss in the United States. Capone built a vast stake in the supply of alcohol throughout the Midwest and made so much money that his influence could be felt in Manhattan.

What all this was worth in monetary terms is difficult to say—figures, for obvious reasons, were not kept. By the early 1930s, one estimate put beer sales in the New York region at $60 million to $100 million a year; another estimate suggested that alcohol sales in Detroit grossed $215 million in 1928. The market in New York, a city bigger than Chicago and Detroit put together, can scarcely have been worth less than $500 million by that time, and if the city's Mafia families, among them, claimed even one-twentieth of that, their profits must have exceeded $5 million a year.

Nothing like it had ever happened before. An entire industry—one of the most important in the country—had been gifted by the government to gangsters.

FOR MOST ORDINARY CRIMINALS, the most striking thing about the liquor business was not so much the money that it generated but the way in which it eroded existing boundaries within the underworld itself. Crime, before 1919, had been largely a neighborhood affair. Gangs struggled for control over small areas of large cities, as the Morellos had done in Harlem and Little Italy, and the gangs themselves were almost always tightly knit. Jewish syndicates fought over the Jewish districts of the Lower East Side; Sicilians and Neapolitans disputed the Italian quarter of Manhattan. Prohibition broke down many of those barriers. The vastly influential, Jewish-run Reinfeld Syndicate included several leaders who had American backgrounds; Waxey Gordon and Dutch Schultz, two of the best-known bootleggers of the 1920s, came from Jewish and German families respectively, and Schultz (whose criminal empire was rumored to turn over $20 million a year) had many allies in the Italian community, including Ciro Terranova, with whom he split the Harlem lottery racket. Some Mafia families even began to admit Neapolitans, a development made considerably more palatable by the demise of the Camorra in New York. Vito Genovese, who became one of the most feared Mafiosi in the city, was the first Naples man to rise to real power in this way. Genovese certainly had Camorra links—according to Sing Sing prison records, he was one of the last men to visit Tony "the Shoemaker" Paretti before his execution for the murder of Nick Terranova. But he was also an ally of Charlie Luciano, who came from Lercara Friddi in Sicily and whose star was rising swiftly in the Mafia.

An influx of new, younger blood certainly helped Sicilian criminals to profit from the opportunities on offer. "Prohibition," said Joe Bonanno, whose own successful Mafia career owed a good deal to the ban on alcohol, "was too good to be true. I didn't consider it wrong. It seemed fairly safe in that the police did not bother you. There was plenty of business for everyone, [and] the profits were tremendous." But, to begin with, little changed. In the early 1920s the bootlegging of alcohol was as much of a neighborhood business as the racketeering that preceded it, and the bootleggers themselves were very often the same gangsters who had infested their local communities for years. North of Central Park, the remnants of the old Morello family seized gratefully on these new opportunities. They were led on this occasion by Vincenzo Terranova, who proved to be so fearsome a competitor that he now acquired the nickname of the Harlem Tiger. He and his brother-in-law Vincenzo Salemi formed a partnership with another bootlegger by the name of Diamond Joe Viserti—a flashy Neapolitan involved in several of the killings at the Murder Stable. Viserti was renowned for his gaudy taste in jewelry and flashed a ten-thousand-dollar stickpin. His links with the Morello family went at least as far back as 1913.

Terranova, Salemi, and Viserti were strong enough to control most of the liquor trade in Harlem, but their influence seems to have run no further south than 106th Street. Further downtown, rival gangs fought over the enclave of Little Italy and the new Italian colonies on the East Side. One was led by the Morellos' old friend and new enemy, Umberto Valenti. Another, even more important, was controlled by yet another influential Mafioso. He was a small, combative, and frighteningly ambitious man who had come to New York from the town of Marsala, on the west coast of Sicily, and had a criminal record that stretched back nearly twenty years. In time, he would prove to be the most important Mafia figure of the Prohibition era. His name was Giuseppe Masseria, but he was better known as Joe the Boss.

Masseria had got his start in crime before the war. His police rap sheet noted arrests on suspicion of kidnapping, sending Black Hand letters, and theft from numerous premises around the Bowery. He and a companion named Lima were convicted of burglary in 1907 (Marie Morello, the Clutch Hand's sister, had married a man called Gioacchino Lima, which hints at one possible connection between Masseria and the Morello family). Then, a few years later, Masseria was caught again, this time breaking into a pawnshop with the assistance of a barman from the Lomonte brothers' Harlem bar. He served four and a half years for this second offense, enough to keep him in prison until late in 1917.

This was scarcely the record of an important Mafioso, and the future boss was still barely more than a petty crook, living in a single room above a bar, when Prohibition came in and changed everything. Without the ban on alcohol, Masseria might never have been heard of. As it was, however, he benefited more than most from the new laws. His territory on Kenmare Street in Little Italy chanced to include an important stretch of sidewalk known as the Curb Exchange—a place where liquor dealers from across New York met informally to buy and sell. Control of the Curb Exchange meant a small slice of a large portion of the city's liquor sales, and within a few months Masseria had reinvented himself as the boss of an influential syndicate. By 1921, allied by now with several other Italian gangs from Brooklyn and Manhattan, he was second in influence only to Totò D'Aquila. His lieutenants included several men destined to be the leaders of a coming generation, among them Joe Adonis, Frank Costello, and Charles "Lucky" Luciano.

Whatever it was that drew men of such undoubted ability to flock around the rising boss, it had little to do with his habits or appearance. Masseria was a glutton who ate far too much. Standing not much more than five feet five, he was squat and chubby, and though (like the great majority of bootleggers) he dressed well, in silk shirts and tailored suits, he lacked the poise to impress even his fellow criminals. Joe Bonanno, a fastidious dresser, found him sloppy in his personal appearance: "His belly protruded from under his half-opened vest," Bonanno wrote after one meeting. "His collar was unbuttoned and his tie loosened. One of his shirt sleeves was buttoned on the wrong holes." Another enemy nicknamed him "the Chinese," because, he said, of his "bloated cheeks, which made his eyes seem like narrow oriental slits." Masseria was neither eloquent nor intelligent. He spoke both English and Sicilian poorly. And, notoriously, he was a messy eater. "He attacked a plate of spaghetti as if he were a drooling mastiff. He had the table manners of a Hun," recorded Bonanno, who professed himself to be repulsed by the mere sight of the new boss at the table. "[He] was vulgar, and puffy . . . the nervous type of eater, an incomplete man inside—the glutton in him compelled him to feed his belly as the bully in him was compelled to feed his ego."

What Masseria did have, though, was something more important than appearance: a reputation for ruthlessness and a long run of good fortune. Chancing to control the territory around the Curb Exchange was only one example of his luck. The fat Sicilian was also famous in the New York underworld for his preternatural ability to dodge trouble and even bullets, and on at least two occasions in the early 1920s, rival gangsters cornered Masseria in ambushes from which the boss emerged miraculously unscathed. These encounters entered underworld legend and leant luster to the gangster's reputation.

From the Morello family's perspective, Joe the Boss had suddenly become a man worth courting. He was, by now, the only Mafioso in Manhattan strong enough to face down Totò D'Aquila, and it was this strength, almost certainly, that attracted Morello himself into Masseria's orbit. Spared, however grudgingly, from his Mafia death sentence, the Clutch Hand still had every reason to fear that the implacable D'Aquila would come after him again. In 1921 he abruptly reemerged as Joe the Boss's right hand man.

It was an alliance that made every kind of sense. The Clutch Hand traded independence for protection, while Masseria benefited hugely from Morello's contacts and his long years of experience. The Terranova brothers also entered the equation. By aligning his fast-rising new syndicate with the remnants of the old Morello family, Joe the Boss expanded his influence to Harlem and gained an important outlet for his alcohol. He also added to his strength in the event of any power struggle.

D'Aquila wasted little time in fighting back against the new alliance. The Masseria-Morello pact was far from welcome to the boss of bosses, and in the fall of 1921 he struck back hard at what remained of the Morello gang. Diamond Joe Viserti was the first to go, shot twice in the back in Little Italy on October 13, but his death was followed a few months later by none other than that of the Harlem Tiger. Vincenzo Terranova fell on May 8, 1922, ambushed as he was walking past an ice cream parlor on East 116th Street, in the heart of the Morello territory. The end was swift; a touring car with its top down sidled up behind the eldest of the Terranovas and pulled up to the curb; two men armed with sawed-off shotguns leaned out and fired buckshot charges, hitting their man repeatedly in the shoulder, back, and lungs. Vincenzo collapsed to the ground, where he had just sufficient strength to raise himself on one arm, draw a revolver from inside his coat, and discharge several hopeless rounds after the disappearing car. Then he fell back to the ground and died, the third member of his family to lose his life to a gang war. He was only thirty-six.

The man responsible for Terranova's death was Umberto Valenti. The Ghost—so it was widely thought—had proved his loyalty to D'Aquila by bringing down an enemy, and that afternoon he struck again, downtown this time, at Masseria. No fewer than five Sicilians were involved in this battle—Joe the Boss and two of his men on one side and two Valenti gunmen on the other. Neither side, it seems, shot straight; five minutes of intermittent gunfire wounded half a dozen passing garment workers, but Masseria escaped unscathed. Valenti tried again a few months later, sending four more men to Joe the Boss's house early in August. This time Masseria spotted them as he came down his front steps; he fled into a nearby shop, dodging one bullet that came crashing through a glass window and two more, fired at close range, that came within inches of killing him. Joe's famous luck was with him once again that day—two bullets had torn holes in his straw hat—but his enemy the Ghost's had finally deserted him. Three days later, on August 11, Valenti was ambushed entering a restaurant at Twelfth Street and Second

Avenue. He made a run for a nearby taxi, but a small group of Masseria's men shot him as he leapt onto the running boards.

Valenti died in hospital an hour later, and though his boss, D'Aquila, did not call a truce for several months, his attempt to curb Masseria's power was thenceforth all but over. There was one further important casualty on the Morellos' side—Lina Morello's brother, Vincenzo Salemi, died on East 108th Street early in 1923, hit four times in the back by bullets fired from a passing car—but the shooting petered out that spring. With his closest ally gone, D'Aquila was forced to admit that Joe the Boss had come to stay. In turn, the balance of power in the Sicilian districts altered irrevocably.

Masseria took the credit, but he owed a great deal to another man. Without Giuseppe Morello, Joe the Boss had lacked the brains to rival Totò D'Aquila, much less to best the boss of bosses so decisively. With Morello as adviser and chief strategist—as counselor, or *consigliere* in the language of the Mafia—he was a better leader. Together, the two men would dominate Manhattan for the next half-decade.

WHAT HAPPENED NEXT is known only in broad outline; the war of 1922 was the last the New York public heard of the Mafia for half a dozen years. Conflict and murder were bad for business, and either D'Aquila or Masseria, or both, decreed that business should again be the priority.

The remainder of the Roaring Twenties passed in a blur of illicit bootleg deals punctuated by occasional murders. The killings, as always, made the press, while the day-to-day rivalries of the various gangs that preyed on the city did not. The FBI, which would eventually claim jurisdiction over many aspects of organized crime, was still a decade away from full effectiveness—not until the mid-1930s did the organization acquire real competence in such investigations—and in the absence of some figure of the stature of Flynn or Petrosino, the New York Police Department lacked both the will and the ability to secure evidence against the powerful, elusive leaders responsible for most Italian American crime. Far less is known of the Mafia's operations in the 1920s and 1930s than was ever discovered about the activities of the Morello family.

A glimpse of the one surviving Terranova brother's place in this criminal firmament comes from the memoirs, unremittingly hostile to the Morello family, of a low-level Mafioso by the name of Joe Valachi. Valachi was no more than a street thug: almost illiterate, and a mere burglar with five arrests and a short spell in Sing Sing to his name when he first encountered Ciro, then "the big man on 116th Street," sometime in 1925. On that occasion, the Artichoke King brokered a truce between the members of Valachi's former gang of burglars—who happened to be Italian—and a group of Irish thieves with whom he had gone to work on his release from prison. Keeping the peace was an important part of a boss's job, and the fact that Terranova ruled in favor of a predominantly Irish gang over the angry protests of Italians suggests that he was forward-looking for the day. The next time that Valachi encountered him, however, Ciro appeared in a very different light. The burglar was back in Sing Sing, serving a nearly four-year sentence, when he heard from another prisoner that a friend, a fellow housebreaker by the name of Frank LaPluma, had been killed. "They shot him sitting on a stoop one morning," Valachi said. "The way I made it out, it didn't make no sense. Well, all I could do is wonder what was going on."

It took a prisoner who understood East Harlem to explain the situation to Valachi. Ciro Terranova, the burglar was shocked to hear, had sentenced him to death.

> "They sold you out," he said. I said I didn't know what he was talking about. "I mean they made peace," he said, "on condition that you and Frank must die. Ciro Terranova fixed the whole thing." Then [he] told me to watch myself. He said that if they got one, they'll get the other—meaning me.

Valachi thought that he was safe in Sing Sing, but he soon discovered that the influence of the Morello-Terranova clan stretched much further in the 1920s than it had a quarter of a century earlier, when a similar prison sentence had kept Giuseppe Di Priemo safe from Morello's wrath.

> Right after this I was mopping up one day in the dormitory . . . another guy who was helping to clean up, his name was Angelo, was in the toilet. Just then there was a knock at the door, and a kid by the name of Pete LaTempa said he wanted to get something from under his bed. I didn't think anything about it. I knew this LaTempa but I never had much to do with him, so I let him in and went about my business with a mop.

All of a sudden I felt a sort of sting—that's the best I can describe it—under my left arm. I looked behind me, and I saw this LaTempa with a knife in his hand. By now Angelo had come out of the toilet and was standing there, looking at me with his eyes bugging out. . . . I put my hand down under my arm where he was pointing, and I kind of felt it go right inside me. Then I saw all the blood. Believe me, it was all over the place. So naturally I went after LaTempa, and he started to yell how bad I was cut, hoping I would forget him and worry about myself. But I just kept going, and when I caught him, I let him have a couple of good raps on the mouth. He was smaller than me, and I would have killed him with my bare hands, but by this time my knees were getting weak.

What saved me was that the hospital was only one flight above the dormitory. . . . When they finished sewing me up, I had thirty-eight stitches running from right under my heart and around to my back. I still got the scar.

Terranova left Valachi alone after that, and his inability to have Valachi killed came as little surprise to many members of the Sicilian underworld. Ciro was feared—his family history, his profitable rackets, and his position as an ally of Masseria all meant that he enjoyed both power and prestige. But the Artichoke King was never held in anything like the same regard as his dead brothers, and for a few irreverent Mafiosi he actually became a figure of fun, a man whose best efforts seemed destined to descend to bitter farce.

The lowest point in Ciro's criminal career came on December 8, 1929, when he attended a formal dinner in the Bronx in honor of Albert Vitale, a noted magistrate with friends on both sides of the criminal divide. Also in the restaurant that night were a number of eminent New York politicians, several other gangsters, and at least one policeman.

Midway through a raucous evening, the festivities were interrupted by a number of gunmen who burst into the room and held up the assembled dignitaries. The politicians lost their wallets, and—more important, as it transpired—the one policeman was relieved of his revolver. That theft had to be reported, and when it was the whole story of the evening made the press. Vitale was pilloried for his underworld associations, the unfortunate policeman for not putting up a fight. In Mafia circles, though, the Artichoke King was generally believed to have been the most embarrassed guest of all. By allowing himself to get caught up in the Vitale scandal, Terranova had drawn a great deal of unwelcome attention to himself. He had given the newspapers an excuse to dredge up old stories about Italian crime in general and the artichoke racket in particular. However inadvertently, he had interfered with business.

A while later, another story about that evening began to do the rounds. According to this new version of events, Ciro had been much cleverer than it appeared and had in fact been the instigator of events. The holdup, it was said, had been staged by the Terranova clan to recover a wildly incriminating piece of evidence: a written murder contract, signed by Ciro himself, that another of Vitale's shady guests had been carrying in his pocket.

The story failed to impress Italian Harlem, nonetheless. In the collective opinion of the underworld, any boss foolhardy enough to let such a document fall into unfriendly hands deserved all the criticism that he got.

PUBLICITY OF THE SORT that attended Ciro Terranova was something that New York's boss of bosses thoroughly abhorred. Totò D'Aquila was obsessively secretive, so much so that, despite a long career as the most influential Mafioso in the country and a criminal record that stretched back to 1906, he remained unknown to the police and press and had never been convicted of a crime. A couple of reports by Flynn aside, practically all that is known of the reclusive Palermitano comes from Nick Gentile. According to Gentile, D'Aquila was brutal and authoritarian, a leader who had men condemned to death merely as "a question of power." He was certainly wary enough of likely rivals to remain wary of Joe Masseria, and with good reason—the most logical explanation for what happened next was that Masseria had decided to remove D'Aquila in order to complete his rise to power.

The assassination of Totò D'Aquila, which took place at dusk on October 10, 1928, went almost unnoticed at the time. In retrospect, however, it plainly marked the end of an era: a period of continuity stretching all the way back to the formation of the Morello gang itself and of the precariously maintained peace among New York's increasingly powerful Mafia families. While D'Aquila ruled in New York, Sicilian criminals still preyed almost exclusively on the Sicilian community. Under his successors, Italian crime became increasingly indistinguishable from New York crime as a whole.

D'Aquila had been boss of bosses for nearly eighteen years when he died, and his killing was thoroughly professional. It had been planned by someone with a good knowledge of his movements; D'Aquila was ambushed on the corner of 13th Street and Avenue A after driving down from his home in the Bronx to keep a regular appointment with his doctor. Leaving the man's office "just as the lamps were being lit," he was shot nine times by three assassins who took good care to harm neither the boss's wife nor any of the four children who had accompanied him downtown. The killers had ensured that their victim would be unable to escape by tampering with the engine of his car. Stranded on the roadside and without a bodyguard, D'Aquila made a vulnerable target. He was hit by a fusillade of bullets fired from point-blank range and died almost instantly.

Morello's stern successor had drawn a cloak of anonymity around himself so tightly that none of the newsmen who reported his murder seems to have had the least idea of its significance; the story was buried on page 48 of the next day's *New York Times,* where the victim was described as a "cheese importer." But someone made it their business to let the single witness to the shooting know exactly who the dead man was. When Louis Realbuto, the owner of a nearby drugstore, first spoke to the police, he admitted to watching the killing and described what happened in considerable detail. The next day, upon mature reflection, the unfortunate pharmacist hurried to change his story. He had not even been in his shop when the murder happened, he now insisted, and he knew nothing whatsoever of the case.

WITH TOTÒ D'AQUILA DEAD, his likely killer, Masseria, succeeded him as boss of bosses by general acclamation.

Masseria was an ambitious and ruthless man who boasted almost all the qualities demanded of a successful Mafioso. He was strong and cunning, violent, and possessed in full measure the ability to terrify opponents that had made Morello such a formidable presence. Perhaps most tellingly of all, in the treacherous world of organized crime, Masseria was noted for his willingness to strike the first, most telling, blow. He had acted decisively in disposing of D'Aquila. None of the city's other Mafia bosses relished the prospect of challenging his accession.

The truth was that they had all gone soft: bloated and sated by the profits of Prohibition, wearied by age, worn down by the strains of gangster life. Masseria was considerably younger than the man he had replaced—forty-one years old to D'Aquila's fifty—and still new enough to leadership to relish it. The leaders of New York's remaining families were mostly closer to D'Aquila's age. Cola Schiro was fifty-six, apparently, and had led the Brooklyn game that bore his name for more than two decades. Manfredi Mineo was fifty and had been a power in the same borough for almost as long. Neither man wanted conflict, and both chose to ally themselves with Masseria. The bosses of two smaller families were younger; Joe Profaci—a thief and rapist from Villabate, Sicily, who emerged late in 1928 as leader of his own family—was a mere stripling of thirty, and Tom Reina, who led the fifth of New York's Mafia gangs from his base in the Bronx, was thirty-eight. Profaci, who had burgeoning interests that extended as far as Staten Island, was less willing than Mineo and Schiro to prostrate himself but just as eager to keep the peace. Only Reina, Masseria's closest contemporary, presented any sort of threat. One well-informed observer, Joe Bonanno—then a rising member of the Schiro gang—thought that "Reina had to be careful not to offend him, and he generally toed the Masseria line. But it was a relationship based on convenience rather than on likemindedness."

The one trait that Joe Masseria fatally lacked was a talent for diplomacy. Tact and the willingness to compromise—to set limited goals and accept something other than unconditional surrender—had long been valued by the Mafia, but Masseria's lack of flexibility surpassed even D'Aquila's, and his authoritarian aggressiveness soon proved to be a crucial weakness. He seems to have reveled in the nickname "Joe the Boss," and as Bonanno was swift to point out, the eagerness with which he embraced the name was highly significant.

Sicilian to the tip of his trigger finger, a traditionalist, a romantic, and a liar even to himself, Bonanno held fast to the notion of the boss as a benevolent "father" whose job it was to shepherd the members of his family. Masseria was not a father of this sort. His English nickname, Bonanno said,

> was something new, and, in hindsight, it reflected the subtle changes already transforming our Tradition in America. The title "boss" represented a corruption of the title "Father." It's regret-

table that in America the term "boss" became the more popular of the two. The terms are not interchangeable. . . . "Boss" connotes a relationship between a master and his servants or his workers. The growing use of the word "boss" when referring to "Father" was one of the earliest indications that in America relationships between a leader and his followers had more of a business than a kinship base. The word "boss" represented a new reality.

Joe the Boss's greatest sin, at least so far as his fellow Mafiosi were concerned, was his attempt to expand the powers of the boss of bosses. In Giuseppe Morello's time, the fragmentary evidence suggests, the boss had been more than anything an adviser and conciliator. D'Aquila had been far more authoritarian, but Masseria took things further still, seizing as much power as possible for himself and demanding more than mere obedience from New York's five families. Joe the Boss, it became clear, wanted to share in all the profits from the city's rackets. In February 1930, a year and a half into his reign, he felt strong enough to press Tom Reina into ceding him a stake in the lucrative Bronx ice racket. When Reina resisted, he was murdered, and perhaps as a result, Masseria's subsequent attempts to grab a substantial share of Manhattan's clothing racket met with little resistance. Soon the boss of bosses began making demands of families as far away as Chicago and Detroit—a privilege that, so far as is known, no New York Mafiosi had ever claimed before. It is scarcely surprising that Masseria's brutal attempts to garner power led first to protests, then to covert opposition, and finally to outright violence on an unprecedented scale.

It would come to be known as the Castellammare War—"Castellammare" because resistance to Masseria was strongest among the Mafia of Brooklyn and led by Brooklyn Mafiosi who had been born in Castellammare del Golfo. The Castellammaresi had a reputation even among other Sicilians as men "renowned for their refusal to take guff from anyone," and Bonanno, who had been born in the town, liked to portray the resistance to Joe the Boss as something that sprang up naturally among the proud Mafiosi of that district: a noble crusade against unjust rule. The truth was rather more complex than that; Masseria was more than a mere autocrat—he was able to persuade the Mafia's general assembly to back him, which suggests the boss was not merely indulging in a personal vendetta. A good number of Masseria's opponents, moreover, came from other parts of Sicily, and men from the same town often supported different sides. Tommaso Gagliano, who succeeded Tom Reina as leader of the Bronx family, had been born in Corleone and so was well known to Morello, who remained loyal to Joe the Boss. It certainly is true, however, that many of Masseria's most determined opponents were drawn from among the Castellammaresi who filled the ranks of Schiro's family—men whom the boss himself saw as "unruly and thick-skulled."

The Castellammare War was an important turning point in Mafia history: the greatest convulsion that the fraternity had known. It was a conflict long remembered by all those who took part in it, and it was Morello, in his role as Masseria's chief strategist, who fired its opening shots and dictated the course of the first six months of hostilities, a period that saw his boss's forces victorious on every front.

According to the Castellammaresi themselves, it was thanks almost entirely to Morello that Masseria scored so much success: "Mr. Joe," Bonanno said, was smug and stupid, and it was the Clutch Hand who was Masseria's "brains trust." The first months of the war were marked by several murderous, clever moves aimed at asserting the Masseria faction's dominance and crippling resistance to his rule. Morello began by sowing dissent between two of the most important families west of New York: the Detroit Mafia gang led by Gaspare Milazzo of Castellammare and the Chicago family of Milazzo's close friend Joe Aiello. Next he kept Aiello busy, playing him off against Chicago's most notorious Italian gangster, Al Capone, while Milazzo was disposed of. On May 31, 1930, gunmen dispatched by the Clutch Hand hunted down and killed the Detroit boss in the back room of a fish restaurant.

Masseria followed up this murder with some deft maneuvering in New York. The boss of bosses demanded and received ten thousand dollars of tribute from Cola Schiro's family, then arranged for the murder of Vito Bonventre, one of the richest of the Castellammare faction. Both incidents, Bonanno thought, bore witness to Morello's touch. "If Masseria had killed Schiro, his Family would surely have sought revenge. However, by intimidating Schiro, a timid man, Masseria stood to domineer us all." And by murdering Bonventre, the Clutch Hand had denied his boss's enemies much of the cash that they would need to fight a war.

New York's Italian underworld, Bonanno thought, resembled a volcanic chamber packed with magma: molten, seething, perpetually ready to erupt. Now, with Schiro humbled and humiliated and Joe the Boss's opponents in disorganized retreat, "a sense of foreboding gripped the Castellammaresi in the city." Masseria had more money, more support, and more men than his enemies. No real attempt had yet been made to coordinate resistance. Yet the situation was now acutely dangerous. Morello and his master had done more than merely declare war on the Castellammaresi—or so the Brooklyn Mafia believed: They had condemned them all to death. Joe the Boss himself had threatened to "eat them like a sandwich." Something had to be done about the situation, quickly.

Cola Schiro, plainly, was too old and far too indecisive to make a decent leader in the coming war, but the Brooklyn boss, mindful, apparently, of Tom Reina's fate, solved this problem by disappearing from the city shortly afterward. Schiro was next heard of back in Italy, and in his place the Castellammaresi chose a younger and more warlike man. Their new leader, Salvatore Maranzano, was forty-two years old and unusually well educated for a Mafioso; he was reputed to speak seven languages and had at one time trained to be a priest. The theft of a number of his family's valuable cattle soon drove him to renounce his vows, however, and with a mother who was the daughter of a powerful boss from the province of Trapani, Maranzano soon found himself initiated into the Mafia. Arriving in the United States sometime before 1926, he became a bootlegger with extensive connections in the north of New York State and rapidly built up a flourishing business, manufacturing alcohol in his own illegal stills and moving quantities of liquor across the border with Canada. "In his own way," Bonanno said, "his was a classic American success story."

Most of those who encountered Maranzano seem to have found him thoroughly impressive. To Bonanno, he was handsome, smartly dressed, and straightforward: "a fine example of the Sicilian male . . . a bold man and a ready fighter, an apostle of the old Tradition." His voice was said to be particularly striking; it had "an entrancing quality," Bonanno said: "When Maranzano used his voice assertively, to give a command, he was the bell knocker and you were the bell." However, Joe Valachi, a far less intelligent man who was recruited to the Mafia in Brooklyn at the outbreak of the war and soon found himself appointed one of Maranzano's bodyguards, was more struck by other aspects of his personality. For Valachi, the new boss was shrewd, well educated, and a first-rate planner, a man who seemingly had little in common with the coarse and poorly educated "soldiers" he was asked to lead: "Gee, he looked just like a banker. You'd never guess in a million years that he was a racketeer."

Morello, too, held his new opponent in high regard. The two men had met in Palermo in 1921, and even before Maranzano properly succeeded Schiro, the Clutch Hand had been anxious to neutralize his threat. "No one," Joe Bonanno would recall,

> as yet knew that Maranzano had committed himself to war against Masseria, not even the people in our family in Brooklyn. People in Masseria's camp, meanwhile, were trying to persuade Maranzano to remain neutral. The other side had already singled out those Castellammaresi who might give them special trouble. As a result, Maranzano was invited to a friendly meeting with Masseria himself.

It was a dangerous suggestion. "Tête-à-têtes with 'Joe the Boss' had a history of ending badly," Bonanno said, and Morello had a well-deserved reputation of his own for savagery. But Maranzano needed more time to prepare for war—to build up his strength and organize his finances—and, if only to delay matters, he agreed to go. The meeting was to take place in a private house "in uptown Manhattan"—probably one of the Clutch Hand's many strongholds. Masseria would be accompanied by his chief adviser, whom the Castellammaresi knew as Peter Morello, "Don Petru," an alias he had adopted after leaving prison. For his part, Maranzano asked Joe Bonanno to attend. The date, apparently, was sometime in June 1930.

> The others looked at me with a mixture of admiration and sorrow, as if to say,
>   —What a lucky bastard! What a dead stiff!
>   The following day, the day of the meeting, I picked up Maranzano at his home, being extra sure I was on time. Maranzano always harped on about punctuality. He didn't say anything to me in the house. I was starting the car when he finally spoke:
>   —*Andiamo e ritorniamo.*
>   —Let's go and let's return.

Once at the meeting place, Bonanno wrote, Masseria and Maranzano

exchanged greetings in the Sicilian manner: cheek-to-cheek, one eye looking at the man and the other looking over the man's shoulder. They and Morello sat at a table by themselves, while I and a couple of Masseria's bodyguards sat to the side. Espresso coffee was served, the steam spiralling out of the demitasse cups. As for the finer points of the discussion, Masseria said,

—Let Don Petru talk for me.

Masseria sat back, yielding the floor to his second, Peter Morello. This Morello had a deformed right hand, from which he got his nickname, "the Clutch Hand." There was nothing of the buffoon about Morello. He had a parched, gaunt voice, a stone face and a claw. It was probably Morello who had advised Masseria to try to neutralize Maranzano.

—Thank you, Mr. Joe, Morello said, nodding slightly at Masseria, who grinned smugly.

Morello congratulated Maranzano, first of all, on his success in America. These repeated references to Maranzano's success were intended to point out that continued success would depend on whether Maranzano had the right friends. Then Morello said he wanted to clarify some recent events which Maranzano, being a Castellammarese, no doubt must be concerned about.

—The Milazzo slaying, Morello admitted, was from our part. We can't deny it.

But Morello accused Milazzo and Aiello of plotting to kill "Mr. Joe." And since Stefano Maggadino [Bonanno's uncle, another Castellammarese and the head of Buffalo's Mafia family] had refused to talk with Masseria, Morello continued, there was every reason to suppose Don Stefano didn't like Mr. Joe either.

—Perhaps you, Morello told Maranzano, can go to Don Stefano and put in a good word for Mr. Joe. Tell him to come see Mr. Joe. We just want to clarify everything, that's all.

Maranzano gave no indication of what he really thought of the suggestion.

—I'll see what I can do, Maranzano said coyly. But really, Don Petru, I'm just a soldier in the House of Cola Schiro, as you know. I have no authority.

—Try, try, Masseria bellowed out of a cloud of smoke.

—Do try, Don Turridru, Morello reiterated.

—It can't hurt to try, Maranzano said. But I can't promise anything.

—If something isn't done, Morello said, there might be bloodshed. And if there is fighting, I think the wisest course for an intelligent man such as yourself would be neutrality. On that we can all agree.

—We understand each other, Maranzano said.

The two had been treating each other gingerly and tactfully. Suddenly, Morello leaned closer to Maranzano and, dropping his voice to a lower pitch, said:

—If you're fooling us, your fight will be against me. In Sicily you have never fought against anyone like Petru Morello.

Maranzano replied quickly in a calm, level voice:

—And you have never fought against anyone like Turridru Maranzano.

They stared at each other for an instant and then tried to smile, to make it appear they had only been kidding.

—What a bunch of comedians, you two, Masseria declared.

MARANZANO MADE READY to strike back.

The members of the old Schiro family, he said, must be an army now. The Brooklyn Mafiosi were divided into squads and placed under the command of handpicked leaders. "Only these group leaders knew who the other group leaders were and their whereabouts." Intelligence would be supplied by an intricate network of informants, many of them cabdrivers from the Italian quarter who could identify the leading members of Masseria's gang by sight. Conscious of what had happened to Milazzo and Reina, Maranzano was determined never to be caught unaware by his enemies.

The new boss's own strategy was straightforward: strike at the leaders of Joe the Boss's gang. "Now we are all one," Valachi was told.

We're only a few here, but in a month we'll be four or five hundred. We have to work hard. The odds are against us. The other side has a lot of money. . . . You will all be placed in different apartments around the city. We will have spotters out on the street. These spotters will have the telephone number of main headquarters. When a call comes in from the Bronx, for instance, that somebody has been spotted, the apartment we have in the Bronx will get a call. And when that call comes, you will have to respond as fast as you can. Of course, you have been given a picture of Masseria. He's the most important one.

We must concentrate on getting their main bosses, and we must get Masseria himself. There will be no deal made with Joe Masseria. The war will go on for ten years if we don't get him.

Every effort was made to give the Castellammare forces a chance against the well-armed opposition. Supplies were brought in and organized: food, equipment, ammunition. Several safe houses were set up, some in New York, others in Yonkers and Long Island, and Maranzano and his bodyguards shuttled among them to evade possible ambushes by Masseria's forces. The new boss had used his contacts in Detroit to equip himself with two armored limousines, with "special metal plates on the side and bullet proof windows," and he rarely moved anywhere without them. The cars traveled in convoy, to make them difficult to ambush, and according to Bonanno, Maranzano himself sat in the backseat "with a machine gun mounted on a swivel between his legs. He also packed a Luger and a Colt, as well as his omnipresent dagger behind his back."

Bonanno, impressed as ever by his soldierly bearing, found Maranzano's meticulous attention to detail both an inspiration and a comfort during long days and nights spent shuttling around New York. But it was the new boss's cool determination that impressed him most:

I watched Maranzano loading shotgun cartridges. I watched him weigh the black gunpowder on a small scale and fill the cartridges with pellets. Maranzano eschewed store-bought shotgun cartridges—he liked to prepare them himself. He did this last thing every night, before turning in.

He performed the loading of the shotgun shells as if it were a sacred ritual, with great precision, even elegance. . . . Then, without looking up at me, he began a hushed monologue.

—To kill a rabbit, to kill a deer, to kill even a bear is simple.

You aim steady and you shoot. But man is the hardest animal to kill. When you aim at a man, your heart flutters, your mind interferes. Man is the hardest animal to kill. If possible you should always touch the body with your gun to make sure the man is dead. Man is the hardest animal to kill. If he gets away, he will come back to kill you.

ONE DECISION THAT Maranzano made at about this time would have a decisive effect on the outcome of the war.

The opposing sides were evenly matched in one respect: Each knew the other very well. Mafiosi on both sides easily recognized their enemies, and there were a number of incidents in which the members of one faction spotted a rival from a car or on the street and were able to give chase to him. On several occasions, scouts noticed leading members of one side or the other disappearing into buildings, and—as Maranzano had foretold—elaborate ambushes were organized to catch the men as they emerged.

The Castellammaresi had a neat solution to this problem, one that simultaneously addressed their lack of manpower: Maranzano initiated a number of new Mafiosi into the ranks of Schiro's family and brought in several gunmen from outside New York. Most of these men had been born in Castellammare del Golfo, though Masseria's threat was far too pressing for this to be a formal requirement; Valachi, a Neapolitan, was one of a number who found himself admitted to the Schiro family in this way. The best were already experienced killers, rendered all the more lethal by their utter anonymity. Among their number was a young gangster from Benton Harbor, Michigan, a "sharpshooter," Valachi said, who had left his home after several relatives fell victim to the local bootleg wars. His name was Sebastiano Domingo, though to the Mafiosi of Brooklyn, with their love of nicknames, he was always known as "Buster from Chicago."

Buster was only twenty-two years old when he came to New York, but he was already heavily scarred by violence. His sister-in-law, Mary, had been "mutilated almost beyond recognition" by a car bomb that detonated as she drove home in September 1927. His brother, Tony, was murdered two years later, shot nine times as he ate at a café, then blown nearly in half by a shotgun placed against his back. Buster himself, remarked Valachi, "looked like a college boy" but was deadly with any sort of weapon. He was, as Joe Bonanno recalled, "the quickest to set up and the best shot among us. He could shoot from any angle and from any direction. His speciality was the machine gun, with which he was a virtuoso."

For Maranzano, Buster from Chicago was a dream come true: deadly, dependable, a loyal Castellammarese, and, best of all, unknown to anyone on Masseria's side. Domingo, he realized, could pass unnoticed anywhere in the city and get close enough to any of Joe the Boss's men to kill before they realized the danger they were in. So far as Maranzano was concerned, one potential target was more important than all the others put together. He would use Buster to remove the brains of Masseria's operation. His new gunman would be dispatched to kill Morello.

"MARANZANO USED TO SAY that if we hoped to win the war we should get at Morello before the old fox stopped following his daily routine," Joe Bonanno would recall. "Once Morello went undercover, Maranzano would say, the old man could exist forever on hard bread, cheese and onions." Then they would have no hope of finding him.

Morello never got the chance to change his diet. At 3:45 P.M. on August 15, 1930, two and a half months after the first shots in the Castellammare War were fired, two killers drove up to the office he maintained in the heart of Italian Harlem. It occupied the second floor of a four-story brownstone at 352 East 116th Street, just seven doors down from the old headquarters of the Ignatz Florio Co-Operative. One of the Castellammarese gunmen was Sebastiano Domingo; the other has never been identified. They were armed with .32- and .38-caliber revolvers.

Maranzano had gotten his timing right. Satisfied with the havoc he had unleashed on his enemies and convinced they were in full retreat, Morello had grown overconfident. There was no security inside the building and no guards. The assassins climbed the stairs and reached the office without being stopped or seen.

Buster found three men at work inside the room. Two of them, Morello and Gaspare Pollaro, were leading members of the Masseria faction. The third man was Pollaro's nephew, Joseph Perranio, a twenty-six-year-old with a conviction for larceny. According to Pollaro, who lived just long enough to tell a policeman what had happened, the three men had been discussing building contracts when they heard a knock. None of them had felt any sort of sense of danger, and they were given no chance to react to the intrusion. When the ever-cautious Morello opened the door a crack, the killers forced their way in and opened fire immediately. Finding more men in the office than they had expected, Maranzano's assassins responded by pumping as many shots as possible into the room. Their excitement compromised their accuracy; at least four bullets missed their intended marks as Morello and his colleagues sought desperately to dodge the fusillade.

Perranio, the least obvious target and perhaps also the farthest man from the door, took two bullets and spun around but was only wounded. He staggered to a window and either jumped or pitched the twenty or so feet into a yard at the rear of the building; the fall completed the work the shots had started. His uncle was also hit. Morello, Buster explained to Joe Valachi, "was tough. He kept running around the office, and [we] had to give him a couple of more shots before he went down."

After seconds that seemed like minutes, the firing ceased. At least a dozen shots had been discharged, perhaps as many as fifteen. The acrid tang of gun smoke hung in the heavy August air.

Pollaro slumped next to a desk, mortally wounded by a bullet in the chest. The broken body of his nephew lay outside. Giuseppe Morello survived long enough to stagger from his office into a dusty room next door. He was trying to reach a window when he collapsed.

America's first boss of bosses lay on his back, head facing north, legs splayed, a gray fedora still on his head. Blood trickled from his mouth and nose. There were bullet holes in his cheek and jaw, his left shoulder, right side, right hip, back, and leg. Two shots had penetrated his lungs, and one of these had sliced through his aorta. Another had shredded his intestines; a fourth had severed his left jugular vein and opened the carotid artery. A considerable hemorrhage distended the skin around his neck, and a quart of blood had pooled inside his chest. He had lived as much as half a minute after being hit, and in that time had bled to death.

EPILOGUE

JOE THE BOSS, BONANNO SAID, "HAD LOST HIS BEST MAN, THE brains of his outfit." And, with the Clutch Hand dead, his prospects took a sharp turn for the worse. While Morello was alive, Masseria had dictated the course of the Castellammare War—and he had been winning it. Now Maranzano and his men seized the initiative. Deprived of Morello's experience and cunning, the boss of bosses was soon cut down to size.

Mafiosi throughout the city sensed that the balance of power was shifting. Defectors began going over to the Castellammarese side. They came mostly from Manfredi Mineo's family at first, then from the Reina family in the Bronx, which by the end of 1930 had begun to work covertly with Maranzano, too. Mineo himself realized that things had changed, and when Joe the Boss asked him to succeed Morello as his adviser and strategist, his first act was to urge Masseria to go into hiding. It was a necessary precaution but also a humiliating admission of weakness and a substantial blow to the boss's esteem. With Morello gone, it was said, the two sides were evenly matched at last.

Mineo certainly lacked his predecessor's guile and subtlety. Masseria's former strategy had been flexible and deadly; following the Clutch Hand's advice, Joe the Boss had struck at the Castellammarese leadership in New York, Detroit, and Chicago and had also undermined his enemies' financial ability to win the war. Mineo's policy, in contrast, boiled down to a single, stark idea: Find Maranzano, and kill him before he could kill Masseria. As a strategy, it made sense; the Castellammare leader was plainly crucial to the rebels' hopes of victory. But as an achievable objective, it was less realistic. The enemy's forces were better disposed and better organized than "Mr. Joe's." If the war was to be won by one side discovering the rival boss's hiding place, the odds favored Maranzano.

It was Joe Valachi who made the next breakthrough for the Castellammaresi, and it came about thanks to the Maranzano "spotting system." The date was November 5, 1930. "They tell me," Valachi said,

> to rent this apartment up on Pelham Parkway [in the Bronx] because they found out this was the address of one of the guys under Masseria. His name was a hard one to say—[Steve] Ferrigno. They wanted me to get this apartment because these other guys don't know who I was. . . . At the time I'm just "proposed"— meaning I'm in line to be a member, but I ain't one yet.
>
> We're in this apartment for I'd say a month, and there's no Ferrigno. I'm beginning to wonder where the hell he is, but they explain that this is only one of the addresses he has and we got to wait. . . .
>
> It was only a few days later that I was out with Buster somewhere and he left me off on the corner of Pelham Parkway in front of the apartment building. Buster left, and another car pulled up in front of me. Now we had all gotten pictures of Masseria to recognize him in case we ever see him. So, to my amazement, I saw Masseria get out of the car. I recognize him fast. This Ferrigno is with him, and they look me over suspicious-like. You got to understand this is a Jewish neighborhood, and they can see that I ain't no Jew.

Obeying orders, Valachi went into the building with Masseria and Ferrigno, even standing with them in the elevator. Then he ran to alert his colleagues. Maranzano's gunmen kept a nervous watch from the apartment as more and more of Joe the Boss's men—more than twenty in all—arrived at Pelham Parkway during the afternoon.

The meeting went on all night and most of the next day; it was not until mid-afternoon that Masseria's thugs began to leave the building in pairs. The Castellammaresi watching them held their fire, scanning faces, looking for the boss. To their intense frustration, Masseria was not among the men who streamed into the street—he had held back, they learned later, so as to be the last man to leave. Valachi and his friends saw

Manfredi Mineo and Steve Ferrigno, though, and behind the blinds they leveled shotguns. According to Joe Bonanno, "Maranzano had already decided that if Masseria eluded our ambush, the sharpshooters were at least to fire on Ferrigno and Mineo. The sharpshooters did their job."

Now Mineo, too, was dead, and his murder, Bonanno thought, robbed Masseria of his last chance for victory. In one sense this was fantasy; even now, with the war going so badly for him, Joe the Boss still controlled more men and had more money than his enemies. In other respects, however, Bonanno was absolutely right. Mafia "wars" are not like conflicts between nations; the participants are weaker, less determined, less committed to a cause. Above all, few are willing, as Maranzano was, to place the achievement of long-term objectives over personal safety and their own short-term profit. The war had already dragged on for half a year, and it was disrupting normal business; hoodlums who were traveling the city in packs, hunting one another, could not be terrorizing unfortunate storekeepers or managing extortion rackets. New York's Mafia families had lost thousands of dollars, and most of the participants yearned for peace.

It would have been dangerous, of course, to say any such thing openly, but one man on Joe the Boss's side acknowledged the truth. Lucky Luciano, who had become, after Mineo's death, the most influential of Masseria's surviving aides, had little in common with veteran Mafiosi such as Morello and Mineo. A short, thin man of thirty-three with a sallow, scarred, and pockmarked face, Luciano had arrived in the United States from the Sicilian town of Lercara Friddi when he was nine, and spoke better English than he did Italian. He was shrewd and ruthless, but more of a businessman than he was a man of action and far from a traditionalist when it came to the vexing question of sharing money and power with non-Sicilians. He was also far less interested in the internal struggles of the Mafia than he was in maximizing profits.

Luciano, more perhaps than any of Masseria's lieutenants, saw no point in fighting for a losing cause. Maranzano realized this. Early in 1931, the Castellammaresi issued a proposal.

It was Bonanno, once again, who told the tale. Maranzano, he said, "let it be known through various intermediaries that he would not seek vengeance on Masseria supporters or soldiers once Masseria was eliminated. In other words, Maranzano was telling the other side that the quickest way to end the war and save their lives was to take care of Masseria themselves." This proposition soon had the desired effect. Luciano made secret arrangements to call on Maranzano.

The meeting took place in a private house in Brooklyn—Castellammarese territory. Bonanno, as usual, was present, and he recalled that

> Maranzano and Luciano engaged in one of those classic Sicilian dialogues in which every word carried manifold implications but nothing is stated directly.
> —Do you know why you are here? Maranzano asked.
> —Yes.
> —Then I don't have to tell you what has to be done.
> —No.
> —How much time do you need to do what you have to do?
> —A week or two.
> —Good, Maranzano said. I'm looking forward to a peaceful Easter.

Maranzano did not get his wish, not quite. Easter that year fell on April 5, and on April 5, Masseria was still alive. But, as Bonanno said, "Joe the Boss had a limited number of meals left to eat in this life," and his last one came not quite a fortnight later, on April 15, a Wednesday. It was lunch at the Nuova Villa Tammara, an Italian restaurant in Coney Island, a spot chosen for him by Lucky Luciano.

According to New York legend, the boss of bosses' murder was accomplished with all the panoply of a fictional Mafia killing. First Masseria was wined and dined by Luciano, "gorging himself on antipasto, spaghetti with red clam sauce, lobster Fra Diavolo, [and] a quart of Chianti." Then the two men settled down to a game of cards. They played a few hands before Luciano excused himself from the table. Once he was safely out of the way—the story went—three assassins, driven to the spot by Ciro Terranova, walked into the restaurant. Masseria had barely time to register their presence; he died at his table, six bullets in his body and "an ace of spades clutched in one bejewelled paw."

The truth, according to police reports, was rather less dramatic: there was no huge meal, no ace of spades, and no sign, apparently, of Luciano or of Terranova. The end result was the same, however. Masseria died, and with his death the Castellammare War was over.

———

TO NOBODY'S SURPRISE, Salvatore Maranzano emerged as the dominant Mafioso in New York. Soon after Joe the Boss's death, he called a general meeting of all the city's families. It was held in a large hall on Washington Avenue in the Bronx, and four or five hundred men attended, as Joe Valachi said. When everyone was gathered, Maranzano addressed the throng.

"Whatever happened in the past is over," he said. "There is to be no more ill feeling among us. If you lost someone in this past war, you must forgive and forget. If your own brother was killed, don't try to find out who did it to get even. If you do, you pay with your life."

In the past, the Castellammare man continued, Joe the Boss "was always shaking down members, right and left." Now things were going to be different. New York's Mafia families were to be reorganized along military lines, "to keep everything businesslike and in line." Some of the families would get new bosses—Luciano took over Masseria's gang. Maranzano himself would be *capo di tutti capi,* boss of bosses.

Years later, Joe Bonanno cautioned against interpreting this title literally (it was a "vulgar, superficial" view, he said, to think of Maranzano as "ruler of all the Sicilian clans"). At the time, though, it appears that few of the Sicilian gangsters in the city saw the new boss as anything but an all-powerful overlord. In victory, Maranzano became as tyrannical as Masseria. Every Mafia family in the country was to pay him tribute—the sum collected after the war came to $115,000. And, much like his predecessor, the new boss of bosses expected to have a stake in every racket: "the Italian lottery, which was very big then, the building unions, bootlegging, bookmaking, all that kind of stuff," Valachi said.

Maranzano was busy now, perhaps too busy. He had to find time for his own businesses, to counsel other families, and to explore new opportunities. He was besieged by supplicants. Short of time and endlessly distracted, he aroused anger among his closest allies by failing to reward them for the risks they had taken on his behalf and profound resentment among the heads of families who were being taxed by him. By September, only five months after the war had ended, he could no longer get along with Luciano or Al Capone, the boss of the Chicago Mafia. "We got to get rid of them before we control everything," he told his bodyguards. When Luciano heard of this, he decided to strike first.

Joe the Boss had died in Coney Island deserted by even his closest friends. Six months later, Maranzano went much the same way. His murder had been carefully planned, and plenty of lesser Mafiosi seemed to have an idea of what was coming; a friend of Valachi's advised him to steer clear of Maranzano's office on September 10, 1931, which was the day set for the murder. When the time came, the boss of bosses was almost alone. Two Jewish hoodlums, hired by Luciano and dressed as police officers, shot and stabbed him to death.

For years afterward, rumors swirled through Mafia circles that Maranzano's murder was only the first killing orchestrated by Lucky Luciano on that day. The boss's death, these stories said, had been swiftly followed by the well-coordinated slaughter of as many as sixty of his followers—loyalists gunned down to clear away the clannish, murderous traditionalists who threatened to embroil their families in endless vendettas. Luciano, in this version of events, ruthlessly engineered the elimination of a number of old-school bosses—the "Mustache Petes"— who were more interested in dominating Little Italy than they were in expanding into larger and more lucrative domains. The dead men were replaced, such accounts went on, by "Americanized" gangsters— Luciano chief among them—who had less objection to working with non-Sicilians, indeed non-Italians, and were interested chiefly in making money. If they were true, Maranzano's murder had marked the most significant shift of the period, from the first generation of Mafiosi to a new and modern Mafia, one able to dominate organized crime in the United States, and not just its Italian neighborhoods, for decades.

It is certainly true that Mafiosi elsewhere in the United States took advantage of events in New York to dispose of rivals loyal to Maranzano. There were killings in Detroit and Pittsburgh and a trio of shootings in New Jersey, which included the murder of one gangster who was thrown into the Passaic River "with an iron pipe hammered up his ass." Proof that these deaths had any connection is lacking, though, and so is evidence that the Mafia of 1931 possessed anything like the resources necessary to coordinate slaughter on so grand a scale. Luciano's rebellion had more to do with the rejection of the rigid hierarchy of bosses that Maranzano and Masseria had both attempted to enforce than it did with any modernizing impulse. Never again would the Mafia acclaim a *capo di tutti capi*.

The Mafia of 1900, Giuseppe Morello's "mob," had, indeed, more in common with Luciano's than is usually realized. The existence of strong links between branches of the fraternity in Sicily and the United States can be traced back to the Clutch Hand's time, as can the admittance of non-Sicilians to the fraternity, as can the existence of a Mafia "council" or "commission," which even Joe Bonanno thought was a creation of the 1930s. Mafiosi who had served under Morello survived and prospered under Luciano, too; Steve La Salle, who was for years among the Clutch Hand's lieutenants, reemerged in the 1930s as the operator of one of the largest numbers rackets in New York.

As for the Mafia's standing as the most fearsome, most efficient, most iconic gang of criminals in the United States, that too owed as much to Morello as it did to the vastly better known hoodlums of the Luciano generation. Mafia history, in the United States, begins not with Maranzano's murder, as it is generally written. Its roots lie several decades earlier, in the dust and blood of Corleone and in the fractured heart of the Morello family. Understanding America's Mafia means understanding that, if nothing else.

GIUSEPPE MORELLO HAD outlived most of his friends and many enemies, chief among them William Flynn, who remained head of the Secret Service until 1917. The Chief was a considerable success, not least in the years leading up to America's entry into the First World War, when, in the absence of the counterespionage organizations that would share responsibility for security in later years, his agency assumed some of the responsibility for rounding up the spies and saboteurs loose in the United States.

Germany was the most active power in this respect, striving not only to influence American opinion but also to prevent its enemies from obtaining munitions and supplies from America. Flynn assigned eleven men to counter these efforts, and they scored some notable successes. The most celebrated incident involved a German diplomat, Dr. Heinrich Albert, whose briefcase one of Flynn's men snatched on a crowded streetcar. Opened, the case revealed an array of incriminating documents, including account books showing that Albert had spent $27 million building up a spy network in the United States. German money had funded dock strikes, attacks on shipping, and bombs planted in munitions plants.

The Albert case and other triumphs made Flynn famous during the war in a way that his years combating counterfeiting had not. He reveled in his celebrity, and it is hard not to conclude that fame went at least a little to his head. Never averse to personal publicity, Flynn had always liked to take a full part in operations and share in any credit that accrued—a predilection more laudable in the chief of a small Secret Service bureau than it was when indulged by the director of a national agency. Now he set to work to rouse the country to the threat of German espionage, delivering scaremongering speeches from New York to California. In one newspaper interview, Flynn said that Germany had 250,000 spies at work in the United States. "Maybe," he added, "one of them is sitting next to you." His wilder claims resembled those of a later and less principled agitator, Senator Joseph McCarthy.

Rabble-rousing statements of this sort underlined Flynn's bulldog patriotism, but they also aroused considerable anger in German and Irish communities. Pressure on the Chief mounted rapidly, and it came as little surprise when he tendered his resignation from the Secret Service in November 1917, saying he was exhausted and had been ordered to rest. It soon emerged that the real reason for Flynn's departure was lack of support in Washington for his hard-line approach to counterespionage. The great detective's nemesis, in this respect, was William Bayard Hale, a newspaperman of German ancestry and pronouncedly pro-German views who had been an influential correspondent in Berlin until America entered the war. Hale returned to New York, where Flynn put him under investigation as a potential threat to national security.

According to a protest the furious reporter lodged with President Woodrow Wilson, this surveillance included a visit from an intimidating Secret Service man who issued threats against his family. When the Justice Department's Bureau of Investigation (forerunner of the FBI) was ordered to check out the complaint and concluded that Flynn had acted "not only without the authority of law, but in defiance of [an] act of Congress limiting activities of [his] service," he had to go. He was replaced by his deputy, William Moran—another veteran Secret Service man, but one who would prove considerably more malleable and, on occasion, actually corrupt.

As things turned out, Flynn would enjoy one last hurrah as a detective, and it would come precisely because he held such firm views on questions of national security. Two years after his departure from the

Secret Service, a tremendous explosion shook the home of A. Mitchell Palmer, the attorney general of the United States, virtually demolishing it. Eight similar devices exploded that same evening across the country, all but one of them at the homes of judges and politicians involved in bringing cases against anarchists and radical socialists; sixteen deadly letter bombs were also discovered at the New York post office, where they had been put aside for bearing insufficient postage. A few months later, in September 1920, there was another terrific detonation on Wall Street, opposite the headquarters of J. P. Morgan & Company. On that occasion, the bombers exploded a huge device that had been concealed on a delivery wagon.

Concerted terrorist action of this sort was unprecedented in America; worse, it came at a time when fear of communism and union agitation was sweeping the country. The shaken Palmer dedicated his Department of Justice to tracking down the men responsible. To fulfill that pledge, he needed a brilliant detective, and Flynn was the obvious choice. Hastily recalled from semiretirement (he had accepted a sinecure as head of the Federal Railway Administration police), the old Secret Service chief was appointed director of the Bureau of Investigation. The task of monitoring suspected radicals Flynn gave to an ambitious Justice Department clerk by the name of J. Edgar Hoover. He himself took charge of hunting down the bombers.

It was an impossible task, rendered harder by the scarcity of information or reliable informants, but Flynn still nearly managed it. In a fine example of the sort of plodding detective work that he had always believed in, his men tracked down a label found in a fragment of clothing outside Palmer's house by calling at every laundry in each of the eight cities where bombs had exploded. In time, they identified the man responsible for the Palmer blast and narrowed their inquiry into the Wall Street atrocity to the point where Flynn felt certain that the men he was seeking were followers of an anarchist named Luigi Galleani. He even called in his old informant Salvatore Clemente and sent him to Italy to try to penetrate the gang. Clemente, posing as an Italian American radical, made some useful contacts but failed to get to Galleani, who had already fled to Switzerland. Flynn kept trying, but he could never obtain the sort of evidence that would stand up in court.

By early in 1921, opinion was shifting against the Bureau of Investigation. Flynn's cheerful public pronouncements, endlessly claiming he was on the verge of breaking the case, appeared increasingly hollow; people wanted arrests, not promises and theories, and the bureau was not providing them. Support within the Justice Department withered, too, as Flynn failed to address the plummeting morale among his staff. To make matters worse, Hoover had launched a series of raids that resulted in the rounding up of ten thousand suspected radicals and the deportation of more than five hundred, without having firm evidence that any of the men involved were criminals. The "Palmer Raids," as they were known, turned into a public relations debacle of such magnitude that there was no way Flynn could keep his job under the new Harding administration. At the end of August 1921 he was replaced as director of the Bureau of Investigation by another famous detective, William Burns—a man renowned in equal measure for catching the radicals who had blown up the *Los Angeles Times* building in 1910 and for running a private detective agency that had been caught jury tampering and specialized in intimidating unions.

It was a sad end to a remarkable career. Flynn remained certain that he had been within an ace of cracking the Wall Street case, and he undoubtedly got closer to the correct solution than did the far more famous Burns, who also failed to make arrests and was convinced from the outset that the culprits were the unions he hated. The loss of his $7,500 bureau salary was, moreover, a severe blow to a man with a large family to support. ("As he has told me, he has half a dozen little Flynns, and he has been working for the Government so long that he has not anything laid by," Palmer had once observed.) Going into business for himself, as the boss of a new New York detective agency, produced some money, but Flynn had to make ends meet by turning to the one other thing that he was good at: For the remainder of his life, he earned much of his living as a writer.

Flynn had been contributing occasional articles to newspapers such as *The Washington Post* and the *New York Herald* ever since 1914, most of them retellings of his greatest cases. After his enforced retirement from the Secret Service, he embarked on a brief career as a crime novelist and a scenario writer for the motion picture industry, turning an acquaintance with the actor King Baggot—forgotten now, but in 1917 the greatest film star in the country—into a commission to write story lines for Theodore and Leopold Wharton. The Whartons were the pioneer producers of movie serials such as *The Perils of Pauline,* a melodrama that was the first to feature what became a popular cliché, the heroine tied to railway tracks by a mustache-twirling villain; they turned Flynn's experiences into a twenty-part spy thriller titled *The Eagle's Eye*. A few years later, the Chief was hired to lend his name to new detective fiction magazine, *Flynn's Weekly*, which he edited with evident relish and which eventually became the longest-running, most successful title of its kind.

It was all too much for the aging detective. Though still in his late fifties, Flynn was very overweight by now, a confirmed smoker of powerful cigars, and beset by family problems that spilled over into his working life. His daughter Veronica and son Elmer, whom he had taken on as partners in his agency, were running the detective business into the ground. Both heavy drinkers, they overspent and upset clients. The pair's increasingly erratic behavior distressed their more abstemious father, and the worry weakened him.

William Flynn expired of heart disease at the age of sixty, in October 1928. He died a disappointed man.

FRANCESCO ORTOLEVA, the man framed by the Corleone Mafia for the killing of Giovanni Vella, was finally released from jail at the end of 1913. Age sixty-five, "broken in body and weighted with years"—so Flynn remarked—he had served twenty-one years of his life sentence for the murder. Taking into account the time that Ortoleva had rotted on remand, awaiting trial, he spent a quarter of a century in jail for a crime that Morello had committed.

Why the prisoner of Palermo was freed at this time remains uncertain. It may be that he simply served out his time and was granted parole; perhaps Flynn intervened on his behalf, as he once claimed. But the Ortoleva family had campaigned long and hard for his release, and they had been given new hope when news reached Corleone of Morello's conviction for counterfeiting. Ortoleva's son, James, came to New York in the summer of 1910 to see Flynn and ask if arrangements could be made for his mother to visit Atlanta; he hoped the sight of a woman who had been cruelly wronged might induce Morello to confess. Flynn was not encouraging—"While Morello is making an effort to have his case appealed, it is very doubtful he would make any admissions which would be detrimental to him," he said—but he took a liking to Ortoleva nonetheless and offered him employment as his confidential secretary.

The next year, James wrote a fruitless series of letters to the federal penitentiary, attempting to persuade the Mafioso to accept responsibility for
Vella's death.

Francesco Ortoleva was healthy enough, after his long incarceration,
to go to New York and live out his last years with his wife and son. He arrived in the city aboard the SS *San Guglielmo* on January 25, 1914. "I
pray for him and his family," Flynn concluded in his account, "and they
give thanks to me and mine."

MOST OF THE THUGS, gangsters, and counterfeiters who likewise
crossed the path of the Morello family faded into obscurity or came to violent ends.

Pietro Inzerillo, the café proprietor who had supplied the barrel in
which Benedetto Madonia's body was placed, fled New York when news
broke of the Secret Service roundup of Morello's counterfeiting operation. He returned to Italy, where in October 1911 one of Flynn's informants stumbled across him unexpectedly in Milan and learned that he had
resumed work as a counterfeiter. Giuseppe Di Priemo did not make it
that far; he died on board ship while traveling home to Sicily sometime
after 1909. But two other American Mafiosi did successfully reestablish
themselves on the island. Carlo Costantino, one of the assassins sent after Petrosino in 1909, stayed on in Palermo as a robber, swindler, and
liquor dealer; he died in the late 1930s, riddled with the syphilis he had
contracted in New York. His associate Antonio Passananti, on the other
hand, outlived every other member of the Morello family. Jailed for
four years for murder in 1911, Passananti went into hiding during a
crackdown on the Mafia in the mid-1920s and continued to crop up
sporadically in Italian police reports until the early 1960s. In the first
week of March 1969, by then ninety years old, he committed suicide by
shooting himself in the head. Passananti had belatedly given up his life of
crime a year or two earlier. The last note in his police file read: "He no
longer associates with criminal figures [and] can no longer be regarded
as a socially dangerous individual."

A little more is known of Ralph Daniello, alias Ralph the Barber, who
pleaded guilty in June 1918 to his part in the ambush and assassination
of Nick Terranova. In recognition of the testimony that had convicted
five of his fellow Camorrists, he was given a suspended sentence. The

Barber did not walk free immediately, however; convinced, with reason, that the surviving members of his gang would kill him, he begged the judge to keep him behind bars until all his confederates had been safely jailed.

Daniello eked out the second chance his sentence gave him for about a year; then, in 1920, he got himself into an argument in a Coney Island bar, lashed out, and was arrested. This time his record as a stool pigeon failed to impress the judge—he served five years for felonious assault. It seems likely that Ralph hoped his half decade in jail would wash away the memory of his betrayals; rather than flee the vengeance of his former colleagues, he moved to New Jersey after his release, purchased a saloon, and lived there openly under his real name, Alfonso Pepe. It was a fatal mistake. Less than a month after his release, Ralph was sitting with a friend outside his Newark bar when a man approached. The stranger drew a gun, remarked, "I've got you now," and fired three times into his body.

Daniello died in agony from a bullet in the gut. His killer jumped into a car driven by two other men and got clean away, aided by a fusillade of fifteen shots he and the second passenger directed back into the crowd. The Barber's assassins were never caught, but, the Newark police declared, their most likely motive was revenge.

Among the many suspects who might have ordered Daniello's murder, Pellegrino Marano, the Camorra boss in Coney Island, was last heard of at the trial of Tony the Shoemaker in July 1926. By then seven years into his sentence of twenty years to life for the Terranova killing, Marano flatly refused to give evidence against his associate. "I won't talk," he told the court. "I don't know anybody." His lieutenant, Giuseppe Vocaro, was just as tight-lipped. "Seven years ago," he said, "I swore on the tomb of my mother that I would never be a witness for or against anybody." The two Camorrists were returned to their cells.

The latter years of Alessandro Vollero, the leader of the Navy Street gang, are better chronicled, thanks largely to the chance that placed Joe Valachi in his Sing Sing cell during the 1920s. Valachi, already a sworn enemy of Ciro Terranova, was delighted to discover that his cellmate was the man who had had Terranova's brother killed. It was the Camorra boss, he recalled, who educated him in the deep-rooted enmity between Sicilians and Neapolitans: "If there is one thing that we who are from Naples must always remember," Vollero preached, "it is that if you hang out with a Sicilian for twenty years and you have trouble with another Sicilian, the Sicilian that you hung out with for all that time will turn on you. In other words, you can never trust them."

Vollero became a mentor to Valachi, even offering the younger man an introduction to a fellow Neapolitan, the Chicago gangster Al Capone. It was he who first hinted at the existence of the secret criminal fraternity called the Mafia—an organization that Valachi, a streetwise Italian American criminal, had not realized existed. He pressed eagerly for further information, but Vollero realized that he had said too much. "Take it easy, kid," he counseled his protégé. "You'll learn all there is to know in good time. It's not for me to say it."

By the time Vollero was released from jail, in 1933, Valachi had fulfilled his cellmate's prediction. Initiated into Tom Gagliano's family during the Castellammare War, the former burglar had become a member of the organization he always referred to as Cosa Nostra, running a numbers racket under the protection of an ambitious hoodlum named Vito Genovese. There was still a good deal the low-ranking Valachi did not understand about the inner workings of the Mafia—"Well, who knows what the hell's going on?" he once complained—but he knew enough to realize that Vollero's life was now in danger. A friend of the old Camorra leader soon appeared to beg Valachi for his help. "The old guy don't know nobody now," the man explained. "But he hears you're with Vito and them others. Can you straighten things out for him?"

Valachi did his best. The days of the Morello-Terranova ascendancy had faded into irrelevance by now, and the forward-looking Genovese was reluctant at first to intervene—"When the hell did this happen, twenty years ago?" Eventually, however, Valachi's boss agreed to speak to Ciro Terranova, and word was relayed that the problem was resolved. Valachi passed the good news to Vollero, who was so grateful that he pressed the younger man to visit him at home. "It was really something," Valachi said. "He had the whole family lined up to greet me. He called me his savior. Well, we ate, and it was the last time I saw him. I heard later that he went back to Italy and died in peace."

IN SICILY, VITO CASCIO FERRO— last seen in New York on the night of the Barrel Murder in April 1903, and last heard of six years later, in Palermo, as a suspect in the Petrosino murder case—returned to his hometown, Bisaquino, to find the local Mafia waxing considerably in strength.

It was a situation that suited the wily and ambitious gangster perfectly. Cascio Ferro worked tirelessly for two decades, first to cement his position as an influential leader in his own district, then to extend the Mafia's rapacious grip over most forms of crime in western Sicily. In doing so, he made a fortune from rustling cattle and turned himself from an all but illiterate peasant into one of the dozen or so most influential men in the whole island. Cascio Ferro, according to one police report dating to 1909, controlled organized crime across three provinces of Sicily and had a number of influential friends in the political establishment. By the early 1920s, it is said, his power in the hinterland beyond Palermo was such that the mayors of towns he was expected to pass through would wait outside their gates to kiss his hand.

It is doubtful whether the Sicilian Mafia has ever had a more respected—even beloved—leader in all its long and fratricidal history. "Don Vito," the Italian writer Luigi Barzini observed, "brought the organization to its highest perfection without undue recourse to violence. . . . [He] ruled and inspired fear mainly by use of his great qualities and his natural ascendancy. His awe-inspiring appearance helped him. He was tall, spare, elegantly but sombrely dressed. A long white beard made him resemble a sage, a New England preacher of the last century, or a respected judge. . . . Being very generous by nature, he never refused a request for aid and dispensed millions in loans, gifts and general philanthropy. He would personally go out of his way to redress a wrong. . . . Under his reign, peace and order were preserved."

Attaining a position of such eminence may have gratified Cascio Ferro, but it has almost always proved dangerous for any criminal to gain such public renown. In May 1926, in the course of a vigorous campaign against the Mafia decreed by Mussolini, Don Vito was arrested. In the Sicily of old, this would have proved no more than a temporary hindrance. But when one of Cascio Ferro's numerous godsons called on a powerful local landowner to solicit his support, he was dismissed with the bleak observation "Times have changed." The Fascist regime took no chances when it came to indicting the old boss. Don Vito was charged with participation in twenty murders, eight attempted murders, five robberies, thirty-seven acts of extortion, and fifty-three sundry other offenses, all of which had been accompanied by threats of violence.

Sentenced, after a brief, one-sided trial, to life in prison, Cascio Ferro disappeared behind the forbidding walls of the Ucciardone Prison in Palermo. There, wrote Barzini, he established an effortless sway over warders and prisoners alike, arbitrating disputes and ending feuds. If true, it did him little good; he died in jail. According to Arrigo Petacco, an Italian journalist and the biographer of Joseph Petrosino, the old don's end was appropriately diabolical; accidentally left behind when his prison was heavily bombed and then evacuated in 1943, "he died of thirst and terror in the gloomy, abandoned penitentiary, like the villain in some old serial story." The truth was less melodramatic. Cascio Ferro expired in his cell of heart failure, in 1942. Don Vito left behind him the words of an old Sicilian proverb, carved painstakingly by hand into the walls: "Prison, sickness, and necessity reveal the heart of a friend." The inscription remained visible until the late 1960s, when it was finally painted over.

CASCIO FERRO'S RISE to eminence in Sicily coincided with the panicked visit Giuseppe Morello and Lupo the Wolf made to the island in 1921. It seems possible that the powerful Mafioso, their ally in New York two decades earlier, was one of the men the pair appealed to in their efforts to have the death sentences imposed upon them overturned.

However the trouble was resolved—whether Cascio Ferro, or Nick Gentile, or some other Mafia boss intervened on the men's behalf— Ignazio Lupo was able to return to the United States in May 1922, his difficulties with Totò D'Aquila at an end. The Mafioso immediately encountered a problem of a different sort, however: A Secret Service agent stationed at Ellis Island recognized his distinctive moon face as he disembarked, and immigration officials on the island detained and held him there for three weeks as a potential undesirable and a likely deportee. It took the production of a copy of the commutation President Harding had signed for him—an impressive piece of parchment affixed with seal and ribbon—to secure his release.

Lupo returned to New York on June 12. There, thanks largely to the protection he received from Ciro Terranova, who also provided him with a handsome sixteen-room home on Brooklyn's swanky Avenue P, he experienced no difficulty in resuming his old trade as an extortionist. By early 1923, the Wolf was hard at work running a wholesale operation, the La Rosa Fruit Company, which supplied grocery stores and restaurants throughout Brooklyn with produce at the usual inflated prices. This business lasted for the best part of a decade, and, when it was sold, Lupo worked as a lemon broker for a while before shifting his attention to the bakery trade. He had long experience of running operations of this sort and soon built up a substantial racket. In 1925, it was reported, he returned again to Italy to bank the money he had made over the last three years, and the total came to $3 million. The bakery delivery round that he opened in 1933 with Rocco, his only son, began trading with a single truck; three years later there were eight, and Lupo had also became the self-appointed president of the Italian Bakers' Association. Payment of the association's dues guaranteed members the chance to run their stores unmolested, though as usual the protection that the Wolf was selling was mostly protection against himself. *The New York Times* wrote that he also controlled Brooklyn's lucrative Italian lottery.

Like his brother-in-law Terranova, the Wolf took pains to present himself as a legitimate businessman and to claim his burgeoning wealth as the product of hard work. "He especially liked to stay home with his family after his business hours and duties and did not congregate in any saloon or meeting place," his brother John would claim. "He always went to bed early so that he would be better able to take care of his business the next morning." Any complaints made about his methods, insisted Salvatrice, his wife, were lodged by rivals who were simply jealous of his success. There is not much truth in this. The reality was that Lupo made good in business by making good his threats. He was a suspect in the unsolved murder of a contractor named Ruggerio Consiglio in October 1930 and was charged a year later with killing a rival who had challenged the monopoly he had established in the Brooklyn grape trade—a racket that had yielded the Sicilian gangster Frankie Uale fifty dollars per carload of wine grapes during the 1920s. On that occasion Lupo was picked out by a witness from a ninety-four-man lineup in Manhattan.

The usual problems, not least the impossibility of finding men brave enough to testify against the Mafia in open court, prevented the DA from bringing prosecutions in these cases. But there was at least one woman in Brooklyn angry and principled enough to take a stand against the Wolf's extortion. Rose Vitale, who ran a bakery shop at 557 McDonald Avenue, had been told to join the bakers' association but refused to pay

Lupo's inflated dues. Threats followed, and when Vitale still proved obdurate, a mysterious fire broke out in her shop. Later one of her delivery trucks was overturned, and stink bombs were used to contaminate the bread in others.

By July 1935, Vitale had had enough, and she went to the police with her complaints. They responded. Ignazio and Rocco Lupo were arrested at their home and held in jail for the next four months. By the time they got out, Vitale had persuaded several of the bakers' association's reluctant members to join her in giving statements. The Lupos replied with more threats and several beatings.

The fact that some of the Wolf's victims had finally found the courage to speak out against him says a good deal about the changing conditions in New York. By the mid-1930s, Lupo was nearly sixty years old and lacked much of his youthful strength and vigor. His son, Rocco, was not cut from the same stern cloth, and their old protector, Terranova, was himself a fading force. The new generation of Mafiosi that came to power in the wake of the Castellammare War had no reason to support a man whose friends and allies were mostly dead and gone, and Vitale may have sensed there was more bluster than real menace in Lupo's threats. The political climate in the city was changing, too. A new mayor, Fiorello La Guardia, was shaking up the police and speaking out against crime and criminals. These factors combined to make Vitale's stand against the Wolf's rackets possible.

Retribution was not far off by now. On January 11, 1936, a few weeks after the Lupos emerged from jail, a formal complaint signed by several Brooklyn bakers was lodged with New York's governor, Herbert Lehman. It alleged that the Wolf and his cub had been operating bakeries and selling goods at cost to undercut their businesses and punish them for their intransigence; the signatories urged Lehman to investigate the Mafioso's "homicidal organization." The governor passed the information to Brooklyn's DA for action, and it was at the district attorney's office that, at last, a chink was found in Lupo's armor. The commutation that the Mafioso had brandished on Ellis Island was not a full and formal pardon, as the Wolf believed; his release had been conditional, and President Harding's decree would remain in force only for as long as Lupo stayed within the law. Should he return to criminal ways, the commutation clearly stated, he could be immediately recalled to prison to serve out the remainder of his term. There was no need for more investigation or a trial; the president reserved to himself the sole right to decide the case.

Acting on Lehman's recommendation, Harding's successor, Franklin Roosevelt, soon signed the necessary order. On July 13, at dawn, Brooklyn police arrived outside the Lupo home. The Wolf was under arrest and on his way back to Atlanta long before his friends or lawyers had any inkling of the danger.

The sound of the federal penitentiary doors slamming behind him was a shocking blow to Lupo. He had 7,174 days, or almost twenty years, of his sentence still to serve, and was not due for release until March 4, 1956—when he would be seventy-nine years old. With no hope of a further commutation and little of parole, his one chance of release was to fight the validity of Roosevelt's summary recall, and a petition for a writ of habeas corpus, aimed at the warden at Atlanta, was filed accordingly in 1937. *Lupo v. Zerbst,* as the case was known, drained much of the Lupo family's finances and was a miserable failure, though it did enough to confirm the president's rights in cases of commutation to be cited in legal textbooks to this day. In the same year, news reached the Wolf that his son had proved incapable of keeping up the bakery business; Rocco Lupo was declared bankrupt at the end of September.

It is scarcely surprising, in these circumstances, that Lupo's physical and mental state seemed parlous to the prison doctor. "Examination reveals . . . an elderly white man, very obese, who enters the examination room promptly, and responds to questions in a lingo, but has a good understanding of the English language," the physician noted. "At the present time he is nervous, irritable, and excitable, with a tendency to self-pity and somewhat lachrymose." The Wolf was diagnosed with a heart murmur and had varicose veins in both legs. According to his brother, he experienced a nervous breakdown at the time of his arrest; examined in Atlanta, his IQ was measured at 70, on the borderline of retardation, and the early symptoms of "senile psychosis" were detected.

During his first term in Atlanta, Lupo had flouted prison regulations. He had been placed in solitary confinement for "crookedness" in 1910, for fraternizing with other prisoners in 1911, and for breaking rules in 1919, and there were other reprimands and warnings. Now, though, he was more or less a broken man. Two minor incidents were recorded in 1936, soon after his return to prison, but the prisoner's record was otherwise spotless. Lupo even earned a commendation from the tailors' shop, where he was put to work, for his exemplary behavior while engaged in sewing flies.

The years passed slowly. There were fewer visits from family and friends; many were already dead, of course, his daughters had married, and Salvatrice, in New York, was too old and too impoverished to make the journey down to Georgia anymore; if there was any truth in the rumors of a fortune banked in Italy, the money was lost when the United States declared war on Mussolini's regime in 1941. There was little companionship; most of the Wolf's fellow prisoners were far younger than him. He kept to himself during exercise periods, circling the vast prison yard alone, and, in his loneliness, became increasingly religious. According to Zia Trestelle, a fellow Mafioso who once took the train to Atlanta to see him, Lupo regularly attended Mass and had come to feel some sort of contrition for the life he had chosen. In a letter to his eldest daughter, Onofria, he wrote: "I am overcome by my memories. All these years in America, sometimes I think they never existed. I'd like to be a boy again in Sicily and die young, very young, and never know all these years of struggle and evil."

The Wolf was still in Atlanta when peace returned in 1945, by now well past retirement age. A year later, on the tenth anniversary of his return to jail, the prison doctor noted that the old man was "failing fast, becoming more and more senile and childish." Lupo's case was reviewed over the summer, and it was recommended that he should be released while his family was still able to take care of him. There was a further legal tussle over the legality of granting a parole violator renewed parole, however, and the old man was not actually discharged from Atlanta until the morning of December 21, 1946. He had $7.83 in his pocket, the sum total of his prison savings. The warden advanced him just sufficient money to get him to New York.

Ignazio Lupo returned to the city in time for Christmas, a living example of the maxim that crime does not pay. A fifty-year career in murder and extortion had left him and his elderly wife quite destitute. At some point in the 1940s, Salvatrice, penniless and alone, had been forced to sell their heavily remortgaged home, and the couple moved into a rented room in Queens, visited occasionally by their children. Lupo the Wolf died three weeks after his release, on January 13, 1947, at the age of sixty-nine. The story failed to make the papers.

―――

THE MATRIARCHS OF the Morello-Terranova clan lived longer but died in the same obscurity as Lupo. Angela Terranova, Bernardo's wife, the mother of four brothers who had terrorized New York, died in Queens in 1941, age ninety-two. Twice widowed, she had survived her second husband by more than three decades; at least seven of her ten children predeceased her, among them all her sons. Angela had lived quietly in the United States for nearly fifty years, and as befitted a Mafia wife, she left no record of her thoughts and feelings. The life had brought her a certain affluence—relative, that is, to the existence she could have expected had she remained in Corleone—but she was certainly not rich; she died in her daughter-in-law's apartment on 222nd Street, where she had lived for just eight months. Whether she believed the violent deaths of three sons and a grandson were a price worth paying for that modest comfort is impossible to say.

Not much more is known of the last years of Morello's wife. Lina of the volcanic eyes never remarried after the murder of her husband, though she outlived him by nearly forty years. She raised four long-lived children, the last of them a sufferer from Down syndrome, and died in New York, at the age of eighty-three, in 1967.

THE LAST MEMBER of the Terranova clan was Ciro. The Artichoke King retained his influence throughout the Castellammare War and remained a significant figure in the New York underworld of the early 1930s. He lived with his family in a large pink house in Pelham Manor, an affluent village on the northern outskirts of the city, kept up his power base in Harlem, and maintained an interest in his old vegetable racket. Under Lucky Luciano, he also kept his stake in the Harlem numbers racket, as a junior partner to Dutch Schultz.

To the casual observer, Ciro appeared serenely untroubled by the vicious undercurrents in the New York underworld. He survived the 1935 murder of his ally Schultz and the upheaval surrounding Luciano's conviction, a year later, for organizing prostitution—an arrest that resulted in a punitive sentence of thirty to fifty years' imprisonment. By then Terranova was popularly supposed to be a millionaire, and certainly the high living continued. He threw a lavish wedding for his daughter Anne in 1935. That same year, a reporter describing the comfortable lives lived by New York's racketeers sarcastically observed that "Ciro Terranova, the high lord of the Harlem rackets, loves a canter in the park or among the lovely hills of Westchester, because you meet such interesting people on the bridle path." In truth, however, Terranova was never quite so rich as he appeared. The artichoke racket, which he passed on to an old subordinate named Joseph Castaldo in 1931, was then reported to gross well under a third of a million dollars a year, and when, after Schultz was murdered, Luciano relieved him of his share in the Harlem numbers racket, he was left without a source of income.

By 1936, Terranova had been "encouraged" to retire, and his lack of ambition—the sheer unlikelihood that he would strike back at the younger bosses who were ousting him—was probably all that saved him from a violent end. In some respects it might have been better for the old Mafioso's reputation if he had been killed. Stripped of his wealth and power, Ciro became an easy prey for a New York Police Department under pressure from Mayor La Guardia to take a tougher stance on crime, and for several years he was harassed every time he came within the city limits. Taking advantage of the fact that Terranova had no visible means of support, the police detained him as a vagrant, subjecting the old boss to repeated humiliation.

"I have to come down here sometimes," Ciro complained to Captain Daniel Courtayne on one of these occasions.

"You are supposed to be a bigshot racketeer," Courtayne taunted him. "You're just a cheap pushcart peddler. That's about your speed."

"I never was a pushcart peddler," snarled Terranova. He was furious.

Ciro was a husk of his old self by now. In 1935, the government began pursuing him for unpaid tax on his earnings—the same ruse that had been employed to convict Al Capone a few years earlier. Two years later, apparently unable to pay a $543 bill, the Mafioso slipped into bankruptcy. His bank foreclosed the mortgage on the house at Pelham Manor, and he moved back with his wife to 338 East 116th Street, the old headquarters of the Ignatz Florio Co-Operative Association, a property that the family had owned for many years. His other assets were listed as two hundred dollars in cash owed to him, two shares in a realty company, and a "possible cause for action for wrongful arrest."

Less than a year later, still only forty-nine, Terranova was crippled by a stroke that left him paralyzed down his left side and incapable of speech. He was taken to Columbia Hospital, where he expired half an hour after midnight on the morning of February 20, 1938, the only one of the four Morello-Terranova brothers who died in bed. The police had long since dropped their campaign of harassment against him. Ciro, an officer told *The New York Times,* died not only virtually penniless but also "criminally, financially and physically irrelevant."

It is hard to imagine a more humiliating epitaph for a Mafia boss from Corleone.

WILLIAM FLYNN, WITHOUT whose efforts practically nothing would be known of the first years of America's Mafia, has no monument in New York or anywhere else. His grave in Valhalla, just north of the city, lies in a family plot that nobody much visits anymore; he himself has been virtually forgotten. Joe Petrosino, on the other hand, survives—if only barely—in the collective memory of the city that he loved. His resting place, in Calvary Cemetery in Queens, is marked by a pillar topped with an elaborate bust. It continues to attract visitors, and a handful of tributes—a card, a withered flower—lie scattered at its base. By an appropriate coincidence, the plot lies less than a policeman's beat away from the bare and unremembered graves in which Giuseppe Morello, Ignazio Lupo, and the Terranova brothers were interred.

In 1987, as a gesture to the policeman's memory, a tiny triangle of land at the junction of Kenmare and Lafayette streets, in Little Italy, was designated Lieutenant Joseph Petrosino Park. A small plaque next to the entrance identifies the place, but the park itself remains unused. It stands forlorn and empty aside from a single tree, and the ground has been concreted over from end to end. To add to the atmosphere of uncaring neglect, both pillars guarding the entrance lean at crazy angles, and the gate that once secured it has disappeared.

A few years after the park opened, with fine irony, an Italian restaurant across the street was purchased by Alphonse D'Arco, a capo in the Lucchese family—one of the five Mafia gangs that had emerged from the Castellammare War, and a family that at one time included several members of the old Morello clan among their ranks.

For many years, Al D'Arco used the restaurant as a secure meeting place where numerous Mafia crimes were planned. In 1991, however, he learned that the bosses he had served so loyally and so long had lost confidence in him and were plotting his murder. Fearing for his life, he ran to the FBI and, to save himself from prison, gave the bureau every scrap of information he possessed about the Luccheses.

Almost all of the details that D'Arco provided were unknown to the bureau and the police. The capo explained in detail how his Mafia family profited from protection rackets in the construction, air freight, and rubbish industries, controlled as many as twenty union locals, and maintained discipline by murdering anyone whom it thought of as an enemy. He also passed the police details that enabled them to close about a dozen unsolved murder cases.

Amid this welter of sensational disclosures, D'Arco supplied one piece of information that went unremarked in the press. The Luccheses, he explained, ran lucrative protection rackets in both of New York's gigantic wholesale produce markets, in Brooklyn and the Bronx. No one in the city sold fruit and vegetables without paying off the mob.

For someone with a sense of history, the disclosure was sobering. Three quarters of a century after Morello and Ciro Terranova had set up the first New York vegetable rackets, their direct descendants in the Mafia were still taking a cut on every single artichoke sold in the five boroughs.

ACKNOWLEDGMENTS

WRITING THE HISTORY OF CRIME POSES UNIQUE CHALLENGES to any author. No more than a handful of records written by participants on either side of the divide between criminals and police survive; private papers are conspicuous by their absence; memoirs are distorted by evasion, fading memories, and special pleading. Worse, few among the participants in the events described had a clear picture of what was going on; fewer still elected to explain their actions, or those of their bosses, in print; and none did so dispassionately. Accurate, reliable, and comprehensive firsthand accounts are, in short, entirely lacking.

I have done my best to surmount these obstacles, though inevitably narrative history is not always the ideal medium in which to explore conflicts in testimony and gaps in information, and my work has been made vastly easier by the unstinting assistance I have received from dozens of people who had no motive, other than kindness, to help.

Recollections, anecdotes, private papers, and photographs provided by members of the Morello, Flynn, and Farach families have, I hope, added depth to my portrayal of characters who are generally depicted entirely one-dimensionally. In this context, I would like to thank Giuseppe Morello's great-grandson Steven Gargiula, Chief William Flynn's grandson William Flynn Sanders, and Carmelo Farach's great-grandnephew Dean Farrish, for their help.

In the United States, my old friend and colleague Dr. Henk Looijesteijn—who fortuitously happened to be in Albany and New York just before I arrived to conduct my own research there—got the search in the New York State Archives and the Municipal Archives, New York, under way on my behalf. I was also the grateful recipient of assistance from

Ellen Belcher of the Lloyd Sealy Library of John Jay College of Criminal Justice; Spencer Howard of the Herbert Hoover Presidential Library in West Branch, Iowa; Richard Gelbke and Gregory Plunges of NARA-Northeast in New York; Arlene Royer of NARA-Southeast in Morrow, Georgia; Leonora Goodlund of the New York Municipal Archives; Stuart M. Cohen, clerk to the New York Court of Appeals, Albany; Bill Gorman of the New York State Archives, Albany; Tiffany Levandowski of Osterhout Free Library in Wilkes-Barre, Pennsylvania; Amy Veracruz-Gregory of the Brazos County Genealogical Association, Texas; Colin Brown and Nancy Abrahams of Brooklyn Heights; and Parry Desmond of Philadelphia. Dino Paternostro, of Corleone, a noted authority on the local Mafia, most generously conducted new research on my behalf in Sicily. In the United Kingdom, Dr. Serena Ferente, of King's College London, was my guide to research on the subject in Italian, Carolyn Keim helped with electronic resources at the Seeley Historical Library, Cambridge, Kevin Brownlow shared his knowledge of William Flynn's brief film career—a fascinating period I would have liked to devote more space to—and Dr. David Critchley, whose knowledge of early American Mafia history is unrivaled in its depth, very generously swapped leads and documents. I owe a considerable debt, too, to Fiona Jerome for her assistance with the plates sections.

My indomitable agent, Patrick Walsh, worked miracles on my behalf and deserves a large slice of the credit for helping me to realize this project on a large scale, and my editors, Kerri Sharpe in London and Tim Bartlett in New York, showed huge enthusiasm for this project from the start; each in turn improved it. Thanks, too, to Tim Rostron at Doubleday in Canada, Diana Fox and Lindsay Schwoeri at Random House, Rory Scarfe at Simon & Schuster, and to Rob Dinsdale and Jake Smith-Bosanquet at Conville & Walsh.

At home, Penny and Ffion provided more support, in every way, than I deserved during a seemingly endless period of writing and rewriting. This book is for them, for the shade of Mollie Callahan, and for every other innocent victim of the Morello family.

NOTES

The First Family is narrative history, but it is also intended to be *good* history. I have provided the most precise source notes that I can. Considerations of space, unfortunately, have meant that the discursive footnotes that accompanied my previous books have had to be omitted. As this is a subject of considerable importance, however, I have written detailed footnotes anyway, amounting to some forty thousand words of additional material—nearly half as much again as the main text of this book. Anyone wishing to find out exactly where I got my information from and why I have interpreted it in the way I have, or who wishes to have a fuller analysis, see transcriptions of original documents and other background material, and read a much more voluminous discussion of various contentious points, is welcome to consult them. Bound copies have been deposited in the Library of Congress, the New York Public Library, and the British Library. Readers can also download the notes, for free, by visiting my *The First Family* pages at www.mikedash.com.

ABBREVIATIONS USED IN THE NOTES

ASP Archivio di Stato, Palermo. These documents are arranged by section (b.), then category (c.), and finally by bundle (f.).

Barrel file New York District Attorney's papers concerning the "Barrel Murder" case of April 1903. File 42841, District Attorney's Closed Case Files 1895–1966, NYMA.

Comito confession "Antonio Comito's statement in re the Morello-Lupo case," August 1910, in "Black Hand confessions 1910," Box 1, Lawrence Richey Papers, Herbert Hoover Presidential Library, West Branch, Iowa. Two versions of the confession, the first 48 pages long and only partial, and the second 109 pages long and complete, are contained in this file; in the notes that follow they are numbered I and II.

Dailies Daily reports of Secret Service agents, summarizing activities, intelligence, and the movements of suspects. These reports have been microfilmed and make up the several hundred reels of National Archives Microfilm Publication T915 in Record Group 87 of NARA at College Park, Maryland. The series referred to are:

Flynn	Reports of William J. Flynn, chief of the New York office 1901–10 (31 vols.)
Hazen	Reports of William P. Hazen, chief of the New York office 1898–1901 (11 vols.)
New York	Reports of successive chiefs of the New York office 1911–18 (30 vols.)
Taylor	Reports of Richard H. Taylor, chief of the New York office 1910–11 (5 vols.)

Federal transcripts Trial transcripts of the U.S. Circuit Court for the District of New York, 1790–1912, held in NARA-NE, New York. These include stenographic records of counterfeiting cases brought in U.S. federal courts. The trials referred to are:

Giallombardo	Transcripts of the trial of Giuseppe Giallombardo, Giuseppe Di Priemo, and others, March 1903, in *USA v. Salvatore Romano, Isidore Crose, Joseph DePrima and Giuseppe Giallombardo*. Case file C–2832.
Morello	Transcripts of the trial of Giuseppe Morello, Ignazio Lupo, and others, Jan.–Feb. 1910, in *USA v. Giuseppe Calicchio, Giuseppe Morello, Nicholas Sylvester, Ignazio Lupo, Salvatore Cecala, and Giuseppe Palermo*. Case file C2–347.

Flynn	William J. Flynn, *The Barrel Mystery*. New York: James A. McCann, 1919.
Gentile interviews	Translations of interviews with Nicola Gentile conducted by Felice Chilanti, 1963, in the Gentile file formerly maintained by the · Federal Bureau of Investigation.
MS	Miscellany Section, part of *The Washington Post*.
NARA	National Archives and Records Administration, College Park, Maryland.
NARA-NE	National Archives and Records Administration, Northeast Region, New York City.
NARA-SE	National Archives and Records Administration, Southeast Region, Morrow, Georgia.
NYMA	New York Municipal Archives, New York.
NYSA	New York State Archives, Albany.
Sealy transcripts	Trial Transcripts of the County of New York 1883–1927, in the

Lloyd Sealy Library, John Jay College of Criminal Justice, New York. The trials referred to are:

Impoluzzo	*People v. Antonio Impuluzzo,* January 4, 1916, trial 3240, reel 400
Giordano	*People v. Antonio Giordano,* March 31, 1919, trial 2597, reel 323
Antonio Morello	*People v. Antonio Morello,* January 19, 1893, trial 33, reel 9
Terranova	*People v. Ciro Terranova,* June 3, 1918, trial 2472, reel 311

SM   *Sunday Magazine,* a supplement of most weekend newspapers of the day.

Terranova files   New York district attorney's papers concerning Ciro and Vincenzo Terranova's trial for the murders of Charles Lombardi and Joe DiMarco. Files 118362 and 23838, District Attorney's Closed Case Files 1895–1966, NYMA.

Trial transcripts   Transcripts of trials before the Court of General Sessions of the Peace for New York County, held among the Records and Briefs of the New York Court of Appeal at the NYSA. The trials referred to are:

Florio	*John A. Philbrick & Brother v. Ignatz Florio Co-Operative Association Among Corleonesi,* 122 N.Y.S. 341 (1910)
Giordano	*People v. Angelo Giordano,* 231 N.Y. 633 (1921), in volume 96 of 1921
Marano	*People v. Pellegrino Marano,* 232 N.Y. 569 (1922), in volume 152 of 1921
Paretti (1922)	*People v. Aniellio Paretti,* 234 N.Y. 98 (1922), in volume 149 of 1922
Paretti (1926)	*People v. Antonio Paretti,* 244 N.Y. 527 (1926), in volume 166 of 1926
Vollero	*People v. Alessandro Vollero,* 226 N.Y. 587 (1919), in volumes 75 and 76 of 1919

A NOTE ON CITATION

In order to keep the length of these notes within reasonable bounds, I have reduced discussion to a minimum. Where lists of several associated newspaper articles appear, I have cited the year only once, at the end of the list, and I have referred to books consulted only in the short form.

CHAPTER 1: The Barrel Mystery

3 **Benedetto Madonia sat eating:** Madonia murder details are from Dailies Flynn, vol. 9 fol. 108, reel 109, April 17, 1903 (physical description); passenger list for SS *Neustria*, January 9, 1901, "Passenger and crew lists of vessels arriving at New York, 1897–1957," T715/168, RG85, NARA (immigration date); *Evening Journal*, April 14, pp. 1, 2, April 15, p. 3, April 16, p. 3, April 24, p. 3, and *World*, April 15, p. 1, and *New York Times*, April 15, p. 2 (last meal, murder, weapons, locations, autopsy); *Evening Journal*, April 18, p. 3 (position of body in barrel); *Herald*, April 17, pp. 3–4, and *Evening Journal*, April 21, pp. 1–2 (reconstruction of murder); *Herald*, April 22, 1903, p. 4 (soft hands); Flynn, pp. 6 (reconstruction of murder), 25 (restaurant interior); Carey, *Memoirs of a Murder Man*, pp. 116–17 (Morello's restaurant); Riis, *How the Other Half Lives*, pp. 41–57 (life in Little Italy).

4 **he required an escort:** Dailies Flynn, vol. 9 fols. 143–44, reel 109, April 21, 1903.

4 **Tommaso Petto:** Petto's real name was Luciano Perrini, and he came from Carini in western Sicily; *Sun*, May 8, 1903, p. 5, *Wilkes-Barre Record*, October 23, 1905, p. 5; see also Dailies Flynn, vol. 9 fol. 144, reel 109, April 21, 1903.

5 **Giuseppe Morello:** "Description and Information of Criminals," vol. 37 of 40 fol. 366, RG87, NARA, and autopsy report, August 16, 1930, Office of the Chief Medical Examiner, file DA4801 fol. 3, NYMA, and Bonanno, *A Man of Honor*, p. 100 (physical description); Comito confession II, 55, and *Herald*, April 17, 1903, p. 4 (intimidating presence); *Herald Tribune*, August 16, 1930, p. 1 (nickname).

6 **had dragged a barrel:** *Herald*, April 16, 1903, p. 4.

6 **one-horse covered wagon:** *World*, April 16, p. 1, and *Evening Journal*, April 23, p. 2, and *New York Times*, May 2, p. 16, and May 9, 1903, p. 6.

7 **Mallet & Handle's lumberyard:** Flynn, pp. 1–6.

7 **What Connors saw:** *Evening Journal*, April 14, p. 2 (Connors interview); *Brooklyn Daily Eagle*, April 14, p. 1 (ooze of blood); *Mail and Express*, April 14, p. 1, and *Herald*, April 15, p. 5, and *New York Times*, same date, p. 2, and *Commercial Advertiser*, May 1, 1903, p. 2 (circumstances of discovery).

7 **examining their find:** *Evening Journal*, April 14, p. 1, and April 21, p. 2; *Tribune*, April 15, p. 1; *Herald*, April 17, pp. 3–4; *Sun*, April 17, 1903, p. 2.

8 **Forensic science:** Lardner and Reppetto, *NYPD: A City and Its Police*, pp. 81–6, 221.

8 **It was left to Detective:** New York papers for May 14 and 15 as previously cited; Carey, *Memoirs*, pp. 113–15; George LeBrun, *It's Time to Tell*, pp. 132–33.

8 **a brief note, written in Italian:** *World*, April 15, p. 14, and *Sun*, April 15, p. 2, and *Evening Journal*, April 21, 1903, p. 3.

8 **Not all of Carey's colleagues:** *Commercial Advertiser*, April 15, 1903, p. 1; LeBrun, *It's Time to Tell*, p. 135.

9 **the Italian sections of the city:** Jackson, *The Encyclopedia of New York City*, pp. 584–85.

9   three-quarters of whom were Irish: Levine, "Police, Parties and Policy: The Bureaucratization, Unionization, and Professionalization of the New York City Police 1870–1917," p. 43.

9   "Chesty George": *New York Times*, November 7, 1908, p. 1, and Lardner and Reppetto, *NYPD*, p. 87 (career, nickname); *Chicago Tribune*, August 24, 1913, section I, pp. 3, 12 (police deficiencies).

10 Sergeant Joseph Petrosino: *Herald*, March 14, 1909, p. 1, and *Sun*, same date, p. 2, and *Washington Post*, June 28, 1914, MS6, and Train, *Courts, Criminals, and the Camorra*, pp. 103–4, 106, and Lardner and Reppetto, *NYPD*, pp. 128–29 (description and career).

10 "W&T": *World*, April 15, p. 14, and April 17, p. 3; *Herald*, April 16, 1903, p. 4; Carey, *Memoirs*, pp. 114–15.

11 the city morgue: *Commercial Advertiser*, April 18, 1903, p. 1; Flynn, p. 8; LeBrun, *It's Time to Tell*, pp. 132–38.

12 allowed a photographer: *Evening Journal*, April 14, 1903, p. 4.

12 reporters could scarcely remember: *New York Times*, April 15, 1903, p. 2; *Evening Journal*, same date, p. 3.

12 William Flynn was chief: *Washington Post*, April 19, 1914, SM1 (recollections of barrel case); *New York Times*, December 8 1912, p. 13 (profile); *Flynn's Weekly*, October 4, pp. 388–400, and October 11, 1924, pp. 618–36 (life and career); Manhattan marriage certificate 13668, September 11, 1895, NYMA (family); Dailies Flynn, vol. 3 fol. 555, reel 106, May 11, 1901 (heads New York office).

12 U.S. Secret Service: Melanson, *The Secret Service: The Hidden History of an Enigmatic Agency*, pp. 3–28.

13 Counterfeiting . . . enclaves: Annual report of the Chief of the Secret Service Division, October 18, 1912, letter 50485, Secret Service letters sent 1899–1918, Box 48 (May 19–October 28, 1911), RG 87, NARA.

14 Flynn had spent the evening: Dailies Flynn, vol. 9 fols. 80–83, reel 109, 13 April 13, 1903; *Washington Post*, April 19, 1914, SM1; Flynn, p. 8.

14 ever since the spring of 1899: Dailies Hazen, vol. 5 fols. 773–74, reel 173, March 19, 1899.

14 caught in Yonkers: Federal transcripts Giallombardo, trial transcript fols. 2–13, 27.

14 Vito Laduca: *Pittsburgh Gazette*, April 17, 1903, p. 1 (arrested); *Herald*, April 16, 1903, p. 3 (disappearance); Dailies Flynn, vol. 9 fol. 175, April 25, 1903, (date of arrival).

15 William Flynn had built his reputation: *Flynn's Weekly*, October 4, 1924, pp. 392, 401–2.

15 "La Cava is a good man": Dailies Flynn, vol. 8 fol. 880, reel 108, March 30, 1903.

16 almost a dozen members: Dailies Flynn, vol. 9 fols. 1–92, reel 109, April 1–14, 1903.

16 Flynn switched his attention to the stranger: Ibid., fols. 93–96, 99, reel 109, April 15, 1903; *New York Times*, April 15, 1903, p. 1 (weather); *Washington Post*, April 19, 1914, SM1 (scene at Laduca's).

17   The evening papers: *Evening World, Mail and Express,* and *Brooklyn Daily Eagle,* all April 14, 1903, p. 1; *Evening Journal,* same date, pp. 1, 4.

18   Get down to the morgue: Dailies Flynn, vol. 9 fols. 93–6, reel 109, April 15, 1903 (orders agents to morgue); *Washington Post,* April 19, 1914, SM1 (sees photograph, cigar, suit color, experiment).

19   the Café Pasticcerea: *Washington Post,* August 2, 1914, MS6 (Petrosino's notes); *Sun,* April 16, p. 1, and *Mail and Express,* same date, p. 1 (café described); *Herald,* April 17, 1903, pp. 3–4 (Inzerillo's age); Carey, *Memoirs,* p. 117 (barrels sold).

20   a briefing on the Morello gang: Dailies Flynn, vol. 9 fols. 99–104, reel 109, April 16, 1903 (meeting, attendees); *Chicago Tribune,* August 24, 1913, section I, p. 13 (police tactics).

23   The two Sicilians had no chance: Dailies Flynn, vol. 9 fols. 100–3, reel 109, April 16, 1903 (events); Federal Transcripts Morello fol. 200 (Agent Henry); *Herald,* April 16, pp. 1, 4, and *Tribune,* same date, p. 1 (police operation); *Herald,* April 17, p. 4 (under guard); *Sun,* April 16, 1903, p. 2 (Petto punched, McClusky jubilant, Flynn bored).

24   It was obvious: Dailies Flynn, vol. 9 fol. 106, reel 109, April 17, 1903; *Sun,* April 16, 1903, p. 2 (correspondence, interrogation); *Tribune,* same date, p. 1 (collar); *Washington Post,* April 19, 1914, SM1 (at the morgue; "redoubled their efforts"); Carey, *Memoirs,* p. 17 (sawdust sample).

25   an anonymous letter: Dailies Flynn, vol. 9 fol. 142–43, reel 109, April 21, 1903.

25   no one in Little Italy: *Commercial Advertiser,* April 18, 1903, p. 1.

25   the name Giuseppe Di Priemo: Passenger list for the SS *Marco Minghetti,* May 25, 1901, "Passenger and crew lists of vessels arriving at New York, 1897–1957," T715/199, RG85, NARA (immigration date); inmate admission register for federal prisoners, Sing Sing correctional facility, 1896–1908, vol. 1 fol. 172, March 17, 1903, B0148-80, NYSA (description, sentence).

25   locked up in Sing Sing: Gilfoyle, *A Pickpocket's Tale,* pp. 42–58, 74; Dash, *Satan's Circus,* pp. 284–89.

26   decided to send Petrosino: *Commercial Advertiser,* April 20, p. 1 (arrival time); *World,* April 21, p. 4 (McClusky sends Petrosino); *Sun,* April 21, p. 1, *New York Times,* same date, p. 1, *Evening Journal,* April 20, pp. 1–3, April 21, pp. 2–3, and *Herald,* April 21, 1903, pp. 1–2, Flynn, pp. 13–14 (details of interview).

27   a photograph of the barrel victim: *World,* April 16, 1903, p. 1.

28   By the time Petrosino got to Buffalo: Dailies Flynn, vol. 9 fol. 142–43, reel 109, April 21 (red ink); *Evening Journal,* April 20, pp. 1–2, and April 21, 1903, pp. 2–3 (at Madonia's house); Carey, *Memoirs,* p. 116 (interview with Mrs. Madonia).

29   had raised a thousand dollars: *Evening Journal,* April 21, 1903, p. 2.

30   "a great society": *Herald,* April 21, 1903, p. 2.

CHAPTER 2. Men of Respect

32   the history of Sicily: Fentress, *Rebels and Mafiosi,* pp. 18–19 (kings' visits, pile of grain); Servadio, *Mafioso,* pp. 3, 9–17 (absentee landlords, conditions); Nelli, *The Business of Crime,* pp. 5–6 (landlords, population, natural disasters); Hess, *Mafia and Mafiosi,* pp. 27–29 (alien police).

33   It would be misleading: Dickie, *Cosa Nostra,* p. 27; Nelli, *The Business of Crime,* p. 9.

34   the *mala vita*: Fentress, *Rebels,* pp. 153, 174; Hess, *Mafia,* p. 25 (murder rates for 1893 by Italian province); Dickie, *Cosa Nostra,* pp. 50–53 (monopoly on violence).

35   the emergence of the Mafia: Servadio, *Mafioso,* pp. 9, 17 (prerequisites); Cutrera, *La Mafia e i Mafiosi,* p. 57 (before 1850?); Fentress, *Rebels,* pp. 2, 22–25, 41–43, 136, 149, 169, 213 (oath swearing and secret societies, networks of power, priests, rebels); Schneider, "On Mafiology," pp. 145–49, and Catanzaro, *Men of Respect,* p. 3 (central leadership?); Ianni, *A Family Business,* pp. 34–36 (facts in dispute); Hess, *Mafia,* p. 29 (banditry, castration).

36   In some tellings of the story: Servadio, *Mafioso,* p. 18; Catanzaro, *Men of Respect,* p. 24; Fentress, *Rebels,* pp. 163, 174; Dickie, *Cosa Nostra,* p. 122.

36   a bit of slang: Ianni, *A Family Business,* pp. 34–35; Catanzaro, *Men of Respect,* p. 5.

36   "so-called Maffia": Dickie, *Cosa Nostra,* pp. 2 (*cosche*), 60–61 (prefect's report), 122 (*cagnolazzi*); Fentress, *Rebels,* pp. 1, 147 ("Maffia"), 148 (organization), 175–76 (territories).

37   initiation ritual: Fentress, *Rebels,* pp. 215–17 (police report); Dickie, *Cosa Nostra,* pp. 36–37 (Masons, teeth).

39   "men of respect": Servadio, *Mafioso,* p. xiii; Ianni, *A Family Business,* p. 31 (men of respect); Catanzaro, *Men of Respect,* p. 26; Bonnano, *A Man of Honor,* p. 19 (men of honor).

39   alliances with landowners and the church: Fentress, *Rebels,* p. 187; Dickie, *Cosa Nostra,* pp. 34, 70–71; Servadio, *Mafioso,* p. 18; Catanzaro, *Men of Respect,* pp. 12–13; Nelli, *The Business of Crime,* p. 12.

39   a summary compiled in 1900: Min dell'Interno, dir gen PS, aa.gg.e.rr atti speciali (1898–1940) b.1, f.1, Archivio Centrale dello Stato, Rome; Dickie, *Cosa Nostra,* pp. 100–27.

39   more than thirty towns: Prefect of Sicily's report to the Minister of the Interior, 1874, in Gambetta, *The Sicilian Mafia,* p. 82.

40   There were significant differences: Fentress, *Rebels,* pp. 16–18, 175 (agricultural towns); Catanzaro, *Men of Respect,* p. 4 (rustling and robbery); Sabetti, *Village Politics and the Mafia in Sicily,* p. xix (Mafia of the coast and highlands); Dickie, *Cosa Nostra,* pp. 26–33 (citrus groves), 128–52 (Notarbartolo and Fontana).

40   the Stoppaglieri: Fentress, *Rebels,* pp. 193–211; Ianni, *A Family Business,* p. 30; Schneider, "On Mafiology," p. 14.

41   in Favera: Fentress, *Rebels,* pp. 214–15; Dickie, *Cosa Nostra,* pp. 79–86.

41 Corleone—"lionheart": Donna Gabaccia, *From Sicily to Elizabeth Street,*
pp. xvii, 11–30 (housing); Ianni, *A Family Business,* pp. 35–37; Dickie, *Cosa
Nostra,* pp. 155–56, 167 (poverty, diet, armed clergy).

42 Exactly when the Mafia: ASP 1885, b.85 c.50 f.133, and Hess, *Mafia,*
pp. 52–55, 61, 116–19 (Valenza); letter to the subprefect of Termini, May 26,
1884, ASP 1885, b.85 c.20 f.107 (Patti); verdict in the Bernardino Verro murder case (Palermo Assize Court 1917), copy in the Archivo di Gramsci,
Palermo (Cutrera); Flynn, pp. 248–50 (Streva).

43 called themselves the Fratuzzi: Fentress, *Rebels,* p. 214.

44 There had been Morellos: Details of births, marriages, and deaths are all drawn
from the records of the Ufficio Anagrafe, Comune of Corleone.

44 his closest and most trusted allies: *Washington Post,* April 14, 1914, SM1.

44 would describe himself as a "laborer": Passenger list for SS *Alsatia,* March 8,
1893, "Passenger lists of vessels arriving at New York, 1820–1897," M237/603,
RG85, NARA.

44 The writer, Bernardino Verro: Dickie, *Cosa Nostra,* pp. 156–64, and Anselmo,
La Terra Promessa, pp. 215–16 (background); verdict in the Bernardino Verro
murder case (1917), copy in the Archivio di Gramsci, Palermo (member of the
Mafia).

45 He was also literate: *Herald,* April 16, 1903, p. 1, *New York Times,* same date,
p. 1, and *Washington Post,* February 5, 1922, p. 64.

45 became involved in cattle rustling: Catanzaro, *Men of Respect,* p. 21; Hess,
Mafia, pp. 55, 98.

45 the Field Guards: Report dated January 15 in ASP 1884, b.77, c.20, f.20
(mayor of Borgetto); Cutrera, *La Mafia e i Mafiosi,* p. 95 ("Frequently a Field
Guard . . ."); Hess, *Mafia,* pp. 22–25 (mixed reputation); *Washington Post,*
February 5, 1922, p. 64 (Vella and field guards); Blok, *The Mafia of a Sicilian
Village,* p. 65, Hess, *Mafia,* p. 60, and Catanzaro, *Men of Respect,* p. 20 (reputa-
tion).

46 Giovanni Vella was not like: James Ortelero to Superintendent, Federal Penitentiary, Atlanta, February 7 and 15, 1911, inmate file 2882, Giuseppe
Morello, Atlanta Federal Penitentiary papers, Records of the Bureau of Prisons,
RG 129, NARA-SE ("brave fearless man," "nearing a solution"); Flynn,
pp. 244–60 (rival candidate, scene at Ortoleva's, Vella murder).

47 Francesco Ortoleva: Dino Paternostro, personal communication, October 25,
2007, author's files.

48 the killing: Mattox et al., *Trauma* (effects of gunshot wound to lung).

50 a woman named Anna Di Puma: *Washington Post,* April 26, 1914, M5; Flynn,
pp. 244–48, 256.

50 Michele Zangara: Flynn, p. 245; Zangara death certificate, January 10, 1904,
Ufficio Anagrafe, Corleone.

51 Ortoleva finally came to trial: Flynn, pp. 255–59.

52 Morello's new idea was counterfeiting: New York Police Department criminal
record, n.d. (1910), inmate file 2882, Giuseppe Morello, Atlanta Federal
Penitentiary papers (conviction and sentence); Fentress, *Rebels,* pp. 170–71,

177–78 (Siino, Giammona, Palermo ring); Dickie, *Cosa Nostra*, p. 164 (Verro's café).

CHAPTER 3. Little Italy

54   **It was a spring day:** Passenger list for SS *Alsatia*, March 8, 1893, "Passenger lists of vessels arriving at New York, 1820–1897," M237/603, RG85, NARA (family members, baggage, occupation, literacy); *New York Times*, March 7, 1893, p. 8 (weather); Ferber, *A New American*, pp. 1–2 (sea voyage; arrival at Ellis Island in March); Bonanno, *A Man of Honor*, p. 19 (Sicilian perceptions of New York upon arrival); Ianni, *A Family Business*, p. 66 (immigrant wealth).

54   **Ellis Island:** Burrows and Wallace, *Gotham*, pp. 1111–12 (size, description); Amfitheatrof, *Children of Columbus*, p. 160 (tests); Burns and Sanders, *New York: An Illustrated History*, p. 271 (12,000).

55   **the Clutch Hand had slipped into:** Federal transcripts, Morello, fol. 456; prisoner's record, February 23, 1910, inmate file 2882, Giuseppe Morello, Atlanta Federal Penitentiary papers, RG 129, NARA-SE (immigration date).

55   **entered the country with six dollars:** *Herald*, April 26, 1903, fifth section, p. 5; Amfitheatrof, *Children of Columbus*, p. 160.

55   **Gotham was an unimaginable metropolis:** Jackson, *The Encyclopedia of New York City*, pp. 582, 1157; Dash, *Satan's Circus*, pp. 24–29.

56   **The number of Italians:** Iorizzo, *Italian Immigration and the Impact of the Padrone System*, pp. 57 ($30 million), 58 (problems in Italy); Bevilacqua et al., *Storia dell'Emigrazione Italiano*, pp. 55–88 (numbers, conditions); Amfitheatrof, *Children of Columbus*, pp. 137–38 ("At the head of everything"; a third of the population); Nelli, "The Italian Padrone System," pp. 157, 160–62 (conditions outside New York); Jackson, pp. 584–5 (immigrant numbers).

57   **regarded with hostility:** *Herald*, April 26, 1903, fifth section, p. 5 ("scum of Southern Europe," SS *Belgravia*).

58   **immune from deportation:** La Gumina, *Wop!*, pp. 89–90 (three-year deportation limit).

58   **Mulberry Bend:** Riis, *How the Other Half Lives*, pp. 30, 46–58; Page, *The Creative Destruction of Manhattan, 1900–1940*, pp. 74–84.

59   **Conditions in the tenements:** Iorizzo, *Italian Immigration*, pp. 59–60 (wages in Italy and New York); Nelli, "Italian Padrone System," pp. 156–67 (workings of padrone system); Burrows and Wallace, *Gotham*, pp. 1122–25 (tenements); Norton, "Chicago Housing Conditions," pp. 519, 528–29 (damp walls); Ianni, *A Family Business*, p. 68 ("More than anything I remember . . ."); Riis, *How the Other Half Lives*, pp. 41–46 (rag picking); Maas, *Valachi Papers*, pp. 40–41 (coal under beds; cement-bag sheets); Amfitheatrof, *Children of Columbus*, p. 161 (rag picking); Orsi, *The Madonna of 115th Street*, p. 28 (women's work).

61   **dimly lit sweatshops:** Burns and Sanders, *New York*, pp. 276–77; Sante, *Low Life*, pp. 307–8.

61   **This sort of casual work:** Iorizzo, *Italian Immigration*, pp. 57, 59–60 (wages, savings, Italian banks).

61 **The crash of 1893:** Rezneck, "Unemployment, Unrest and Relief," pp. 324-45; Steeples and Whitman, *Democracy in Desperation,* pp. 142-65.

62 **traveled south, to Louisiana:** Federal transcripts, Morello, fol. 456 (locations); *Washington Post,* July 12, 1914, MS6 (Morello in Louisiana); Scarpaci, "Italian Immigrants in Louisiana's Sugar Parishes: Recruitment, Labor Conditions, and Community Relations, 1880-1910," pp. ii, 16-20, 32, 35, 97, 99-100, 107, 124-6, 139-31, 146 (conditions); Iorizzo, *Italian Immigration,* p. 59 ($3). The approximate date of the family's arrival in Louisiana can be fixed by the marriage records of Plaquemines Parish, which show that Lucia Terranova married Antonio Saltaformaggio there on February 3, 1894; private information from the Saltaformaggio family.

64 **to an agricultural community in Texas:** Federal transcripts, Morello, fols. 456-57 (location); Valentine Belfiglio, *The Italian Experience in Texas,* pp. 81-88 (conditions in Brazos County, Corleone colony).

65 **The decision to return north:** Federal transcripts, Morello, fols. 456-57 (timing, malaria, business ventures); passenger list for SS *Alsatia,* March 8, 1893, "Passenger lists of vessels arriving at New York, 1820-1897," M237/603, RG85, NARA; and death certificate of Calogero Morello, April 17, 1912, Manhattan 12458, NYMA (two Calogeros).

65 **New York's Italian neighborhoods had changed:** Jackson, *Encyclopedia,* pp. 584-85, 605 (numbers); Iorizzo, *Italian Immigration,* p. 57 (remittances).

66 **the criminals of the Italian districts:** *Brooklyn Daily Eagle,* May 30, 1899, p. 4 (kidnapping craze); Pitkin, *The Black Hand,* p. 31 (Giovanni Branchi), 67 (extemporized gangs), 87 (Petrosino's estimate); Jackson, *Encyclopedia,* pp. 604-5 (total immigrants); *New York Times,* March 3, 1907, SM10 (1:300); Nelli, *The Business of Crime,* pp. 85, 90 (1:250, 1:5).

67 **Extortion rings:** Gambetta, *Sicilian Mafia,* pp. 28-33 (Sicily); Pitkin, *The Black Hand,* p. 46 (New Orleans); Landesco, *Organized Crime in Chicago,* p. 108 (Chicago).

69 **"the Black Hand":** Lombardo, "The Black Hand," p. 395 (representatives, negotiations); *New York Times,* February 7, 1907, p. 1 (J.P. murdered), March 9, 1909, p. 1, and March 26, 1910, p. 4 (Caruso), March 3, 1907, SM10 (three hundred killings); Sacco, "Black Hand Outrage," pp. 59-63 (methodology); Landesco, *Organized Crime,* p. 108 (Black Hand letters); Pitkin, *The Black Hand,* p. 89 (no national gang); *San Francisco Call,* October 18, 1905, p. 4 (twelve cities).

CHAPTER 4. "The Most Secret and Terrible Organization in the World"

70 **Tunisia, which had long been:** Pitkin, *The Black Hand,* p. 134; Flynn, pp. 83-84.

71 **were not sent there by their superiors:** Bonanno, *A Man of Honor,* pp. 19-28; Ianni, *Family Business,* p. 66; Fentress, *Rebels,* pp. 196-98.

71 **For all this, even the most conservative analysis:** *St. Lawrence Herald,* May 1, 1903, p. 1 (Boston); Morello, *Before Bruno,* pp. 4 (Luzerne County, 1880s),

6, 8, 13 (Sciaccatani, DiGiovannis, counterfeiting); Fox, *Blood and Power*, p. 64 (Men of Montedoro); Cutrera, *La Mafia e i Mafiosi,* pp. 25–30 (Sciaccatani); *Sun,* September 20, 1903, p. 8; *New York Times,* August 17, 1921, p. 1 (Detroit); *Philadelphia Inquirer,* December 3, 1903, p. 1 (early report of a Mafia in Philadelphia); *New York Times,* May 5, 1891, p. 1, *Chicago Tribune,* February 22, p. 1, February 23, 1901, p. 3, and Nelli, *The Business of Crime,* pp. 125, 134–36 (Chicago); Gentile, *Vita di Capomafia,* p. 33 (Pittsburgh).

71 **Rocco Racco:** Louis Warren, *The Hunter's Game,* pp. 21–45.

72 **It was a killing that took place in New Orleans:** Smith, *The Crescent City Lynchings,* pp. 39–41 (rates of pay, ambush), 47 (Red Light club), 49 (murders of Sicilians), 53–65 (Provenzano trial; "soak the levee"); Hunt and Macheca, *Deep Water,* pp. 86–88, 188–91, 201–5 (vendetta murders); Gambino, *Vendetta,* p. 153 (ambush arrests); Nelli, *The Business of Crime,* pp. 24–46 (Provenzano-Matranga feud and Mafia claims).

74 **It was the Italian authorities:** "Relazioni di Rosario La Mantia," Ministero di Grazia e Giustizia dir gen.le aa pp, misc 1879.b.55, f.620, Archivio Centrale dello Stato, Rome; Fentress, *Rebels,* pp. 193–211.

74 **a Mafia in New Orleans:** New Orleans *Daily Picayune,* May 16, 1891 (mutual accusations); Smith, *The Crescent City Lynchings,* pp. 57–58 (threatening letters), 59 ("Stoppiglieri"), 102 (Provenzano), 104–5 ("They're people that work for the Matrangas . . ."), 247 ("a great deal . . . ," Vandervoort).

75 **"They've got the Mafia Society":** *New York Times,* October 20, 1890, p. 1; Smith, *The Crescent City Lynchings,* pp. 39, 103–4 (Matranga and the domino); 47–48 (Vandervoort); 237–38 (repeats Provenzano's allegations); 247–48 (no evidence at trial); Hunt and Sheldon, *Deep Water,* pp. 201–02, 206, 298–99 (Matranga as leader).

75 **information about Joseph Macheca:** Hunt and Sheldon, *Deep Water,* pp. 7, 10, 85–87.

76 **Hennessy himself appeared:** Gambino, *Vendetta,* pp. 1–5 (murder); Smith, *The Crescent City Lynchings,* pp. xxii–xxv (day leading to the murder, the shooting), 34–35 (character and history); Baiomonte, " 'Who Killa de Chief' Revisited," p. 122 ("dagoes did it").

77 **When the chief's words reached:** Smith, *The Crescent City Lynchings,* pp. 80–115; Gambino, *Vendetta,* p. 41–95 ("We find them . . .").

77 **Whipped up by the mayor:** Smith, *The Crescent City Lynchings,* pp. 213–32 (events); Gambino, *Vendetta,* pp. 78–95 ("snapping fire," "hang the dagoes," execution squad).

79 **an outbreak of violence:** Scarpaci, "Italian Immigrants in Louisiana's Sugar Parishes," pp. 246–49.

80 **Matranga, who had found:** Nelli, *The Business of Crime,* p. 64; Smith, *The Crescent City Lynchings,* p. 289.

80 **dark rumors still swirled:** *Winona Republican Herald,* October 18, 1890, p. 1 (murder officials); Scarpaci, *Italian Immigrants,* p. 247 (spate of murders).

81 **the biggest Mafia scare of the century:** *Morning Oregonian,* August 2, 1890 (Boston); *Brooklyn Daily Eagle,* December 7, 1892 (Denver); *Milwaukee*

Sentinel, July 18, 1897 (Milwaukee); *Ogden Standard Examiner,* December 7, 1898 (San Francisco); *Chicago Tribune,* October 29, 1888, p. 3 (Drummond, Rosso), and October 6, 1892, p. 6 (Wheeler, Lewis, and Duranto).

81 **Only in New York:** *New York Times,* September 22, p. 5, September 30, 1857, p. 1, and March 28, 1891, p. 2 (early rumors); May 16, 1893, p. 9; *Brooklyn Daily Eagle,* October 4, 1889, p. 6 (barber).

81 **the Secret Service:** *Sun,* April 19, 1903, second section, p. 15.

82 **Raymond and Carmelo Farach:** *Brooklyn Daily Eagle,* February 18, 1877, p. 4 (Raymond Farach and a murderous counterfeiter), April 7, p. 4 (murder, appearance, Flaccomio under police surveillance, barber's statement), April 8, p. 2 (several wounds), 4 (partners), April 11, 1884, p. 4 (no positive identification), July 25, p. 16 (stabbed in back, left-handed, visit to Raymond Farach, "If he does . . ."), and October 21, 1886, p. 6 (Carmelo involved in counterfeiting); *Richmond County Standard,* April 12, 1884, p. 4 (circumstances of body's discovery); private information from the Farach family (date of immigration).

83 **Flaccomio had spent:** *New York Times,* October 22, p. 8 (bread knife, premeditated, Byrnes statement, informant, vow, Quarteraro surrenders), October 23, 1888, p. 8 (witnesses talk), March 27, 1889, p. 3 ("Mafia murder," trial, Carlo escapes, evidence); March 29, p. 2 (lack of proof), March 30, p. 8 (since 1881), April 3, p. 8 (blame prosecution witnesses); Pitkin, *The Black Hand,* pp. 26–27 (failed to convict); Lardner and Reppetto, *NYPD,* pp. 79–89 (Byrnes background).

86 **As it was, however:** *New York Tribune,* March 15, 1891, p. 1; Pitkin, *The Black Hand,* p. 27 ("Kill each other").

CHAPTER 5. **The Clutch Hand**

88 **their choice of residence:** Federal census, 1900 (Terranova); Dailies Hazen, vol. 5 fols. 773–4, reel 173, March 19, 1899 (Morello).

89 **attempts to make his mark:** Federal transcripts, Morello, fol. 457.

89 **he maintained a wide correspondence:** Dailies Hazen, vol. 9 fols. 127–28, reel 174, June 17, 1900; fols. 136–37, June 18, 1900; fol. 198, June 27, 1900.

89 **the first faint whiff of trouble:** Dailies Hazen, vol. 5, fols. 773–74, reel 173, March 19, 1899 (Mastropole); fol. 789, March 20, 1899 (Brown's search).

89 **John Wilkie, the director:** *New York Times,* January 29, 1911, SM3; Melanson, *Secret Service,* pp. 26–27.

90 **Several miles uptown:** Dailies Hazen, vol. 9, fol. 5, reel 174, June 1 (where notes passed), fols. 74–83, June 9 (Gleason), fol. 92, June 11 (East 106th Street), vol. 8 fols. 879–82, May 24, vol. 9 fols. 1–8, June 1; fols. 13–14, June 2, fols. 38–39, June 7; fols. 71–84, June 9, fols. 122–25, June 15, fols. 139–40, June 20, 1900 (members of gang).

91 **Mollie Callahan:** Dailies Hazen, vol. 9, fol. 74, reel 174, June 10, 1900 (sees plates, murdered); *Tribune,* June 12, 1900, p. 14 (disappeared December 1899, police report).

92 **Morello had the counterfeiting operation:** Dailies Hazen, vol. 8, reel 174, fols.

872–76, May 23 (Kelly arrested buying drawers), vol. 9, reel 174, fol. 3, June 2 (in threes or fours, North Beach, Brown talks); *Tribune,* June 12, 1900, p. 14 (total printed, side shows).

93   **the Secret Service did things differently:** Dailies Hazen, vol. 9, reel 174 fols. 2–7, June 2 (arrests, transferred, Tyrrell), fols. 13–14, June 3 (trail Thompson, drunks), fols. 50–51, June 8 (Kelly interviewed), fols. 76–80, June 10, 1900 (arrests, Morello booked).

95   **brought before Judge Thomas:** "Description and information of criminals," fols. 348–49, 371, vol. 37 of 40, RG87, NARA (sentences, Morello goes free).

96   **were recruited from Corleone:** *Washington Post,* May 19, 1914, SM1 (approval required); Flynn, pp. 15–16 (from hometown), 211 ("All of Corleone"); Dickie, *Cosa Nostra,* p. 205 (Carini, Villabate, Lercara Friddi).

96   **thirty strong:** *Sun,* April 16, 1903, p. 2.

96   **working as a waiter:** Federal transcripts, Morello, fols. 459–60.

97   **Vito Laduca:** *Pittsburgh Gazette,* April 17, 1903, p. 1 (arrested Pittsburgh, January 17); *New York Sun,* August 13, p. 1, August 14, p. 5, August 15, p. 1, August 17, p. 3, and August 18, 1904, p. 10 (alias, kidnapping); *Canton Commercial Advertiser,* August 16, 1904, p. 2 (naval career, Italian prison sentence, ransom); *New York Times,* August 19, p. 1, and August 20, 1904, p. 1 (age, ransom of only $500 paid); *Sun,* March 29, 1905, p. 3 ("dread bulwark"); *Evening World,* February 22, 1908, p. 1 (wealthy in Italy).

97   **Others made the same journey:** Dailies Flynn, vol. 9 fol. 176, reel 109, April 25, 1903.

97   **letters of recommendation:** Critchley, *The Origin of Organized Crime,* pp. 62–63; Dickie, *Cosa Nostra,* p. 219; *New York Times,* May 8, 1903, p. 7 (example letter).

98   **Vito Cascio Ferro:** Passenger list for SS *La Champagne,* September 9, 1901, "Passenger and crew lists of vessels arriving in New York 1897–1957," T715/225, RG85, NARA; Dailies Flynn, vol. 6 fols. 615, reel 108, May 7, (Morello associated with Fraute), and fols. 763–68, May 22, 1902 (Cascio Ferro arrested with Fraute gang); "Description and information of criminals," vol. 39 of 40, fol. 370, RG 87, NARA (arrest details, description); Petacco, *Joe Petrosino,* p. 94 ("plate of macaroni"), 95 (proffers advice).

98   **Ignazio Lupo:** Queens death certificate 524, January 13, 1947, NYMA (correct spelling of name).

98   **Ignazio Lupo had been born in 1877:** Comito confession II, 68 (voice); federal transcripts, Morello, fols. 462–64 (youth, Palermo murder, emigration, New York businesses); Flynn, p. 28 ("business man of the two"); prisoner's criminal record (Palermo murder) and admission summary, August 5, 1936 (education, lachrymose), both inmate file 2883, Ignazio Lupo, Atlanta Federal Penitentiary papers, RG 129, NARA-SE; dailies Flynn, vol. 35 fol. 723, reel 591, June 4, 1912 (relative in Palermo Mafia); *New York Times,* February 17, p. 4, *American,* February 20, 1910, p. 3 (lachrymose); *Washington Post,* May 17, 1914, p. 47 (voice), February 5, 1922, p. 64 (intelligent, looks, touch like poison); Selvaggio, *The Rise of the American Mafia in New York,* pp. 51–53 (buggy,

Trestelle, office, working habits); "The Mafia and the Secret Service—the Elizabeth Street Syndicate," in Frank Wilson collection, box 10, folder 370, American Heritage Center, University of Wyoming ("Field agents . . .").

99 **a prosperous grocery shop:** *New York Times,* December 5, 1908, p. 1 (pretentious), December 31, 1911, SM5 (branches); Flynn, p. 24 (branches).

100 **run by a Calabrian named Giuseppe D'Agostino:** *Washington Post,* July 12, 1914, SM6.

101 **"Lupo was the business man":** Dailies Flynn, vol. 9 fol. 135, reel 109, April 20, 1903 (first noticed); *Herald,* April 16, 1903, p. 4 (inner councils); *Washington Post,* February 22, 1922, SM1 ("Lupo was the business man . . .").

101 **The wedding took place:** Manhattan marriage certificate 251, December 22, 1903, NYMA (details of marriage); 1910 and 1930 federal censuses (family); Salvatrice Lupo to Myrl Alexander, director, Social Service Unit, n.d. (July 1936), inmate file 2883, Ignazio Lupo, Atlanta Federal Penitentiary papers, RG 129, NARA-SE (husband's qualities).

101 **Morello had lived a largely solitary:** Dailies Hazen, vol. 5 fol. 789, reel 173, March 20 (neighbors do not know him), vol. 9 fol. 92, reel 174, June 11, 1900 (East Harlem); dailies Flynn, vol. 9 fol. 6, reel 109, April 2, 1903 (Chrystie Street; sleeps in); *Herald,* April 16, 1903, p. 1 (squalid, live as man and wife); *New York Journal,* April 22, 1903, p. 2 (elusive, move about); Flynn, pp. 177–79 (illegitimate child, "shortly before the Barrel Murder").

102 **time to find her son a second wife:** Passenger list for SS *Sardegna,* September 23, 1903, "Passenger and crew lists of vessels arriving at New York, 1897–1957" T715/396, RG85, NARA (literate, dowry, youngest, brother and sister, age); thirteenth census of the United States (1910) for 218 East 90th Street, Borough of Manhattan (no English, children); *Washington Post,* July 12, 1914, MS6 (death of first wife); *Herald,* April 16, 1903, pp. 3–4 (does not live with son); Flynn, p. 177 ("notion to get married," death of daughter); private information from Morello family (chosen from photographs); Lina-Morello correspondence, 1910–20, inmate file 2882, Giuseppe Morello, Atlanta Federal Penitentiary papers, RG 129, NARA-SE (passionate, sharp temper, self-worth).

102 **a pair of sisters named Salemi:** Manhattan marriage certificate 249, December 27, 1903, NYMA (Vincenzo marries Lucia); *New York Times,* June 20, 1923, p. 4 (Vincenzo Salemi and organized crime).

103 **Lupo's grocery empire:** *New York Times,* March 3, SM10, and May 25, 1907, p. 18 (Costa); March 17, p. 1 (Manzella), and November 29, 1909, p. 2 (extortion schemes; extorts $4,000); *New York Herald,* October 12, 1905, p. 1 (Costa).

103 **Veiled threats soon gave way to violence:** Bowen and Neil, *The United States Secret Service,* pp. 37–38 (poisoning); *New York Times,* March 17, 1909, p. 1 (bombing, extortion).

104 **smuggling the counterfeits:** Dailies Flynn, vol. 9 fol. 349, reel 109, May 24, 1903 (quantity of notes); *Annual Report of the Chief of the Secret Service Division,* 1903, p. 8, *New York Times,* April 3, 1910, SM6, "The Mafia and the Secret Service—the Elizabeth Street Syndicate," Frank Wilson collection,

Walter Page, ed., *The World's Work,* 1913, p. 35, *Washington Post,* April 26, 1914, M5, and Flynn, p. 18 (smuggled from Italy).

104 **Flynn was aware:** *Sun,* April 16, 1903, pp. 1–2 (Flynn aware since spring 1902); dailies Flynn, vol. 8 fol. 699, reel 108, March 2, 1903 (agents collect samples); federal transcripts, Giallombardo, trial transcript fol. 11 (spelling mistakes).

104 **when Vito Laduca was captured:** *Pittsburgh Gazette,* April 17, p. 1, and *Evening Journal,* April 23, 1903, p. 2.

105 **Giuseppe Catania:** *Brooklyn Daily Eagle,* July 24, p. 1 ("bled a gallon," hogtied, family, no enemies, quarrel, multiple killers), July 25, p. 2 (address), July 26, p. 18 and July 30, 1902, p. 18 (vendetta); October 5, 1902, p. 5 (police say Mafia killing); *Brooklyn Standard Union,* July 28, 1902, p. 2 (last seen in Manhattan); *Herald,* July 24, 1902, p. 1 (Dead Man's Cove); dailies Flynn, vol. 9 fol. 93, reel 109, April 15, and fol. 135, April 20, 1903 (drunkard, killed by Morello gang, last seen with Lupo); federal transcripts, Morello, 469 (Lupo admits to knowing Catania).

106 **caught in Yonkers:** Federal transcripts, Giallombardo, trial transcript fols. 2–13, 27 (circumstances, origins, arrival in U.S.); evidence of John Rossi (separately typed and filed with the Bill of Exceptions), fols. 1–4 (events in Rossi's shop); inmate admission register for federal prisoners, Sing Sing correctional facility, 1896–1908, vol. 1 fols. 171–73, March 17, 1903, B0148-80, NYSA (Di Priemo, Crocevera, Giallombardo personal details); passenger list for SS *Marco Minghetti,* May 25, 1901, "Passenger lists of vessels arriving at New York, 1897–1902," T519/199, RG85, NARA (Di Priemo arrival, hometown); *Washington Post,* April 26, 1914, M5 (circumstances, boodle carrier); *Flynn's Weekly,* October 4, 1924, pp. 401–2 (butchers' grease).

107 **Flynn tried one last subterfuge:** *Washington Post,* April 26, 1914, M5 ("I kept Di Priemo . . ."); dailies Flynn, vol. 9 fols. 149, 152, reel 109, April 22, 1903 (common knowledge).

108 **wrote to New York to request money:** *Evening Journal,* April 20, pp. 1–2, April 21, p. 3, April 22, p. 1, and April 23, 1903, p. 1; *Sun,* April 21, p. 1, and April 23, 1903, p. 1; *Herald,* April 23, 1903, p. 6; *Chicago Tribune,* April 23, 1903, p. 5.

CHAPTER 6. Vengeance

109 **"Clear the court":** *Sun,* April 17, April 20, p. 1 (court cleared), and April 21, 1903, p. 1 (word arrives); Dash, *Satan's Circus,* p. 11 (description of court).

110 **Morello stood flanked:** Dailies Flynn, vol. 9 fol. 107, reel 109, April 17 (Lupo arrest); *Sun,* April 20, p. 1 (Le Barbier in court); *Sun,* April 23, p. 1, and *New York Times,* same date, p. 16 (Laduca knife); *Commercial Advertiser,* May 1, 1903, p. 2 (Genova); dailies Flynn, vol. 9 fol. 176, reel 109, April 25, 1903 (minor members).

110 **the legal fees had been met:** *Evening Journal,* April 21, 1903, p. 2 ($10,000); *St. Lawrence Herald* (Potsdam, N.Y.), May 1, 1903, p. 1 (Boston).

111   **Barlow opened the proceedings:** *Sun,* April 20, p. 1 ("I ask . . ."; "I am sure . . ."); dailies Flynn, vol. 9 fol. 160, reel 109, April 23, 1903 (Morello on the stand); *Herald,* April 21, 1903, p. 4 (same); *Washington Times,* same date p. 1 (Lupo; third degree).

112   **proof Morello knew the barrel victim:** *Sun,* April 21, p. 1 (Garvan's paper); *Evening Journal,* April 22, 1903, p. 1 ("In the Mafia . . .").

113   **had brought Salvatore Madonia:** *Evening Journal,* April 22, 1903, p. 2 (more evidence, Petrosino and Madonia, "I believe . . .").

114   **he would not stay in New York:** *Evening Journal,* April 23, 1903, p. 2 (Illich, "If I stay here," train).

114   **felt that he should try to help:** Dailies Flynn, vol. 9 fol. 182, reel 109, April 26, 1903 (discovers ticket); *New York Times,* April 26, 1903, p. 2 (bail; Carey redeems ticket; bail revoked; McClusky's call; arraigned); Carey, *Memoirs of a Murder Man,* pp. 116–17 (pawnbrokers), 119 (Morello as king); *Herald,* May 2, 1903, p. 5 (Inzerillo and Fanaro cracking).

117   **the Barrel Murder inquest:** *New York Times,* May 2, p. 16 (difficulties, jurors' names, Zacconi, "gruesome objects"); *Herald,* April 28, p. 5 ("made no secret"), May 2, p. 5 ("Evident misgivings"), and May 8, 1903, p. 5 ("remarkable exhibition"); *Evening World,* April 27, 1903, p. 1 (insufficient jurors), and January 29, 1904, p. 2 (Petto discharge); *Sun,* January 30, 1904, p. 12 (Petto discharge); Carey, *Memoirs,* p. 120 (intimidation of Inzerillo, the Madonias, Di Priemo); LeBrun, *It's Time to Tell,* p. 138 ("I had difficulty . . ."). The outcome of the inquest is detailed in *Tribune,* May 9, 1903, p. 6.

120   **left few clues to his true character:** Private information from the Morello family (sons' names); Dickie, *Cosa Nostra,* p. 205 (unique structure); Comito confession II, 74 (overrules others); *Washington Post,* February 5, 1922, p. 64 (Flynn on Morello).

121   **Salvatore Especiale:** *Brooklyn Daily Eagle,* December 14, p. 22, *Brooklyn Standard Union,* December 13, p. 1, and December 14, p. 18 (informant; barrel case; Catania; Condon; details of shooting), *San Francisco Call,* December 14, 1903, p. 3 ("dread penalty").

122   **The victim on this occasion was Tommaso Petto:** *Evening Word,* January 29, 1904, p. 2 (release); *Wilkes-Barre Record,* October 23, p. 5 (circumstances, other arrests, wounds "large enough to admit a teacup"), and *Sun,* October 24, 1905, p. 5 (Luciano Perrini, five bullets, revolver, Di Priemo out); inmate admission register for federal prisoners, Sing Sing correctional facility, 1896–1908, vol. 1 fol. 172, March 17, 1903, B0148-80, NYSA (parole date); *Washington Post,* April 26, 1914, M5 (Flynn on release date; "act of vengeance").

123   **Morello as the killer, wreaking vengeance:** *American,* February 23, pt. 2, p. 2, and *Brooklyn Daily Eagle,* February 27, 1908, p. 3 (Laduca murder); *Washington Times,* July 22, p. 6 (Zacconi killed by barrel murderers), *Sun,* July 28, p. 2 (face blown away), and *Chicago Tribune,* July 29, 1909, p. 7 (Genova murder, "the police explain").

124   **had grown almost pathologically cautious:** Dailies Flynn, vol. 10 fol. 373, reel 109, October 27, 1903 (mail) and fol. 395, October 30, 1903 (movements).

124   **Flynn was extremely perturbed:** *Chicago Tribune,* August 24, 1913, p. 13 ("Too many policemen").

124   **"The detectives used to come around":** Federal transcripts, Morello, fols. 457–58.

125   **Detective Sergeant Antonio Vachris:** Pitkin, *The Black Hand,* p. 44.

125   **this new Italian Squad:** *New York Times,* December 30, 1906, SM21 (Petrosino described; long hours; office, rogues' gallery; "almost entirely separate"), and March 14, 1909, p. 2 (numbers increased, files in head); *Sun,* March 14, 1909, p. 2 (eight men); McAdoo, *Guarding a Great City,* p. 154 (created by McAdoo); Pitkin, *The Black Hand,* pp. 56–57 (members), 66 (Italian), 81–83 (Alfano, kidnapping, fingerprinting); Lardner and Reppetto, *NYPD,* pp. 129 (more teeth than a dentist), 131 (dates of formation and expansion).

126   **an especially bloody murder in the Bronx:** *Sun,* March 14, 1909, p. 2.

126   **Enrico Alfano:** *New York Times,* March 12, p. 16, April 1, 1911, p. 5, and July 16, 1922, E6 (case details); Pitkin, *The Black Hand,* p. 82 (demi-god).

127   **Joe Petrosino:** *Sun,* March 14, 1909, p. 2 ("short fat man," disguises).

129   **The family burned ten thousand:** Dailies Flynn, vol. 9 fol. 349, reel 109, May 24, 1903.

129   **the loose ends of the Yonkers investigation:** Dailies Flynn, vol. 9 fol. 204, reel 109, April 30, 1903 (Canadian case); vol. 10 fol. 123, reel 109, September 19, 1903 (watch begins again), and fol. 259, October 10, 1903 (agents' trial); *Annual Report of the Chief of the Secret Service Division,* 1903, p. 8 (mail fraud); Flynn, pp. 226–38 (Canadian case); *Washington Post,* February 5, 1922, p. 64 ("enveloped in mystery . . .").

130   **Flynn's Secret Service bureau:** *Washington Evening Star,* August 24, 1889, p. 9 (Washington HQ, rogues' gallery, number of agents); dailies Hazen, vol. 9 fol. 72, reel 174, June 10, 1900 (lack of manpower); dailies Flynn, vol. 6 fol. 702, reel 108, May 16, 1902 (number of operatives in N.Y.); vol. 9 fol. 161, April 23, and fol. 430, June 4, 1903 (Brancatto); *Chicago Tribune,* August 24, 1913, I3 ("A detective force of a hundred"); *New York Times,* February 6, 1911, SM14 (wide variety of Secret Service agents); *Time,* April 1, 1929 (Richey); *New York Times,* March 11, 1939, p. 21 (Rubano); Flynn, p. 24 (keeps watch); Melanson, *Secret Service,* p. 3 (waiting list); Johnson, *Illegal Tender,* p. 33 (Brancatto); Dash, *Satan's Circus,* pp. 49–52, 55–56, 62–66, 114, 376 (police corruption).

132   **gave Flynn a large advantage:** Dailies Flynn, vol. 9 fol. 11, reel 109, April 3, 1903 (intercept post); *Washington Post,* April 26, 1914, M5 (followed to New Orleans); Flynn, pp. 38–39 (hires room).

CHAPTER 7. **Family Business**

134   **Salvatore Marchiani:** Passenger list for SS *Neckar,* March 15, 1905, "Passenger and crew lists of vessels arriving at New York, 1897–1957." T715/544, RG85, NARA (arrival in New York); *Brooklyn Daily Eagle,* February 20, p. 1 (discovery, scene of crime, mutilations), February 21, p. 1 ("desanguination," informer,

Pigtown), February 23, p. 1 (Fanaro arrested), and February 27, 1908, pp. 1, 3 (police theories); *Brooklyn Standard Union,* February 21, 1908, p. 1 (mutilations); *New York American,* February 21, p. 4 (mutilations), and February 23, 1908, p. 2 (in U.S. three years, father's letter, Fontana, Petrosino); *Herald,* February 21, 1908, p. 5 (Sicilian vengeance); *Evening World,* February 22, 1908, p. 2 (Fontana connection); *Sun,* February 23, 1908, p. 2 (Fanaro); Kings death certificate 3956, February 20, 1908, NYMA (spelling of name; age).

135   **gang led by Paul Kelly:** Thompson and Raymond, *Gang Rule in New York,* p. 361 (Morello protection); Territt, *Only Saps Work,* pp. 30–33, and Downey, *Gangster City,* pp. 3–11 (career); Sante, *Low Life,* pp. 217, 223 (numbers, career).

135   **death of Meyer Weisbard:** *Evening Journal,* January 16, pp. 1, 5, and January 17, 1901, p. 1 (circumstances, $300); April 15, 1903, pp. 1, 3 (links to Mafia); *Herald,* January 17, p. 1, and January 18, 1901, p. 5 (circumstances); *Sun,* April 19, 1903, second section, p. 15 (links to Mafia).

135   **Louis Troja:** *Evening World,* April 19, 1902, p. 8 (circumstances); *Herald,* April 16, 1903, p. 4 (Mafia link).

135   **"Diamond Sam" Sica:** *American,* January 13, 1908, p. 6 (circumstances); *Herald,* May 9, 1922, p. 1 (Terranova a suspect); Manhattan death certificate 12266, January 12, 1908, NYMA (name, place of death).

135   **did not scruple at killing women:** Dailies New York, vol. 36 fols. 120–21, reel 591, July 18, 1912.

136   **"Sometimes the system":** *Tribune,* November 28, 1917, p. 16; Downey, *Gangster City,* pp. 35–36 ("Sometimes the system . . .").

136   **botching the killings:** Terranova files; Sealy transcripts, Terranova, fols. 2, 97, 107; Thompson and Raymond, *Gang Rule,* pp. 5–6.

137   **"There is a wood":** *Herald,* January 7, 1917, SM2.

137   **a killer named Lulu Vicari:** Dailies New York, vol. 36 fols. 66–67, reel 591, July 11, 1912.

137   **Rival gangs had their own:** *New York Times,* December 15, 1906, p. 18 (Sperlozza's place in underworld); *Harper's Weekly,* May 8, 1909, pp. 7–8 (chalk mark); *Herald,* November 10, 1909, p. 1 (holdup man).

138   **Barnet Baff:** *New York Times,* November 25, p. 1, November 26, p. 5, November 27, 1914, p. 5 (killing, cartel), February 11, 1916, p. 20 (gunmen, $100); *New York American,* October 8, 1915, p. 5 (Greco); Critchley, *The Birth of Organized Crime,* pp. 73–76, 100–11 (significance of Baff case).

138   **a set of nine regulations:** Flynn, pp. 199–202.

139   **It was Nicola Gentile:** Gentile, *Vita di Capomafia,* pp. 7–71 (career, "boss of the bosses"); FBI Gentile file, interview 2, fols. 1–4 (early years) and interview 3, fol. 6 (Mafia diplomat); Dickie, *Cosa Nostra,* pp. 213–23 ("the classic raw material").

140   **families in eight or ten large cities:** Gentile, *Vita di Capomafia,* pp. 1–75 (boss of bosses, Philadelphia, Pittsburgh, Kansas City, San Francisco, Chicago, Los Angeles); FBI Gentile file, interview 2, fol. 4 (Cleveland, Kansas City, Pittsburgh); *Winona Republican Herald,* February 22, 1901, p. 1 (New Yorker

at Chicago murder); *Winona Republican Herald,* December 2, p. 1, and December 4, 1903, p. 1 ("admitted in court"); Celeste Morello, *Before Bruno,* I, 4–46 (Philadelphia); *Sun,* April 19, 1903, p. 15 (Boston, Chicago); *Winona Republican Herald,* February 22, 1901, p. 2 (Chicago); *Ogden Standard Examiner,* December 7, 1898, p. 8 (Di Franchi and San Francisco); Bonanno, *A Man of Honor,* pp. 19, 63, and Critchley, "Buster, Maranzano, and the Castellammarese War," p. 56n (Buffalo); *Los Angeles Times,* February 10, 1916, section II, p. 1, December 20, 1917, section II, p. 1, February 27, 1919, section II, p. 1, and Warner, "The First Mafia Boss of Los Angeles?" (Los Angeles, Mike Marino).

142 **Morello's influence in New Orleans:** *New York Times,* May 8, 1903, p. 7 (F. Genova); *Herald,* May 8, 1903, p. 5 (Genova letter).

142 **to deal with an Italian hotelier:** *New York Times,* April 3, 1910, SM6 (four-day visit; "the offending Italian"); *Washington Post,* April 26, 1914, M5 (knotted handkerchief, death sign).

142 **likely ordered other murders:** *New York Herald,* February 22, 1908, p. 1; *Evening World,* same date, p. 2 (suggestive cases).

143 **"the Commission":** Dickie, *Cosa Nostra,* p. 219 ("It was made up . . ."); for Morello's, see Flynn, pp. 207–14; Bonanno, *A Man of Honor,* pp. 126, 141, 159–61 (commission in 1930s); Raab, *Five Families,* pp. 117–24 (every five years).

144 **"pretty rough in those days":** Maas, *The Valachi Papers,* pp. 39–40.

144 **"dipping the beak":** Petacco, *Joe Petrosino,* pp. 93–94 (introduced to New York); Celeste Morello, *Before Bruno* I, 39 ("With the Mafia").

144 **that Mafiosi were somehow benefactors:** Bonanno, *A Man of Honor,* p. 62.

145 **"Good morning":** *Washington Post,* February 5, 1922, p. 64.

145 **Salvatore Romano:** Flynn, pp. 174–98.

146 **his discharge from prison:** Dailies Flynn, vol. 9 fol. 584, reel 109, June 27, 1903.

147 **stole horses and wagons:** Dailies New York, vol. 34 fol. 729, reel 591, March 13, 1912; Comito confession II, 86–87; McAdoo, *Guarding a Great City,* pp. 144–45.

147 **Kidnapping, too, enjoyed a vogue:** NYPD criminal record for Giuseppe Morello, inmate file 2882, Atlanta Federal Penitentiary papers, RG 129, NARA-SE (arrests); *New York American,* March 7, p. 1, and March 8, 1906, p. 5 (Bozzuffi); *Washington Post,* July 26, 1914, M6 (Morello's involvement); File 01097-02C, line 910476, Division of Old Records, New York Country Clerk's Office (Bozzuffi knows Morello).

147 **theft of fifteen watches:** Comito confession II, 86.

148 **"band of incendiaries":** Comito confession II, 59–61 (poor, methods); Atlanta Federal Penitentiary inmate file 2880 (Cecala's physical description); *Washington Post,* May 3, 1914, M8 (Lupo relative, from Corleone).

149 **almost entirely risk-free profits:** Comito confession II, 60 (police corrupted, political corruption, "Morello knows"); *New York Times,* March 9, 1900, p. 1 ($3 million a year).

150 **larger and more profitable rackets:** Terrett, *Only Saps Work,* pp. 78–87 (poultry racket), 93 (wet wash); Nelli, *The Business of Crime,* p. 244 (labor racketeering).

151 **Terranova brothers became increasingly involved:** Manhattan marriage certificate 18591, July 23, 1913, NYMA, and dailies New York, vol. 35 fol. 913, reel 591, June 22, 1912 (Vincenzo); dailies Taylor, vol. 4 fol. 92, reel 277, January 9, 1911 (Ciro); dailies New York, vol. 34 fol. 729, reel 591, March 13, 1912 (Nick); Dash, *Satan's Circus,* p. 24n (New York ice trade).

151 **Morello began making investments:** *Evening Journal,* April 22, 1903, p. 2 (barbershop, cobbler's); Flynn, pp. 28–29 (multiple stores, $200,000).

152 **It was Lupo:** *Washington Post,* February 22, 1922, p. 64.

152 **Ignatz Florio Co-Operative Association:** File 01097-02C, line 910476, Division of Old Records (incorporation, directors, shareholdings, extraordinary meeting); *New York Times,* March 7, 1905, p. 14, June 21, 1905, p. 12, June 30, 1905, p. 13, December 29, 1905, p. 14, March 4, 1906, p. 16, March 11, 1906, p. 16, July 1, 1906, p. 16, August 19, 1906, p. 12, February 22, 1907, p. 16, and September 26, 1907, p. 13 (lots and mortgages), April 22, p. 13, June 24, p. 9, July 10, p. 9, September 24, p. 11, and October 7, 1908, p. 12 (sued by creditors); *New York Times,* May 7, p. 11 (Supreme Court), June 25, 1909, p. 16 ($8,032); *Washington Times,* December 2, 1910, p. 6 (need for more funds becomes urgent); *Washington Post,* April 26, 1914, M5 (shares $3, $5; Mississippi to the Gulf; embezzlement, legal actions); *John A. Philbrick & Brother v. Ignatz Florio Co-Operative Association Among Corleonesi,* 137 Appellate Division 613 (1910), 122 N.Y.S. 341, fols. 1–99 (disputes with suppliers); Flynn, pp. 183–84 ($5 down, Romano holding, dividends); Carmine Altieri to William Moyer, August 24 and 29, 1912, in inmate file 2882, Giuseppe Morello, Atlanta Federal Penitentiary papers (staggered on); Salvatore Cina statement in dailies New York, vol. 38 fols. 472–3, reel 592, February 11, 1913 (menaced by shareholders); Dickie, *Cosa Nostra,* pp. 111–17 (Ignatz Florio of Palermo); Sante, *Low Life,* p. 26 (cost of building).

154 **The depression of 1907:** Bruner and Carr, *The Panic of 1907,* pp. 105–15 (extent); Iorizzo, *Italian Immigration and the Impact of the Padrone System,* p. 123 (effects in Little Italy).

156 **Lupo's problems:** *New York Times,* December 5, 1908, p. 1 (mortgages and remortgages); March 17, p. 1 (grocery business fails), and November 17, 1909, p. 1 (Petrosino beating, stock value, losses); *Herald,* November 13, 1909, p. 7 ($38,000 loss); *Washington Post,* July 12, 1914, MS6.

157 **back in the counterfeiting business:** *Washington Post,* April 26, 1914, M5.

CHAPTER 8. Green Goods

158 **Antonio Comito had decided:** Comito confession I, 1–37; confession II, 1–46 (most details); federal transcripts, Morello, fols. 20–32 (home, in Italy and Brazil, Katrina, Philadelphia, Cecala, Cina, Sylvester, journey to Highland, Giglio, stone house, pornography), 89 (age), 119 (languages), 132–34, 138–41

(Katrina's name, journey, $5, age); *Washington Post,* May 3, M8 (Cecala background), and May 10, 1914, M8 (Comito physical description).

164 **In an anonymous apartment:** Dailies Flynn, vol. 33 fols. 517–18, reel 590, November 24, 1911 (Antonio Milone; engraving the plates; Florio Society); Comito confession II, 38–40, 43 (zinc plates, description of notes, advantages of $5 bills); Lynn Glaser, *Counterfeiting in America,* pp. 192–94 (photoengraving techniques).

166 **Snow blanketed the woods:** Comito confession II, 37–42 (snow, boredom, illness, plates and paper, threats, branches of society).

169 **Zu Vincenzo told the printer more:** Comito confession II, 48–52 (story); Flynn, p. 114 (former banker).

172 **They printed the Canadian:** Comito confession II, 39–43 ($5 plates, silkless, orders, print targets), 45 (other families), 53 (completion date, macaroni box, $2 colors), 65–66 (printing time, sentries); federal transcripts, Morello, fols. 42 (days per plate), 45, 53 (total printed, box).

174 **"He was wrapped up":** Comito confession II, 54–59.

175 **Giuseppe Calicchio:** Federal transcripts, Morello, fols. 317–19 (background); Comito confession II, 65–66 (poorly dressed); prisoner records for Giuseppe Calicchio, inmate file 2881, Atlanta Federal Penitentiary papers, RG 129, NARA-SE (appearance), dailies Flynn, vol. 28 fols. 5–8, reel 116, January 7, 1910 (Calicchio's account of his time in Highland).

176 **But the men waiting on the doorstep:** Comito confession II, 68–71 (date and time, guns and ammunition, Petrosino, hiding out).

CHAPTER 9. "See the Fine Parsley"

178 crime rates rising in Little Italy: *Sun,* November 16, 1908, p. 3; Pitkin, *The Black Hand,* pp. 74 (accounts book), 80, 92 (White Hand).

179 **"See the fine parsley!":** Petacco, *Joe Petrosino,* p. 40.

179 **The only real solution:** Pitkin, *The Black Hand,* pp. 61–62 (Stanton Street Petrosino quote, detective bureau in Italy), 83–84 (new immigration law, list of criminals); *San Francisco Call,* October 18, 1905, p. 4, *New York Times,* same date, p. 20, and Train, *Courts, Criminals, and the Camorra,* pp. 226–27 (five thousand former convicts, new treaty on deportation).

180 **Theodore Bingham:** Pitkin, *The Black Hand,* pp. 63–65 (career, one leg); Lardner and Reppetto, *NYPD,* pp. 141–42 (riffraff, Italian Squad); *North American Review,* September 1908 (ethnic crime); Petacco, *Petrosino,* pp. 68–69 (Petrosino's report).

181 **a "secret service" branch of the police department:** *Herald,* February 20, 1909, p. 6.

182 **thirty thousand dollars of private funding:** *Winona Republican Herald,* March 13, 1909, p. 1.

182 **Petrosino had married:** Manhattan marriage certificate 33618, December 30, 1907; Petacco, *Petrosino,* pp. 70–71 (courting, "You too"), 110 (daughter).

183 **Petrosino left New York:** Petacco, *Petrosino,* pp. 118, 123 (liner, mood, Vachris); Pitkin, *The Black Hand,* pp. 109–10 (mission background).

183 **the alias of Simone Velletri:** Petacco, *Petrosino,* pp. 119–22 (alias, digestive, deportee, recognized, Delli Bovi).

185 **his absence had already been noticed:** Nelli, *The Business of Crime,* p. 97. *L'Araldo's* article appeared as early as February 9.

185 **Petrosino's first inkling:** *Herald,* March 14, 1909, p. 4 (meets journalists, followed); Petacco, *Petrosino,* pp. 123–32 (Rome, Padula, letter to brother).

186 **travel to Palermo:** Petacco, *Petrosino,* pp. 133–45 (certificates, bank account, typewriter).

187 **Ceola found himself underwhelmed:** Petacco, *Petrosino,* pp. 130, 139.

188 **his presence in the capital was already too well known:** Comito confession II, 69 (Mafia knowledge); *Washington Herald,* March 14, 1909, p. 6 (Alfano, Baltimore Black Hand); Fiaschetti, *The Man They Couldn't Escape,* pp. 276–78 (Camorra); Petacco, *Petrosino,* pp. 158–59 (*Il Mattino*).

188 **the difficulty of killing the policeman:** Comito confession II, 81.

189 **Carlo Costantino and Antonio Passananti:** *New York Times,* December 31, 1911 SM5 (work for Lupo); anonymous letter to Ceola, March 16, 1909, in Petacco, *Petrosino,* p. 168 (bosses pay fare, visit Cascio Ferro); report of Baldassare Ceola, reprinted in Petacco, *Petrosino,* pp. 170–74 (passage, creditors, activities, aliases, Milone and Fontana).

189 **he had made his escape from New York:** Dailies Flynn, vol. 9 fol. 117, reel 109, April 18, and fol. 132, April 19, 1903.

190 **According to the recollections:** *Sun,* March 14, 1909, p. 1 (blood, two men); Petacco, *Petrosino,* pp. 146–50, and Dickie, *Cosa Nostra,* pp. 199–200, 209–11 (shots, wounds, carriage, gaslights).

192 **They rounded up:** *New York Times,* March 15, p. 1, March 16, 1909, p. 1 (initial investigation), and January 17, 1911, p. 1 (Costantino); *Chicago Tribune,* March 21, 1909, p. 1 (140 arrests); Petacco, *Petrosino,* pp. 150–63 (Schillaci, Militano, Cascio Ferro, anonymous letters); Dickie, *Cosa Nostra,* p. 211 (Cascio Ferro's alibi).

192 **a pair of telegrams:** *American,* November 17, 1909, p. 9; *New York Times,* December 31, 1911, SM5 ("whiskers"); Petacco, *Petrosino,* p. 125 ("I Lo Baido").

193 **letters and telephone calls:** Petacco, *Petrosino,* pp. 167–69.

194 **"Lieutenant Petrosino's arrival":** Cited in Petacco, *Petrosino,* pp. 165–66.

194 **Cascio Ferro's story was not enough:** Petacco, *Petrosino,* pp. 175–79.

194 **cost Baldassare Ceola his job:** *Sun,* November 17, 1909, p. 3 (release); Petacco, *Petrosino,* pp. 178–79 (Ferrantelli, retirement).

195 **there were rumors:** *Richmond Times Dispatch,* January 11, 1910, p. 11 (Pennsylvania); *New York Times,* July 2, 1909, p. 1 (Mexico).

195 **the first official telegram:** *American,* March 14, 1909, p. 1 (Bishop's telegram).

195 **Most New Yorkers felt a sense of outrage:** *Tribune,* March 14, 1909, p. 1.

195 **Adelina Petrosino:** *Herald,* March 14, 1909, p. 4 (wife); *Winona Republican Herald,* March 13, 1909, p. 1 (tears).

196   Petrosino's funeral: *New York Times,* April 13, 1909, p. 1; *Sun,* same date, p. 1; *Tribune,* same date, p. 1.

CHAPTER 10. **Sheep and Wolves**

197   **The news of Petrosino's death:** Comito confession II, 80–81.
198   **Production of the counterfeits:** Comito confession II, 75, 79, 82 ($2 notes, retouching $5 million); Flynn, pp. 121, 126, 134–35 (rate of work, more paper).
198   **the problem of the five-dollar bills:** Comito confession II, 73.
198   **became abusive:** Comito confession II, 72 (rifle), 73, 80, 84–85 (burn notes, "damn brains," grabbed by the throat).
200   **to engrave new plates:** Comito confession, II, 97.
200   **As the pace of work increased:** Comito confession II, 71 (towns), 73 (twenty-five cents on the dollar), 74 (barely profitable), 87 (orders), 102 (promised $500, $13,500 order); dailies Flynn, vol. 28 fol. 824, reel 116, January 7, 1910 (others charge ten cents on the dollar); Flynn, pp. 34–35 (thirty-five cents on the dollar), 135–36, 142 (proofs, orders).
201   **Work was finally suspended for the summer:** Comito confession II, 102–4.
201   **Read of the arrest:** Comito confession II, 105.
201   **to improve the Secret Service's efficiency:** Dailies Flynn, vol. 27 fol. 1002, reel 116, November 1, 1909, and vol. 28 fols. 600–1, reel 116, December 19, 1909 (new informants); federal transcripts, Morello, fol. 274 (Rubano service); *New York Times,* March 11, 1939, p. 21 (Rubano career); *Washington Post,* July 7, 1912, SM1 (five informants, "here, there and everywhere"); Bowen and Neil, *The United States Secret Service,* p. 39 (Rubano infiltrates Morello organization).
202   **Giuseppe Morello had been placed:** Federal transcripts, Morello, fol. 308 (first man suspected); *New York Times,* April 3, 1910, SM6 (life surveillance, "The oftener Morello was arrested . . ."), and February 6, 1911, SM14 ("ideas are big . . .").
203   **the first forged bills appeared:** Dailies Flynn, vol. 29, fol. 168, reel 116, February 20, 1910 (first seen May); Comito confession II, 58 ("Do I not take"); federal transcripts, Morello, fol. 302 (bankers and shopkeepers); Flynn, p. 31 (cities notes circulated in).
204   **his first real breakthrough:** Dailies Flynn, vol. 27, fol. 396, reel 116, September 11, 1909 (description of Boscarini); vol. 29, fol. 168, reel 116, February 20, 1910 (Locino and Boscarini; no testimony); federal transcripts, Morello, fols. 222–23 (233 East 97th St.); *Washington Post,* April 26, SM5 (fear premature arrests), May 3, 1914, M8 (Boscarini, marked bills, meet behind boxes), and February 22, 1922, p. 64 (Ignatz Florio); Flynn, pp. 32–42 (Pittston; Flynn's pursuit; hired room).
207   **The network so painstakingly unraveled:** *Washington Post,* May 3, 1914, M8 (pyramid, six deputies); Flynn, pp. 33, 35–36 (Corleonesi, obtain sanction).
208   **It was Lupo who:** *Sun,* November 13, 1909, p. 6 (mind disturbed, Black Hand threat); *Washington Post,* May 10, 1914, M8 (trailed to Ardonia); Flynn,

pp. 39–40 ("Like malignant spirits"); dailies Flynn, vol. 27 fols. 394–97, reel 116, September 11, 1909, and fol. 1002, November 1, 1909 (a second lead).

209   **It was time to move in:** Dailies Flynn, vol. 28 fols. 161–72, reel 116, November 16, 1909 (apartment raid, names and addresses; Italian Squad; Black Hand letters found; Cecala's marked bills); *New York Times,* November 16, 1909, p. 1 (Black Hand notes; $3,600 in counterfeits); *Sun,* same date, p. 1 (buckshot); federal transcripts, Morello, fols. 285, 301 (Lupo arrest); *Washington Post,* February 5, 1922, p. 64 (nine guns, Lina, diapers); Flynn, pp. 206–7 (Gallagher); Bowen and Neal, *The United States Secret Service,* pp. 44–45 (Callaghan's encounter with Morello).

214   **Lupo was picked up:** Dailies Flynn, vol. 28 fols. 811–12, reel 116, January 6, fols. 859–60, January 9, and fols. 867–88, January 10, 1910.

214   **Bail had been set:** Dailies Flynn, vol. 28 fols. 184–85, reel 116, November 17, 1909; *Sun,* November 17 1909, p. 6.

215   **It's not certain when Flynn:** Dailies Flynn, vol. 28 fols. 600–1, December 19, 1909, and fols. 795–808, reel 116, January 5, 1910 (Mazzei, arrest date); vol. 30 fol. 990, reel 117, September 5, 1910 (full name); federal transcripts, Morello, fol. 122 (nine men); *Washington Post,* May 10, 1914, M8 (expected evidence, no counterfeits, kindness); Comito confession II (detailed evidence).

217   **to pay the costs of a defense:** *Sun,* January 27, 1910, p. 1.

217   **Cecala, for example, made:** Federal transcripts, Morello, fols. 424, 427–28.

217   **an elaborate alibi:** Federal transcripts, Morello, fols. 345–50 ("This is the way it was done . . ."); 428–30 (Brancatto); Flynn, pp. 181 (sixty patients), 186–87, 93 (hypochondriac), 187–93 (mother, meeting with Terranova, "pale as a ghost").

220   **including Giuseppe Boscarini:** Dailies Flynn, vol. 31 fol. 892, reel 117, December 7, 1910.

220   **"a rabble of Italians":** *New York Times,* April 3, 1910, SM6.

220   **crude attempts at intimidation:** *New York Times,* April 3, 1910, p. 1; *Sun,* January 27, p. 1, and January 28, 1910, p. 12.

220   **548 in total:** Pitkin, *The Black Hand,* p. 135.

221   **The printing press lay:** Dailies Taylor, vol. 4 fol. 236, reel 277, January 22, 1911 (plates); dailies New York, vol. 34 fol. 113, reel 591, January 16, 1912 (Mrs. Cina), and fol. 792, March 18, 1912 (New Paltz River); dailies New York, vol. 38 fols. 347–48, January 30, 1913 (Lupo buries counterfeits).

221   **The diminutive Calabrian:** *Sun,* January 27, 1910, p. 1 ("thin, nervous youth," Morello's looks).

221   **Comito dared not meet:** *Sun,* January 29, 1910, p. 12.

222   **were shaken to the core:** *Sun,* January 27, 1910, p. 1.

222   **a price of $2,500:** *Washington Post,* May 10, 1914, M8.

222   **portray Comito as a bloodthirsty:** Comito confession II, 107.

222   **Lupo did testify:** Federal transcripts, Morello, fols. 462–72.

222   **charged with perjury:** Dailies Flynn, vol. 30 fol. 76, reel 117, June 11, 1910 (Brancatto trial); Flynn, pp. 172–98 (Romano grand jury testimony and trial).

223   **sentences pronounced:** Dailies Flynn, vol. 29 fol. 166, reel 116, February 20,

1910 (forty-five minutes); federal transcripts, Morello, fols. 317 (Calicchio's age), 576–78 (verdicts); cumulation of verdicts recorded in "Description and information of criminals," vols. 39 and 40 of 40, RG 87, NARA (typical sentences); *New York Times,* February 20, 1910, pp. 1, 2 (court cleared, tears, convulsions, outside the court, Flynn's comment); *Sun,* same date, p. 1 (most severe sentences, Calicchio aged, slid rather than walked); *American,* same date, p. 3 (haunted looks, "words of the judge"); *Chicago Tribune,* April 24, 1913, I3 (sentences reflect earlier crimes).

CHAPTER 11. **Mob**

225   **The prison that was to house:** *New York Times,* April 3, 1910, SM6 ("spaghetti or garlic"); *Washington Post,* May 15, 1910, MT4 (conditions).

226   **the earliest date:** Prisoner records for Giuseppe Morello, inmate file 2882, and Ignazio Lupo, inmate file 2883, Atlanta Federal Penitentiary defense (fund, defense, Cockran), June 7, 1914, SM1 (other Mafia families).

226   **the hope that their appeal:** Dailies New York, vol. 33 fols. 563–64, reel 590, November 28, 1911, and fols. 892–93, December 30, 1911 (political clout); vol. 34 fol. 245, reel 591, January 27, 1912 (lack of funds); vol. 35 fols. 27–28, April 4, and 51-52, April 6, 1912 (politics).

227   **"it affected him so much":** Dailies Flynn, vol. 30 fols. 1024–25, September 9, 1910.

227   **There remained the prospect of escape:** Dailies Flynn, vol. 30 fols. 958, reel 117, September 1, 1910 (bribe guards); dailies New York, vol. 36 fol. 68, reel 591, July 11, 1912; *Plattsburgh Sentinel* (N.Y.), July 10, 1912, p. 2 (guard doubled); dailies New York, vol. 47 fol. 666, reel 595, July 14, 1915 (too much influence).

227   **There were other ways:** *Atlanta Constitution,* February 25, 1912 p. 13, and *Richmond Times Dispatch,* same date, p. 1 (letter to Ray); *World,* June 3, 1912, p. 1, and *Washington Post,* July 7, 1912, SM1 (Secret Service protection, children warned, Flynn assassination plot); *Herald,* June 2, 1912, p. 3 (hundred feet from home); Dailies New York, vol. 35 fol. 980, reel 591, July 1, 1912 (Ciro quote), and vol. 36 fols. 458–59, reel 591, August 20, 1912 (kidnap plot); dailies New York, vol. 35 fols. 692–96, June 1, 1912; fols. 710–11, June 3, both reel 591; *New York Times,* June 3, 1912, p. 9; *World,* June 2, pp. 1, 3.

227   **Nick Terranova's prudence:** Dailies New York, vol. 36 fols. 458–59, reel 591, August 20, 1912.

228   **when it came to Antonio Comito:** *New York Times,* May 23, 1910, p. 1, and May 24, p. 10, *Brooklyn Standard Union,* May 23, p. 1, *Washington Times,* May 23, p. 1 (mutilated body in Brooklyn); dailies Flynn, vol. 30 fols. 10–11, June 3, 1910, reel 117 (relative menaced); fol. 398, July 19, (Mexican border); dailies New York, vol. 32 fol. 127, June 14, 1911, reel 590, fol. 269, June 28 (revolver) and fol. 319, July 3 (leaves country); Flynn, pp. 217–20 (bounty, Rubano).

229   **Both men became morose:** Prisoner's record, inmate file 2883, Ignazio Lupo (disapproving comments); Angela Piazza and Lina Morello to Warden, May 14,

1912 (buried alive); J. Calvin Weaver (prison physician) to Warden, February 7, 1914 (indigestion), and July 22, 1915 (heart trouble, weight gain); Morello to Lina, June 1, 1913 ("You are wrong"); Lina to Morello, May 25, 1915 (complaints), all inmate file 2882, Giuseppe Morello.

229   **Lina, though, was finding life no easier:** Dailies Flynn, vol. 30 fol. 1009, reel 117, September 7, 1910 (feather business, pawn tickets); dailies New York, vol. 49 fol. 655, reel 596, February 1, 1916 (silver); Lina to Morello, February 15, 1915, inmate file 2882, Giuseppe Morello (weekly allowance).

229   **upset by his surliness:** Lina to Morello, July 1, 1915 ("Listen, Giuseppe"), July 1, 1916 ("Somewhat surprised"), and August 6, 1916 ("My always adored"), all inmate file 2882, Giuseppe Morello.

230   **It was time to talk:** Dailies Flynn, vol. 29 fols. 168–69, reel 116, February 20, 1910 (predicts men will talk); *New York Times,* January 17, 1911, p. 1, and *Atlanta Constitution,* same date, p. 2 (Morello confession); dailies Taylor, vol. 4 fol. 236, reel 277, January 22, 1911 (burial site); dailies New York, vol. 33 fols. 517–22, reel 590, November 21, 1911 (Sylvester, Lupo, Morello, Cina, burial site), and fol. 665, reel 590, December 8, 1911 (commutation, Cecala), vol. 34 fol. 113, January 12, 1912, and fol. 769, March 16, 1912, reel 591 (Terranova's plans, burial site), vol. 43 fol. 406, reel 594, May 13, 1914 (Giglio dies).

231   **they dared not divulge:** Dailies New York, vol. 34 fol. 215, reel 591, January 25, 1912, and vol. 36 fol. 466, reel 591, July 11, 1912.

232   **Sam Locino:** *Washington Post,* May 3, 1914, M8.

232   **Others were less fortunate:** Dailies New York, vol. 33 fol. 664–65, December 8, 1911, reel 590 (search for informants); dailies Flynn, vol. 30 fol. 86, June 12, 1910, and fol. 148, June 18, both reel 117 (potential informant refuses to cooperate); Manhattan death certificate 34140, November 17, 1911, NYMA, and dailies New York, vol. 33 fol. 472, November 18, 1911, reel 590, *World,* November 18, 1911, p. 3, and *New York Times,* same date, p. 7 (Bono murdered); *Washington Post,* February 5, 1922, p. 64 (ritual incisions, "Morello's enemy").

232   **Even Nick Sylvester:** Dailies New York, vol. 33 fols. 517–18, November 21, 1911, reel 590 (engraver, plates and burial site), vol. 34 fols. 792–93, March 18, 1912, reel 591 (location of plant, Flynn intervenes), and vol. 41 fol. 787, December 6, 1913, reel 593 (Vincenzo Terranova); "Letters sent" and commutation of sentence, October 23, 1913 (correspondence with Flynn, release date), both inmate file 2885, Nicholas Sylvester, Atlanta Federal Penitentiary papers, RG 129, NARA-SE.

233   **especially Charles Mazzei:** Dailies New York, vol. 33 fol. 796, reel 590; vol. 34 fols. 111, 113, reel 591, January 16, 1912, fol. 184, January 23, 1912, and fol. 852, March 22, 1912.

233   **His name was Salvatore Clemente:** "Description and information of criminals," vol. 30 of 40 fol. 172, April 1895, RG87, NARA (description, first conviction); Dailies Flynn, vol. 3 fol. 615, reel 106, and fols. 763–68, May 22, 1902 (Secret Service knowledge of Clemente gang); vol. 31 fol. 13–14, reel 117,

October 4, (recruited); fol. 57–58, October 8 (given trial); fol. 61–62, October 10, 1910 (commences work for Flynn).

233 **Clemente began to prove:** Dailies New York, vol. 34 fol. 215, reel 591, January 25, 1912; vol. 36 fols. 458–59, reel 591, August 20, 1912.

233 **since he refused to cede power:** *Washington Post,* February 5, 1922, p. 64 (runs gang from cell); Dailies New York, vol. 34 fols. 7–8, reel 591, January 3, 1912 (letters).

234 **the Lomonte brothers:** Dailies Flynn, vol. 30 fol. 994, reel 117, September 5, 1910 (relationship); Manhattan death certificates 16903, May 24, 1914, and 29667, October 13, 1915, NYMA (ages); *World,* October 14, 1915, p. 22 (feed store); *Washington Post,* February 5, 1922, p. 64 (runs family from cell, Lomontes succeed Morello).

234 **had lost its leaders:** *New York Times,* June 3, 1912, p. 9.

235 **Eugene Ubriaco:** Manhattan death certificate 18702, September 7, 1916, NYMA.

235 **DiMarco . . . Verrazano:** Dailies New York, vol. 36 fols. 120–23, reel 591, July 18, 1912; fols. 165–66, July 23, 1912; *Herald,* July 21, 1916, p. 1 (cards held); Sealy transcripts, Terranova, fols. 89–90, 97, 107 (plot details).

235 **Pasquarella Spinelli:** Dailies New York, vol. 33 fol. 522, reel 590, November 2, 1911 (informant); fol. 653–54, December 7, 1911 (Nick's blacksmith's shop); *Herald,* March 21, 1912, p. 1 (murder, address), January 7, SM2 (money), and November 30, 1917, pt. 1 p. 2 (police informant, Murder Stable); *American,* March 21, 1912, p. 7 (murder), and October 8, 1915, p. 5 (police knowledge of horse theft ring); Mondello, *A Sicilian in East Harlem,* p. 17 (Rex, extortion ring); Selvaggi, *The Rise and Fall of the Mafia in New York,* pp. 24–38 (Naples, character, illiterate, coal, moneylending); Manhattan death certificate 9128, March 20, 1912, NYMA (age); Manhattan death certificate 5755, February 19, 1914 (Lazzazzara murder, spelling of name); *New York Times,* February 20, 1914, p. 6 (Lazzazzara murder circumstances).

237 **Morello's only son was also killed:** *Herald,* April 14, 1912, p. 7 (shooting), and June 2, 1912, p. 3 (informant); *American,* April 14, 1912, p. 1 (shooting); dailies New York, vol. 35 fols. 174–75, reel 591, April 17 (Clemente information), fol. 206, April 20 ("butcher every one of them"), fols. 258–59, April 25 (Terranova's first killing), fol. 275, April 26, fols. 327–28, May 1 (Clemente's information, breaking news to Morello), fols. 569–70, May 22 (Madonia relative), fols. 739–40, June 6, 1912 (Terranova's second murder), and fols. 843–44, June 17, 1912 (alibi).

239 **Terranova grew:** Dailies New York, vol. 35 fols. 827–28, reel 591, June 14, 1912; vol. 36 fols. 458–59, reel 591, August 20, 1912.

239 **The Lomontes, for their part:** Dailies New York, vol. 34 fol. 442, reel 591, February 14, 1912 (saloon with Lima), fol. 729, March 13, 1912 (give it up).

239 **Giosue Gallucci:** Passenger list for SS *Wertundam,* March 11, 1892, M237/583, RG85, NARA, and Manhattan death certificate 33625, May 21, 1915, NYMA (date of arrival, age); passenger list for SS *Aller,* August 8, 1899,

"Passenger and crew lists of vessels arriving at New York, 1897–1957," T715/77 (Neapolitan); *Herald,* May 18, 1915, p. 7 (appearance, jewelry, influence, lottery, theft of winnings, legitimate and illegal businesses, shot in leg), and October 14, 1915, p. 22 (Lomontes as Gallucci allies); *New York Times,* same date, p. 22 (moneylender); *Herald,* November 30, 1917, pt. 1, p. 2 (lottery in basement, winners robbed); Fiaschetti, *The Man They Couldn't Escape,* pp. 111–18 (stool pigeons, army of men, workings of Royal lottery scam, spits); Cotillo, *A New American,* p. 20 (swaggered about, "All people were hirelings"); Nelli, *The Business of Crime,* pp. 129–30 (political influence).

241 **The Lomontes' fall:** Manhattan death certificate 16903, May 24, 1914 (injuries); dailies New York, vol. 43 fol. 528, reel 594, May 26, 1914 (shot, location); fol. 537, May 27 (no clues to killer).

242 **his own brother, Gennaro:** *Herald,* November 15, 1909, p. 1 (murder and background); Manhattan death certificate 33625, November 16, 1909, NYMA (time in New York; wounds)

242 **ten men had died:** *Herald,* May 18, 1915, p. 7.

242 **The assassins' chance came:** Trial transcripts, Marano, fols. 246, 738; Sealy transcripts, Terranova, fol. 97. *Herald,* May 18, 1915, p. 7 (bodyguards, circumstance); Fiaschetti, *The Man They Couldn't Escape,* pp. 116–17 (crime scene, deathbed); *Washington Post,* November 28, 1917, p. 3 (murdered by Morellos).

243 **Tom Lomonte was murdered:** *Herald,* October 14, 1915, p. 22 (murder, chase, East 109th Street); Sealy transcripts, Impoluzzo, fols. 3–14, 475–92 (circumstances, Impoluzzo defense, no motive).

244 **one suspect stood out:** *Brooklyn Standard Union,* September 8, 1916, p. 3.

CHAPTER 12. **Artichoke Kings**

245 **left the Morellos the dominant force:** *Herald,* May 18, 1915, p. 1 (rackets); trial transcripts, Vollero, vol. 75 fols. 113–15, and Marano, fols. 235–39, and Nelli, *The Business of Crime,* p. 131 (Morello rackets as of 1916).

245 **Royal Lottery:** *Herald,* May 18, 1915, p. 7 (robbed); Fiaschetti, *The Man They Couldn't Escape,* pp. 107–9 (profitable; Gallucci reputation).

245 **Black Hand crime:** Sacco, "Black Hand Outrage."

245 **increasingly, narcotics:** *American,* November 29, 1917, p. 3.

245 **not to one family, but to four:** Dailies New York, vol. 34 fols. 546–47, reel 591, February 25, 1912 (four families; leaders; affiliations); Bonanno, *A Man of Honor,* pp. 63 ("bland, compliant"), 84 ("not preordained"), 93–94 (Schiro character), 121 (size of Mineo family); Critchley, "Buster, Maranzano, and the Castellammare War," pp. 55, 61 (Schiro and Mineo ages).

246 **Its leader was Nicola Schiro:** Dailies Flynn, vol. 34 fols. 546–47, reel 591, February 25, 1912 (exists); Critchley, "Buster, Maranzano, and the Castellammare War," p. 61 and note (Schiro emigration date); Bonanno, *A Man of Honor,* pp. 63, 93 (character, rich).

246 **Manfredi Mineo:** Dailies Flynn, vol. 34 fols. 546–47, reel 591, February 25, 1912 (exists); Bonanno, *A Man of Honor,* pp. 84. 116, 141 (largest in 1930).

247 **Salvatore "Totò" D'Aquila:** Dailies Flynn, vol. 34 fols. 546–47, reel 591, February 25, 1912 (exists, can summon meetings, joint approval of members), and vol. 41 fols. 483–84, reel 593, November 11, 1913 (strongest, opposes other three families); *New York Times,* October 11, 1928, p. 20 (confidence man); Dickie, *Cosa Nostra,* p. 223 (Palermo Mafia dominance); Gentile, *Vita di Capomafia,* p. 70n; Critchley, *The Origin of Organized Crime,* pp. 36, 156–58 (structure and importance).

248 **Among those who joined:** Dailies New York, vol. 41 fols. 472–73, reel 593, November 10, 1913 (Fontana killed); fols. 483–84, November 11, 1913 (D'Aquila's dominant position); fols. 678–79, November 27, 1913 (Fanaro killed).

249 **DiMarco had feared:** Dailies New York, vol. 36 fol. 81, reel 591, July 18, and fols. 165–66, July 23, 1912 (DiMarco a Terranova ally, marked for death); *Herald,* July 21, 1916, p. 1 (murdered, poker hand); Manhattan death certificate 21421, July 20, 1916 (place and time, injuries); trial transcripts, Vollero, fol. 119, and Marano, fol. 249, and Sealy transcripts, Terranova, fols. 6–9, 44–48, and *American,* June 4, 1918, p. 13 (Terranovas responsible); Thompson and Raymond, *Gang Rule in New York,* pp. 4–5 (plot).

251 **Salvatore's murder:** Queens death certificate 4413, October 13, 1913 (place and date, injuries); *Herald,* October 14, 1916, p. 5 (body found, auction).

251 **The Camorra, a criminal society:** Di Fiore, *La Camorra e le Sue Storie,* pp. 1–100 (history, organization); trial transcripts, Marano, fol. 53, and *New York Times,* June 30, 1926 (nationwide).

252 **Vollero's boss:** Trial transcripts, Vollero, fols. 117–24 (Marano, Ricci), Paretti (1922), fol. 80 (Vollero, Marano), Marano, fol. 52 (Marano is overall New York boss).

252 **Thanks in large part:** Trial transcripts, Marano, fols. 52–53 (initiation), 58, 117, 242–45 (members drift in); 254 (organized only from 1916), 255, 281 (numbers).

253 **Relations between:** Trial transcripts, Paretti (1926), fols. 45–46 (background), Vollero, fols. 124, 130 (peaceful relations), fol. 130–31, and trial transcripts, Marano, fols. 64, 208 (move in on Harlem rackets), 232 (Morellos expand into Bronx), 238 (Harlem rackets), 252 (cocaine trade), 269 (Morellos kill Vollero friend).

254 **Vollero was actively plotting:** Trial transcripts, Vollero, fol. 117–18 (three weeks, Marano instigates), 121 (seek Navy Street consent), 122 (Lauritano opposes), 123 (want three Morello rackets); trial transcripts, Marano, fol. 64 (incensed by Morello involvement in policy), 188 ("wear diamonds").

254 **persuade the Navy Street gang:** Trial transcripts, Vollero, fols. 119 (DiMarco killing), 121–24 (Lauritano's trust), 130 (save Ricci, "You must consent . . . ," Vollero and Ricci).

255 **to plot the Morellos' deaths:** Trial transcripts, Vollero, fols. 117 (three weeks),

132 (fix witnesses), 135 (garlic and pepper, special cupboard); Nelli, *The Business of Crime,* p. 131 (invitation).

255 **Terranova's willingness:** Trial transcripts, Vollero, fols. 146–47 (pale, Moxie).

256 **Terranova was the first to die:** Sealy transcripts, Terranova, fols. 67–68 (pale); *Brooklyn Daily Eagle,* September 6, p. 8 (weather); *Herald,* September 8, p. 7, and *New York Times,* same date, p. 18 (location, circumstances), and *American,* September 9, 1916 (half-drawn revolver).

256 **Michael Mealli:** Trial transcripts, Vollero, fols. 152.

256 **soon lost another half-dozen:** Trial transcripts, Vollero, fols. 193 (attempt to hire rooms), 198–99 (bomb plot), 200 (poison plot); trial transcripts, Paretti, 1922, fols. 76–140 (Nazarro murder); Sealy transcripts, Giordano, fols. 5–9, and Terranova, fols. 69–71 (Verrazano and Nazarro murders), 82–84 (bomb plot), 84–85 (poison plot); trial transcripts, Vollero, fols. 185–87 (Verrazano murder); Nelli, *The Business of Crime,* pp. 130–34 (Philadelphia); trial transcripts, Marano, fols. 230 (no choice but to pursue Morellos), 239 (bomb plot).

257 **Vollero himself only narrowly:** Trial transcripts, Vollero, fols. 201–2.

257 **moving in on the Morellos' operations:** Trial transcripts, Vollero, fols. 172 (*zicchinetta*), 173–75 ($50 a car, gambling payments in Brooklyn), 176–78 (policy negotiations); trial transcripts, Marano, fols. 178 ($150 a week), 216 (80 percent), 225 (60 percent). 293–95 (artichoke dealers resist), 298 (policy men will close down games).

257 **"Are you crazy?":** Trial transcripts, Marano, fols. 292–94.

258 **"pretty hard characters themselves":** Trial transcripts, Vollero, fol. 73.

258 **hand control of the Harlem lottery back:** Trial transcripts, Marano, fols. 303–4.

258 **Ralph the Barber:** Sealy transcripts, Terranova, fols. 53–60, 94 (career); trial transcripts, Vollero, fols. 116 (career), 206, 212, 233, 247–51 (career, pay, surrenders to police); trial transcripts, Paretti (1922), fols. 126 (kills seven in Italy), 129–30 (in Reno, sends letters); trial transcripts, Marano, fols. 242–43 (in U.S., barber till 1914), 322 (change of name, charges faced); *American,* November 28, 1917, p. 6 (confession, scar, twenty-three murders, "Different methods"); *Washington Post,* same date, p. 3 (Gallucci killing); *Newark Star-Eagle,* August 17, 1925 (criminal record).

260 **police officers were taking bribes:** Trial transcripts, Vollero, fols. 152–53, 158 (police "fixed"); *New York Times,* September 24, 1911, SM8 (Carrao), and February 16, 1918, p. 6 (Mealli).

260 **Vincenzo and Ciro were arrested:** Sealy transcripts, Terranova, fols. 5, 10, 246–55 (Littleton defense); Terranova files (arrests, almost a dozen, most released, "possess influence," first trial halted, "entirely hopeless"); *American,* June 4, p. 13, and June 8, 1918 (second trial, discharge); Lloyd Stryker, *The Art of Advocacy,* pp. 155–75 (Littleton background, greatest American jury lawyer).

261 **protracted series of prosecutions:** See trial transcripts, Vollero (1919), Marano (1922), and Paretti (1922) and (1926); *Brooklyn Daily Standard Union,* June 18, 1918, p. 8; *New York Times,* July 1, 1926, p. 7.

261 **when Tony the Shoemaker unwisely returned:** Trial transcripts, Paretti

(1926), fols. 125–34, 192–288, 453–78 (evidence); *New York Times,* June 30, 1926, p. 7; Downey, *Gangster City,* p. 36.

262 **Andrea Ricci died in 1917:** Kings County death certificate 22069, November 14, 1917, NYMA.

CHAPTER 13. The Eighteenth Amendment

263 **The world had changed:** Jackson, *The Encyclopedia of New York City,* pp. 605, 921; draft cards for Vincenzo and Ciro Terranova, June 1917, RG 163, NARA-SE.

264 **Joe Masseria:** Critchley, "Buster, Maranzano, and the Castellammare War," p. 55.

264 **Umberto Valenti:** Gentile, *Vita di Capomafia,* pp. 55–71 (two thousand associates, "the Ghost").

265 **fled the country:** Gentile, *Vita,* pp. 70–71 (D'Aquila, sentence, a dozen men); Ignazio Lupo, inmate file 2883, Atlanta Federal Penitentiary papers, Records of the Bureau of Prisons, RG 129, NARA-SE (release date); Dickie, *Cosa Nostra,* pp. 217–20; Gentile, *Vita,* pp. 70–71; *New York Times,* February 23, 1938, p. 40; *Washington Post,* February 5, 1922, p. 64 (Newport News, dates); *New York Times,* June 13, 1922, p. 1 (return date for Lupo).

265 **hiding around Palermo:** Bonanno, *A Man of Honor,* p. 100.

267 **Alcohol had been outlawed:** Sinclair, *Prohibition,* pp. 205–6 (Prohibition Bureau), 212 (quarter of a million), 220 (exports), 231 (N.Y. juries), 244–48 (market size); Jackson, *Encyclopedia,* p. 944 (speakeasies).

269 **Ciro Terranova, with whom:** Downey, *Gangster City,* pp. 38, 199, 202.

269 **Vito Genovese:** Maas, *The Valachi Papers,* pp. 128–31; Critchley, *The Origin of Organized Crime,* pp. 132–34 (Paretti).

269 **"Prohibition was too good to be true":** Bonanno, *A Man of Honor,* p. 65.

269 **"so fearsome a competitor":** *New York Daily News,* May 9, 1922 (Harlem Tiger); trial transcripts, Paretti (1926), fol. 205 (Viserti and the Murder Stable); Critchley, *The Origin of Organized Crime,* pp. 102 (Viserti), 138–41, 154–56 (background of Italian bootlegging).

270 **His name was Giuseppe Masseria:** *New York Times,* April 16, 1931, p.1 (criminal record); Critchley, *The Origin of Organized Crime,* pp. 154–56 (background and rise; Curb Exchange).

270 **Whatever it was:** Bonanno, *A Man of Honor,* pp. 84–86 (appearance, gluttony, "the Chinese," messy eater), 100 ("his belly . . .").

271 **From the Morello family's perspective:** Critchley, *The Origin of Organized Crime,* p. 155.

272 **Diamond Joe Viserti was the first to go:** *New York Daily News,* October 14, 1921 (Viserti death), and May 9, 1922, pp. 2, 14 (Vincenzo Terranova murder); Manhattan death certificate 13893, May 8, 1922, NYMA (Terranova wounds); *New York Times,* May 8, 1922, p. 1 (Terranova circumstances), and April 16, 1931, p. 15 (attack on Masseria; straw hat); *Herald,* May 8, 1922, p. 1 (Masseria shooting), and August 12, 1922, p. 1 (Valenti murder); Downey, *Gangster City,* p. 139 (Viserti and Masseria linked), 140–41 (Masseria's gun

battles); Gentile, *Vita di Capomafia*, p. 79 (Valenti responsible for killing Terranova); Critchley, *The Origin of Organized Crime*, pp. 155–56 (Valenti's attacks on Masseria).

273 **one further important casualty:** Manhattan death certificate 17260, June 19, 1923; *New York Times*, June 20, 1923, p. 4 (Salemi murder). My thanks to David Critchley for supplying the latter reference.

273 **surviving Terranova brother's place:** Maas, *The Valachi Papers*, pp. 53–54 (brokers truce, sets up burglars); *New York Times*, December 28, 1929, p. 1, and January 16, 1930, p. 1 (Vitale dinner, murder contract); Terrett, *Only Saps Work*, p. 33 (Vitale's criminal connections).

276 **The assassination of Totò D'Aquila:** *New York Times*, October 11, p. 20, and October 12, 1928, p. 22 (criminal career, cheese importer, unknown as Mafioso, witness changes story); Gentile, *Vita*, pp. 70–71 (authoritarian, from Palermo); Critchley, *The Origin of Organized Crime*, pp. 161–64 (murder and aftermath).

278 **wearied by age:** *New York Times*, October 11, p. 20 (D'Aquila); Critchley, "Buster, Maranzano, and the Castellammare War," pp. 55, 61n (Mineo, Schiro); Maas, *The Valachi Papers*, p. 65 (Reina); Bonanno, *A Man of Honor*, pp. 84–85 ("careful not to offend").

278 **the boss as a benevolent "father":** Bonanno, *A Man of Honor*, pp. 63, 76–77, 85.

279 **Masseria took things further still:** Maas, *The Valachi Papers*, p. 65, Critchley, "Buster, Maranzano, and the Castellammare War," pp. 44, 75.

279 **the Castellammare War:** Critchley, "Buster, Maranzano, and the Castellammare War," p. 61n (origins); Bonanno, *A Man of Honor*, p. 86 (guff), 88 (thick-skulled).

280 **"brains trust":** Bonanno, *A Man of Honor*, p. 100.

280 **Morello began by sowing dissent:** Bonanno, *A Man of Honor*, pp. 87–88 93–94 (Milazzo murder, Aiello, Capone), 100 (Morello and Milazzo), 102 (tribute, Bonventre murder); Critchley, "Buster, Maranzano, and the Castellammare War," p. 63 (Milazzo murder).

280 **resembled a volcanic chamber:** Bonanno, *A Man of Honor*, p. 95 ("In a war between . . ."), 101 (sandwich), 102 (condemned).

281 **solved this problem by disappearing:** Bonanno, *A Man of Honor*, p. 102 ("If Masseria"); Critchley, "Buster, Maranzano, and the Castellammare War," p. 61n (Schiro leaves for Italy).

281 **"classic American success story":** Bonanno, *A Man of Honor*, p. 74.

281 **Most of those who encountered Maranzano:** Bonanno, *A Man of Honor*, pp. 71 (appearance, voice), 100 (and Morello); Maas, *The Valachi Papers*, p. 74 (Valachi's views); Critchley, "Buster, Maranzano, and the Castellammare War," pp. 56–61 (background, immigration, and D'Aquila).

282 **knew as Peter Morello:** Critchley, "Buster, Maranzano, and the Castellammare War," p. 63n (alias); Manhattan death certificate 19631, August 15, 1930, NYMA (correct identity).

283 **at the meeting place:** Bonanno, *A Man of Honor*, pp. 98–99.

284   Maranzano made ready: Bonanno, *A Man of Honor,* pp. 95, 104.

284   "We're only a few": Maas, *The Valachi Papers,* p. 77.

285   Every effort was made: Maas, *The Valachi Papers,* p. 77, Bonanno, *A Man of Honor,* pp. 104–5 (limo, machine gun).

285   "I watched Maranzano loading": Bonanno, *A Man of Honor,* p. 117.

286   "Buster from Chicago": Maas, *The Valachi Papers,* p. 77 (Valachi's initiation); Critchley, "Buster, Maranzano, and the Castellammare War," pp. 46–51 (Buster identified); Bonanno, *A Man of Honor,* p. 105 (virtuoso).

287   "Maranzano used to say": Bonanno, *A Man of Honor,* p. 107.

287   Morello never got the chance: *New York Times,* August 16, 1930, p. 1; *Daily News,* same date, pp. 2, 4; *Herald Tribune,* same date, pp. 1, 4 (details); autopsy report, August 16, 1930, Office of the Chief Medical Examiner, file DA4801, NYMA (wounds); Maas, *The Valachi Papers,* p. 67, and Bonanno, *A Man of Honor,* p. 107 (events of murder).

Epilogue

289   "had lost his best man": Bonanno, *A Man of Honor,* p. 107.

289   Defectors began going over: Bonanno, *A Man of Honor,* pp. 120–21.

289   as his adviser and strategist: Bonanno, *A Man of Honor,* p. 116.

290   the next breakthrough: Bonanno, *A Man of Honor,* p. 120 ("Maranzano had already decided . . ."); Maas, *The Valachi Papers,* pp. 68–71 ("to rent this apartment . . ."; Masseria spotted, Mineo shot).

291   Lucky Luciano: Bonanno, *A Man of Honor,* pp. 121–22.

292   "limited number of meals": Bonanno, *A Man of Honor,* p. 120.

292   the boss of bosses' murder: *New York Times,* April 16, 1931, p. 1 (circumstances); Critchley, "Buster, Maranzano, and the Castellammare War," pp. 64–65 ("ritual" aspects dismissed).

293   Maranzano emerged as the dominant: Bonanno, *A Man of Honor,* pp. 123–27 (aftermath, national conference, family heads), 131 ("more comfortable . . ."); Maas, *The Valachi Papers,* pp. 84–88 (numbers at meeting; "Whatever happened in the past . . ."; $115,000; "control everything").

294   Maranzano went much the same way: Maas, *The Valachi Papers,* pp. 89–90.

294   For years afterward, rumors: Thompson and Raymond, *Gang Rule in New York,* pp. 374–75 (purge day); Nelli, *The Business of Crime,* pp. 179–218 (no evidence); Critchley, "Buster, Maranzano, and the Castellammare War," pp. 44–78 (events in context); Maas, *The Valachi Papers,* p. 96 ("They got Jimmy Marino . . .").

295   Steve La Salle: Terranova files (Morello associate); Maas, *The Valachi Papers,* p. 111 (numbers racket); Critchley, *The Origin of Organized Crime,* pp. 111, 113.

295   his agency assumed some: *Flynn's Weekly,* November 8, 1924, pp. 253–67 (cases); Melanson, *The Secret Service,* pp. 37–38 (manpower); Fox, "Bureaucratic Wrangling over Counterintelligence, 1917–18" (agencies).

296   he tendered his resignation: *Washington Post,* December 24, 1917, p. 4,

and December 30, 1917, p. 2 (dates, exhausted); McCormick, *Hopeless Cases,* pp. 44–45 (Hale).

296 **William Moran:** *New York Times,* December 23, 1917, p. 1 (New York).

297 **appointed director of the Bureau of Investigation:** Ackerman, *Young J. Edgar,* pp. 27–30 (abilities, reaction, FRA police), 256–57 (investigation); McCormick, *Hopeless Cases,* pp. 8, 45–46, 108–9, 118–19, 125–27 (Wall Street, Clemente, resignation, Burns).

298 **"As he has told me":** Ackerman, *Young J. Edgar,* p. 28 (Palmer quote).

298 **writer for the motion picture industry:** Dumaux, *King Baggot,* pp. 99–102, 243; information from Kevin Brownlow.

299 **running the detective business:** Private information from the Flynn family.

299 **William Flynn expired:** *New York Times,* October 15, 1928, p. 23; *Chicago Tribune,* same date, p. 32.

299 **Francesco Ortoleva, the man framed:** Dailies Flynn, vol. 30 fols. 202–3, reel 117, June 25, 1910 (mother); James Ortoleva to William Mayer, Warden, Atlanta Federal Penitentiary, February 7 and 15, March 23, 1911, inmate file 2882, Giuseppe Morello, Atlanta Federal Penitentiary papers, RG 129, NARA-SE (works for Flynn; pressurize Morello); passenger list for SS *San Guglielmo,* 25 January 1914, "Passenger and crew lists of vessels arriving at New York, 1897–1957," T715/2254, RG85, NARA (arrives N.Y.); Flynn pp. 259, 260–61 (weighted; mutual prayers).

300 **Most of the thugs:** Dailies New York, vol. 39 fol. 17, reel 592, April 3, 1913 (Inzerillo); *Washington Post,* April 26, 1914, SM5 (Di Priemo); Petacco, *Joe Petrosino,* pp. 190, 192 (Costantino and Passananti).

300 **Ralph the Barber:** *Brooklyn Standard-Union,* June 12, 1918, p. 8 (begs to stay in jail); *Newark Star-Eagle,* August 17, 1925, and Alfonso Pepe death certificate, August 18, Essex County, N.J., 3346 of 1925 (murder); *New York Times,* June 17, 1929, p. 19 (killed within a month).

301 **Pellegrino Marano:** *New York Times,* July 1, 1926, p. 7.

301 **Alessandro Vollero:** Maas, *The Valachi Papers,* pp. 55, 60–61, 101.

302 **Vito Cascio Ferro:** Barzini, *The Italians,* pp. 263–66 (career and influence); Petacco, *Joe Petrosino,* p. 195 (incorrect details of death); Hess, *Mafia,* p. 51 (charges); Ianni, *A Family Business,* pp. 32 (inscription), Servadio, *Mafioso,* pp. 60–63 (Mafia career); Dickie, *Cosa Nostra,* pp. 176, 185–86 (death); "Description and information of criminals," vol. 39 of 40, fol. 370, RG 87, NARA (physical description).

304 **Ignazio Lupo was able to return:** *Washington Post,* June 13, 1922, p. 5; *New York Times,* same date, p. 1, and February 23, 1938, p. 40.

304 **handsome sixteen-room home:** *New York Times,* July 17, 1935, p. 42, and July 16, 1936, pp. 1, 3.

304 **resuming his old trade:** "Statement of parole violator," n.d. (July 1936?) (La Rosa Fruit, bakery, working habits); Salvatrice Lupo to Myrl Alexander, director, Social Services Unit, Atlanta Federal Penitentiary, n.d. (July 1936) (bakery trade, jealousy); John Lupo to Alexander, July 22, 1936 (hardworking); copy of Lupo's NYPD record, July 21, 1936 (homicide arrest); "Office memorandum,"

December 18, 1946 (commutation), all in inmate file 2883, Atlanta Federal Penitentiary papers, Records of the Bureau of Prisons, RG 129, NARA-SE; *New York Times,* October 9, 1930, p. 29 (Consiglio), July 17, 1935, p. 42 (Rose Vitale), July 16, 1936, pp. 1, 3 (lottery), January 22, 1937, p. 42 (bakery racket), and February 23, 1938, p. 40 (violence, grapes); *Atlanta Constitution,* July 18, 1936, p. 1 (banks $3 million, runs at cost); *Washington Post,* August 29, 1931, p. 8 (grapes racket); Terrett, *Only Saps Work,* p. 96 (Uale's grapes racket); Reppetto, *American Mafia,* pp. 154–55 (LaGuardia).

306 **Retribution was not far:** Harding commutation, October 29, 1921, presidential warrant, July 10, 1936, and "Record of Court Commitment," July 31, 1936, in inmate file 2883; *New York Times,* July 16, 1936, p. 1 (Lehman); *Atlanta Constitution,* July 18, 1936, p. 1 (hurried arrest).

307 **writ of habeas corpus:** *Lupo v. Zerbst,* 92 F.2d 362, October 19, 1937; *Lupo v. Zerbst,* April 2, 1937, inmate file 2883.

307 **Rocco Lupo was declared bankrupt:** *New York Times,* September 29, 1937, p. 39.

307 **physical and mental state:** "Record of Ignatio Lupo," undated; "Admission summary," undated (medical, time to serve); presidential order, July 10, 1936 (recall); John Lupo to Myrl Alexander, July 22, 1936 (breakdown); Ignazio Lupo to Joseph Sanford, warden, June 8, 1938; "Special progress reports" of June 27 and August 31, 1940; A. Hughes (parole assistant) to Sanford, October 14, 1946 (visits); Sanford to director of prison service, July 15, 1946; Sanford to Walter Urich, parole executive, Bureau of Prisons, July 19, 1946 (recommendations); "Clinical record," December 1946; "Institutional memorandum," December 26, 1946 (funds at release), all in inmate file 2883; Selvaggi, *The Rise and Fall of the Mafia in New York,* pp. 65, 70 (religion, exercise, letter to daughter).

308 **daughters had married, and Salvatrice:** "Admission summary: Lupo, Ignatio," undated (1936); Salvatrice Lupo to Myrl Alexander, director, Social Services Unit, Atlanta Federal Penitentiary, n.d. (July 1936); all in inmate file 2883.

308 **the money was lost:** Cf. Mondello, *A Sicilian in East Harlem,* p. 9.

308 **a rented room in Queens:** Queens death certificate 524, January 13, 1947, NYMA.

309 **Angela Terranova:** Queens death certificate 4526, June 20, 1941, NYMA.

309 **last years of Morello's wife:** Private information from the Morello family (Down syndrome); index to New York City death certificates 1950–82, New York Public Library (date of death).

309 **The Artichoke King retained:** Maas, *The Valachi Papers,* pp. 110–11 (Schultz and the numbers racket); *New York Times,* February 3, 1933, p. 8 (new artichoke king), July 29, 1935, p. 17 (wedding), November 10, 1935, SM6 (canter), June 5, 1936, p. 20 (police harassment), May 14, 1937, p. 6 (foreclosure and bankruptcy), February 20, 1938, p. 26 (stroke and death).

311 **His grave in Valhalla:** Private information from the Flynn family (Valhalla); Selwyn Raab, *Five Families,* pp. 492–501 (D'Arco, vegetable rackets); author's visits to Petrosino Park, March 2006 (neglected) and Calvary Cemetery, July 2007 (Petrosino and Morello graves).

BIBLIOGRAPHY

ARCHIVAL SOURCES

Italy

ARCHIVIO CENTRALE DELLO STATO, ROME
  Papers of the Ministero di Grazia e Giustizia (Ministry of Justice)
ARCHIVIO GRAMSCI, PALERMO
  Verdict in the Bernardino Verro murder case, Palermo Assize Court, 1917
ARCHIVIO STATO, PALERMO
  Police reports in the papers of the Gabinetto Prefettura (Prefectural Cabinet), 1861–1905
UFFICIO ANAGRAFE, COMMUNE OF CORLEONE
  Registers of births, marriages, and deaths

New York State

LLOYD SEALY LIBRARY, JOHN JAY COLLEGE OF CRIMINAL JUSTICE, NEW YORK CITY
  Trial transcripts of the County of New York, Court of General Sessions of the Peace,
  1883–1927
NATIONAL ARCHIVES AND RECORDS ADMINISTRATION, NORTHEAST REGION,
NEW YORK CITY
  RG 276 Records of the U.S. Court of Appeals
  U.S. Circuit Court for the Southern District of New York, 1790–1912
NEW YORK CITY MUNICIPAL ARCHIVES AND RECORDS CENTER
  Certificates of births, marriages, and deaths, 1885–1949
  District Attorney's Closed Case Files, 1895–1966
  District Attorney's Record of Cases, 1895–1966
  New York Police Department photograph collection
  Office of the Chief Medical Examiner Death Records, 1918–46
  WPA Italians of New York
NEW YORK COUNTY CLERK'S OFFICE, DIVISION OF OLD RECORDS
  Company records
  Naturalization certificates

New York Public Library
    Index to New York City death certificates, 1950–82
New York State Archives, Albany
    B0148 Inmate admission register for federal prisoners, Sing Sing Correctional Facility, 1896–1908
    J2002 New York State Court of Appeals, cases and briefs on appeal, 1847–1995
Westchester County Archives, Elmsford
    Naturalization certificates, 1808–1927

Elsewhere in the United States

American Heritage Center, University of Wyoming
    Frank Wilson papers
        Box 10, folder 370, "Secret Service stories"
Federal Bureau of Investigation, Washington, D.C.
    Nicola Gentile file
Hoover Presidential Library, West Branch, Iowa
    Lawrence Richey papers
National Archives and Records Administration, Southeast Region, Morrow, Georgia
    RG129 Records of the Bureau of Prisons
        Inmate files, Atlanta Federal Penitentiary
    RG163 Selective Service System Draft Registration Cards, 1917–18, M1509
National Archives and Records Administration, College Park, Maryland
    RG 29 Federal censuses of 1910, 1920, 1930
    RG 85 Passenger Lists of Vessels Arriving at New York, 1820–97
        Passenger and Crew Lists of Vessels Arriving at New York, 1897–1957
    RG 87 Secret Service papers
        Letters sent, 1889–1918
        Description and information of criminals, 1863–1906
        Daily summary reports of agents, 1875–1936

OFFICIAL PAPERS

Annual Reports of the Chief of the Secret Service Division. 1892–1912.
Organized Crime: 25 Years After Valachi. Hearings Before the Permanent Subcommittee on Investigations of the Committee on Governmental Affairs, United States Senate, 100th Congress, Second Session. Washington, D.C.: U.S. Government Printing Office, 1988.
Papers Relating to the Foreign Relations of the United States, Transmitted to Congress with the Annual Message of the President, December 9, 1891. Executive documents of the House of Representatives 1891–1892. 53rd Congress, First Session. Washington, D.C.: U.S. Government Printing Office, 1892.

UNPUBLISHED DISSERTATIONS

Iorizzo, Luciano. "Italian Migration and the Impact of the Padrone System." Ph.D. diss., Syracuse University, 1966.

Levine, Jerald. "Police, Parties, and Polity: The Bureaucratization, Unionization, and Professionalization of the New York City Police, 1870–1917." Ph.D. diss., University of Wisconsin, 1971.

Scarpaci, Jean Ann. "Italian Immigrants in Louisiana's Sugar Parishes: Recruitment, Labor Conditions and Community Relations, 1880–1910." Ph.D. diss., Rutgers University, 1973.

NEWSPAPERS AND PERIODICALS

Published in New York City unless otherwise stated.

American
Atlanta Constitution
Brooklyn Daily Eagle
Brooklyn Daily Standard Union
Canton Commercial Advertiser (Canton, N.Y.)
Chicago Tribune
Collier's Weekly
Commercial Advertiser
Daily News
Daily Picayune (New Orleans)
Daily States (New Orleans)
Evening Journal
Evening Star (Washington, D.C.)
Evening World
Flynn's Weekly
Harper's Weekly
Los Angeles Times
Mail and Express
Milwaukee Sentinel
Morning Oregonian (Portland)
Newark Star-Eagle (Newark, N.J.)
New Castle News (New Castle, Pa.)
New York Herald
New York Herald Tribune
New York Times
North American Review
Ogden Standard Examiner (Ogden, Utah)
Philadelphia Inquirer
Pittsburgh Gazette

Plattsburgh Sentinel (Plattsburgh, N.Y.)
St. Lawrence Herald (St. Lawrence, N.Y.)
San Francisco Call
Sun
Time
Tribune
Washington Herald
Washington Post
Washington Times
Wilkes-Barre Record (Wilkes-Barre, Pa.)
Winona Republican-Herald (Winona, Minn.)
World

PUBLISHED WORKS

Ackerman, Kenneth. *Young J. Edgar: Hoover, the Red Scare, and the Assault on Civil Liberties.* New York: Carroll & Graf, 2007.

Albini, Joseph. *The American Mafia: Genesis of a Legend.* New York: Appleton-Century-Crofts, 1971.

Amfitheatrof, Erik. *The Children of Columbus: An Informal History of Italians in the New World.* Boston: Little, Brown, 1973.

Anselmo, Nonuccio. *La Terra Promessa: Vita e Morte di Bernardino Verro e del Movimento Contadino Nel Feudo.* Palermo: Herbita, 1989.

Arnesen, Eric. *Waterfront Workers of New Orleans: Race, Class, and Politics, 1863–1923.* New York: Oxford University Press, 1991.

Asbury, Herbert. *The Gangs of New York: An Informal History of the Underworld.* New York: Thunders Mouth Press, 1998.

Baiomonte, John. "'Who Killa de Chief?' Revisited: The Hennessy Assassination and Its Aftermath, 1890–1991." *Louisiana History* 33 (1992).

Barzini, Luigi. *The Italians.* New York: Atheneum, 1964.

Behr, Edward. *Prohibition: The Thirteen Years That Changed America.* London: Penguin, 1998.

Belfiglio, Valentine. *The Italian Experience in Texas.* Austin, Texas: Eakin Press, 1995.

Bevilacqua, P., A. De Clementi, and E. Franzina, eds. *Storia dell'Emigrazione Italiana. Arrivi.* Rome: Domzelli, 2002.

Blok, Anton. *The Mafia of a Sicilian Village, 1860–1960.* New York: Harper & Row, 1974.

Bonanno, Joseph. *A Man of Honor: The Autobiography of Joseph Bonanno.* New York: Simon & Schuster, 1983.

Bowen, Walter, and Harry Edward Neal. *The United States Secret Service.* Philadelphia: Hilton, 1960.

Bruner, Robert, and Sean Carr. *The Panic of 1907: Lessons Learned from the Market's Perfect Storm.* Hoboken, N.J.: John Wiley & Sons, 2007.

Burns, Ric, and James Sanders. *New York: An Illustrated History*. New York: Alfred A. Knopf, 1999.

Burrows, Edwin, and Mike Wallace. *Gotham: A History of New York City to 1898*. New York: Oxford University Press, 1999.

Carey, A. A. *Memoirs of a Murder Man*. Garden City, N.J.: Doubleday, Doran, 1930.

Catanzaro, Raimondo. *Men of Respect: A Social History of the Sicilian Mafia*. New York: Free Press, 1992.

Chandler, David. *Brothers in Blood: The Rise of the Criminal Brotherhood*. New York: E. P. Dutton, 1975.

Critchley, David. "Buster, Maranzano, and the Castellammare War, 1930–1931." *Global Crime Journal* 7 (2006).

———. *The Origin of Organized Crime in America*. New York: Routledge, 2008.

Cutrera, Antonino. *La Mafia e i Mafiosi: Origine e Manifestazioni*. Palermo: Alberto Reber, 1900.

Dash, Mike. *Satan's Circus: Murder, Vice, Police Corruption, and New York's Trial of the Century*. New York: Crown, 2007.

Dickie, John. *Cosa Nostra: A History of the Sicilian Mafia*. London: Hodder & Stoughton, 2004.

Di Fiore, Gigi. *La Camorra e le Sue Storie*. Turin: UTET, 2005.

Downey, Patrick. *Gangster City: The History of the New York Underworld 1900–1935*. Fort Lee, N.J.: Barricade Books, 2004.

Dumaux, Sally. *King Baggot: A Biography and Filmography of the First King of the Movies*. New York: McFarland, 2002.

Fentress, James. *Rebels and Mafiosi: Death in a Sicilian Landscape*. Ithaca, N.Y.: Cornell University Press, 2000.

Ferber, Nat. *A New American: From the Life Story of Salvatore A. Cotillo, Supreme Court Justice*. New York: Farrar & Rinehart, 1939.

Fiaschetti, Michael. *The Man They Couldn't Escape: The Adventures of Detective Fiaschetti of the Italian Squad*. London: Selwyn & Blount, 1928.

Flynn, William. *The Barrel Mystery*. New York: James A. McCann, 1919.

Fox, John. "Bureaucratic Wrangling over Counterintelligence, 1917–18." *Studies in Intelligence* 49 (2005).

Fox, Stephen. *Blood and Power. Organized Crime in 20th Century America*. New York: Morrow, 1989.

Gabaccia, Donna. *From Sicily to Elizabeth Street: Housing and Social Change Among Italian Immigrants, 1880–1930*. Albany: State University of New York Press, 1984.

Gambetta, Diego. *The Sicilian Mafia: The Business of Private Protection*. Cambridge, Mass.: Harvard University Press, 1993.

Gambino, Richard. *Vendetta: A True Story of the Largest Lynching in U.S. History*. Toronto: Guernica Editions, 2000.

Gentile, Nicola. *Vita di Capomafia*. Rome: Editori Riuniti, 1963.

Gilfoyle, Timothy. *A Pickpocket's Tale: The Underworld of Nineteenth-Century New York*. New York: W. W. Norton, 2006.

Glaser, Lynn. *Counterfeiting in America: The History of an American Way to Wealth.* New York: Clarkson N. Potter, 1968.

Hess, Henner. *Mafia and Mafiosi: The Structure of Power.* Lexington, Mass.: Lexington Books, 1973.

Hunt, Thomas, and Martha Macheca Sheldon. *Deep Water: Joseph P. Macheca and the Birth of the American Mafia.* Lincoln, Neb.: iUniverse, 2007.

Hunt, Thomas, and Michael Tona. "The Good Killers: 1921's Glimpse of the Mafia." *The On the Spot Journal* (Spring 2007).

Ianni, Francis, and Elizabeth Reuss-Ianni. *A Family Business: Kinship and Social Control in Organized Crime.* London: Routledge & Kegan Paul, 1972.

Jackson, Kenneth. *The Encyclopedia of New York City.* New Haven, Conn.: Yale University Press, 1995.

Johnson, David. *Illegal Tender: Counterfeiting and the Secret Service in Nineteenth-Century America.* Washington, D.C.: Smithsonian Institution, 1995.

Kurtz, Michael. "Organized Crime in Louisiana History: Myth and Reality." *Louisiana History* 24 (1983).

La Gumina, Salvatore. *Wop! A Documentary History of Anti-Italian Discrimination in the United States.* Toronto: Guernica Editions, 1999.

Landesco, John. *Organized Crime in Chicago: Part III of the Illinois Crime Survey, 1929.* Chicago: University of Chicago Press, 1968.

LeBrun, George, as told to Edward Radin. *It's Time to Tell: On His Hundredth Birthday the Originator of the Sullivan Law Relates His Own Story of Persons Noted and Notorious; of Crimes and Inquests; of Politics in New York City from the Gay Nineties through the Great Depression.* New York: Morrow, 1962.

Lombardo, Robert. "The Black Hand: Terror by Letter in Chicago." *Journal of Contemporary Criminal Justice* 18 (2002).

Lowenthal, Max. *The Federal Bureau of Investigation.* London: Turnstile Press, 1951.

Lupo, Salvatore. *Storia della Mafia: Dalle Origini ai Giorni Nostri.* Rome: Donzelli Editore, 2004.

Mattox, Kenneth, David V. Feliciano, and Ernest E. Moore, eds. *Trauma.* New York: McGraw-Hill, 2000.

McAdoo, William. *Guarding a Great City.* New York: Harper & Bros., 1906.

McCormick, Charles. *Hopeless Cases: The Hunt for the Red Scare Terrorist Bombers.* Lanham, Md.: University Press of America, 2005.

Melanson, Philip. *The Secret Service: The Hidden History of an Enigmatic Agency.* New York: Carroll & Graf, 2005.

Mondello, Salvatore. *A Sicilian in East Harlem.* Youngstown, N.Y.: Cambria Press, 2005.

Morello, C. A. *Before Bruno: The History of the Philadelphia Mafia, Book 1—1880–1931.* Philadelphia: privately published, [c. 1999].

Nelli, Humberto. "The Italian Padrone System." *Labor History* 5 (1969).

———. *The Business of Crime: Italians and Syndicate Crime in the United States.* Chicago: University of Chicago Press, 1976.

Norton, G. P. "Chicago Housing Conditions: Two Italian Districts." *American Journal of Sociology* (1913).

Orsi, Robert. *The Madonna of 115th Street: Faith and Community in Italian Harlem.* New Haven, Conn.: Yale University Press, 2002.

Page, Max. *The Creative Destruction of Manhattan, 1900–1940.* Chicago: University of Chicago Press, 1999.

Panteleone, Michele. *The Mafia and Politics.* New York: Coward-McCann, 1966.

Petacco, Arrigo. *Joe Petrosino.* London: Hamish Hamilton, 1974.

Pitkin, Thomas. *Black Hand: A Chapter in Ethnic Crime.* Totowa, N.J.: Littlefield, Adams & Co., 1977.

Raab, Selwyn. *Five Families: The Rise, Decline, and Resurgence of America's Most Powerful Mafia Families.* New York: St. Martin's Press, 2005.

Repetto, Thomas. *American Mafia: A History of Its Rise to Power.* New York: Henry Holt, 2004.

———. *Bringing Down the Mob: The War Against the American Mafia.* New York: Henry Holt, 2006.

Repetto, Thomas, and James Lardner. *NYPD: A City and Its Police.* New York: Henry Holt, 2000.

Rezneck, Samuel. "Unemployment, Unrest, and Relief in the United States During the Depression of 1893–1897." *Journal of Political Economy* 61 (1953).

Rosenberg, Daniel. *New Orleans Dockworkers: Race, Labor, and Unionism, 1892–1923.* Albany: State University of New York Press, 1988.

Russo, Ferdinando, and Ernesto Serao. *La Camorra: Origini, Usi, Costumi e Riti dell'Annorata Soggietà.* Naples: Ferdinando Bideri, 1907.

Sabetti, Filippo. *Village Politics and the Mafia in Sicily.* Quebec, Canada: McGill's-Queen's University Press, 2002.

Sacco, Vincent. "Black Hand Outrage: A Constructional Analysis of an Urban Crime Movement." *Deviant Behavior* 24 (2003).

Sante, Luc. *Low Life: Lures and Snares of Old New York.* London: Granta Books, 1998.

Schneider, Peter. "On Mafiology." *Journal of Modern Italian Studies* 7 (2002).

Selvaggi, Giuseppe. *The Rise of the Mafia in New York City: From 1896 to World War II.* Indianapolis: Bobbs-Merrill, 1978.

Servadio, Gaia. *Mafioso: A History of the Mafia from Its Origins to the Present Day.* London: Secker & Warburg, 1976.

Sinclair, Andrew. *Prohibition: The Era of Excess.* London: Faber & Faber, 1962.

Smith, Dwight. *The Mafia Mystique.* New York: University Press of America, 1990.

Smith, Tom. *The Crescent City Lynchings: The Murder of Chief Hennessy, the New Orleans "Mafia" Trials, and the Parish Prison Mob.* Guilford, Conn.: The Lyons Press, 2007.

Spillane, Joseph. "Making a Modern Drug: The Manufacture, Sale, and Control of Cocaine in the United States, 1880–1920." In Paul Gootenberg, ed., *Cocaine: Global Histories.* London: Routledge, 1999.

Steeples, Douglas, and David Whitman. *Democracy in Desperation: The Depression of 1893.* Westport, Conn.: Greenwood Books, 1998.

Stryker, Lloyd. *The Art of Advocacy: A Plea for the Renaissance of the Trial Lawyer.* New York: Cornerstone Library, 1954.

Terrett, Courtenay. *Only Saps Work: A Ballyhoo for Racketeering*. New York: Vanguard Press, 1930.

Thompson, Craig, and Allen Raymond. *Gang Rule in New York*. New York: The Dial Press, 1940.

Train, Arthur. *Courts, Criminals, and the Camorra*. London: Chapman & Hall, 1912.

Warner, Richard. "The First Mafia Boss of Los Angeles? The Mystery of Vito Di Giorgio, 1880–1922." *The On The Spot Journal* (Summer 2008).

Warren, Louis S. *The Hunter's Game: Poaching and Conservationists in Twentieth Century America*. New Haven, Conn.: Yale University Press, 1997.

INDEX

PHOTOGRAPH CREDITS

Page numbers refer to the pages in the photo insert.

Archivio Stato, Palermo: Corleone street scene, p. 2

David Critchley: Ralph "the Barber" Daniello, p. 15

New York City Municipal Archives: the remains of Gaspare Candella, p. 16

William Flynn Saunders: William Flynn, p. 10

U.S. Library of Congress: Joe Petrosino, p. 8; Petrosino funeral procession, p. 9

U.S. National Archives: Giuseppe Morello, p. 1 and title page of book; Calogero Maggiore, Don Vito Cascio Ferro, Chas Brown, John "Red" Duffy, and Edward R. Kelly, p. 3; Salvatore Clemente, p. 12

U.S. National Archives—Northeast: forged notes, p. 9

U.S. National Archives—Southeast: Anthony Cecala, Salvatore Cina, and Giuseppe Calicchio, p. 7; Ignazio Lupo, p. 15

Zarcone Family/David Critchley: Giovanni Zacconi, p. 7

Author's collection: Calogero Morello, p. 12; Nick Terranova, p. 13; Nicolena Salemi Morello, p. 15

ABOUT THE AUTHOR

MIKE DASH is a historian with an M.A. from the University of Cambridge and a Ph.D. from the University of London. A former professional journalist whose work has appeared in numerous national newspapers and magazines, Dash is the author of seven books, including *Satan's Circus, Thug, Batavia's Graveyard,* and *Tulipomania.* He lives in London with his wife and daughter.

This book was set in Bulmer, a typeface designed in the late eighteenth century by the London type-cutter William Martin. The typeface was created especially for the Shakespeare Press, directed by William Bulmer; hence, the font's name. Bulmer is considered to be a transitional typeface, containing characteristics of old-style and modern designs. It is recognized for its elegantly proportioned letters, with their long ascenders and descenders.